The New Dictionary of Spiritual Thought

The New Dictionary of Spiritual Thought

Carol E. Parrish-Harra

SPARROW HAWK PRESS
Tahlequah, Oklahoma

First Edition 1994 by Sparrow Hawk Press

Editing and design by Mary Beth Marvin
Type composition and design by Raymond John
Illustrations by Raymond John and Marianne Sansing

Library of Congress Cataloging-in-Publication Data
Parrish-Harra, Carol E.
The New Dictionary of Spiritual Thought
Over 3,000 Western and Eastern esoteric and spiritual terms and concepts; by Carol E. Parrish-Harra.
Includes biographies, symbols, illustrations, bibliography.

ISBN 0-945027-22-2: $24.95
1. Spiritual dictionary. 2. Religion—Esoteric Christianity. 3. Western and Eastern spiritual, philosophical thought. 4. Wisdom teachings. 5. Hermetic principles. I. Title.

Library of Congress Catalog Card Number 2002 141254

Manufactured in the United States of America.

Dedicated to Sophia

I, Wisdom, have created prudence,
And I possess knowledge and reason.
I love those who love me;
And those who seek me shall find me.

Proverbs 8.12,17

From the Publisher

This new dictionary, triple in size to the first edition, does much more than define terms unique to spiritual studies. It enlightens its user with concepts and mythology that gave rise to these terms. Use it as your faithful companion as you progress on the Path; you will find it an indispensable key to understanding the esoteric wisdom of the ancients.

Prepared by the highly respected mystic, Dean of Sancta Sophia Seminary, Carol E. Parrish-Harra, this exceptional compendium is the result of the author's nearly forty-year pursuit of the ageless wisdom teachings. This search has led her to a guru high in the Himalayas, to sacred sites in Peru, across the former USSR, to Egypt, the Orient, the Gobi Desert for Wesak, and the Yucatan and Guatemala for study of the Mayan culture under the tutelage of the wisdomkeeper Hunbatz Men, whose lineage predates Columbus. Her pilgrimage to Turkey—with its rich heritage of early Christianity, of twelve to seventeen early civilizations, and of Islam—adds dimension to help integrate early Western wisdom for the benefit all of humanity.

Dr. Parrish-Harra is a popular lecturer across the U.S. and in many countries, most often in the U.S., Russia, and now Turkey and the British Isles. In 1981 she established a spiritual community in the foothills of the Ozark Mountains near Tahlequah, Oklahoma, which includes the campus of Sancta Sophia Seminary where she works tirelessly to disseminate the practical and enduring wisdom of the ancient teachings.

Other works by Carol E. Parrish-Harra

The New Age Handbook on Death and Dying
Messengers of Hope—The Walk-in Phenomenon
The Aquarian Rosary—Reviving the Art of Mantra Yoga
The Book of Rituals—Personal and Planetary Transformation
Adventure in Meditation—Spirituality for the 21st Century, Vols. 1, 2, 3
How to Use Sacred Space for Problem-Solving and Inner Guidance
Reflections (compiled by Maggie Webb-Adams)

Editor's Notes

Because of their unique importance in the practical esoteric teachings of Sancta Sophia Seminary, Agni Yoga, Kabalah, Esoteric Christianity, Psychography, and astrology references, as well as references to the above Sitchin and Trigueirinho works, are designated throughout the dictionary by the symbols of a flame, the kabalistic Tree, a chalice, a spiral, and a star, respectively. For the unique preview of Zecharia Sitchin's work we have used the ancient Sumerian symbol of the 12th planet, and for the teachings of Trigueirinho we use a symbol of his center, Figueira, in Brazil.

In the interest of completeness and to suggest further study, relevant major literary works are cited at the end of their authors' biographical entries. Throughout the text cross-referenced words and terms are designated by "small caps." A consistent effort has been made to avoid sexist terms and constructions where possible, without altering meaning or compromising grammatical usage (except, of course, in quoted references).

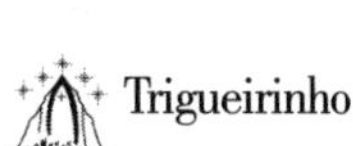

A truly useful reference work must, by its very nature, reflect countless sources and authorities, both well-known and esoteric. We wish to express our particular indebtedness to The Holy Bible from the Ancient Eastern Text, George M. Lamsa's Aramaic translation from the

Peshitta (A. J. Holman Company, 1933) for biblical references (unless otherwise noted); Webster's New World™ Encyclopedia (New York: Prentice Hall General Reference, 1993); *The Kybalion—A Study of the Hermetic Philosophy of Ancient Egypt and Greece,* by Three Initiates (Yogi Publication Society, Chicago, 1912), an important source for the sacred wisdom teachings said to have originated with Hermes Trismegistus. We are further indebted to these important references for biographical information: Oxford Dictionary of the Christian Church (Oxford University Press, 1974) and Dictionary of Bible and Religion (Abingdon Press, 1986).

Acknowledgments

I wish to recognize the many people who have prompted me to define words we have come to depend upon in order to examine concepts that bring new awareness, knowledge, and peace of mind to many who are in a process of searching for a greater meaning and purpose to life.

The first time someone said to me, "I need a dictionary if I am going to hang out with you," I had no idea someday I would indeed create one. But now I have, and to Grace Bradley who said it to me first, I say, "Thank you!"

My second thank you is to Mary Beth Marvin who has edited it for and with me. When I thought I could not define one more word, Mary Beth, with her fine journalistic manner, persisted. So the accomplishment belongs to us both. We have loved creating this book; it has been more fun than a jigsaw puzzle.

I wish to acknowledge my dear friend and colleague Sarah Leigh Brown—known to us as Sally—for her permission to integrate data gathered for her new book, *Cosmic Fire Revealed—A Student Guide to Alice A. Bailey's* A Treatise on Cosmic Fire. Sally wrote this excellent dissertation for her Doctor of Theology degree through Sancta Sophia Seminary. Her insights add significantly to the value of this revision.

I would like to express my appreciation to Grace B. Bradley, Carol Joy Phelps, and Doris Southwick for their research assistance. Each has been gracious and helpful when called upon. Thank you, Ann Knight, for lending your touch to the Sitchin material, which she has also enjoyed studying after our taking his workshop together. For your expertise and dedication to our project and for your artistic flair in design and typesetting, thank you, Raymond John, our graphic artist.

It is appropriate also to acknowledge the contributions of fine kabalists to our perceptions of life in other dimensions. Particularly helpful is Z'ev ben Shimon Halevi's definitive work concerning the angelic kingdom, included both for its scholarship and for its contemporary explanation of the Judaic line of Kabalah. He is the author of twelve books. Additionally, I thank kabalist Jim Judd for his contribution to today's kabalistic studies and lessons

Two very special sections of profound teachings begin on page 334—some of the most current ideas regarding the origins and the development of planet Earth and her inhabitants:

Terms of growing significance in Zechariah Sitchin's research have been selected from his six volumes of Earth Chronicles. As they gain acceptance, they will provide a great amount of information for the integration of science and spirituality. See "Humanity's Genesis: A Space Chronicle."

Another pioneer, Josè Trigueirinho, of Brazil, offers unprecedented concepts of the inner world (so called in older writings, now known as higher dimensions) regarding other kingdoms within the Earth and from beyond. This modern delivery, challenging humanity to stretch its awareness and reclaim its cosmic identity, emphasizes building subtler bodies in order to experience other realities. The work—we have entitled it "Etheric Dimensions: The Expanding Reality"—is some of the finest I have seen concerning the divine feminine and new realities. These teachings provide keys to the transformation of humanity and renew our hope for the fully human–fully divine future to which we aspire, as well as interaction with spacial beings.

It is my hope that these concepts bless those who explore them. May Light descend on Earth!

Introduction

When I began to receive impressions during meditation before I even knew what meditation was, my mind would fill with an awareness beyond my rational grasp. I might "know" something, but I lacked words to interpret the concepts. I struggled quietly. As I attempted to share these promptings, I quickly learned my thoughts were not understood by others and that I appeared awkward as I attempted to explain beyond-words ideas. Yet, the inner life persisted.

In the presence of the Light Being during my near-death experience, realizations had come. In that wondrous time, it all seemed so clear. It would be several years before, again, I would touch the fount of wisdom I felt was mine to share. In time, my quest led to wise teachers who would encourage me by sharing their precious inner lives and personal revelations.

Recapitulation was a time of joy—finding words for the knowingness. Each new concept strengthened the conviction of my spirit, giving form to the expanding mind map in the back of my head. Gradually I would be able to pass on to others ancient and ageless truths that illumine the path. May they be as a lamp offering clarity upon your way.

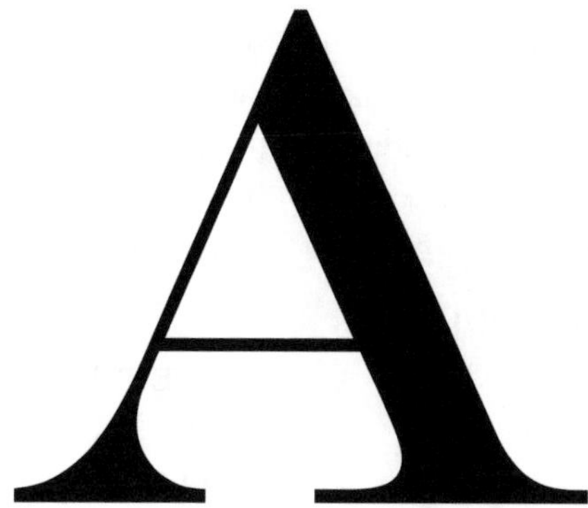

Aarati. A portion of Hindu worship when fire—usually small wicks burning ghee (purified butter)—is waved in front of an image of a deity for the purpose of devotion. The smoke is to carry prayers, adoration, and requests heavenward.

Abashkarel. A Hebrew word analogous to ASHRAM or temple; a place where spiritual awareness is consciously sought.

Abaton. A huge dream incubation temple in Epidaurus, Greece, where pilgrims slept, requesting a specific kind of dream for healing or contact with the deceased. The vast sleeping hall was called "canes" or "klinis," the Greek word from which "clinic" is derived.

Abstinence. As a SPIRITUAL DISCIPLINE, the choice to refrain from a particular function for a time—often refers to sexual activity. Many religious approaches suggest practicing periodic restraint. The goal of occasional sexual restriction is for partners to go beyond satisfying compulsive sexual craving and learn to express love, appreciation, and affection in ways other than just intercourse. Sexual energy is not to be taken for granted. Here we learn to rest in our love to form the foundation of a relationship and not just use physical excitement.

Abstract Mind. Higher aspect of the mental plane, where we conduct conceptual thought, think in theoretical terms, and generate plans and purposes. The level of the mental plane into which impulses and purposes of the soul flow. That which is formulated by abstract mind eventually crystallizes and descends into CONCRETE MIND. The work of the fifth ROOT RACE, the ARYAN wave of consciousness, is to develop the powers of abstract mind.

ABUNDANCE, LAW OF. A concept of prosperity that acknowledges richness of supply on each level: physical, emotional, mental, and spiritual. Operating in harmony with giving and receiving brings much to us. "The abundant life" conveys ample challenge and opportunity, and the growth that results.

ABYDOS. Site of the Temple of Seti I on the Nile in the Old Kingdom of upper Egypt. A hieroglyph of the sacred KESTREL, or Sparrow Hawk (the logo used by Sparrow Hawk Village), was found there.

ABYSS. A vast divide separating the world of time and space from the triune Godhead (the supernal triad in KABALAH)—the invisible, incomprehensible creative nature of God. The separation can only be bridged by a holy consciousness—the CHRIST-WITHIN in Esoteric Christianity or DAATH in Kabalah—the gnosis, or wisdom, gleaned as one advances on the PATH OF INITIATION.

ACCELERATED LEARNING. A state of exceptional acquisition of skills or ability, used particularly in an area of techniques or tools to facilitate the acquisition of knowledge at such enhanced rates that the information can be easily measured. Several techniques were introduced by the human potential movement in the late 20th century to demonstrate the human capacity to learn and retain.

ACCUMULATION. The part of each life experience that is carried forward in the EGOIC LOTUS from incarnation to incarnation.

ACTIVE IMAGINATION. An exercise developed by Carl JUNG as an aid to understanding personal symbology in a dream, vision, or meditation. The explorer imagines the symbol, then, orally or in writing, describes a dialogue between any two objects: self and the symbol, two symbols, or a significant other person and the symbol.

ACTIVE INTELLIGENCE. The RAY 3 quality of energy, acknowledging the conscious process of aptitude by differentiating it from innate or subconscious intellect at work in life without developed conscious awareness.

ACTIVE MEDITATION. *See* Meditation, active; Meditation, passive.

ACTUALISM. A school of ESOTERIC thought derived from AGNI YOGA teachings. Writer, poet, and teacher Russell Paul SCHOFIELD established Schools of Actualism across the U.S. to promote the realization that humanity must free itself at all levels of consciousness from image-mechanism manipulation in order to express the Actual SELF. *Imprint Unmistakable,* 1969.

ACUPRESSURE. A definitive system using pressure on specific points of the body for balancing or stimulating the energy flow of the ETHERIC BODY in health-supportive ways.

ACUPUNCTURE. A system using a variety of needles on specific points of the body to balance or stimulate the energy flow of the ETHERIC BODY in health-supportive ways.

ADAMIC ROOT RACE. *See* Root race.

ADDICTIONS. Emotionally backed demands or a dependency that by habitual indulgence

Adam

The biblical name given by the Creator to the human creature and applied to human consciousness in its development in each of the four WORLDS of KABALAH—in accordance with the subtle forces of each world:

ADAM, ARCHETYPAL. In Kabalah, the prototype of wo/man created by the ELOHIM and held in the highest world of ATZILUTH.

ADAM KADMON. The collective soul of humanity (wo/man), according to the Kabalah; the Adam of the creative world of BRIAH, wherein we are all one. In the Christian tradition, the "heavenly man" or the "mystical body of Christ wherein we are all one."

ADAM BELIAL. In Kabalah, the androgynous nature of humanity held in the psychological world of YETZIRAH, the astral and mental planes combined.

ADAM PROTOPLASTES. In Kabalah, the human incarnated in the physical world of ASSIAH—male or female, any color or stature.

over-rides CELLULAR INTELLIGENCE and the power of BASIC SELF.

ADEPT. An OCCULT degree of soul-realized being cultivating the understanding and ability to use the laws of inner reality—divided into two classes: one group demonstrates outward use of inner forces in human life and consciousness; the other creates reservoirs of energy to sustain forces of nature, providing direction to ELEMENTALS, etc., to support outer manifestation. An advanced INITIATE, considered to have taken the fourth INITIATION in ESOTERIC CHRISTIANITY.

ADI. First, primeval, or divine.[1]

ADONAI. A Hebrew name meaning "Lord" used in place of the four-letter name of God, the TETRAGRAMMATON, YOD HEH VAU HEH (YHWH). Only rabbis were permitted to use the name *Adonai;* lay people used the word *Hashem,* meaning "the Name."

ADONAI INTERNA. In the Western mysteries, the GOD-WITHIN.

ADORATION. An important practice of Christianity for PURIFICATION of the astral body. Adoration lifts emotion to devotion; the next step from devotion to adoration raises the emotional focus to the highest levels of astral reality. Through the power of ASPIRATION, we connect with inner guidance. The archetypes, deities, and saints we revere link us to energies of higher realities at this high level of the ASTRAL PLANE. The passion of adoration purifies.

ADVANCED ORDERS OF ARCHANGELS. These archangels work under the supervision of the SILENT WATCHERS BEFORE THE THRONE: *Dominions* who obey the Thrones holding Higher Will and the Plan as directed toward lower worlds; *Principalities* who watch over and seek to guide in an orderly fashion the nations and the development of group minds; *Powers* who serve under the Lords of Karma to fulfill purpose executing cause and effect; *Virtues* who honor integrity and bestow miracles (grace).

ADVENT. This commencement of the Christian year begins four Sundays before Christmas day as we prepare to celebrate the historical birth of Jesus. We contemplate specific concepts weekly: 1) expectancy, 2) purification and preparation, 3) hope and joy, 4) identification, reminding us of humanity's long journey from awakening to awareness of the birth of the holy within. THE PATH OF INITIATION is the way to achieve God's Plan.

ADVENT WREATH. Five candles (three purple, one pink, one white) usually on greenery, one of which is lighted each of the four Sundays before Christmas, the pink always on the third Sunday of ADVENT, with the white center candle to be lit on Christmas eve or day.

ADYAR. City in India where the THEOSOPHICAL SOCIETY was established and still maintains headquarters (as well as in Wheaton, Illinois).

AEROFORMS, PLASMATIC. A term for biological UFOs, a form of life previously unknown to official science: invisible biological aeroforms or organisms living in the sky. This theory, originated by Meade Layne, was developed by Trevor James Constable of Hawaii, merchant marine radio-electronics officer, internationally known aviation historian, and long-time researcher in borderline science. He claims to have captured on film a form of life offering startling new data for all fields, believing he has proven these life forms exist in the PLASMA state. They are not solid, liquid, or gas, but exist in the fourth state of matter—plasma—as living heat-substance at the upper border of physical nature (the esoteric term would be "etheric"), looking like unicellular life forms, complete with nuclei, nucleoli, and vacuoles. Others have coined names such as plasmoids, ideoplasms (Constable calls them "critters"). The important point is to realize this life form exhibits animal-like behavior.[2] *See* Critters hypothesis.

AFFECT BRIDGE. A REGRESSION technique in which the client, in an altered state of consciousness, is guided from present to past by way of a feeling, emotion, or memory, as defined and practiced in PSYCHOGRAPHY.

AFFECTIVE. Defines techniques used to expand the illumination of the heart, emotions, and feelings attributed to an idea, such as focusing a light on the heart or the emotional nature as one amplifies positive feelings—love for the world, compassion for the restricted.[3] *See* Spirituality, approaches to Christian.

AFFIRMATION. A statement said repeatedly to program the basic nature to a new reality. A tool for change, for reprogramming the unconscious mind and BASIC SELF. A mental discipline.

AGAPE. The love of God for humanity. Also, a spiritual bond, usually understood as unconditional love of soul for soul; the spontaneous

AGNI YOGA—AN INTRODUCTION

Agni Yoga writings were received by transmission through the Russian Christian mystic, Helena ROERICH, the AMANUENSIS for MASTER MORYA of the PLANETARY HIERARCHY. Agni principles employ the use of virtues and themes to propose guidelines (rather than rigid dogma) for living an ethical life. In this book Agni terms are designated by the symbol of a flame, the meaning of *agni.*

When Helena's husband, Nicholas, designed the Banner of Peace, introducing it to the world in 1929, he stated that the three red disks—encircled by a red ring on a field of white—represent art, science, and religion. Through a synthesis of these three, culture can unite humanity in peace.

Art is a science when we are able to define the discipline, the structure, and the controllability within set boundaries.

Science is an art when its creativity and true purpose of experimentation are allowed to flow and be acknowledged.

Banner of Peace

Religion can be practiced as both an art and a science, as well as a path of devotion. The true purpose of religion is to realign us with the source of life. When we worship God following a defined format of commandments, dogmas, and practices (inner or outer), we utilize the collective power of the religion to assist us in the ascension of consciousness. Our theology must support and sustain us in our journey toward spirituality.

An ignorant person must be civilized first of all, then educated, after which he becomes intelligent. Then comes refinement and realization of synthesis, which is crowned by the acceptance of the idea of culture. Not a single narrow specialist, no matter how high his professional skill, can be considered a cultural leader. Culture is synthesis. Culture knows and understands the foundations of life and creativeness, because it is the cult of worship or reverence for the creative fire, which is life.

—Nicholas Roerich

Also see Roerich; Yoga, Agni.

love expressed freely without calculation of cost or gain to the giver or reward to the receiver. The highest manifestation of love. In Greek, "The good disposition of the soul wherein it prefers nothing that exists to the knowledge of God," according to Maximus the Confessor, an early church father. *See p. 159,* Love.

AGE, AN. Determined by the orbit of Earth through the influence of a constellation, usually considered to be 2,150 to 2,250 years in length. The movement is reverse of that of the sun through the ZODIAC: We are currently leaving the age of Pisces and traveling into the age of Aquarius, whereas monthly sun progression moves from Pisces into Aries. *Also see* Aquarian Age; New Age; Piscean Age.

AGE, GREAT, OR GREAT YEAR. In spiritual science and astrology, a cycle of 12 ages—each ruled by a zodiacal constellation. A Great Age is approximately 24,000 to 26,000 years in length.

AGELESS WISDOM TEACHINGS. *See* Ancient wisdom teachings.

AGE OF FLOWERS. The MAYAN name for the forthcoming era, about 2,150 to 2,250 years long. Also known as the AQUARIAN AGE or GOLDEN AGE of Enlightenment.

AGNI. Literal meaning, "fire," in yogic practices, emphasizing the burning away of blocks and barriers, or PURIFICATION. Lord Agni is the Great Lord of Light and Fire in Hinduism.

AGNICHAITANS. *Agni* meaning "fire," *chaitan* meaning "builder," devas (the holding spark) are builders in densest form, the seventh sub-plane of the cosmic physical plane.[4]

AGNI INVISIBILAE. The bioelectric energy that enters and acts upon the body of one attuned to higher realities and seeking to purify and illumine consciousness. These invisible energies of transcendence, symbolized as a fire of purification and illumination, ignite the divine potential within and burn away distortions to clear the mental and emotional bodies of GLAMOURS and ILLUSIONS. The fire, released into individual lives, cleanses and elevates with a discriminating fiery force, analogous to the experience of PENTECOST.

AGNI, LORD OF FIRE. A Hindu God. "Lord Agni," a reference from the Vedas, correlates to the concept, "Our God is a fiery God," "For our God is a consuming fire" (Heb. 12.29), and "Goeth over before thee; as a consuming fire" (Deut. 9.3). This concept of fire as creator also is natural to Kabalah's world of ATZILUTH—the world of creative fire and the world of ARCHETYPES.

AGNISHVATTAS. *Agni* meaning "fire," *vatta* meaning "spark," or "lightning," builders on the fifth gaseous sub-plane of the cosmic physical plane. Important as the builders of consciousness.[5]

AGNISURYANS. *Agni* meaning "fire," *surya* referring to the sun, a lord, a god. Builders on the sixth sub-plane of the cosmic physical plane, the astral plane, reflected from buddhic level.[6]

AGNI THEMES. Values, rather than commandments, laws, or rules, guide the Agni practitioner: striving, humanity, self-sacrifice, future, freedom, harmony, community, responsibility, service. *See individual themes.*

AGNI VIRTUES. Twelve qualities are suggested as necessary aspects the disciple must build within the self in the quest for enlightenment. Each virtue corresponds to a zodiacal influence, from Aries to Pisces, respectively: enthusiasm, beauty, universality, leadership, love, purity, reverence, transformation, harmlessness, fearlessness, humility, joy. *See individual virtues.*

AGNI YOGA. *See p. 5*; Roerich; Yoga.

AGNOSTIC. A person of any heritage or belief system who questions dogma and defined

AIN, AIN SOPH, AIN SOPH AUR

Kabalistic terms for the veils of pure spirit, pure love, and pure light that are the very source of life. From this point—"about which naught can be known"—the Creator emanates mysteries through four WORLDS, or levels of vibration, into Creation as we know it. Three partial circles are depicted above the kabalistic TREE OF LIFE: the friction of the first ring (Ain) against the second ring (Ain Soph) created sound, which in turn produced Ain Soph Aur, light.

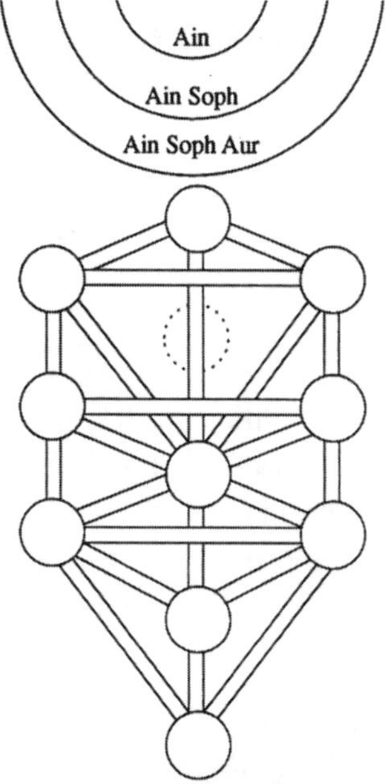

AIN. The Ring Cosmos from which the whole cosmos was created. As the Ring Cosmos spun, diffused light began to concentrate into a still center where all is one. Also known as SIRIUS, the Central Sun of the universe from which our solar system is drawn. Short definition: *Negative existence, the No-thing from which all has come.*

AIN SOPH. Ring Chaos is the thrust block for the secondary movement of Ain, Ring Cosmos. Opposing Ring Cosmos in movement, Ain Soph tends toward diffusion with a flow toward the unmanifest from which it has been pulled. Short definition: *Limitless expansion.*

AIN SOPH AUR. The RING-PASS-NOT is the wide neutral center within which all creation takes place, stabilized by Ring Chaos on the outside and Ring Cosmos in the center. Short definition: *Limitless light.*

teachings, considering him- or herself a freethinker, reserving the right to examine independently.

Agnus Dei. Latin for "Lamb of God," a favorite and familiar symbol of Jesus Christ, epitomizing his innocence. John 1.29 records, "Behold the Lamb of God, who takes away the sins of the world."

Aha. This common expression refers to an insight or realization that comes in a perceptive moment of integration. When certain barriers in the psychological nature dissolve, bits and pieces of life shift and blend rapidly before the mind's eye—an aha. An interesting aside: For an experience to become an aha, it must register or resound to something within us (perhaps as knowledge from an earlier incarnation); hence, the revelation becomes conscious and impacts our awareness.

Ahimsa. The term for "nonviolence," as used in the Jain tradition for a goal pursued to remarkable lengths and applications. Gandhi, in his interfaith approach, once said, "Ahimsa, love, is the very law of our being."

Ahura Mazda. The name of God in the Zoroastrian tradition; also called "Ormazd." The God of Truth and Light of ancient Persia is depicted as a bearded deity roaming the skies within a Winged Disc.

Aïvanhov, Omraam Mikhael. b. Bulgaria, 1900, d. 1986. Prolific writer, teacher, and seer. He gave his followers the Surya, or Solar Yoga, Yoga of the Sun, which teaches that we draw our energies from the Christ who dwells in the sun. Adherents practice a discipline of witnessing the sunrise to meditate and pray in order to live in daily harmony, drawing the courage and will to transform. A scholar well-grounded in physical sciences, he taught that all natural laws and phenomena are translations on the physical plane of those existing on the spiritual plane—the Law of Correspondence; *As Above, So Below.* Visions of God led him to "choose the path of light, the path of selflessness and sacrifice, because God who is all those things is also the greatest and most perfect beauty. . . . With divine knowledge, you can never be the same; as soon as you know even a few aspects of the truth, you are transformed, and are capable of helping others." His concept is quite similar to Agni Yoga. However, he envisioned the center of the Earth to be a hollow region, Agartha, inhabited by an advanced race of beings with a utopian political system, who, concerned about humanity, are alien visitors reported widely as ETs. His teachings are preserved in 300 volumes of lectures. *The Second Birth,* 1976.

Ajna. Sanskrit for the brow center. *See* Chakras.

Aka, or Aka cord. The etheric or psychic bond that continues to exist between two power sources after contact and is sustained by frequent emotion or thought. Often used to direct healing to another at a distance. A term derived from the Huna tradition.

Akasha. Primordial, spiritual substance, which is to ether what spirit is to matter. Emotion and thought imprint easily upon the subtle substance commonly known as the reflective ether, the light ether, the love ether, and the chemical ether—part of the physical plane. These ETHERS combine with the astral dimension to form the ETHERIC BODY.

AKASHIC RECORDS. The chronicle of events mentally and emotionally imprinted upon the reflective ETHERS of the Earth to which every being contributes; individual and group memory of all planetary life. The etheric level records and reflects a living chronicle of life, the story of the planetary being, and all life upon the planet.

AKHENATON. An evolved pharaoh of Egypt, perceived as semi-divine, clearly and qualitatively superior to the masses around the world. Many rulers were acknowledged as having both human and divine qualities. Akhenaton, however, is particularly remembered as the pharaoh who perceived the presence of the One God above all gods, establishing monotheism in Egypt around 2000 B.C. The concept was short-lived and his work destroyed, but the belief in the One God was now firmly anchored on the planet.

ALCHEMY. From the Arabic *al-khem,* meaning "out of Egypt." A term often used as a substitute for KABALAH or other esoteric systems of TRANSFORMATION. The TRANSMUTATION of one substance into another (as in turning base metals into gold), symbolic of the transmutation of matter into spirit that causes new birth (through regeneration) within the individual. A process by which ego extracts the conscious soul or ultimate spiritual essence through life experiences while in physical body. The result of practical application of Kabalah, Esoteric Christianity, or esoteric practice of YOGA, seeking to realize the PHILOSOPHER'S STONE or PEARL OF GREAT PRICE. Sometimes called the "royal art" or "yoga of the West." After the earlier term "magick," "alchemy" came into use; today we use "transformation." *Be ye transformed by the renewing of your mind.* (Rom. 12.2)

ALCHEMY, SPIRITUAL. Acknowledging every individual has the four earthly elements within him- or herself plus three heavenly ones, the ancients viewed each person as a microcosm of the macrocosm—the doctrine of CORRESPONDENCE. Symbolic higher elements are veiled by using Earth elements to preserve the mystery of the process of TRANSFORMATION. Mercury, known as quicksilver or living silver, could participate in all realms and serve as an agent of transformation between all elements, the androgynous. Salt is perfected earth, feminine quality, the philosopher's stone representing transcendence and direct knowledge—matter made completely aware. Sulfur, known as brimstone or burning stone, is given active masculine characteristics, the Sun, energy, and spirit of nature.

ALDER, VERA STANLEY. b. England, 1898, d. 1984. Author of seven books on the WISDOM TEACHINGS, translated into numerous languages. An original member of the DINA group taught by MASTER DJWHAL KHUL through Alice BAILEY. (DINA dictations are largely contained in Bailey's *Discipleship in the New Age,* volumes 1 and 2.) Vera Stanley Alder almost single-handedly maintained the Order of World Guardians from her private office. She was recognized as having a rare gift for synthesizing the essentials of esoteric teachings. *The Finding of the Third Eye,*

1938; *The Initiation of the World,* 1939; *From the Mundane to the Magnificent,* 1979.

ALIENS. Those not of the human evolution. Aliens exist due to laws of creation, according to mystic Rabbi Shimon bar Yochai of the kabalistic tradition, Master Djwhal Khul in Alice Bailey's *Initiation Human and Solar,* Ann Manser of the Shustah materials, and many others. The seven lower sephiroth of the kabalistic Tree combine to project holographic worlds that exist in parallel universes with life forms within each of these dimensions. Others explain planes and frequencies as home to these worlds of other beings. *Also see pp. 349–55,* Etheric Dimensions; Extraterrestrial; Evolutions, other; *pp. 337–47,* Humanity's Genesis.

ALIGNMENT. Attuned to, on a wave length with, working in consort with.

ALLAH. The name for "the One God" from the Islamic tradition.

ALL IS READY, MASTER. COME. This special chant used at Wesak celebrations is most significant when, as representatives of humanity, we stand ready to receive outpourings of grace passed from the Buddha to the planetary Christ for distribution through the planetary hierarchy to all of humanity.

ALMS, GIVING OF. A spiritual discipline emphasizing the awareness of right relationship to all; a reminder that we are all one, and since we are one, we have an innate responsibility to those who have less or are in need. The practice helps us recall, *There but for the grace of God go I.*

ALOHA. This familiar Hawaiian greeting literally conveys, "I salute the divine presence within you," *alo* meaning "presence" and *ha* meaning "divine breath" (as in Hindi). This salutation holds the same concept as Namasté.

ALPHA AND OMEGA. As the first and last characters in the Greek alphabet, these letters symbolize totality in the One in whom creation began and by whom it will end. To Christians, it represents the omnipresence of the Christ.

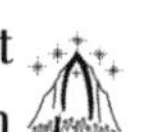

ALPHA SPACECRAFT. "From one standpoint Alpha Spacecraft could be described as an immense mobile work base of the stellar awareness for healing, harmonization and transformation of the species, according to the parameters of its divine archetypes. Space Gardeners and healers work through this base. On the other hand, it is a state of consciousness which synthesizes information about healing processes existent in the confederated universes. In its expression closest to the material levels, it is known as the 'Floating City' because of its size. The presence of this spacecraft in the Earth's orbit concerns the evolution of the planet and not of specific individuals. However, due to needs on a wiser level, many rescuable [advanced] beings are taken, generally as a group, into its aura, where they undergo profound transformation. Among the tasks carried out by Alpha Spacecraft, one could mention: transmutation of energies, change of genetic code and modification of the energetic system in human beings, as well as diverse transformations in representatives of other kingdoms of Nature.

One of the most complete within the network of healing in the cosmos, Alpha Spacecraft presently has Aurora intraterrestrial center as support for its operations."[7] *Also see pp. 349–55,* Etheric Dimensions.

ALPHA VESSEL. The external manifestation of a great consciousness that resides in the Central Sun of a distant galaxy. It expresses itself to the Earth as a traveling light in the skies, yet it never loses contact with its immaterial origin. It has a working relationship with Mirna Jad. *See pp. 349–55,* Etheric Dimensions.

ALTA MAJOR CENTER. The nerve center at the top of the spine where the cranium and spine connect. Here, impressions rush in. Along with the brow and crown centers, the point forms the mental triad. This hollow (you can feel it) is often called the "mouth of God." Impressions registered here are considered "as if I heard the voice of God" or spiritual beings.

ALTERED STATE OF CONSCIOUSNESS. Commonly used to imply any status of reality other than beta (rational or outer).

ALTRUISM. An awareness closely related to unconditional love expressed as humanitarian or unqualified giving—"no strings attached."

AMANUENSIS. A person who takes dictation and/or functions almost as a servant to an authority. In spiritual thought, one who receives the messages dictated by a holy one (note the *manu* portion of the word)—usually a teacher in spirit—and becomes the outer-world representative. Examples from the esoteric tradition are Alice A. BAILEY for MASTER DJWHAL KHUL and Helena ROERICH for MASTER MORYA.

AMARTIA. In Greek, "to miss the mark"; most often translated "sin."

AMEN. "So be it"—approval or affirmation. *Also see* Om.

AMHAJ. The name given to the Figueria Center, explaining that it is the consciousness known as EL MORYA that expresses in many dimensions and planes (pronounced phonetically: *Ah Mahr). Also see pp. 349–55,* Etheric Dimensions.

AMRITA. Sanskrit for sweetness, the nectar or elixir of life, or life essence.

ANANDA. Hindu, meaning "bliss." Often attached to a name to indicate one who has realized a high state of consciousness.

ANATOLIA. From Greek *anatole,* meaning "east." A region east of Greece called Asia Minor (Anatolia in the past), now mostly in the country of Turkey.

ANCHOR. The source for this Christian symbol of hope and steadfastness is Heb. 6.19: "That promise is like an anchor to us; it upholds the soul so that it may not be shaken, and it penetrates beyond the veil of the temple." Anchors are found in many inscriptions in the catacombs of Rome. They were often carved on old Christian gems and remind us of Jesus the Christ, "fisher of men," to whom we can anchor our lives, a symbol of security.

ANCHORESS. A person called to a solitary life—however, one who is not cut off from the world but anchored in it.

ANCHORITISM. The spiritual practice of withdrawing to live in seclusion, practicing constant prayer to awaken to the presence of God. An anchorite often adds KATOPHATIC (imaginal, mental images of what is not actually present) and AFFECTIVE (emotional, feeling) approaches to spirituality as well.

ANCIENT WISDOM TEACHINGS. A body of knowledge preserved traditionally for those deemed ready, revealed to those who can penetrate to the inner temples or teachers and share these truths to help others understand the laws of life and how to live in harmony with high principles. Also known as mystery, ageless wisdom, SOPHIANIC, spiritual, or esoteric teachings, or shortened to "the teachings." This practical wisdom—inner knowing revealed individually to intuitives with the powerful sense of recognition to affirm the source—underlies all religions and cultures but is obscured by materialistic and rational thinking. Includes folk wisdom, archetypes, myths, and allegories that seek to explain the mysteries of life. Wise ones pass the knowledge on, understanding they must accept the karmic responsibility for what they share.

ANDES CENTERS. Anchoring places in the Andes Mountains of South America for the powerful incoming feminine energies of the higher worlds to move the planet forward in evolution and into the new era, identified and recorded by Trigueirinho.[8] *Also see pp. 349–55,* Etheric Dimensions; Planetary centers, new.

ANDROGYNY. The balance of masculine and feminine qualities within a personality.

ANDROID. A robot-like being appearing as a human being.

ANGEL. From the Greek word *angelos,* meaning "messenger." This devic evolution is androgynous and evolves parallel to humanity upon planet Earth, with similar levels of initiation, and living in the astral dimension. The CHRIST is teacher of angels and humanity. MOTHER MARY, a MASTER, is an advanced one in this kingdom and known as Queen of Heaven and of Earth. Angels are the celestial rulers of the zodiacal sign of Aquarius.

ANGELIC KINGDOM. The realm of the angels—known in the East as the kingdom of the DEVAS, or "shining ones." These active, inventive form-builders of objective creation are in ceaseless action behind the scenes as designers and directors, artists and producers. The personifications associated with angelic beings are not to be regarded as physical realities, rather as a parallel kingdom with diversified expression or its own path of evolution, dwelling in the astral with the densest manifestation in the etheric realm. These invisible but omnipresent intelligences—from NATURE SPIRITS to ARCHANGELS—bring divine thought into form without interfering with individuality. One of three major EVOLUTIONS (parallel to the human kingdom and the spacial kingdom), this intelligent lifestream is in charge of life principles. The angelic kingdom creates, builds, and maintains forms in the dense world.

ANGEL OF THE PRESENCE. An angelic THOUGHTFORM who mediates the glory of the Divine for human consciousness. This powerful presentation of the oneness, deity, and eternal life waits beyond the threshold and steps down Divinity to us as we can best perceive it. When overly personified, it becomes the distorted image of the exaggerated good s/he embodies—that saintly self we aspire to be, all goodness and light. Each individual and each collective develops an archetypal outpicturing of itself—perfect, as it would wish to be perfect. Counterpart to the DWELLER ON THE THRESHOLD, both form unrealistic self-images on the astral (emotional) level—one excessively good, the other excessively bad. Reality lies somewhere in between.

ANGELOLOGY. The story and study of ANGELS their history, roles, and names, as recorded down through time by ancient MYSTERY TEACHINGS: *The Book of Enoch,* the ESSENE tradition, the Bible, as well as KABALAH and Eastern references to the DEVAS. These invisible (to most) beings are considered a parallel family evolving on Earth, anchored in the ASTRAL world; at times, they densify to reveal themselves to humanity.

ANGER. Distorted love. A barrier to spiritual growth; an ego creation of contorted astral energy that seems a natural reaction to threat. Neither bad nor good, this emotional reaction generates power with which to defend and protect ego, or nonself. It may be expressed outwardly or turned against oneself.

ANIMA. A Jungian term denoting the feminine aspect of our inner nature, usually hidden and gradually discovered and developed. *Also see* Animus.

ANIMA MUNDI. The WORLD SOUL, the One in whom all manifestation occurs.

ANIMISM. A religious approach that honors the spirit of animals in worship. The spiritual perception of paleolithic man, wherein an awareness of God through nature was realized. Nature was perceived to be animated by spiritual power, and humanity could interact with those powers via ceremony and sacrifice. As human consciousness enlarged and the sense of self-operating within the race solidified, the religion of the Great Mother or Earth Mother arose.

ANIMUS. A Jungian term denoting the masculine aspect of the inner nature, usually hidden and gradually discovered and developed. *Also see* Anima.

ANKH. *See* Crosses.

ANNO LUCIS. In Latin, *anno* means "year" and *lucis* means "light." A term from an early dating system used by Masons to memorialize the founding of the ancient craft of Masonry in 4000 B.C., the "year of light"—(A.L.). *See* Freemasons.

ANNUNCIATION. The feast day of the Christian tradition commemorating Angel Gabriel telling the VIRGIN MARY she had been chosen to be the mother of a holy child to be called Jesus. He greeted her, "Blessed art thou among women," and Mary accepted the role, "Let it be done to me according to thy word." (Luke 1) This exchange forms the basis of the HAIL MARY prayer.

ANTAHKARANA. A combination of three threads linking higher and lower minds, also called the "rainbow bridge." These threads—the life thread (SUTRATMA) and consciousness thread (also called antahkarana) are inherent;

the CREATIVE THREAD is to be built in mental matter by the aspirant—collectively weave the antahkarana, the communication mechanism between each individual's SOUL, SPIRITUAL TRIAD, and LOWER MIND. In *The Voice of the Silence* H. P. Blavatsky expresses it, "that path which lies between thy spirit and thy self."[9]

Also spelled "Antaskarana, the term has various meanings, which differ with every school of philosophy and sect. Thus Sankaracharya renders the word as 'understanding'; others, as 'the internal instrument, the Soul, formed by the thinking principle and egoism'; whereas the Occultists explain it as the *path* or bridge between the Higher and the Lower Manas, the divine *Ego,* and the *personal* Soul of man. It serves as a medium of communication between the two, and conveys . . . all those personal impressions and thoughts which can, by their nature, be assimilated and stored by the undying Entity, . . . these being the only elements of the evanescent *Personality* that survive death and time. It thus stands to reason that only that which is noble, spiritual, and divine in man can testify in Eternity to his having lived."[10]

"A compound word: *antar,* "interior," "within"; *karana,* sense-organ. Occultists explain this word as the bridge between the higher and lower Manas or the spiritual *ego* and *personal* soul of man. Such is H.P. Blavatsky's definition. As a matter of fact there are several Antahkaranas in the human septenary constitution—one for every *path* or *bridge* between any two of the several monadic centers in man. Man is a microcosm, therefore a unified composite, a unity in diversity; and the antahkaranas are the links of vibrating consciousness substance uniting these various centers."[11]

ANTHROPOMORPHIC. The concept of the Creator possessing human qualities. Humanity seeking to understand nature forces as human qualities, i.e., storms become God expressing anger.

ANTHROPOSOPHY. Literally, "human wisdom." Rudolf STEINER'S system of ageless wisdom within the esoteric Christian tradition. Steiner began in the THEOSOPHICAL SOCIETY but established his own, more Christian position, closely resembling ROSICRUCIANS. His centers emphasize EURYTHMY, gardening, and COMMUNITY. WALDORF SCHOOLS have their origin in Steiner's teachings.

ANTICHRIST. The focused force or intelligence that seeks to counteract expansion of consciousness or the love-light that encourages maturity. This restrictive consciousness may be individual, collective, or embodied by a personality.

ANTONY OF EGYPT. *See pp. 246–51,* Saints.

ANT PEOPLE. A name given by North American natives, the Hopi, to the survivors of an earlier world period. Their legends suggest a group of ant people emerged from the hollow of the Earth. *Also see pp. 349–55,* Etheric Dimensions; Hollow Earth Theory; Intraterrestrials.

ANUBIS. "In Egyptian mythology, the jackal-headed god of the dead, son of Osiris. Anubis presided over the funeral cult, including

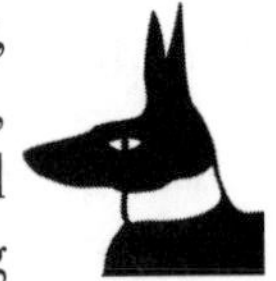

embalming, . . ."[12] guiding the departed through the lower world to the appropriate place where they create their after-life.

ANUNNAKI. Cosmic astronauts from Nibiru—"the gods of heaven and earth," as stated in ancient Sumerian texts, who landed and stayed on Earth—revered by the "humanoids," as humanity was known. *See pp. 337–47,* Humanity's Genesis.

ANU TEA. A PLANETARY CENTER (in the etheric) now activated between Japan, Australia, and Oceania.[13] *See pp. 349–55,* Etheric Dimensions.

APOCALYPSE. Meaning "uncovering," as some possibilities; that which has been hidden is now to be revealed, to teach us what can be. Traditionally, the revelation or Armageddon, what will occur in the last days of a particular world. In MYSTERY TEACHINGS this refers to the closing period of an era, wherein its revelations and KARMIC lessons are satisfied.

APOCRYPHA. This Greek noun means "things hidden." Also, a group of books printed as an "addendum" to some Bibles. Despite their Jewish or Christian origin, sometimes quite ancient, these tracts have not been included in the canon of Scriptures; they are considered to be on the fringe of the Old and New Testaments. The Old Testament Apocrypha should be defined as a closed and focused collection. Catholic and Protestant theologies concur on the New Testament Apocrypha, i.e., the Apocryphal Gospels, Acts of the Apostles, Epistles, and apocalypses. All were written in a Semitic language in Palestine except for the Wisdom of Solomon and the two Maccabees, which were written in Greek (probably in Alexandria). While they are numerous, more important discoveries were made in the 20th century. *Also see* Dead Sea Scrolls; Gnostic Gospels; Nag Hammadi.

APOLLONIUS OF TYANA. b. Tyana, Cappadocia (part of today's Turkey), (dates range from 16 C.E., d. 98 C.E. to 200 A.D.) Torkom SARAYDARIAN and the THEOSOPHICAL SOCIETY recognize Apollonius as the next incarnation of Jesus. "Legends say that He was born in Tyana, 'a town in southern Cappadocia [now Turkey], in the mid-eastern part of Asia Minor.' His biographer says that He was born at the winter solstice of a virgin, that angels appeared, and so on. He was very intelligent and extremely handsome."[14]

According to Dennis Hauck, a boy named Balinas was transformed when he ran his fingers over the EMERALD TABLET. At 16, the child, conversant on any subject in several different languages, felt an intense need for absolute truth. The authorities publicly proclaimed him an incarnation of Proteus, the shape-shifting god of the Greeks. When Balinas happened upon a statue of HERMES TRISMEGISTUS, he knew this was the tutor for whom he hungered. He fell to his knees and whispered, "Teach me, Hermes!" and thereafter conversed with the cold marble as if it were alive. When his intolerant parents sent him away for formal studying, he discovered the writings of PYTHAGORUS (said to be directly descended from Hermes). After years of studying and healing, the ascetic sage became known as Apollonius of Tyana, after the Greek sun god Apollo, bringer of enlightenment. His primary message was that union

Aquarian Age

The 26,000-year cycle (Great Year) contains a period when Earth is subject to the influence of the constellation Aquarius for approximately 2,150 to 2,250 years. The 12 periods, or ages—each approximately 2,250 years long—in a Great Year characterize the 12 zodiacal signs. Now completing the age in which energies from the constellation Pisces dominated, planet Earth is entering the Age of Aquarius, which emphasizes inner and outer peace, cooperation, interdependence, and global community. *See* Aquarian Age, vision for the; New Age.

"Viewed in relation to the dating of the astronomical Age of Aquarius, there is an overlapping with the New Age. [*See* 195.] This has led many to mistakenly identify the New Age with the Age of Aquarius. By following the retrograde movement of the vernal point (the zodiacal location of the Sun on March 21) through the constellations/signs of the zodiac, it is possible to date the Age of Aquarius quite precisely. The present location of the vernal point is slightly more than 5 degrees in the sign of Pisces, which means that we are still in the Age of Pisces.[19] Since each sign is 30 degrees in length, and since the vernal point retrogrades one degree every 72 years, the zodiacal ages are each 2,160 (30x72) years long. To retrograde through five degrees will take 360 (5x72) years; and in fact, measured from the year 2000, it will take the vernal point precisely 375 years to reach 0 degrees Pisces and enter the sign of Aquarius (=30 degrees Aquarius), because in the year 2000, the vernal point is at 5 degrees 12 ½ minutes in Pisces. . . .

"Astronomically, the Age of Aquarius will begin in 2375 and will last 2,160 years, ending in the year 4535. The end of the Age of Aquarius, therefore, occurs shortly after—actually 136 years after—the end of the New Age. This means that the New Age embraces the last part (a little more than the last fifth) of the Age of Pisces and almost the whole of the Age of Aquarius. The New Age thus leads over into the Age of Aquarius.

"With the start of the New Age in 1899, something of the Sophianic culture of the Aquarian Age already began to flow in. It was in the year 1900 that three young Russians, inspired by the great Russian philosopher Vladimir Soloviev, came together: Andrei Belyi, Aleksandr Blok, and Sergei Soloviev (nephew of Vladimir)—the first two acknowledged as great Russian poets. They felt a new era dedicated to Sophia was beginning, and that they were the heralds or prophets of this New Age.[20]

"Eighteen-ninety-nine was also the year in which Rudolf Steiner—at that time thirty-eight years old—underwent a profound spiritual experience that changed the course of his life. This experience, which he alludes to in his autobiography,[21] transformed him into a spiritual teacher and bearer of Anthroposophia, the Western spiritual counterpart to the Russian stream of Sophiology that arose under Soloviev's influence. . . .

"Against this chronological background, both SOPHIOLOGY and ANTHROPOSOPHY are examples of Sophianic spiritual streams arising at the beginning of the New Age, evincing the beginning of a new revelation of the Divine Feminine that will culminate in the Age of Aquarius. The new, inflowing impulse of the Divine Feminine will grow stronger and stronger as we approach the Age of Aquarius. Already now, at the end of the 20th century, a widespread awakening to the Divine Feminine is apparent, whether in the guise of a new interest in the Divine Mother,[22] in the Divine Sophia,[23] or in the apparitions of the Virgin Mary.[24] These and many other signs and phenomena all bear witness to the unfolding of a new revelation of the Divine Feminine."[25]

AQUARIAN AGE, VISION FOR THE. Humanity is to become aware of unseen life in a way unrecognizable until advanced spiritual senses evolve. As it reaches new heights of vibration, the devas will teach humanity: how to nourish the physical body from the ethers, telepathy, and new uses of color and sound. New mystery schools will emerge as the externalization of the Hierarchy occurs and a golden age of cooperation and humanitarian values is realized. This is but a glimpse of the promises toward which people of the Aquarian era are to strive! *Also see* New Age.

with God, the One Mind of the whole universe, is possible for each of us. A man who owned nothing, his will contained a summary of the tenets of the EMERALD TABLET. It is said that his body rose directly to heaven.[15]

Saraydarian continues, "He studied philosophy and became a close friend of the priests of the various temples in Greece and Rome and was initiated into their mysteries. The priests loved Him as He was able to see in their Teaching the common denominator. He ate only fruits and vegetables, did not drink wine, went barefoot, let His hair grow long, and dressed in linen. Once He took a vow of silence for five years. He traveled to Rome, Crete, Greece, Babylon, Nimus, Antioch, Selencia, Asia Minor, Spain, Africa, Egypt, Nepal, and the Ganges, visiting temples and monasteries of wise men. All this time He was overshadowed by the Christ and impressed by Him to further His evolution and to serve Humanity. 'His teaching was pure. He healed the sick, cured the blind, even raised dead men to life, cast out demons, stilled tempests and prophesied the future events . . .' He had His disciples but He left them freedom in their choice of life and never imposed His mode of life on others. Apollonius was worshiped in the beginning of the fourth century under the name of Hercules.'

Archangels

These advanced beings of the angelic kingdom have risen above the limitations of individuality and entered universal, or cosmic, consciousness, as do adepts from the human kingdom. Highest among this group are the seven solar archangels, the Seven Mighty Spirits before the Throne. A vast group of beings, archangels are the directors of the evolution of life and form in every dimension; they step down and bestow energies upon the physical, etheric, and astral world, including the bodies of human beings. The four best-known archangels guide humanity through the seasons of the year: Raphael, spring; Uriel, summer; Michael, autumn; and Gabriel, winter. Since the time of Abraham, Kabalah teaches, Raphael, Uriel, Michael, and Gabriel are the traditional guardians of those who walk the way of Kabalah.

The Four Mighty Archangels

Raphael. Archangel of spring equinox. Considered a major influence in the field of healing, Raphael is in charge of both lesser healing angels and the energies of rejuvenation.

Uriel. Archangel of summer solstice, Uriel paints faces in the clouds and colors the flowers. He brings the blessings of fulfillment.

Michael. Archangel of fall equinox and considered the fierce defender of justice and faith. Michael reminds us to note the seeds we plant and thus what we will harvest in the long run. Acknowledged in the Christian tradition as the principal helper of the Christ.

Gabriel. Archangel of winter solstice. The guardian of mothers and the young of both the human and animal kingdoms and said to be the teacher of Mother Mary. His angelic assistants conduct the celestial music at the time of winter solstice and Christmas, we are told.

"The dates of the births of Jesus and Apollonius have been recorded as very close to each other . . . .

"Apollonius led a victorious life as a Fifth Degree Initiate, and all His teachings paralleled the teachings of Christ. . . . Apollonius surpassed the human kingdom and, through the Fifth Initiation, entered into the kingdom of God. He demonstrated His love toward man and God, and now He was a Master, over-shadowed by the Prince of Peace, the Christ."[16]

Apophatic. An approach to Christian spirituality that is negative, denying, emptying.[17]

Apparition. A visitation of an entity perceived by individuals, as if in physical body having form and density. Not necessarily witnessed by all present but "real" to those who sense the presence.

ARCHANGELS

From the kabalistic perspective: "The hierarchy of angelic beings conforms to the order of the Worlds. . . . The highest entities of the angelic World of Creation are the holy spirits of the inner council, under Metatron; on the central pillar, the great archangels Michael and Gabriel . . . are vehicles of Grace through which the Divine Metatron communicates to Sandalphon at the level of man . . . ," according to Z'ev ben Shimon Halevi.[26] The nature of angel creatures is said to be like creatures below, except they have no physical functions and no individual will. The archangels reside in the world of Briah and take their stations in the sephiroth thereof.

Briah: World of Adam Kadmon and Principal Archangels

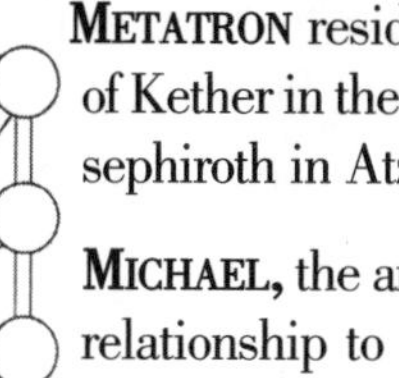

METATRON resides at Tiphareth in the world of Atziluth and is the archangel of Kether in the world of Briah. The ELOHIM surround him at each of the other sephiroth in Atziluth.

MICHAEL, the archangel of Tiphareth, on the center pillar holds special close relationship to humanity, for through Michael and Gabriel, Metatron communicates to Sandalphon at the level of humanity to the self or the psyche.

GABRIEL, assigned to Yesod on the center pillar, assists Michael in the care of humanity as it births its higher nature.

SANDALPHON is the archangel assigned to Malkuth. This densest sephirah is located on the central pillar and cooperates with Gabriel and Michael to assist humanity to receive the energies of the higher sephiroth at the level of the psyche.

Other archangels of Briah assigned to particular sephiroth and their roles:

RAZIEL, assigned to Chokmah, dispenses creative ideas and deep inpulses.

ZAPHKIEL, assigned to Binah, is one of the hosts of Elohim assigned to contemplations.

ZADKIEL, of Chesed, under the hosts of Yahweh; vibrates forces of good and benevolence.

SAMAEL has a special assignment, the archangel of Geburah, under the hosts of ELOHIM. LUCIFER, or Samael, the destructive aspect of divine judgment and the leader of the hosts that test creation, is said to have been one of the highest of archangels until he refused to submit himself to Adam, as even Michael, the captain of the host, had done. Lucifer—also known as Satan, the tester of humanity—may be redeemed at the End of Days in proportion to his state of submission.

HANIEL, assigned to Netzach, bestows grace from above.

RAPHAEL, assigned to Hod, receives and distributes healing energies.

(Paraphrased from the works of Z'ev ben Shimon Halevi, above.)

APPARITIONS, FACILITATED. Intentional contact expedited through the use of a mirror technique to manifest a being from the world of spirit. A term coined by Dr. Raymond Moody, author of *Reunions—Visionary Encounters with Departed Loved Ones.*[18]

APPORT. An object materialized by spirit through the use of unknown laws of manifestation, often accompanying a SEANCE or contact with a powerful nonphysical being.

APPROPRIATE RESPONSE. A phrase bequeathed by mystery teachings acknowledging we must weigh many factors and consciously create a reaction that witnesses to inner awareness, as well as outer. The conscious shaping of a reaction that produces the greatest possible good for all concerned, formed as a result of a thorough evaluation and guided by our highest intuition.

ARCANA. Information, language, or knowledge veiled or protected by symbol so that preparation or initiation is needed to perceive the true, often-hidden meaning, e.g., the tarot arcana.

ARCANE. Secret, veiled, known only to the initiate.

ARCHETYPAL LOGOS. The great being who supervises the divine PLAN for a given group of solar systems and who holds the Plan while other Logoi bring it into manifestation at their levels of command.

ARCHETYPAL WORLD. The great reservoir of prototypical energies from which the ELOHIM created humanity, directing ideas and forces to every level. In kabalistic teachings, the highest world, ATZILUTH.

ARCHETYPE. Greek from *arche,* meaning "old, original, basic," and *typos,* meaning "form." A pattern or blueprint held in the inner planes to guide and assist the lower planes in forming and evolving. The container of subtle energies—basic symbols of consciousness—to be used in modeling oneself. As defined by Carl JUNG, belonging to a collective language of religion or myth. Preserves a more personal energy that can transform or act upon the nature of one who keys into it.

ARCHON. In Greek, "ruler." Invisible, godlike rulers of the world of appearances. Often depicted as a hierarchy ruling from the astral dimension and given names of the Old Testament God, e.g., Adonai, Sabaoth.

ARHAT. A title given by Buddha for his selected core of disciples. It has since come to mean "advanced" or one who has attained the fourth INITIATION and is now preparing for the next level. Purification of human traits is primary; the DWELLER ON THE THRESHOLD must be dissolved. Pain (physical, emotional, or mental) is a principal tool until will aligns to higher influences. This stage is to SOLAR INITIATION as PROBATIONER is to first human initiation.

ARJUNA. The initiate being instructed by KRISHNA, as found in the BHAGAVAD GITA.

ARK OF THE COVENANT. The "Throne of SHEKINAH," kept in the Mosaic tabernacle and the great temple of Solomon, is a reference from the Hebrew tradition and Kabalah to what Christians call the HOLY GRAIL.

ARYAN ROOT RACE. *See* Root race.

AS ABOVE, SO BELOW. The HERMETIC PRINCIPLE of Correspondence, one of seven postulates underlying the spiritual laws of creation. A major concept is that the dense world of physical manifestation is a reflection of the higher; therefore, as we reach a greater understanding of ourselves and our world, we apply it to other realities as well. Examples: *Know thyself if you would know another;* or, microcosm/macrocosm; or, humanity stands equidistant between inner space and outer. *Also see* Macrocosm.

ASANA. A physical posture designated by HATHA YOGA as significant for the stimulation of life energy.

ASCENDANT. Located on the horizon at the time of birth, this constellation is calculated according to birth date, time, and location and of prime importance to the determination of the personal astrological trinity. This sign sits on the eastern horizon, or first house cusp, in an individual's natal chart, or horoscope. Also known as "rising sign."

ASCENSION, THE. The fifth step in the esoteric Christian PATH OF INITIATION; in the life of Jesus, the Christ, when the body was lifted into higher vibrations and was no longer apparent from a physical perspective. Also called the revelation.

ASCENT. The EVOLUTIONARY arc out of dense matter toward subtler realities, marking the journey of the MONAD, or SPARK OF GOD within, toward the higher world on its return to the Source.

ASCESIS. One's work on the self to heal the past and to heal the soul, restoring full potential. Such a practice is rarely taken seriously today. From this word comes "asceticism," conveying the idea of denying oneself pleasure; its true meaning is to undergo exercises necessary to become a different kind of being. Ascesis comes in many forms but particularly physical, psychological, and NOETIC—in other words, "wisdom ways" or transformation.

ASHLAG, RAV YEHUDA. b. 1882, d. 1955. A profound kabalist and mystic of the 20th century who rendered the first Hebrew translation of the ZOHAR from its original Aramaic. His work, *Entrance to the Zohar,* provides an introduction to mystical teachings of Rabbi Shimon bar YOCHAI of 2,000 years ago and the Zohar in *The Sulam.* He also wrote 16 volumes on *The Ten Luminous Emanations*—the SEPHIROTH, which correlate to the CHAKRA system. He wrote,

> *The root of all corruption is the will to receive,*
> *a diverse phase in opposition to that of the Creator*
> *in Whom no such will exists.*

ASHRAM. A spiritual center especially designed for the advancement of consciousness according to a specific practice.

ASIA. Derived from *Assuwa,* thought to be the name of the region in HITTITE texts.

***AS IF* TECHNIQUE.** A conscious choice to work *as if* a desired reality already exists, affirming that it will come to pass, at the same time responding to lessons to be learned as if it were already so.

ASKLEPIOS. A revered Greek god, considered the son of Apollo, a physician who was elevated to the status of divinity after his death. It was believed that at night he entered the hall of the healing temple dedicated to him, wearing a fur coat and carrying the CADUCEUS, offering tender concern, and healing through dreams. Many dramatic cures are said to have occurred.

ASPECT. In astrology, the placement of or relationship between two or more planets is considered "in aspect." The degree of the angle determines whether the relationship is harmonious, inharmonious, or challenging.

ASPIRANT. One who consciously seeks acceptance to the spiritual path. More specifically, a person on the PROBATIONARY PATH, the initial stages of conscious spiritual growth.

ASPIRATION. High ideals or images used for focusing and lifting emotion to devotion; use of higher values and models to uplift human values.

ASSAGIOLI, ROBERTO. b. Venice, 1888, d. 1974. Young colleague of FREUD and JUNG in psychoanalytic studies who formulated a new concept in transpersonal psychology called PSYCHOSYNTHESIS. He believed that, in addition to the individual, conscious self, or "I," every person experiences spiritual realities to be used on the evolutionary path to higher consciousness. He founded the Institute of Psychosynthesis in 1926 and in 1932 began teaching with Alice BAILEY at her school on Lake Maggiore, considered to be of the Agni Yoga tradition. Incarcerated by Fascists during World War II, he began life-long investigations into advanced techniques of meditation and altered states of consciousness, training many in techniques of telepathy and CLAIRVOYANCE. *Psychosynthesis: A Manual of Principles and Techniques,* 1965; *Act of Will,* 1973.

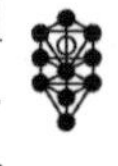

ASSIAH. In Kabalah the physical, material world of form—the dense field of human endeavors; the world of lowest vibration or action.

ASSUMPTION. A Christian term for the translation of the physical body of MARY, MOTHER OF JESUS, into a less dense vehicle and its ascent into heaven. Celebrated on Aug. 15 annually in the Roman Catholic tradition.

ASTRAL. Literally "starry," for bursts of activity and energy that collect in this sensitive, feeling level of being. When the animator level of self is ignited through emotion, it serves desires of personality until purified; then it becomes the battery of the heart-mind connection to serve the soul.

ASTRAL BODY. This nonphysical but feeling vehicle—which can separate from the physical body and travel alone through the etheric/astral reality—looks like the physical manifestation. This emotional, or "starry," body is easily imprinted by energies in the vicinity, as well as by the collective. As the emotional disposition, by nature unstable and powerful, is cleared, the astral body serves as a battery of energy to assist the soul in fulfilling its purpose. *Also see* Chains and rounds.

ASTRAL DIMENSION. This nonmaterial world (world of illusion or desire) consists of the emotional and lower mental planes and is subject to laws other than those operating in the physical world or in the higher worlds of mind and spirit. This reflected plane of being, of a different nature than the etheric dimension, flows through the physical world, interpenetrating the etheric regions of the physical and influencing the activities of this sphere. Composed of what may be described as force-matter, this dimension is one of sensitive ethers of life, feeling, and emotion. As they assume tangible form in this force-matter, feelings, sensations, and emotions each have a particular form, color, and rate of vibration. The combined emotional and lower mental states of humanity form a globe-encircling, globe-penetrating cloud, or aura, that constitutes a world of its own—the astral dimen-

The study of the influence on humanity and planetary life of the vibratory radiations of the sun, the moon, and other celestial bodies in their various positions and relationships. The practice of astrology is considered both an art and a spiritual science. *Also see* Celestial hierarchies; Planets.

ASTROLOGY CHART, THE, or natal horoscope, is a map or diagram of the heavens calculated to present information regarding the impact and influence of the sun, moon, and other planets upon specific people and/or events. A chart is constructed according to the exact date, time, and location of the event.

ASTROLOGY, ESOTERIC. Deals with the qualities and aims of the soul as it encounters Earth-plane experiences; seeks to assist one to comprehend the hidden influences acting upon the personality and its resulting responses.

ASTROLOGY, EVOLUTIONARY. The study of indicators suggesting why a soul projected a personality, what particular shifts in consciousness are the goals of this incarnation. According to evolutionary astrology, one moves from the nadir influences of a chart to the midheaven, ascending in consciousness as climbing a learning ladder. This is the first of three definitive markers this branch of astrology uses to study soul purpose in a given incarnation; the other two are the direction indicated by the south node–north node indicator and advancement from the planet behind the moon to the one before the moon.

ASTROLOGY, EXOTERIC, OR MUNDANE. Addresses the characteristics and qualities of the personality and outer aspects of a life.

ASTROLOGY, HORARY. A particular school of astrology utilizing specific techniques to refine the time of birth or an event by the study of the timing of other events in one's life. A quite detailed and exacting form of astrology.

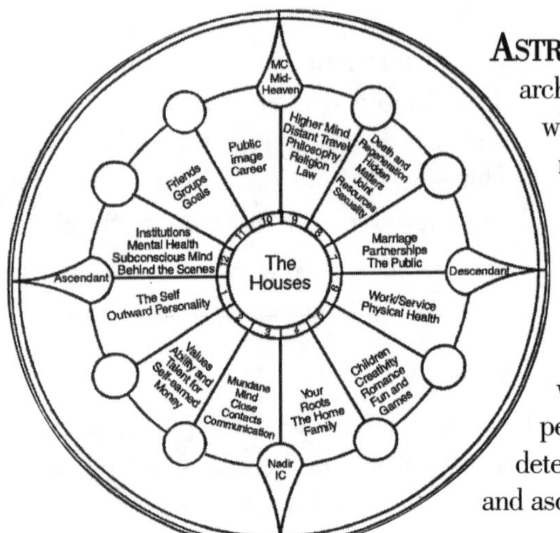

ASTROLOGICAL SUN SIGN PROFILES. Great archetypes help us understand the energies to which we are attuned. Each person has three major personality influences—sun, moon, and ascendant—to be integrated for personal growth.

AGNI YOGA suggests the influences under which a person is born reveal what the soul has designated as virtues upon which one is to focus in this lifetime. Each person has three major qualities to develop, determined by assigned virtues of sun, moon, and ascendant. *Also see* Agni virtues.

ARIES (approximately March 20–April 20). Recognized strengths: youthfully vital, warm, bright, dynamic, independent, assertive, courageous; initiator and leader. Potential weaknesses: impatient, headstrong, arrogant, intrusive; lacks perseverance, quick to over-react. Element: fire. Hidden helper: Libra. Virtue: enthusiasm. Ruled by Mars. Motto: *I am.*

TAURUS (approx. April 20–May 20). Recognized strengths: hard-working, stable, persistent, responsible, determined, patient, reliable, slow to anger; cherishes nature and loves to create beauty. Potential weaknesses: stubborn (as a bull), materialistic, slow, selfish; sexual nature may dominate. Element: earth. Hidden helper: Scorpio. Virtue: beauty. Ruled by Venus. Motto: *I have, I hold.*

GEMINI (approx. May 20–June 20). Recognized strengths: quick-minded, versatile, alert, inventive, chatty, adaptable, sociable, energetic. Potential weaknesses: fickle, judgmental, easily scattered; over-commits. Element: air. Hidden helper: Sagittarius. Virtue: universality. Ruled by Mercury. Motto: *I think.*

CANCER (approx. June 20–July 20). Recognized strengths: nurturing, supportive, home-loving; patriotic, sensitive, tenacious; listens well. Potential weaknesses: possessive, over-reactive, evasive, emotional. Element: water. Hidden helper: Capricorn. Virtue: leadership. Ruled by moon. Motto: *I feel.*

LEO (approx. July 20–Aug. 20). Recognized strengths: courageous, perceptive, generous, affectionate, creative, receptive, self-confident; seeks the limelight. Potential weaknesses: egocentric, selfish, domineering, proud, over-bearing. Element: fire. Hidden helper: Aquarius. Virtue: love. Ruled by sun. Motto: *I will.*

VIRGO (approx. Aug. 20–Sept. 20). Recognized strengths: detail-oriented, intelligent, discerning, self-disciplined, analytic, hardworking, unassuming; self-examiner. Potential weaknesses: judgmental, negative, critical, skeptical; low self-esteem. Element: earth. Hidden helper: Pisces. Virtue: purity. Ruled by Mercury. Motto: *I analyze.*

LIBRA (approx. Sept. 20–Oct. 20). Recognized strengths: perceptive, charming, sociable, diplomatic; negotiator; lover of harmony, justice, and beauty. Potential weaknesses: indecisive, codependent, quick to swing to opposite pole; unexpected rigidity. Element: air. Hidden helper: Aries. Virtue: reverence. Ruled by Venus. Motto: *I balance.*

SCORPIO (approx. Oct. 20–Nov. 20). Recognized strengths: enduring, intense, sexually alluring, introspective, practical, never superficial; admirable recuperative powers. Potential weaknesses: secretive, vindictive, purposefully mysterious, sexually excessive, lacking in self-understanding. Element: water. Hidden helper: Taurus. Virtue: transformation. Ruled by Pluto. Motto: *I desire.*

SAGITTARIUS (approx. Nov. 20–Dec. 20). Recognized strengths: analytical, philosophical, straightforward, friendly, optimistic, honest, independent, fun, enthusiastic, direct, quick-witted; loves travel and freedom. Potential weaknesses: fickle, disloyal, sharp-tongued or blunt, truthful to a fault; can be shattered. Element: fire. Hidden helper: Gemini. Virtue: harmlessness. Ruled by Jupiter. Motto: *I perceive.*

CAPRICORN (approx. Dec. 20–Jan. 20). Recognized strengths: stable, progresses slowly, goal-oriented, obedient to rules and regulations, achieving, self-disciplined, reliable, persevering. Potential weaknesses: materialistic, fearful, conservative, excessively ambitious, overly cautious; needs recognition, may be melancholy. Element: earth. Hidden helper: Cancer. Virtue: fearlessness. Ruled by Saturn. Motto: *I see.*

AQUARIUS (approx. Jan. 20–Feb. 20). Recognized strengths: generous, inventive, detached, progressive, tolerant, ingenuous, open-minded, social, creative; problem-solver, humanitarian. Potential weaknesses: unconventional, eccentric, changeable, independent to a fault, unsteady, aloof. Element: air. Hidden helper: Leo. Virtue: humility. Ruled by Uranus. Motto: *I know.*

PISCES (approx. Feb. 20–March 20). Recognized strengths: imaginative, sensitive, spiritual, sympathetic, compassionate, charming, dramatic, humorous, impressionable, kind, gentle, graceful. Potential weaknesses: depressive, addictive, evasive; low vitality, may lack will power. Element: water. Hidden helper: Virgo. Virtue: joy. Ruled by Neptune. Motto: *I believe.*

sion. Its dominant laws are attraction, repulsion, METAMORPHOSIS, and TRANSFORMATION. This realm is inhabited by innumerable sensate beings—i.e., devas, discarnates, elementals, as well as empty shells—who operate in diverse subtle ways to influence humanity through desires and emotions. Dominated by desires and living without physical form, they are still capable of influencing others and growing themselves. A living record of feelings, pictures, sounds, and colors of the happenings of all planetary life is preserved in this reflecting ether.

ASTRAL LIGHT WORKERS. Awakened ones who actively distribute light and love and healing through their consciousness as a service to those in need. These helpers may be in physical embodiment or may serve invisibly from the spiritual realms, i.e., healing angels and beings of inspiration, such as the saints.

ASTRAL PLANE. The reflective ETHERS that record the sensitive, feeling level of individuals and of the collective—the emotional nature. The seven astral sub-planes from the highest are archetypes (though distorted); moral codes (distorted); music, color, and artistic forms; objects of devotion; emotionally charged values of self and others; appetites and sexual agitations; wishes and fantasies. *Also see* Planes, cosmic.

ASTRAL PROJECTION. Purposeful separation from the physical body of a person, usually when at rest, to experience at the nonphysical level. One may become conscious at this astral dimension. A conscious projecting may be mastered by some who, through the power of strong emotion, withdraw their ASTRAL BODY at will and "travel" to locations other than where the physical body is located—often for purposes of healing, comforting, or other world services at times of trauma. The astral body contains correspondences to the five physical senses and experiences at the level registered upon them "as if" one were in her/his physical nature. Also called OUT-OF-BODY EXPERIENCE (OOB).

ASTRAL SENSES. Faculties that psychically perceive the subtler or less dense frequencies, i.e., feelings or thoughts free of physical limitation, such as time and space. They are to the feeling nature what physical senses are to dense bodies.

ASTRAL TRAVEL. The experience of the separate dream-body, motivated by desire, that leaves behind the physical form to move about in the nonphysical reality behind the veil of sleep. Also called "astral projection." *See* Out-of-body experience.

ASTRAL VEHICLE. This feeling body, less material than the physical body, consists of emotional matter, or the desire nature, interpenetrating the physical body.

ASTRAL WORLD. The combined feeling and thinking nonphysical reality that permeates the matter world and its etheric body, charging it with emotions and impressions. It extends beyond the densified reality to form the astral body of the planet.

ATHEISM. A belief system acknowledging no deity or supreme creator; an approach to the unfolding of life as rational and mechanistic—nonspiritual.

ATLANTEAN ROOT RACE. *See* Root race.

ATLANTIS. Legendary continent believed to have been located in the Atlantic Ocean, now submerged. Having reached a high civilization, it destroyed itself through misuse and abuse of power. Its downfall is usually noted to be in three parts: 50,000 years ago, 30,000 years ago, and the latest about 10,000 years ago at the time of the Flood. Mayans believe this to be their original home.

ATMA. The self; the universal spirit of life, or highest divine frequency of the septenary constitution of every human being. *See* Monad.

ATMAN. A Hindu term for the inner being, the spark of life residing within, "the Supreme Self"; also called the Self, the True Being. In Christianity, corresponds to the CHRIST-WITHIN—the Hope of Glory—or in humanistic psychology, the TRANSPERSONAL SELF.

ATMIC PLANE. The more highly vibrating plane of divine will flowing directly from the MONADIC PLANE of the Trinity, the Supernal. Here divine will is expressed in seven sub-influences, or sub-planes, as (from the highest) the will to initiate, will to unify, will to evolve, will to harmonize or relate, will to act, will to cause, and will to express. *Also see* Planes, cosmic.

ATOM. Esoterically, a vortex ring or a positive nucleus of energy surrounded with electrons

AUROBINDO, SRI GHOSE

b. Calcutta, 1872, d. 1950. Philosopher, mystic, educator, and poet, the guiding force behind AUROVILLE ASHRAM. He and his disciple, Mira RICHARDS, known as "the Mother," delivered to the world a set of teachings called INTEGRAL YOGA. Its purpose was to bring about the salvation of society by individual attainment of higher consciousness. *The Life Divine,* 1940; *The Synthesis of Yoga,* 1948; *Aurobindo on Himself,* 1953.

A mass of new material is flowing into us; . . . the remote and dateless past which seemed to be dead is returning upon us with an effulgence of many luminous secrets long lost to the consciousness of mankind but now breaking out again from behind the veil.

For centuries you have waited for this time. Now it has come: the hour of the unexpected, the hour of God, when the Spirit moves among men and the breath of the Lord is abroad upon the waters of your being, when even a little effort changes destiny.

I see the Omnipotent's flaming pioneers come crowding down the amber stairs of births—forerunners of a divine multitude. Out of the paths of the morning star they come. I see them cross the twilight of an age, the sun-eyed children of a marvelous dawn, the massive barrier breakers of the world carrying the magical word, the mystic fire, swimmer of Love's laughing fiery floods and dancers within rapture's golden doors.

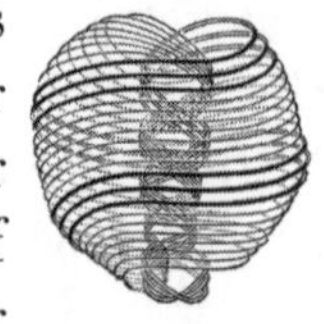

or negative corpuscles, thus subdividing the atom of earlier science into numerous lesser bodies. Exoterically, phase of electrical phenomena; a center of energy active through its own internal make-up and emitting energy, heat, or radiation.

Atomic planes (and sub-planes). Frequencies used by the MONAD to emanate its will toward the denser reality to be conveyed by the soul. The lowest level of monadic and the highest level of soul intermingle in expression.

At-one-ment. The state of unity with the one Source of which humanity is capable, whereby the parts of creation become whole, or one.

Attached entity. *See* Spirit attachment.

Attachment. A tie or bond to a person, thing, or idea—positive or negative in nature—that becomes a barrier to illumination due to a conscious or unconscious refusal to release in order to embrace the new.

In Psychography one or more entities appended to an incarnate soul (rather than advancing on their own soul pattern of growth), influencing the incarnated one by adding conditions of the attached one, thus restricting the freedom of the host. When positive, the attachment may act as a guardian for a period of time but must release or be released when the challenge passes or it will become negative. For example, a deceased mother who stays with and attempts to watch over her child is no longer on her path and may unconsciously impact her will on the

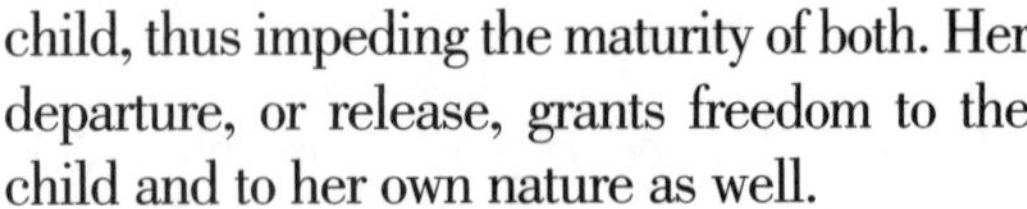

child, thus impeding the maturity of both. Her departure, or release, grants freedom to the child and to her own nature as well.

Attribute. A characteristic associated with various aspects of our being. Specific traits combine to form keynotes of an individual existence.

Attunement. A technique for becoming "one in vibration with . . . . . ." The natural state of blending with our surroundings.

Atziluth. The subtlest fiery world, as known in Kabalah.

Augoeides. It is said the soul is encased within a subtle oval of fiery, radiant matter, delicate as the evanescence of a sunset, frequently pictured as a rainbow of colored light, the AURA, around an advanced human. This light of the soul becomes the light of the human as s/he becomes increasingly SOUL INFUSED. "The celestial or perpetual vehicle of the soul—its 'robe of glory'."[27]

Augustine. *See pp. 246–51,* Saints.

Aum. *See* Om.

Aura. A subtle emanation of the energy pattern of a soul shining through the physical and etheric bodies, the emotional nature, and the mental make-up, as well as the soul in its field of activity.

Aurascope. A precise reading of the human aura wherein the history of an individual's soul is recorded in color and vibration. A technique created by Ann MANSER; she studied the aura of her subject by remote viewing and then wrote an extensive analysis of her findings.

AURORA. A PLANETARY CENTER (in the etheric) now activated in the intra-terrestrial region of Salto, Uruguay. *Aurora* means "dawn."[28] *Also see pp. 349–55,* Etheric Dimensions.

AUROREAN ROOT RACE. *See* Root race.

AUROVILLE ASHRAM. A spiritual community at Pondicherry, (French) India, from which the teachings of INTEGRAL YOGA were delivered to the world by Sri Ghose AUROBINDO.

AUSTERITY OF SPEECH. A SPIRITUAL DISCIPLINE of consciously limiting speech to important interactions; related to but not a practice of total silence, rather saying what is necessary without frills or social amenities.

AUTHENTIC. From a Greek word meaning "one who acts independently." Genuine, accurate presentation, entitled to acceptance or belief; trustworthy, reliable.

AUTOHYPNOSIS. A technique wherein an individual directs the self from an altered state of consciousness.

AUTOMATIC WRITING. The act of a DISCARNATE utilizing a person in the physical to write through either guidance or information. Usually the person is in a light trance, and the entity uses the arm and hand to relay its message. Considered risky, for the entity need not be very evolved to achieve this.

AUTOMATISM. The "manipulation of the medium's body—most often the vocal cords, sometimes the arms, and occasionally the entire body—by a controlling agent other than the will of the medium. . . . in deep trance."[29]

AUTOPILOT. Often referred to as "getting our buttons pushed"; no conscious thought occurs, just unconscious reaction. When stimulated, this tender point in the unconscious brings instant reaction. In the millisecond between experience and response, autopilots communicate unconscious patterns from past experiences created to protect us.

AUTOSUGGESTION. A thought existing in the unconscious mind causing specific and immediate attitudes, actions, or bodily conditions.

AVALOKITA. Sanskrit for "the Lord who is perceived or recognized." The spiritual entity whose influence is recognized; the Soul unfolded and expressing, as in ADEPT or MASTER.

AVALOKITESHVARA. The masculine version of the BODHISATTVA OF COMPASSION; translates "one who looks down from on high."

AVATAR. One who is not bound by the WHEEL OF REBIRTH but comes to humanity in its spiritual growth. Divine potency embodied in an avatar acts as a regenerative power for humanity and appears approximately once each age, usually near the beginning of an era. In Sanskrit, literally "he descends" (avator in Hindi); said to be an incarnation of God; the descent of Divinity into human form. More specifically, an avatar is an incarnation of Vishnu in the Hindu tradition. (It is taught there have been nine avatars, with the tenth still to come). The concept originated about the 6th century B.C. Totally different from a human being who becomes enlightened, avatars are born perfect and in a supernatural way; they have no karma, remember their previous lives, and are conscious of their mission from birth.

AVATAR OF SYNTHESIS. An Agni term. The expected one who will be the guiding consciousness of the new era. Little can be said of this Great Mystery except that the consciousness of this forthcoming avatar will overlight and reinforce the work of the CHRIST. The avatar will influence us through the mental plane, promoting good will, harmony, unity, seeking to eradicate separativeness.

AWAKENED ONES. Those aware of deity and desirous of interacting with higher realities.

AWAKENING. Secondary influence of human nature that stirs and becomes conscious of a path to high consciousness (the primary influence being survival). A capacity for fresh insights and intellectual awareness; a state of liberation from conventional thought and openness to a new perspective enters the consciousness. *See* Divine discontent.

AWARENESS. The capacity for cognizance transcending limitations of physical senses and gathering information or experiences in areas considered unreachable by many.

AYURVEDA. A popular name for the body of health and medical knowledge originated by the Eastern tradition that has been preserved from ancient times and now is being revisited by many for its valued contributions to the body-mind-spirit field.

AZTECS. A strong native people of Mexico who followed the Maya into power. Known for their ferocity, they conquered many cities and states throughout Central and South America.

B

Baal. The most active and prominent of all Canaanite deities, Baal was the god of storms and fertility, whose name means "Lord" and is an epithet of the god Hadad, the thunderer. The fertility of the land depended on the rain Baal supplied. The Baal sect, a cult of the goddess, provided the greatest, most persistent threat to the establishment of exclusive Yahweh worship in ancient Israel.

Baba. Father, in Hindi.

Babaji. A name of endearment given many Hindu saints meaning "dear father" or "holy father."

Babaji Herakhan. This saint, who reincarnates in the northern Himalayas, is said to create a body without physical parents or birth, appearing and disappearing at will, merely calling his physical form into manifestation as needed. He remains visible to a small number of people on Earth. He specifically incarnated in 1970 through 1984 when he took MAHASAMADHI, returning to spirit, and is considered the supreme guru of the Self-Realization Fellowship. Babaji's disciple, Lahiri Mahasaya, received KRIYA YOGA from him to pass on as a means to "control sensory mind and intellect; and to banish desire, fear, and anger." Kriya Yoga is cited twice in the Bhagavad Gita. For modern introduction see Paramahansa YOGANANDA'S *Autobiography of a Yogi,* 1946, or *I Am Harmony* by Radhe Shyam, 1989.

Babel, Tower of. *See* Tower of Babel.

Babylon. Means "Gate of the Gods." Often used as a reference akin to "sin city." In Revelation we are told the kings of the Earth must face temptation from the "whore of Babylon," meaning adulterated materialism,

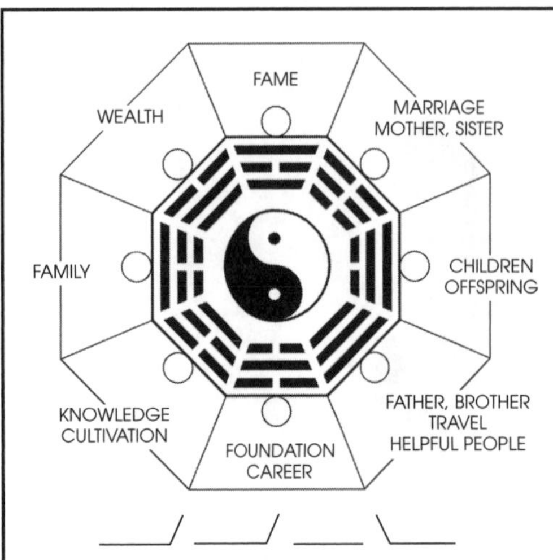

BAGUA. In FENG SHUI, a "map" (left) used to determine the placement of nine life issues as represented in a space. Feng Shui is based on the principle that your space mirrors your life. When the bagua is correctly placed and enhanced, your life will manifest harmony, good health, and good fortune. The map is placed at the entrance of a building, room, or specific space (e.g., one's desk) and detailed directions fulfill the "art of placement." Feng Shui practitioners are trained to guide in the application of the bagua.

distorted values of the physical world. Located on the lower Euphrates River in what is now Iraq.

BAHA'I. A more contemporary religion, founded in Iran in 1844 by the Bab who proclaimed the faith and was followed by Baha'u'lla, the chosen prophet to bring the faith to fruition. Baha'i has a strong dedication to love of humanity and world service. Similar to esoteric traditions and quite interfaith, along the line of modern Sufism, except it does not accept the doctrine of reincarnation.

BAILEY, ALICE A. b. Manchester, England, 1880, d. 1949. Theosophist and spiritualist writer. She was first visited in 1919 by MASTER DJWHAL KHUL, spiritual guide also called "the Tibetan," who dictated the ancient wisdom teachings to her over a 30-year period. These "Bailey books" comprise 20 volumes. In 1923, she founded the Arcane School in New York, seeking to establish a world-wide organization unifying traditions of East and West. *Light from the Soul,* 1927; *The Great Invocation,* 1937; *The Reappearance of the Christ,* 1948, are gifts of this school of thought.

BALLARD, GUY WARREN. b. Kansas, 1878, d. 1939. Founded the "I AM" religious activity, an offshoot of ROSICRUCIANISM. He claimed to have been visited by Comte de St. GERMAIN, the ascended MASTER, who had come to initiate the Seventh Golden Age of Eternal Perfection on Earth and to disseminate teachings on the Great Law of Life. With his wife, Edna Anne Ballard, he established the Saint Germain Press and the Saint Germain Foundation, giving rise to a number of like-minded groups and much channeled material. *Unveiled Mysteries,* 1934; *The Magic Presence,* 1935; *The "I AM" Discourses,* 1936.

BALL OF KNOWLEDGE. The understanding and awareness gathered through many experiences (other lives) and retained by the High Self. Data that can be brought to consciousness largely through meditation, particularly guided approaches, to assist one in a current life.

BAPTISM. A Christian sacrament invoking spiritual forces and guardians—both physical and nonphysical—to assist us as we encounter life's challenges. The rite opens the aura to environmental influence. Parents and godparents commit to consciously assist the soul in its growth. In baptism, as the aura (our natural protective covering) is ruptured, the ritual invokes grace to foster spiritual awareness.

BARDO. The after-life reality through which we travel as we process our life review, confronting emotional situations and unfinished business to see if we have sufficiently satisfied seeds of KARMA to be freed from their influence. A significant share of the *Tibetan Book of the Dead* relates to the bardo. An old and excellent volume is *The 49 Days of Death* by Bill S. Ballinger, 1969.[1]

BARRIERS (TO ILLUMINATION). Emotional or mental in nature, GLAMOURS and ILLUSIONS that restrict and constrict consciousness while reinforcing distortion and limitation within the consciousness of the carrier.

BASIC SELF. (Also, basic nature, lower self, or SELF with lower-case s). The personality we choose for this life, possessing certain characteristics, such as masculine and feminine traits and unique RAY influences that modify the physical, emotional, and mental natures to form and reform the character. More than the subconscious nature, it includes our specific emotional and mental patterns, intuitive capacities, likes and dislikes, and so on.

BEACON OF ACHIEVEMENT. An Agni term. One who stands purified and radiant with the manifestation of cosmic fire. "Few understand how the dwellers themselves can be like beacons."[2] Thus Agni yogis contain within their centers the cosmic fire that transforms them into beacons.

BEAUTY. Agni virtue for Taurus. Beauty is sustenance to the emerging spirit. It bestows the ability to see and apprehend splendor in the world. Knowing beauty is in the eye of the beholder, we usually see first the beauty of things, then nature, then we come to behold the light in another. As we do so, we learn to see the beauty in ourselves and how to be the beauty needed to illumine the world.

BEHIND EMOTIONS DWELL FEELINGS; BEHIND INTELLECT AWAITS KNOWING. A saying to remind us that emotions veil deeper feelings, and when the emotional nature is clear, we can contact the true feelings of the self. Further, the intellect conceals our inner knower until we become conscious of subtle impressions that provide profound wisdom.

BEING. Allowing awareness and consciousness of the true self to take form through the uniqueness of the moment and personality. Centered in the here and now, the true being just is. Being and doing are often seen in opposition to one another, with doing causing us to create a false identity as to our own nature.

BEINGNESS. Beingness concerns qualities of the true self we bring to life situations and the integration of levels of self in practical, honorable, and serving ways.

BERMUDA TRIANGLE. A certain territory east of the southern U.S. in the Atlantic Ocean. Many peculiar incidents are said to occur in this area, believed by many to be a place of time-space warp and/or an opening to other planes or dimensions.

BESANT, ANNIE WOOD. b. London, 1847, d. 1933. Theosophist, feminist, and president of the Indian National Congress in 1919. Noted for her stand in favor of birth control in such an unlikely era as the 1870s and for founding the Freethought Publishing Company with Charles Bradlaugh. A devoted student of Madame BLAVATSKY'S ancient wisdom teachings and investigations into the occult, she collaborated with C. W. Leadbeater on *Man: Whence, How and Whither*, 1913, an examination of human history as an evolutionary journey; *The Ancient Wisdom*, 1897; *Esoteric Christianity*, 1901; *The Spiritual Life*, 1912.

BETROTHAL. *See* Disciplines, sexual.

BHAGAVAD GITA. Sacred writing of the Hindi, part of the great epic Mahabharata. A teaching segment excerpted as hallowed text is translated into English as *The Song of God.*

BHAKTI YOGA. *See* Yoga.

BIBLIOMANCY. The use of the Bible for guidance or in response to a query. The practice of opening the Bible without looking, putting one's finger on a verse, and using the Scripture as divination.

BILOCATION. The seeming ability to appear and be recognized in more than one place at a time. A phenomenon recorded in stories of certain saints and holy ones. A modern example is PADRE PIO (1887–1968).

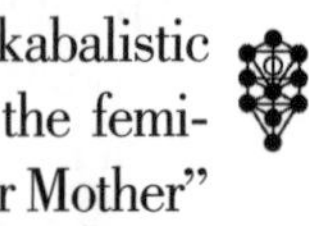

BINAH. The third SEPHIRAH on the kabalistic TREE and the highest sephirah on the feminine PILLAR; also called the "Superior Mother" and noted as the home of the HOLY SPIRIT.

BINGEN, HILDEGARD OF. *See pp. 246–51,* Saints, Hildegard of Bingen.

BIOENERGETICS. The invisible energy system by which the human organism can be understood. Acting as both receiver and transmitter, the subtle body can be facilitated in healing and clearing techniques and acupuncture, as well as serving as the etheric vehicle wherein centers of consciousness exist.

BIOFEEDBACK. A process of registering subtle changes in physiology of autonomic functions, such as heart beat, brain-wave frequencies, minute body temperature, or skin resistance as states of consciousness change, i.e., at rest or asleep, stressed, etc. A tool useful in learning to manipulate or control unconscious reflexes by conscious design for certain benefits, particularly health improvement.

BIOPLASM. Psi energy.

BIORHYTHM. A system of measuring and plotting the flow of energy in the physical, emotional, and mental dimensions of our nature; often used to study oneself.

BLACK MAGIC, OR BLACK ARTS. The selfish use of power to enhance ego or materialism or to manipulate others; thus, the misuse of spiritual powers for ego gratification. *Magick*, an old term, meaning "transformation or transformational powers"—could be positive or negative. As the term fell into abuse, the term "alchemy" emerged.

BLACK MOON. In alchemy, the feminine point opposite the WHITE SUN. *Also see* Unicorn eye.

BLACK SUN. In alchemy, an astrological reference similar to our notion of HELL.

BLAVATSKY, HELENA PETROVNA. b. Ukraine, 1831, d. 1891, the first Russian woman to become a naturalized American citizen (1878). Widely acclaimed occultist, psychic, and adept who in 1875, with Henry Steel Olcott, founded the THEOSOPHICAL SOCIETy to "promote universal brotherhood, study various religions of the world, and investigate psychic phenomena." *The Secret Doctrine*—cited as the "authentic sourcebook" for the birth, structure, and evolution of the universes, solar systems, and our Earth's humanities—is considered her great work. A disciple of MASTER MORYA, she imparted his teachings as Theosophy, formalizing concepts of REINCARNATION and KARMA, spiritual hierarchy, and the divine Plan. She taught that theosophy was "divine ethics" and that the way must be prepared for the coming of the Lord MAITREYA who would issue in a new cycle in human evolution. *Isis Unveiled,* 1877; *The Secret Doctrine, The Key to Theosophy, The Voice of Silence,* all published 1889.

BLENDED HEART. An Agni term. A clue to a prerequisite for spiritual advancement—the integration of thinking and feeling, of mind and heart. A blended heart is able to perceive, empathize, understand, and adjust to demands consistent to unfolding spiritual maturity.

BLISS. The nature of the inner spirit. Resonance to the holy within bestows bliss, joy, grace.

BLOOD OF THE HEART. This symbol of outer life stands for personality desires; it represents the grief and suffering through which the heart frees itself of desire domination.

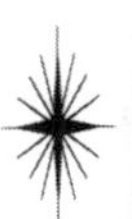

BLUE MOON. In astrology, a second full moon in any given sun sign period—an infrequent occurrence at irregular intervals. Whether a Blue Moon is the second full moon in a sun sign or in a month is disputed.

BODHI. In Sanskrit, "to awaken."

BODHISATTVA. World Teacher, a pure being carrying a high RAY 2 love-wisdom energy. Sanskrit for one who carries BUDDHIC energy and in a future incarnation will become a BUDDHA (enlightened to NIRVANA), or one whose consciousness has become enlightened intelligence, or BUDDHI. Used much like Western spiritual traditions use "Christed." Bodhisattvas choose to remain close to humanity and the planet to continue to assist sentient beings.

BODHISATTVA OF COMPASSION. An oriental title given most frequently to the personification of the DIVINE FEMININE, KUAN YIN, in the way "Queen of Peace" refers to Holy Mary, Mother of Jesus. The masculine version of the Bodhisattva of Compassion is AVALOKITESHVARA, translating "one who looks down from on high," or AVALOKITA, Sanskrit for "the Lord who is perceived or recognized." *Also see* Mothers and Goddesses of the World.

Bodhi Tree. The specific tree under which Gautama Siddhartha, the Buddha, sat and meditated until he reached enlightenment. It is so called for the service it rendered to the Bodhisattva, the Buddha.

Body-consciousness. Recognition of the intelligence in-dwelling the physical body and nonphysical SHEATHS used by soul in anchoring a personality in the dense world. CELLULAR INTELLIGENCE—the purposeful intelligence of organs and systems, as well as collective intelligence of the physical body—is now acknowledged, especially appreciated in body-mind-spirit communication.

Boehme, Jakob. b. Germany, 1575, d. 1624. A simple medieval cobbler of peasant stock who became a revered Christian mystic. As a youth, he discovered the ability to enter altered states of consciousness and see into the astral light. Though apprenticed as a shoemaker, he was able to read and write and, in 1612, recounted the visions he had experienced from boyhood.

"The Protestant mystic while in prayerful meditation passed through a series of remarkable mystical experiences. It seemed to him that the physical atmosphere which surrounded him was actually opaque, but with the eye of his soul he was able to clear away the material mist and behold the splendors of the superphysical realms. He was in the midst of a living light which flowed and moved in patterns of celestial colors. Space was filled with spirits administering the physical phenomena of the universe. He could endure such visions for only a short time and allowed the veil to close, but the memory of what he had seen remained with him; these glimpses of reality were incorporated in his philosophy and sustained him through long years of adversity."[3]

As foretold by a stranger under mysterious circumstances, he was maligned and persecuted throughout his life. Boehme advocated an esoteric, cosmic understanding of Christ and maintained his writings described only what he had learned from divine illumination; that no one needed assistance from the established church to find fulfillment in Christ. When in a meditative state, Boehme often perceived Sophia. He became a major source for Sophia writings, inspiring theologians and poets for centuries. He believed that God reconciles all opposites, is the basis of all being, and the source of all energy; that all existing things carry the signature of God. *The Signature of All Things,* 1621; *Mysterium Magnum,* 1623; *The Way to Christ,* 1623. *See pp. 268–77,* Introducing the Sophia Teachings.

Bonaventure. *See pp. 246–51,* Saints.

Book of Changes. Another name for the *I Ching,* a Chinese system of wisdom based on 64 hexagrams, patterns of six lines, and accessed by a particular formula of coins or yarrow stalks. The inquirer forms questions before throwing. The book contains interpretations of the meaning of each hexagram.

Born again. A spiritual birth that occurs during incarnation. The empowerment of "babes in Christ," candidates for the teachings, to whom spiritual reality extends—attaining "eyes with which to see and ears with which to hear." The second (and nonphysical) birth is the birth of the Christ-Within. The third is realized by initiates of a disciplined nature when they achieve soul maturity, at which time they become an Arhat.

Bottomless Cauldron, the. The Well of Transformation, or the Holy Grail in Celtic lore, sacred to the goddess Ceriddwen.

Brahma, or Brahman. In Hinduism, the essential divine reality of the universe; the eternal spirit from which all beings originate and to which all return. Also, a name applied to the highest caste—originally comprising only priests, now more diverse.

Brain. The physical instrument designed to respond to the messages of higher intelligence and the impressions of mind. This physical mechanism constitutes a tool of both individuals and the planetary deity as collective humanity becomes the mind of the planet. *See* Hemispheres, right and left, of the brain; Three-brain concept.

Brandwein, Rav Yehuda. b. Safed, 1904, d. 1969; 20th century kabalist, disciple of Rav Yehuda Ashlag. A gentle and kind soul who paved the way for kabalistic teachings to be released to the masses.

Briah. The second of four worlds in Kabalah, the World of Creation, also called Khorsis, the World of Thrones, and the world of Adam Kadmon. Here, the energies of the sephiroth manifest through the ten archangels. The sephiroth, regarded as emanations of deity, represent a group of exalted ideas, titles, and attributes. A hierarchy of angelic spiritual beings abides here, guiding the devic family developing in its own dimension parallel to humanity.

Bridge techniques. Exercises used in Psychography to move a client in an altered state of consciousness from the present to the past. *Also see* Affect bridge; Linguistic bridge; Mental bridge; Somatic bridge.

Bro, Harmon. b. Nanking, China, 1919, to missionary parents; d. Sept. 13, 1997, West Yarmouth, Mass. "He served a unique role in the Association for Research and Enlightenment (ARE) community because of the time he spent working and studying directly with Edgar Cayce. In recent years, Bro and his wife June Avis Bro have been the only living eyewitnesses to hundreds of Cayce's readings."[4] Bro had degrees from Harvard and the University of Chicago with emphasis in world religions. A psychotherapist, he practiced a Jungian-based psychotherapy for over 40 years. His doctoral dissertation and a biography of Cayce, *A Seer Out of Season,* were based on his time spent with Cayce. He wrote seven books and many articles for various publications. Bro was a columnist for *Venture Inward* during the '80s.

Brotherhood, Dark. A formation of strong egos that seeks to restrict human evolution, tempting humans to amplify their love of power rather than to open the heart, learning love and service. These influences strengthen the forces of duality and individuality, catering to those in search of personal power and will, magnifying personality ego rather than yielding to higher will.

BROTHERHOOD (THE). The Hierarchy of ELDER BROTHERS BEFORE THE THRONE, as called in Christian tradition: saints and holy ones who have emerged from the human condition into greater oneness with the Christ. Having passed certain tests at first initiation, aspirants are deemed worthy of the attention of this HIERARCHY, also known as the Great White Brotherhood.

BROTHERHOOD, WHITE (or White Lodge). The Hierarchy of elders leading humanity on its evolutionary path. The term "white" is used as in "white magic" or positive transformation—the enhancing of ego—versus the path of darkness.

BRUJO. Central and South American shaman or wise one. A term used by Carlos Casteneda.

BRUNTON, PAUL. b. 1898, d. 1981. "British philosopher, mystic, and traveler. He left a successful journalistic career to live among yogis, mystics, and holy men, and studied a wide variety of Eastern and Western esoteric teachings. With his entire life dedicated to an inward, spiritual quest, he felt charged with the task of communicating his experiences to others and, as the first person to write accounts of what he learned in the East from a Western perspective, his works had a major influence on the spread of Eastern mysticism to the West. Taking pains to express his thoughts in layperson's terms, Brunton was able to present what he learned from the Orient and from ancient tradition as a living wisdom. His writings sum up his view that meditation and the inward quest are not exclusively for monks and hermits, but will also support those living normal, active lives in the Western world."[5]

BUDDHA. An "enlightened one" who has developed the buddhic principle of spiritual discrimination. There have been many buddhas, so teaches the East, but the one most remembered and recognized in this era is Gautama Siddhartha, whose birth prompted many holy events. This Buddha anchored the wisdom principle for humanity upon the Earth, say occult teachings, and lived a long life teaching the FOUR NOBLE TRUTHS and the EIGHT-FOLD PATH. Improperly used as a personal name, it is a title, as is "the Christ." It is said that on the night of his enlightment he recalled all his previous lives—some 900,000 of them.

BUDDHA BUMP. A ridge or mound currently developing on the heads of certain human beings, indicative of the evolving physical form, allowing more room in the cranial cavity for the expected "fourth" brain, or PRE-FRONTAL LOBE.

BUDDHA CONSCIOUSNESS. Correlates in Eastern thought to Christ consciousness, meaning an "enlightened state of consciousness" experienced as "unlimited holy awareness."

BUDDHA, GAUTAMA SIDDHARTHA. ca. 563–483 B.C. Called "The Blessed One" or "The Enlightened," Buddha taught that the true self is God and God is the true self. His most important revelations concern the causes of suffering and the way in which salvation from suffering may be achieved. Buddhism teaches, he experienced 24 lives as a BODHISATTVA while on the path, choosing to remain in the world to teach. The next bodhisattva to achieve buddhahood, we are told, will be MAITREYA.

BUDDHAHOOD. A state of enlightenment achieved by Gautama Siddhartha and other Buddhas before him. Similar to "Christ consciousness" or "holy consciousness."

BUDDHI. Sanskrit, meaning intellect at the level of spiritual subjectivity. The love and cognition flowing through the spiritualized heart useful in softening the destructive mind. Often refers to the energy of heart and mind blended and balanced.

BUDDHIC PLANE. The intuitive, spiritual or CHRIST CONSCIOUSNESS level of expression that is the door to COSMIC CONSCIOUSNESS. Ideas stream from this intuitional plane of pure reason or true love in a manner comparable to the outpouring of the Holy Spirit in traditional Christian terms. A spiritual level of mind that perceives higher will, intelligence, and love and is able to vibrate these energies to the maturing soul. The seven buddhic sub-planes are (from the highest) divine will; divine compassion; divine intelligence; awareness, or direct knowing; blueprints beamed to humanity; divine archetypes; and divine symbols. *Also see* Planes, cosmic.

BUDDHISM. A world religion that has grown from the teachings of Gautama Siddhartha, who lived about 500 years prior to Christ. Siddhartha became the Buddha and anchored the wisdom principle, just as Jesus became the Christ and anchored the love

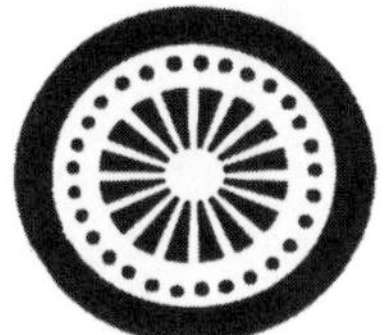

principle. Buddhism emerged fromHINDUISM, just as Christianity grew out of Judaism. It consists of three major schools of Eastern thought: HINAYANA, MAHAYANA, andVAJRAYANA. As Buddhism spreads throughout the world, these schools are becoming universal in nature.

BUILDING THE CUP. The gradual creation and expansion within the human mental body of a receiver-container for the droplets of wisdom that come from the CLOUD OF KNOWABLE THINGS usually during meditation, when teaching or inspired. The cup, or CHALICE, makes it possible to retain and record inspiration so that it does not merely dissipate without being anchored or noted.

BYZANTINE EMPIRE. A.D. 395–1453, powerful in Southeast Europe and Southwest Asia, centered in Constantinople. Today's Byzantine Christian tradition helps the Christian world relate to Eastern traditions, retaining many teachings of the early church and the esoteric. In A.D. 1054, the church divided into the Roman church and the Eastern or Byzantine branch.

BYZANTIUM. Pertaining to Christian Orthodox or Byzantine rites of Eastern Christianity. Primordial Christianity, prior to the split in the 11th century, included a system of self-transformation that led to THEOSIS, the dissolution of the individual self into the Godhead. This system consisted of meditation techniques, purification work, detachment, and icon viewing—described by some as Christian yoga. As the Western branch of Christianity rejected the pursuit of individual experiences of the divine, the mystical tradition was largely retained by the Byzantium and is currently being rediscovered as a hunger has developed in the West for personal spirituality and more contact is occurring between branches.

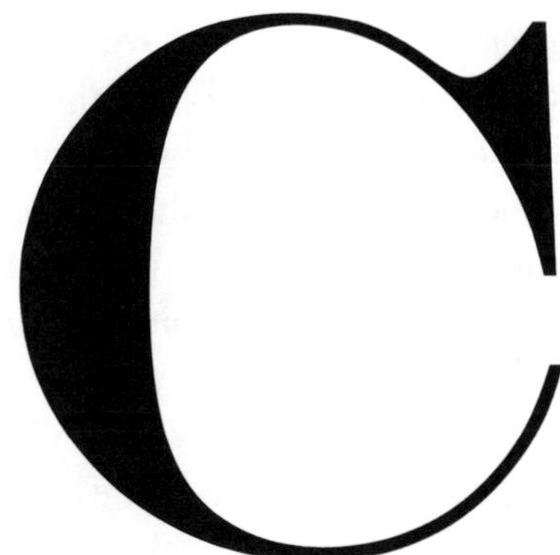

CADUCEUS. This familiar symbol of the medical profession represents the harmonizing of the physical body systems, enabling the body to enjoy wellness. Esoterically, this symbol depicts the balance of spirit and matter within the consciousness of an initiate and is the focus of meditation work at spring EQUINOX.

CALCINATION. In ALCHEMY, the reduction of a substance to ashes, representing the burning off of the dross of the personality to reveal one's soul. To perfect the soul, we must expose it to the painful process of releasing ego and its attachment to the material world. Torkom SARAYDARIAN called this stage, "cooking."

CAMELOT. The legendary and most romantic of King Arthur's castles. Researchers believe it may mean "castle of the waves" or "castle of the hammerer." Most say Camelot was situated near Carlisle by Loch Ryan; others place it in widely scattered areas of the British Isles. Lord Tennyson described Camelot best in his *Idylls of the King:*

> So when their feet were planted on the plain
> That broaden'd toward the base of Camelot,
> Far off they saw the silver-misty morn
> Rolling her smoke about the royal mount,
> That rose between the forest and the field.
>
> At times the spires and turrets halfway down
> Prick'd thro' the mist,
> At times the great gate shown only,
> That open'd on the field below,
> Anon, the whole fair city had disappear'd.[1]

CAMPBELL, JOSEPH. b. New York City, 1904, d. 1987. Educator, author, and foremost authority on the mythologies of the world. It was said that he knew "the vast sweep of humanity's panoramic past as few have ever known it." His profound knowledge and extensive scholarship traced current themes from sacred scriptures and mythologies of the world's broadly divergent races and cultures, which he believed (as did Carl Jung) to be the master keys to the human psyche, "capable of bridging the past and future and the worlds of East and West." *The Masks of God,* Vols. 1–4, 1959–1967; *Myths, Dreams and Religions,* 1970; *Myths to Live By,* 1972.

CANON. A set of rules accepted as dogma and forming the character of a tradition.

CAPPADOCIA. A region of central Turkey known for its unusual terrain and vast underground cities. During early Christian persecutions, many sought shelter here and lived with a variety of traditions in a life not unlike that of other hermits, monks, or Christian communities. Many Cappadocian saints have been recognized for their wisdom. The amazing site bears witness to a bygone era. *See pp. 246–51,* Saints: Gregory, Polycarp.

CARRYOVERS. Negative memories held as attitudes, sensations, or feelings that need to be dissolved and replaced by pure or positive energy.

CATHOLIC. Latin for "universal, all-inclusive." Adopted by the early Christian religion as its name, due to its open invitation to all people regardless of background to follow the way of Jesus, who was accepted as the historical Messiah or Christ, long awaited by the Jews.

CAUSAL BODY. An older term sometimes used for the overlap of higher mind (MANAS) and the intuitive body (BUDDHI), forming the area wherein the EGOIC LOTUS develops. From here, the soul projects itself into the denser sheaths of the personality—mental, emotional, and physical bodies. PERMANENT SEED ATOMS within the causal body (abstract mind and lower intuitive) are the *cause* behind personality. From the subtlest level of the mental body, the SOLAR ANGEL impresses personality. Levels one and two, it is taught, are the home of Solar Angel, which projects its influence downward into the opened mind. This center is formed by the union of buddhi and manas.

CAUSE AND EFFECT (HERMETIC PRINCIPLE OF). Known also as the law of KARMA: every thought, every belief, every action has a reaction, an effect. Noted in the Christian tradition as "casting bread upon the water" to return in due time; also as the concept that we reap what we have sown, Eccl. 11.1 and Gal. 6.7–9, respectively. *See* Hermetic Principles.

CAYCE, EDGAR. b. Kentucky, 1877, d. 1945. The clairvoyant and psychic diagnostician, known as the "Sleeping Prophet," was of humble birth and limited education. His inexplicably accurate readings astonished contemporary physicians: while in a self-induced trance state, he was able to identify specific health problems and their remedy; he often provided information on previous incarnations. His work is commemorated by the Association for Research and Enlightenment, Virginia Beach, Virginia. Biography by Thomas Sugrue, *There Is a River,* 1942; *Auras,*

Celestial Hierarchies

A group of intelligences responsible for the framework of the cosmos and for transmitting the qualities of the Triune God to humanity. A series of graded beings, comprising three triads that, in descending order are: Seraphim, Cherubim, Thrones; Dominions, Powers, Virtues; Principalities, Archangels, and Angels. These great beings represent and are sustained by the divine Source and are most often referred to as angels, from a Greek word meaning "one who acts as messenger from the celestial realms to the world of humankind." Within this structure twelve zodiacal hierarchies are charged to distribute cosmic creative energies and to project specific archetypal ideas and influences into the universe, which then are registered in human consciousness and translated into action according to each person's evolutionary status. A person living consciously uses these energies to enhance life and grow spiritually.

The name of the hierarchical rulers of the **constellation of Aries** is not given, though this celestial hierarchy is related to the **Lords of Fire.** The vibration of this powerful group—said to hold the archetype of the new Christed human being who will be increasingly manifested in the coming era—is considered to be too high to be relayed to humanity at this time.

The rulers of the **constellation of Taurus** work under a hierarchy whose name is unrevealed. They teach form-building through the use of sound, or the Word, to vibrate and to create. This holy order delivers divine will through the **Lords of Karma** (also known as the LIPIKAS) who impress each soul with its purpose for incarnation. Parallel to the THRONES of the angelic kingdom, these Lords assist in bringing about divine justice through the universal law of cause and effect, reminding us that "as we sow, so shall we reap." Currently humanity is satisfying much of the KARMA of the past in preparation for the new era.

The **Lords of Mercury,** the celestial hierarchy of the **constellation of Gemini,** also known as the SERAPHIM, whose power and grandeur surpass all description, guide humanity toward initiatory work. These fiery, enthusiastic beings are among the most advanced of the angelic kingdom and a part of the CLOUD OF SILENT WATCHERS. The word *seraphim* comes from the Hebrew word *seraph,* meaning "love." This third aspect of the Holy TRINITY, known as the Holy Spirit, the deliverer of gifts of the spirit, influences meditations, often bringing profound revelations.

The hierarchical rulers of the **constellation of Cancer,** the **CHERUBIM,** are among the most advanced of the angelic kingdom and a part of the CLOUD OF SILENT WATCHERS. Their most important work is to protect sacred places. Coworking with Capricorn and the archangels, these forces, often called the "waters of life," blend the mystical energies of spirit and matter.

THE LORDS OF FLAME (OR LOVE), one of the great hierarchies of spiritual beings who guides the solar system, rule the **constellation of Leo.** These exalted beings of love, light, and spiritual power inspire humanity in its journey to higher consciousness, toward self-mastery. With their assistance we can comprehend our inherent capability to demonstrate loving attributes responsibly in our lives. They are said to have taken control of the evolution of humanity 18 million years ago, during the middle of the Lemurian, or third, ROOT RACE.

The hierarchical rulers of the **constellation of Virgo,** the **LORDS OF WISDOM,** hold the power by which life ensouls form. They enter into perfect attunement so that mind and matter can become as one. The comic Madonna, symbol of Virgo, sacrifices (makes sacred) herself to nurture and sustain life on the planet as a place for souls to incarnate.

The hierarchical rulers of the **constellation of Libra** teach humanity to translate assertiveness into cooperation. These **LORDS OF INDIVIDUALITY** help us live the ideal of the greatest good for the greatest number, while appreciating our unique gifts, value, and capabilities.

The **LORDS OF FORM,** hierarchical rulers of the **constellation of Scorpio,** have created patterns of cosmic thoughtforms for humanity that hold profound energy for change, rejuvenation, and revitalization, the key elements for healing and renewal.

The hierarchical rulers of the **constellation of Sagittarius,** the **LORDS OF MIND,** are waiting until humans develop enough to be able to use wisely the power of divine mind. These arcing, dancing, mental powers stimulate intellect and invention. Higher human initiates capable of responding to this influence cut the path for us all; these trailblazers discover and anchor the potentials for the benefit of all of humanity.

In the **constellation of Capricorn** we most often relate to initiation, tests, and anchoring changes into the physical plane. **ARCHANGELS** are the guardians of rank and initiation, each holding a pattern humanity must assimilate. Gradually the initiate passes the tests and acquires the many facets needed to become the MASTER.

The **constellation of Aquarius** is the home of the celestial hierarchy of the **ANGELS** and of those who pass from Earth in infancy, until time for the next life arrives. Many disciples are guided by angelic forces without outer awareness, while others work consciously with light beings under the tutelage of this hierarchy. The energy of the Aquarian Age encourages right-relationship between humanity and the angelic kingdom. We have much to learn about etheric reality from them—certainly in one of their most important areas, healing.

The celestial hierarchy of the **constellation of Pisces** is known as the **LORDS OF COMPASSION.** Having learned the power of unconditional love, these advanced ones in whom BUDDHI of the heart is activated hold the human kingdom in a balance of love and wisdom to stimulate unconditional love within the group mind. Bequeathing light and love impartially, they nurture humanity in its painful condition, loving the imperfect and the ignorant without shirking and leading the human kingdom toward super-human evolution, also called the "KINGDOM OF SOULS."

1945; *What I Believe,* 1946; *Edgar Cayce on Atlantis,* 1968.

CEIBA TREE. Sacred tree of the MAYA.

CELESTIAL. Describes subtler, nonphysical realities—worlds, planes, or bodies.

CELESTIAL HIERARCHIES. *See p. 43–5.*

CELIBACY. The practice of sexual self-discipline by nonparticipation. In the best sense of the word, celibacy results when one raises spiritual forces often spent in sexual expression to another level of creativity. The primary function of celibacy is to help the practitioner break the automatic instinctual gratification of the sexual self and learn to relate on higher levels to another. *See* Disciplines, sexual; Periodic abstinence.

CELLULAR INTELLIGENCE/MEMORY. The imprint of life within even the smallest atom that retains a record of purpose and experience, usually unconscious or instinctual.

CELTS. The ancient indigenous people of Western Europe whose religion was matriarchal and nature-based. Often referred to today as DRUIDS, the title given their priests and scholars. They worshiped outdoors, often in oak groves; the tree and mistletoe were sacred symbols. The Druids—chiefs, judges, magicians—form the basis of most European shamanistic religions.

CENTERED AND BALANCED. Implies a state of equilibrium and harmony between spirit and matter, inspiration and expression.

CENTERING. A technique to harmonize our lower nature, making it sensitive to the presence of the nonphysical nature.

CHAINS AND ROUNDS. Aeons of time in the process of planetary and solar system evolutions, per *Treatise on Cosmic Fire* by Alice A. BAILEY (p. 258). Seven root races equal one round; seven rounds equal one globe; seven globes equal one chain; seven chains equal one scheme equals one solar system; seven schemes equal three solar systems.

Great cosmic beings use these forms as their successive physical incarnations. These incarnations are of vast and varying lengths of time, with much overlapping between them. Intervening periods of PRALAYA may also be of indeterminate length, so that the law and order underlying all manifestation may not be discerned by the human mind.

o	o	mental
o	o	astral
o	o	etheric
o		physical

CHAIN ILLUSTRATION

CHALDEANS. An ancient Semitic tribe occupying Chaldea, South MESOPOTAMIA in the Bible. The Chaldeans appeared in 9th century B.C. as a distinct people, well-established but with uncertain origins. Having a reputation for wisdom and counsel throughout the Persian and early Hellenistic periods, their influence remained in the administration of affairs of the empire. Biblically the Chaldeans were a people with whom Judah sought an alliance condemned by God's people, using images of lust and harlotry. (Job 1.17 and Ez.

Chakra

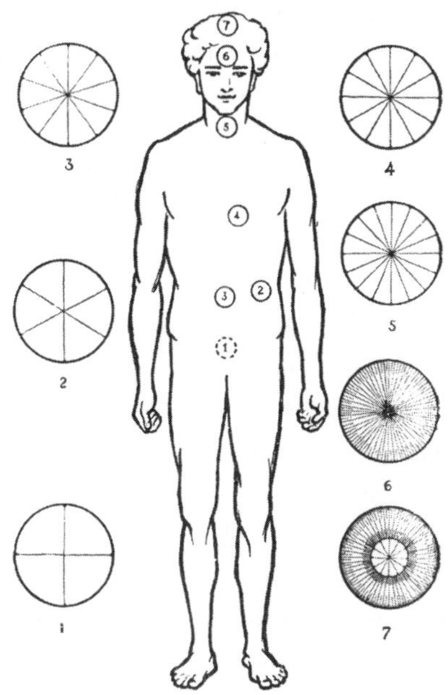

Literally, "wheel." A Sanskrit term designating energy centers, actual vortices of force latent within the etheric body of every human: crown, brow (AJNA), throat, heart, solar plexus, abdomen, root. Corresponding to different levels of consciousness and controlling the physical condition of the area of the body that they influence, the centers activate as we awaken to nonphysical reality and as we become increasingly aware of higher vibrations and extended realities. Eastern and Western concepts and portrayals vary slightly.

Major Chakras and Their Correspondences to Glands[2]

Crown — pineal body (not recognized as endocrine)
Brow — pituitary
Throat — thyroid and parathyroid
Heart — thymus
Solar Plexus — adrenals (dual) and pancreas (dual)
Sacral or Spleen — spleen (not recognized as endocrine)
Base or Sacrum — gonads, prostate, etc.

Minor Etheric Chakras[3]

Location on the Physical Body

2 There are two in front of ears, close to where the jawbones are connected.
2 There are two just above the two breasts.
1 There is one where the breast bone connects, close to the thyroid bland. This, with the two breast centres, makes a triangle of force.
2 There are two, one each in the palms of the hands.
2 There are two, one each in the soles of the feet.
2 There are two, just behind the eyes.
2 There are two, also connected with the gonads.
1 There is one close to the liver.
1 There is one connected with the stomach; it is related, therefore, to the solar plexus, but is not identical with it.
2 There are two—one at the back of each knee.

"There is one powerful centre which is closely connected with the vagus nerve. This is the most potent and is regarded by some schools of occultism as a major centre; it is not in the spine, but is no great distance from the thymus gland.

"There is one which is close to the solar plexus and relates it to the centre at the base of the spine, thus making a triangle of the sacral centre, the solar plexus, and the centre at the base of the spine."

23.23) Abraham is said to have been from Ur of the Chaldees.

CHALICE. Symbolically, the developed receptive nature ready for spiritual growth, guidance, and blessing. The open high consciousness that can accept inspiration, vision, and direct knowledge—a consciousness built in order to contact and receive the energies of the spiritual triad. Soul energy flowing earthward creates a vortex of energy, resembling a cup, on the higher mental plane. Later, in this center will emerge the jewel, a spark of the divine fire, of the MONAD—the real Self. The chalice is anchored by the SOLAR ANGEL, who leads the individual to an awareness of the true SELF through the process of awakening and initiations. The human soul communicates through the chalice with personality. Agni Yoga uses the EGOIC LOTUS, or the Temple of Solomon.

CHANGELING. A stolen human infant that is replaced by a fairy child; the fairy child is raised by the human family but does not quite fit it. In time, the fairy qualities surface, and the identity is discovered. Although the children may be returned to their families, both are forever tainted by the experience of the other realm.

CHANNELING. A technique in which a person brings through information or influence from one dimension to another when in a particular state in which consciousness flows from level to level. Practitioners often were called "trance mediums" in the past. Channeling lends itself to GLAMOUR and abuse, as well as wisdom.

CHANTING. Repetitive vocalizing—spoken or sung—designed to penetrate the subconscious to affect the life of an aspirant. The vibrations impress the subtle bodies and are particularly effective (when properly designed) to balance the chakras, to calm and comfort.

CHAOS. An Agni term. When used without capitalization, simply "disorder and confusion," the customary meaning; however, when capitalized, refers to the "primordial substance of creation, the *prima materia* of the alchemists, the first outpouring," theosophically. Chaos, as the destroyer aspect, is known as KALI, one expression of the third aspect of the Trinity in Hinduism—also the divine feminine, corresponding to BINAH in KABALAH, raw materials such as in unmanifested potential.

CHAOS, THE LAW OF. Manifestation disintegrating back to the elements of creation. We live in a time of rediscovering certain laws of operation that apply at times of dissolution. These patterns presently are defined by physics, as well as by metaphysics and quantum physics, as the "laws of chaos."

CHAPELS OF SILENCE. Disciples are admitted at this initial point of specialized training behind the veil of sleep after some advancement has been attained. Here they are exposed to currents, archetypal energies, and other stimuli to awaken inner forces, thus assisting those deemed ready to advance more rapidly toward spiritual maturity through testing their inner knowledge. Some are aware and some unaware of this intimate and privileged environment.

CHAUCS. In the Maya belief system the four great lords who hold the physical dimension stable—one at each corner of the Earth.

CHELA. The dedicated student of a GURU; literally, a servant, i.e., handmaiden or servant of the Lord.

CHEMICALIZATION. The condition resulting as various vehicles of expression—such as thought, emotion, or inspiration—mingle within the etheric body. The resulting balance or imbalance greatly influences higher consciousness as it seeks to express through the personality.

CHEOPS. Greek name for Egyptian Pharaoh Khufu.

CHERUBIM. These angels supervise the elementals, emanate wisdom, intone truth, perceive the will, and hold the form for the PLAN. These great beings are responsible for the form side of nature and for the motherhood of all life—a feminine, nurturing influence acting upon evolving life forms. As the celestial hierarchy of the constellation Cancer, they express clear truth and enlighten humanity with the energies of love and wisdom.

CHESED. The fourth SEPHIRAH on the kabalistic Tree is designated as Mercy and considered the home of the MASTERS. The teachings say we cannot comprehend mercy until we have experienced severity. When we have integrated the lessons of severity and are able to comprehend love in its many modes and phases, including tough love and the love "that underlies the happenings of the times,"[4] we can then grant mercy, for we have learned the purpose of discipline. Mercy can appropriately bequeath justice.

CH'I. Ancient Chinese term for "PSI energy," the universal life force. Sometimes "breath," as in "breath of life."

CHILD-LIKE. The ability to experience the innocent basic nature of enthusiasm, spontaneity, trust, and openness, as do undamaged children filled with awe and wonder at the mystery of life. Freedom and joy abound without false limitations in the child-like state.

CHILD-WITHIN. The basic nature (more than the subconscious) that retains childlike, enthusiastic, fresh, energetic qualities often hidden under programming, fears, false ideas, or distortions from earlier events. The forever-young–child part of us that can be set free to experience the events of life with freshness. Much healing can be accomplished on this level, often distorted and wounded. Psychospiritual efforts to restore this basic level of self aid in physical and emotional health maintenance and improve the ability to trust and to expand comprehension, as well as increased joy in living. *See* Inner child.

CHIRON. This minor planet discovered in 1977 confirms a quirk of human nature that prevents us from recognizing something until we are ready for it. The centaur for whom Chiron is named is a union of opposites, like a bridge between heaven and Earth. Chiron promises transmutation of matter (the ordinary) and the pot of gold (the quest, enlightenment). For this reason it is often said to represent the RAINBOW BRIDGE (ANTAHKARANA) to higher consciousness. Chiron is dubbed "wounded healer"

The Christ—many meanings

Christ, the cosmic. The second aspect of the triune Godhead, also known as the Word or the Son, is associated with love-wisdom. The divine creative center of the Supreme Being that disseminates the love and light of God throughout creation. God creates and Christ formulates, while the Holy Spirit activates. Every particle of physical life or energy responds to our visible sun, while all spiritual life force comes from the invisible sun or the central spiritual sun, also known as the cosmic Christ. *See* Sun behind the Sun.

Christ, the. Head of Hierarchy, teacher of angels and of humanity. The primary position of power for planet Earth, this living flame guides all life on this sphere in evolution, reflecting perfectly the will of the Creator into a lower vibrating plane. In esoteric teachings, this holy consciousness is acknowledged as the deity of many major religions, though called by many names. The Christian faith considers the great initiate Jesus to have elevated his consciousness, connected with the Christ, and anchored that love principle within humanity and for all humankind. Hence, he is known as Jesus the Christ or the historical Christ. Also known as the Planetary Christ.

Christ, the planetary. The Archangel Christ who descended from the spiritual sheath of the sun into the body of Master Jesus at the Baptism. The Lord Christ took upon himself the mission of transmuting the astral envelope of the Earth so more purified substance would be available for humanity to build its subtler bodies. The Christ—head of Hierarchy—incarnated in the body of Master Jesus to effectively alter and stimulate the planet and all life upon it. At the Crucifixion, this energy penetrated into the Earth, claiming the Earth as his. The planetary Christ functions as a Solar Angel for Earth life, guiding and guarding all kingdoms.

Christ, the historical. Master Jesus, the Wayshower of the Christian Path of Discipleship. Each major event in his life correlates with a step along the Initiatory Path. Master Jesus built a purified form that was given to serve the Christ at the Baptism. The title of "the Christ" was given to the high initiate, Jesus, as he served the Christ (planetary) in this unique way.

CHRIST, THE MYSTICAL. Refers to the love aspect of the unfolding divine spirit within humanity. The divine life of the Logos forms the garment of the Soul in each person, that humanity may know eternal life. The Christ principle that resides in every human heart is the Christ to be formed in each of us. This Immanent Spirit is born again and again in the heart and can never die but continues to develop throughout evolution until it is fully expressed in human life. Also known as the CHRIST-WITHIN.

CHRIST-WITHIN. Also known as the Mystical Christ, the Christ Immanent, Inner Christ, HOPE OF GLORY. The divine nature incarnate within a human being; a spark or seed of the divine potential brought into increasingly conscious awareness. We unfold the Christ-Within by practicing high consciousness in daily life. The Christ principle abides *in potentia* in the heart chakra as a golden flame. This immanent spirit can never die but continues to develop throughout evolution until each human life fully expresses it.

because wherever it falls in our astrology chart, it clues us to the area where personal healing is needed and, after we have done it, how we can in turn assist others.

CHOHAN. A Lord, MASTER, or chief; a high ADEPT who has taken initiations beyond the five major initiations of the human kingdom, making him or her a "Master of Wisdom." These high adepts—who distribute the force of each RAY, using many sub-departments and offices—serve as the heads of the Rays and are sometimes referred to as the Seven Great Officials of the Rays.

Ray	1	Morya
Ray	2	Kuthumi
Ray	3	The Venetian
Ray	4	Serapis
Ray	5	Hilarion
Ray	6	Jesus
Ray	7	St. Germaine

CHOKMAH. The second SEPHIRAH on the kabalistic Tree, known as Wisdom, is the highest center on the masculine pillar of "force." The knowing or pure, nonverbal thought that comes directly from the right hemisphere and the aspect of wisdom carried within one's awareness.

CHRIST CONSCIOUSNESS. A term the Christian tradition has used for intuitive knowing or the realization or attainment of high consciousness. The pure level of consciousness in which the mind, love, and will of God are made known to the enlightened person.

CHRISTED. A state of enlightened awareness modeled by JESUS the CHRIST, to be achieved by those who follow Christian teachings. To reach spiritual maturity and to complete the human initiations, each is to develop "Christ in you, the hope of glory" (Col. 1.27), according to Esoteric Christianity. This correlates to ENLIGHTENMENT in Hinduism or BUDDHA CONSCIOUSNESS in Buddhism.

CHRISTHOOD (OR BUDDHAHOOD). The state of consciousness that aligns us with the hierarchy of Earth, led by the Christ as teacher of angels and of humanity and realized by wise ones of all traditions after the path of human initiation is completed.

CHRISTIAN INITIATION. A process within Esoteric Christianity describing stages of growth; these seven major steps are birth, baptism, transfiguration, Crucifixion, revelation, decision, and Resurrection. Often spoken of as five because these are experienced within human form or working with humanity. The last two can be for service and growth in other dimensions. *Also see* Initiation.

CHRISTIANITY. The world religion that arose from the life and teachings of Jesus, the historical Christ. It gradually became formalized through the teachings of his apostles, often presented as dogma and doctrines. In the family of world religions, a branch of the Judaic tradition. Christianity like Judaism is inescapably communal from the early church until today. Teachings proclaim Christ, through Jesus, began establishing a new collective bond between those who practice love and service—a community, one body with many parts.

CHRISTIANITY, ORTHODOX. *Ortho* means "straight, hold in order." With the separation of the Christian church in A.D. 1054, two major branches were established: the Eastern, or Orthodox, and the Western, or Roman. While the West acknowledges the pope in Rome as Christ's vicar on Earth, Eastern Orthodox is organized by national identity, e.g., Russian or Greek, an Ecumenical Patriarch being its highest rank official.

CHRIST LIGHT. The illumination of God that emanates from the holy consciousness refocused within the subtler planes and experienced when we perceive and receive the energies of the divine Source through this center. *See* Christ-Within.

CHRISTMAS. The birth of Jesus, the initiate, was celebrated for three days at WINTER SOLSTICE until formally set at Dec. 25. The principal festival of the WATER MYSTERIES and the festival of light for the Christian tradition.

CHRISTOGENESIS. TEILHARD DE CHARDIN introduced this term to define the goal of the human journey toward the omega point—the same goal recognized in many traditions as a perfected being or Christed one.

CHRISTOLOGY. The philosophy and doctrine of the Christ to be reflected within the lives of incarnate wise ones. We are presently creating the Christology of the 21st century.

CHRISTOS. In Greek, "anointed." The anointed consciousness capable of demonstrating a state of holy wisdom.

CHRISTOSOPHIA. Translated most commonly as love-wisdom. In Esoteric Christianity the holy consciousness of one in whom a state of balance, the love of the Christ and the wisdom of Sophia, expresses through the human nature. This term acknowledges the Christ (love) born within as it evolves to reveal an inner wisdom (Sophia), thus blending heart and mind becomes the CHRIST CONSCIOUSNESS. *See* Homo noeticus; Hope of glory; Soul infusion; Theosophia.

CHRISTOSOPHY. The study of the philosophy of and about the CHRIST.

CHROMOTHERAPY. Color therapy; a developing tool using subtle energies to effect change on a physical level, i.e., healing, attitudes, or vibrations.

CHRYSALIS. Symbolically, the unfolding soul encased in human form. Literally, a stage in the development of a butterfly in which the evolving life form is enclosed in a cocoon from which it must free itself if it is to fly.

CHURCH. A literal translation of the term *eclesia* (quoting Elaine Pagels), a "meaningful assembly." People bonded through faith in the Christ. Not a building, but a collective identity or state of consciousness. A secular term for the building Christians use for worship.

CHURCHES OF THE AQUARIAN ERA. More akin to the early church than the organized church of the Middle Ages. In keeping with the challenging ideas of INITIATION, that greater power is received as earned through each step. All are to be truly:

APOSTOLIC: Participating in spiritual lineage all the way back to the Christ. Lineage established by awakening spiritual gifts. Enlightenment is the evidence.

CATHOLIC: Truly universal in nature, knowing in Christ all are one, that the same spirit exists within every being.

EVANGELICAL: Sharing the spirit; witnessing to the world through living ethical lives.

REFORMED: Renewed, reworked, made new and different by the ability to accept and adjust to the new incoming energies of the era.

CHURCHIANITY. A derogative term suggesting church dogma or canon has replaced the message of and the striving to be like the Christ.

CIPHER OF GENESIS. A book by Carlo Suares representing 40 years of biblical research wherein he concludes that "the first five chapters of the Bible were written in code, . . . and cannot be understood without the key, the 'cypher,' to that number/letter code."[5]

CIRCLE. Representing eternity, without beginning or end, the hoop or ring signifies perfection, continuity, and completeness. The OUROBORUS is the FEATHERED SERPENT of the Western way, the circle of creation enclosing the WORLD SOUL.

CLAIRAUDIENCE. Clear-hearing; the facility of spiritual hearing psychically without limitation of matter, time, and space. Related to the throat center. Extrasensory data perceived as sound; often considered a facet of clairvoyance.

CLAIRSENTIENCE. Clear-feeling; the facility of spiritual feeling and sensing, without limitation of matter, time, and space. Extrasensory data perceived as heightened feeling or inner awareness. Related to the solar plexus center.

CLAIRVOYANCE. Clear-seeing; the facility of the spiritual eye that can see psychically, without limitations of matter, time, and space. Extrasensory sight that provides an awareness of physical objects or events.

Cloud of Silent Watchers

Holy ones who care for humanity from higher planes. Often a reference to the archangels; similar to Elder Brothers of Humanity. *See* Watcher.

This highest angelic group in the hierarchy of the angelic kingdom are guardians of the angelic ranks and initiations:

Seraphim
Cherubim
Thrones

The next four advanced orders:

Dominions
Principalities
Virtues
Powers

The concluding orders of the angelic kingdom are:

Archangels
Angels

Cloning. A scientific technique of exact genetic duplication of living forms through the use of DNA from the original donor—animal or person. Legend has it that Atlantis reached such a capability at its peak but lost respect for the gift of life; they believed the replicated beings did not have souls, thus justifying mistreatment.

Cloud of Knowable Things. Thoughtforms contacted on higher levels of the mental plane from which can be drawn great beauty, wisdom, and inspiration; partly created by reflections of advanced thinkers who may be contacted telepathically. Also, the vast storehouse of knowledge into which flows the mind, love, and will of God from which the aspirant can receive inspiration through the awakening perceptions of high consciousness, thus finding that which is needed for the ongoing pattern or evolution. Some earlier Christian mystics used the term, "Unknowable," as such material awaited expanded consciousness to be discerned. Also known as DHARMA LIGHT.

Cluster thinking. A unique change in the mental process of an experiencer of the light, NDE, profound meditation, etc., where, instead of linear, rational thought, a creative flash occurs with numerous realizations, ideas, and impressions occurring concurrently.

Cocreate. When the energies of two or more contribute in cooperation.

Codependency. This modern term describes a personality contingent upon others' responses to shape his or her self-evaluation, self-esteem, and actions. Generally, codependency is developed between two needy people, neither of whom has healthy personal boundaries or a strong center; therefore, each is defined by the other's expectations. The person suffering this constraint seeks another equally needy to help define or reinforce lifestyle choices due to lack of inner conviction.

Collective unconscious. Sum total of all levels of mind existing below the threshold of conscious awareness for all of humanity.

COLLINS, MABEL. Mrs. Keningale Cook, 19th century theosophist and writer of a series of books of occult rules on self-knowledge and self-mastery published by the Theosophical Society. She said she received her prolific writings from the inner world. *Light on the Path* and *Through the Gates of Gold,* 1887; *When the Sun Moves Northward: The Way of Initiation,* 1923.

COLOR THERAPY. The use of color for its corrective influences on the physical, etheric, emotional, and/or mental body.

COMEASUREMENT. An Agni term. The appropriate combination of energies through which purpose is achieved. A beautiful definition is given by Frances Moore of Meditation Mount, Ojai, California: "Understanding that which is great and that which is small; what is distant and what is near; what we can attain and that which we would be fools to attempt . . . comeasurement is a true sense of proportion." Consideration of factors to be brought into right-relationship in order to achieve positive results.

COMMANDMENTS. Rules established for practitioners of particular spiritual paths.

COMMON GOOD. An Agni Yoga term for that which facilitates the evolution of the human family.

COMMUNICATION. Thought clothed in mediums to convey a message—gently, sensitively, or harshly. Words are chosen according to intent. Artists convey thoughts through drawings and color. Composers and musicians deliver messages and feelings through the use of sound. Tones, touches, gestures, and body language are used as well to share thoughts.

COMMUNION, HOLY. In this Christian rite we experience the sacred meal, often called the Lord's Supper or more formally the Eucharist by those committed to oneness with the Lord Christ in their innerworld and oneness to each other. The celebrant stands as the representative of Christ and blesses the bread, wine, and water. Words of power are spoken, and accordingly the substance is changed. The full power of the ritual is disputed by some denominations of the Christian faith, but esotericists believe this is the science of sacred contact; the transubstantiation will be to the degree acknowledged by the receiver.

COMMUNITARIAN. One who lives in a community, sharing commitment and relationship to other members and embodying this reemerging concept.

COMMUNITY. A group of people united by a particular keynote or effort, joining consciousnesses of similar vibration for the purpose of being one in orientation. Each supports the others, and all acknowledge the oneness of their reason for being. Relationship is established by the realization of the similar inner nature and by the commitment to support that essence in each other as they mature.

As an Agni theme: the family is the prototype of communal life personifying cooperation, the Hierarchy, and all conditions of brotherhood/sisterhood, but such families are rare. Community is creating a spiritual family around a like-minded understanding or shared values. The ties, not just on the physical plane, extend to subtler levels as well. In Agni Yoga the hierarchy of chohans is called "the community," individuals bonding in response to a keynote. Correlates to the energy and influence of RAY 7 and the number 7. *See* Numerology.

COMPANY OF JUST ONES MADE PERFECT, THE. Comprising the 12 spiritual types of humanity, perfect and centered in the Oneness, this group (the 12 zodiacal signs) collectively represents God's own concept of humanity—archetypal ADAM OF ATZILUTH—in conscious union with God.

COMPASSION. A blend of love and wisdom, the realization of "THINKETH IN THE HEART AND FEELETH IN THE MIND," sometimes considered a form of unconditional love.

COMPASSION, BODHISATTVA OF. *See* Bodhisattva of Compassion; Mothers and Goddesses of the World.

COMPETITIVE THINKING. Smart, rational; "I versus you."

CONCENTRATION. The power of focus; the ability to focus by will in such a way that we can burn through confusion and distraction to reach a centered point.

CONCRETE MIND. This aspect of mind deals with concrete reality: tangible objects, knowable facts, measurable qualities. A lower level of mind with reference to ABSTRACT MIND; the mid sub-plane(s) of the mental plane.

CONCRETIZED. Denotes the loss of flexibility, a rigid form of thought solidified into what is called "illusion" in esoteric terms.

CONFESSION. A sacrament of the Christian tradition in which errors or offenses are acknowledged and the grace of repentance sought. Special prayers or acts of goodness may be performed as penance. Now often called the "sacrament of reconciliation," though known as "confession" for centuries, it is a rite of forgiving and invoking healing and new life force to help the initiate proceed on the spiritual journey. One of the seven sacraments of the Christian tradition. *See* Sacraments.

CONFIRMATION. A public rite in which one bears witness that s/he is knowledgeable and courageous enough to defend the faith. As part of the ritual, one is struck gently upon the cheek to attest to this inner resolve. In some churches a spiritual name is chosen to evoke the grace and power the name bestows. One of the seven sacraments of the Christian tradition. *See* Sacraments.

CONFLICTING THOUGHT. A difference between heart and mind that creates a contradiction between how we think and what we feel, or when our head holds one belief and our heart holds another.

CONFRONTATION, LOVING. An imperative of the new era. Part of what we learn as we reconcile the duality of our inner and outer realities. We come to understand the technique called "mirroring"; by reflecting to one another differing points of understanding, we force integration or separation. Loving confrontation enables us to lift our consciousness to a higher level and bring a new grasp of reality to play in daily life. Loving confrontation overcomes denial or avoidance as we grow and provoke growth in others.

CONFUCIUS. b. Lu, Shantung Province, 551 B.C., d. 479. China's most revered moral teacher, philosopher, and statesman. Carefully training the young men entrusted to him, he urged them to become models of manhood, possessing *jen,* benevolent love, *shu,* reciprocity and wisdom. He taught that true manhood means both "to realize the true self and to restore *li,*" or "rightness, virtue, faith, and proper conduct in all things." *The Analects.*

CONJUNCTION. In astrology, two or three planets located within an orb of 7 degrees—usually within the same or adjacent sign. Principal impact is to strengthen the sign, can be either favorable or not, according to specific planets involved.

CONJURING. Procedure for calling upon the spirits of the dead, sometimes included in old medical materials, leading to the possibility that physicians once used this as a form of grief counseling.

CONSCIOUSNESS. From two Latin roots, *com* and *scire,* meaning "with knowledge." A registration and response to any impression, through light of the human intellect, operating on the mental plane. Consciousness expands as our intelligence operates on higher levels, with subtler substance and within larger fields. Consciousness is not intellect, rather the result of interaction between intellect and matter—a lighted area in which things are perceived, seen, and sensed; it is created when the intellect of the soul touches matter. While intellect is the positive pole and matter (etheric, physical, astral, and mental) is the negative, consciousness is the lighted area created by their contact. The spark of divinity in the human; the ensouling energy that is the root of all awareness.

Awareness is the capacity for perceiving and feeling, according to John White, who quotes Alan Watts from *The Way of Zen,* "the power of thought enables us to construct symbols of things apart from the things themselves. . . . Because the idea is so much more stable than the fact, we learn to identify ourselves with the idea of ourselves. . . ." White continues, "We cannot define consciousness, yet every day's living confirms its reality. . . . [C]onsciousness is everywhere and is the foundation of all existence—the organizing principle behind the physical universe. Call it the Logos, the Tao, God. . . .

"As the fully formed egoic state of consciousness became the immanent, or subjective, mode of awareness, there arose a bifurcation of mind, a 'split-mindedness' recorded as science versus religion and faith versus knowledge, the analytical recorded as the Aristotelian mode and the intuitive mode called the Platonic. Each has a way of seeing the world, but each is also incomplete. Albert Einstein once said, 'Science without religion is lame; religion without science is blind.'"[6]

CONSCIOUSNESS RESEARCHER. An investigator well-versed in the field of mind sciences who seeks to test and integrate various experiences, phenomena, and discoveries to see how they can be comprehended within the context of developing theories. Usually one who reviews quantities of data seeking a synthesis that reveals how the new and the known fit together.

CONSCIOUSNESS THREAD. A common term for the antahkarana anchored in the physical brain and the thread through which consciousness flows. One of three etheric threads—SUTRATMA, ANTAHKARANA, CREATIVE—that connect soul, the spiritual triad, and the lower mind of each individual. The RAINBOW BRIDGE is a contemporary reference to these three interwoven threads.

CONSTELLATION. A group of fixed stars considered to resemble and named after various mythological characters, inanimate objects, and animals. The zodiac consists of twelve constellations contained in the ecliptic, the apparent path of the sun through the heavens.

CONTEMPLATION. Similar to meditation; the act of holding a thought or object before the mental vision and observing the thought from many perspectives.

CONTINUITY OF CONSCIOUSNESS. The capability linked to the crown CHAKRA for an advanced state of consciousness, wherein we can slip in and out of the physical body without losing conscious awareness of the happenings on the physical plane, recognizing two levels of life simultaneously occurring. Achieving union with one's eternal Self, thus having free access to one's record of experiences on other levels and dimensions.

COPTIC. A member of an ancient Egyptian order that adopted Christianity in the 1st century and refused to convert to ISLAM after the Arab conquest. Today the Copts form a small minority, about 5 percent, of Egypt's population. The Coptic community, found in small numbers outside Egypt as well, continues a strong dedication to mysticism and the divine feminine. Some believe they are related to the early ESSENES.

CORD, SILVER. The SUTRATMA that the soul extends to the personality as it is being created. When this connection is broken, the physical life is finished.

CORRESPONDENCE (HERMETIC PRINCIPLE OF). The concept of mirroring demonstrated by "AS ABOVE, SO BELOW" and, in a more personal way, "KNOW THYSELF if you would know another." *See* Hermetic Principles.

COSMIC CHRIST. *See* Christ, the Cosmic.

COSMIC CONSCIOUSNESS. A profound event of timelessness in which we experience expanded reality. A perspective from a different point of consciousness, rather than the usual, profoundly changing limited awareness to an expanded outlook.

In the classic, *Cosmic Consciousness,* Richard M. Bucke says, "Cosmic consciousness will become more and more universal earlier in the individual life until the race at large will possess this faculty. The same race and not the same; for a cosmic conscious race will not be the race which exists today anymore than the present race of men is the same race which existed prior to the evolution of self-consciousness."

COSMIC EGG. An ancient creation myth that the world evolved from a primordial egg, also known as the eternal egg, world egg, egg of the universe. A symbol of the cosmos in its original abstract conception or innermost state of existence prior to the periods of involution and evolution; also known as the OUROBORUS.

COSMIC HEART, OR GREAT HEART. An Agni term. The spiritual heart of the universe from which pour life-giving emanations of **L**ots **O**f **V**ital **E**nergy; considered feminine. Mother of the World is a symbol of this fount of love energy.

COSMIC INITIATION. A third set of great initiations awaits after human initiations and solar initiations have been fulfilled. We understand little or nothing about the challenges of the distant future except they apply to the life of the evolved MONAD.

COSMIC MAGNET. In Agni Yoga, the God consciousness or spiritual high point that harmonizes all life with Higher Will. When we open to FOHAT, a strong consciousness, a purified heart, and a fiery magnetism develop within, corresponding in conscious cooperation with the Cosmic Magnet. The teachings tell us this point of consciousness maturing within us is our sacred power. Esoteric Christianity would use "the Christ-Within"; in KABALAH the developing inner consciousness would be DAATH, responding to the Great Magnet of High Consciousness (Cosmic Magnet) that will in time draw all the lower kingdoms into oneness.

COSMIC RELATIONSHIPS. The experience of individuals brought together for purposes of the greater good—for the collective of which they are a part, rather than for the satisfaction of personal karma. Such individuals will realize karmic benefit for their service. *Also see* Karmic relationships; Soulmate; Worthy opponent.

COSMIC SONG. A poetic label given to the combined vibrations of the whole cosmic symphony. Also known as the music of the spheres.

COSMOGONY. The method of describing in the form of a myth(s) the creative action and the primordial events to which the world owes its existence. These myths, found in almost all cultures, vary in composition and complexity according to place, time, and degree of maturity of the culture. In astronomy, the study of the evolutionary behavior of the universe and the origin of its characteristic features. From the Greek words *kosmos* (universe) and *gonos* (origin).

COSMOLOGY. The metaphysical understanding of the nature of the cosmos and its interacting influences as one aspect impacts another. The doctrine of interlocking relationships of all pieces to the whole throughout the cosmos.

COSMOS. The vast space containing all universes, their component solar systems and planets, all material and spiritual existence. While "universe" usually refers to only our solar system, cosmos includes all universes.

COURSE IN MIRACLES, A. Channeled material offering guidance and keys for spiritual growth and life-styling. The course seeks to remove the "blocks to the awareness of love's presence, [our] natural inheritance," providing a framework for student and teacher. It is the training of the mind through certain exercises that develops the true perception that has no limits. Published by the Foundation of Inner Peace in 1975.

Coven. A congregation of witches. Sometimes males, usually called warlocks, are accepted.

Covenant. A promise or commitment; used in spiritual language for its binding power, i.e., the covenant between God and humanity.

Coworkers. Those working in conscious cooperation, vibrating to a harmonious keynote, and serving one goal. Spiritually supportive participants of the same vision; a state of consciousness in which all workers identify with the same goal and do their part without hindering the work of others. An alignment of energies toward a unified purpose.

Craft, the. A commonly used synonym for Wicca or witchcraft.

Cranial-sacral therapy. A therapy utilizing the manipulation of the energy of the head and head centers. A sensing of the imbalance is determined by the trained therapist and a slight pressure applied to the etheric body encouraging adjustment. Effects are often noted immediately and found helpful for attitude and for release of tension and discomfort.

Creation. That which was conceived by the Creator and given expression through matter, reflecting the Creator's nature: life, love, and purpose.

Creative thread. One of three threads known collectively as the antahkarana. This thread is woven as an individual responds to life experiences, sometimes called "the Path." The other two threads are known as sutratma and antahkarana. *Also see* Rainbow bridge.

Creative workers. A category of world servers who work through integrated head, heart, sacral, and root chakras to step down the higher Plan for humanity.

Cremation. A method using fire to dispose of the physical shell after death. Commonly used by ancient traditions and highly recommended to free the soul of its attachment to the physical plane. It is becoming more conventional, perhaps for its hygienic value and for preserving burial space on Mother Earth.

Critical mass intentionality. A modern term coined to acknowledge the power of the group mind to achieve for the benefit of all.

Critters hypothesis. The name given by Trevor James Constable to living organisms, invisible biological aeroforms living in the sky (so his developing research shows), existing in a plasma (etheric) state, not solid or liquid, but a living heat-substance at the upper border of physical nature and exhibiting animal-like behavior. Also called plasmoids, aeroforms, ideoplasms, and elementals. *See* UFOlogy.

Crone. A term, not derogatory, for an elderly female, acknowledging wisdom gleaned by life's experiences. Also referred to as a hag or wise woman. *Also see* Goddess, Triple.

Crop circles. Unique designs of unproven

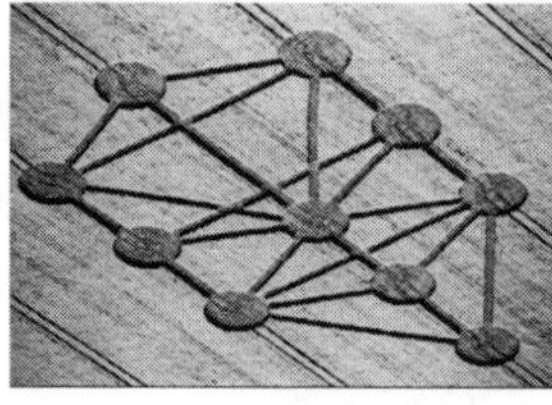

origin appear seemingly miraculously in fields of growing crops. While patterns have appeared in a

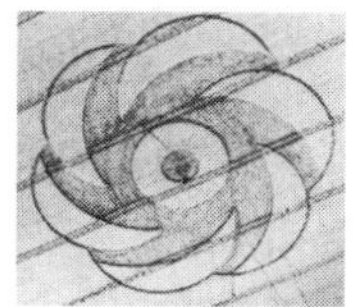

number of countries, the majority have been in the area of Glastonbury, Ashbury, southern British Isles.

These crop circles of the kabalistic Tree and the lotus appeared while this author was guiding a tour through Wales and Southern England—a day after local people had said it was too early for crop circles. These are two symbols of Sancta Sophia Seminary

CROSSES. *See p. 62.*

CROWN. To esoteric traditions this symbolizes the highest CHAKRA, correlating to Egyptian headgear, Native American headdress of feathers, antler horns on Viking and Mongolian helmets, elaborate feather dressings of the MAYA. This head ornamentation was conferred as a sign of high consciousness, awakened leadership, one with God—victory, majesty, sovereignty, and dominion. A symbol used for Christ the King by traditional Christians.

CROWN OF THORNS. The crown placed on the head of Jesus the Christ to ridicule him during his persecution prior to the Crucifixion. A symbol reminding us that each initiate has to pierce through to higher mental awareness to be Christed. The first of three crowns to be won on the Path of Initiation. *Also see* Laurel crown; Lotus crown.

CRUCIFIXION. The fourth initiation consists of two parts (Crucifixion and the emergence of the true Self) and is most often associated with Jesus, the Christ. Crucifixion is a method of torture wherein the body is placed on a cross, sometimes upside down, until death. Crucifixion can be on nonphysical levels of self where torture or extreme pressure is brought to bear upon the psychological nature.

CRYSTAL GAZING. Also called "SKRYING," a technique of activating the inner eye, or clairvoyance.

CRYSTALLIZATION. Definite or permanent in form. Stabilization or fixation of thoughts, ideas, or physical realities held in dense form or lower vibration. According to the law of fixation that governs the mental plane, the result of crystallization is an inevitable shattering so that the indwelling life can be freed for further progress.

CRYSTAL SKULLS. Head-shaped carved crystal sculpture, mysterious in origin. All known skulls have been located in Mayan temple ruins and are considered to have been used in initiation rites. Hunbatz Men, prince of the Maya, says they came from the stars and were on the altars of Atlantis. "Max," a well-known skull has been at Sparrow Hawk Village a number of times, and individuals have had many experiences of expanded reality in its presence.

CUBIC STONE. A part of the SACRED GEOMETRY of space is both the subject and the solution of the third rubric of the EMERALD TABLET. Drawings depict First Matter as a square stone or cube dangling by a rope. PARACELSUS wrote, "Know therefore that the said First Matter is ultimately nothing but an [invisible] box full of great force and power."

CULT. A body of believers gathered around a charismatic leader, attracted by a personality to which obsessive devotion is projected. A

Crosses

Ankh. This cross of ancient Egypt symbolizes the energy pattern of the human body and means "life."

Aquarian. An equal-armed cross with an open, rectangular center containing the VESICA PISCIS symbol of two interlinking circles. It is the perfectly balanced symbol of the Christ consciousness and is now a focus for the second coming of that energy on Earth. It represents the principles of the law of One demonstrated by Master Jesus in his universal, nondenominational teachings.

Botonnee. With arms ending in a graceful trefoil design that suggests the Holy Trinity, the popular Botonnee cross has been widely used on royal and aristocratic coats-of-arms as a reminder of service to humanity and to God. To kabalists the top TREFOIL represents the highest three SEPHIROTH and the long, vertical bar, the descent to Malkuth, the kingdom of matter, signifying that our work is to bring the kingdom of God to Earth.

Celtic. The original Celtic crosses were found in Great Britain and Ireland where they were erected as wayside and cemetery crosses. The circle is an emblem of life everlasting, no beginning and no end. The Celtic cross is also known as the Cross of Iona because it is thought to have been taken by Celtic Christians from Ireland to the Island of Iona in the 6th century, before the Roman arm of Christianity arrived.

Equal-Armed. The vertical arm represents the high consciousness of which we are capable as we align to the Holy. The horizontal bar represents the outer plane of consciousness in which we ground our expression and service. Each awakened one seeks to stand at the center point and mediate the two realities harmoniously. This effort explains the origin of the term "centered and balanced." When a circle encloses the equal-armed cross, it is considered protected. In astrology the equal-armed cross encircled is the symbol for the Earth.

Jerusalem. A specialized form of the Cross Cantonnee, consisting of a central cross surrounded by four smaller crosses of the same design. The five crosses symbolize the five steps of INITIATION in the Christian path. Like the five-pointed star, we are reminded to dedicate the physical, emotional, mental, social, and spiritual aspects of our lives to the Christ when mastery of personality and spiritualized consciousness is sought.

Rose. A single rose marks the cross arms, designating the heart center on this simple cross. Rosicrucians use this single rose on a cross as their symbol.

standard cult characteristic is sameness, lack of individuality. Members must adhere to a defined belief system, behavior is dictated, expectations and routine are defined, and allegiance is expected or commanded. A cult is empowered primarily by the strong allegiance that binds the organization or group. The cult concept is anathema to free thinkers or occultists. *Also see* Occult; Occultism.

CULTURAL CREATIVES. A collective of American adults comprising an awakening subculture of about one-quarter of the population committed to reframing how we view ourselves in context with one another and planetary life. They thrive on authenticity, spirituality, and bringing important issues into public life.

CUNEIFORM. A wedge-shaped script identified as the earliest writing, usually with Sumerian and Hittite culture, related to the Akkadian language, the mother tongue of all the Semitic languages. *See pp. 337–47,* Humanity's Genesis.

CUPID. Originally a symbol of the indwelling self effecting a union between emotion and desire. Also, the Roman counterpart of the Greek god Eros. In Roman literature a playful cherub shooting arrows of passion.

CURSE. The conscious projection of negative energy toward another, especially when accompanied by harmful words, thoughts, or visualization.

CUSP. The overlapping period of astrological-houses or signs, when the two create an intensified period of energy as primary influences recede and incoming influences build. In an ASTROLOGY chart, the sign found on each house demarcation that, with its ruling planet, affects or modifies the activities of the house. Similarly, events that occur or placements that reside within the last or first degrees of a sign are affected by the energies of both the sign of actual degree and the proximate sign. For those born near a change of signs or houses within the cusp period, astrologers find significant challenges. Each sign contains 30 degrees: 0 degrees of any sign will express that sign most radically; the 29th degree of any sign intensifies the need to display the qualities or influences of that given sign.

CYBERSPACE. The destruction or breakdown of fixed time and space identities. As people from one part of the world relate to others, the question of time and distance begins to dissolve. All of us have THOUGHTFORMS built of separate realities; cyberspace demands we merge and acknowledge that we know of tomorrow's events today if we are talking to someone on the other side of the dateline.

CYCLE, ASTROLOGICAL. The orbit of a celestial body; a time interval in which it completes a revolution around another body on a regular basis. Each planet adheres to its particular rotation, dependent upon the speed of the planet and the distance it travels to complete an orbit, e.g., the moon takes approximately 28 days to complete one cycle, the Earth takes about 365 days to orbit the sun, and the sun about 365 days to complete one cycle of the zodiac (28–30 days each to pass through the twelve zodiacal signs). Also, all life is cyclic, in accord to the principle, "AS ABOVE, SO BELOW." Just as planetary cycles exist, so do the rhythms and cycles of human life, seasons of the years—"what goes around, comes around." With wisdom applied, gentle shifts can be achieved.

NUMEROLOGY also offers ways and means of studying the rhythms of life with meanings applied to vibrations in numerical frequencies.

CYCLE, PLANETARY. A stage building upon the past and moving automatically forward. The Earth is entering a new cycle that will take it to a more luminous process in which it will be governed by higher laws and express a more harmonious life within the cosmos. Current conditions of purification and chaos are preparatory to this next cycle for planetary life.

CYCLORAMA. In sacred geometry a curved wall or curtain suggesting unlimited space; may be part of a VESICA PISCIS.

DAATH. The consciousness of an individual soul's evolutionary pattern, portrayed on the kabalistic tree as a dotted circle, indicating its form is incomplete, still in process. As we learn to weigh our options and correctly choose what is appropriate for the occasion, according to the teachings, we earn a "dot." Daath, GNOSIS, and SOPHIA have the same esoteric meaning: wisdom or consciousness ascending. *See* Tree.

DAILY REVIEW. *See* Nightly review.

DALAI LAMA. A Buddhist title meaning "Exalted Ocean" or "teacher who is an ocean of wisdom." The current spiritual leader of Tibetan Buddhism, b. Takster, 1935, is now in exile in India. He was designated the 14th Dalai Lama in 1937 by the monks of the Gelugpa order of Lhasa, who were convinced he was the reincarnation of the Compassionate Buddha. Forced into exile after China's savage suppression of the Tibetan National Uprising of 1959, he remains the spiritual and temporal head of Tibet, an eloquent, unique spokesman for Buddhism around the world.

DARK AGES, THE. The early medieval period of intellectual darkness and barbarity in West European history, specifically 476–800 when there was no emperor in the West, generally refers to the period between A.D. 500–1000 marked by frequent warfare and a virtual disappearance of urban life. Rarely used by historians today because of the unacceptable implied value judgment.

DARK FORCES. Energies that restrict one to ego consciousness (personality level). Usually regarded as bad; better considered as selfish or self-centered. When such influences limit some level of personality, expansion of consciousness is inhibited.

Dark night of the soul. A painful period of testing when the soul must stand alone, demonstrating its own strength or light. "Many spiritual seekers describe [this as] a time when preexisting beliefs and personality constructs are shed, released, or destroyed, and new ones emerge to replace them. The interim period between one state of being and the next is often characterized by confusion, lack of clarity or direction, and even depression."[1] A profound inner experience occurring in the life of those who, seeking knowledge of God, penetrate beyond the realm of knowable things into the invisible and incomprehensible nature of God experienced as the void, darkness, or emptiness.

Darshan. An Eastern practice at which pupils sit in silence in the presence of a revered person or of God incarnate. There may be preliminary prayers or invocations or a blessing at the conclusion, but the true exchange (blessing) takes place at the inner level about "those things which are eternal." A verbal exchange seldom takes place.

Davening. A rhythmic spinal flexion and nodding motion that "happens" while saying ritual prayers, included in the practices of Orthodox Judaism, Islam, and others. A movement sacred in context.

Daykeeper. A wise one in the Mayan tradition, particularly in reference to understanding their complex calendar system; also, shaman or "wisdomkeeper."

Dead Sea Scrolls. Ancient texts written in Hebrew, Aramaic, or Greek on papyrus or leather found 1947–56 near the north end of the Dead Sea. "Dead Sea Scrolls" is used in both a narrow and a broad sense. The narrow definition is restricted to manuscripts found in 11 caves in the vicinity of Khirbet Qumran. The broad usage includes documents found at Masada, Wadi Murabba'at, Nahal Hever, Nahal Se'elim, and Nahal Mishmar. Their primary importance is the understanding they provide of Judaism around the turn of the era. The scrolls illustrate the variety of Judaism and provide a wealth of comparative material that will occupy New Testament scholars for a long time. They depict a religious movement that helps us reconstruct the climate of early Christianity and of the mission of John the Baptist, shedding light on the constitution of the primitive Church. The scrolls do not contain an anticipation of or parallel to the distinctive Christian doctrines of Incarnation, Vicarious Atonement, or Communion. The dates believed to be attributed to the composition of the scrolls vary between 250 B.C. and A.D. 68. *Also see* Nag Hammadi Scrolls.

Death. The most commonly used term for shedding the physical form. A great misunderstanding of life stems from ignorance, for death is confused with "the end," or oblivion. Indeed, birth (entering limitation) is death, and death (a return to our spirit nature) is birth. *See* Mota.

Death and dying, stages of. The process experienced as one adapts to cope with trauma of great change, as in death, loss, divorce, and so on. Five definitive steps are experienced (not always in the clearly defined order and with some overlap):

DENIAL — Rejection of change

ANGER — Distorted and/or confused love goes awry, often exhibited in destructive and painful ways

BARGAINING — Balancing or negotiating painful or distressing change, yet still able to summon hope; often a time of experimenting with new approaches or ideas

DEPRESSION — A despondent response to the struggle with change, energy directed inwardly more than outwardly

ACCEPTANCE — At peace with inevitable changes and able to respond in a loving and wise manner

DEATH REVIEW. *See* Life review.

DEE, JOHN. d. 1608. Alchemist, kabalist, and visionary, considered historically as the founder of the ROSICRUCIAN Order, author of *The Rosie Crucian Secrets,* a voluminous work. He coined the word "Britannia" and developed a plan for the British Navy. A philosopher to Queen Elizabeth, did her horoscope and determined her coronation date astrologically. He was instrumental in theater, arts, and architecture. It is said he avowed he communed with angels.

DÉJÀ VU. A conscious "knowing" that a familiar event has been experienced before, recalled from another point of time and space. A phenomenon similar to lucid dreaming but occurring in an awakened state. In French, literally, "already seen." *Also see* Future.

DELINEATING. In astrology, interpreting a chart.

DELPHIC ORACLE. *See* Oracle of Delphi.

DELUGE. The Great Flood of the Bible (Gen. 7) for which Noah is said to have built the ark for survival.

DELUSION. Distortion in the astral nature that blinds human beings to their true nature. The "unreal" through which we must pierce to perceive the greater values life offers.

DEMON. An entity of destructive influence that has never had a physical form but conveys negativity to a human being. The term often is used for LUCIFER or SATAN due to the tests it creates as it comes into contact with a human being. To demonize is to make a demonic image of another.

DENSE BODY. The physical body.

DENSE WORLD. The lowest sub-plane of the physical world; commonly, reality consisting of matter visible to the human eye. To many, the "real world."

DESCENT INTO MATTER. The soul and its projected personality experience becoming enveloped in denser and denser realities/forms/wrappings, culminating as physical or materialized.

DESERT FATHERS. From the earliest days of the Christian tradition, ascetics and hermits have sought to live simple lives in relative isolation, going into the desert, forests, or mountains to detach themselves from the values of society, to discipline their appetites and their desires, and to focus their full attention on God. The world delighted in hearing of their travails, their feats of self-denial, purported miracles, and their combat with demons in both horrible and alluring disguises. The desert fathers' tradition was well-established by the 4th century throughout the Mediterranean region, even as far as Cappadocia, Turkey, in Asia Minor. Their influence continues to inspire others as they seek a deeper spiritual life. *See pp. 246–51,* Saints: Antony of Egypt, Evagrius Ponticus.

DESIRE BODY. This name applied to the human astral form acknowledges its strong emotional or feeling nature.

DESIRELESSNESS. An Eastern term relating to the goal of nonattachment to material realities so that spiritual reality might emerge more clearly.

DESTINY. The pattern for a life or experience held by the soul or HIGH SELF, usually veiled from personality.

DESTRUCTIVE BEHAVIOR. Usually the result of an inversion of higher energies flowing down into image-laden personality systems.

DETACHMENT. The capacity to disidentify from people, places, events, or things, or to disengage oneself. Non-attachment is a state of awareness that affirms all phenomena of life are in continuous change, and one realizes a greater state of freedom by relating impersonally to the form side of life. From this state one loves and cares but is not subject to manipulation by the emotional or illusionary nature.

DEUNOV, PETER. b. Nickolaevka, Bulgaria, 1864, d. 1944. Spiritual name: Beinsa Douno. Studied in U.S. as a young man, receiving certificates from Harvard, among others. The creator of PAN EURYTHMY, his spiritual practice is expressed largely through music, movement, and prayer to integrate spiritual, physical, ecological, and musical dimensions. The spirit of Jesus, the Christ, appeared to him in 1912 and said, "Give me your body, your heart, and your mind, and work for me." He viewed his work as continuing the mission of Christ through teaching the keynotes of love, wisdom, and truth. He said, "The one who speaks down the centuries is always the same. At all times, it is God who reveals himself to humanity. The forms through which he manifests are different, but he is One." In Europe he established the White BROTHERHOOD for the planet in 1900; it has since spread over the American continents as well.

DEVACHAN. A Sanskrit (Tibetan) word meaning "happy place." The heavenly world or dwelling place of the gods; spirit reality where weary souls rest, refresh the spirit, and experience no pain between lives.

DEVAS. In Sanskrit literally a "shining one." Also called "ANGELS," these comprise a parallel evolution to humanity and often interact. Devic forces, known as the "builders of form" or "NATURE SPIRITS," command many forces of nature. They work with the lesser kingdoms evolving on Earth and cowork effectively with humans of stable temperament and advanced in understanding spiritual law. Devas usually guide the work of elementals, serving humanity and more advanced angels on a line of hierarchical advancement. Much work has been undertaken to counterbalance humanity's 5,000 years of unconsciousness. Now their participation must be invoked consciously by human beings advanced enough to summon, wisely and respectfully, the forces of these creative intelligences.

DEVEKUT. In Judaism, a high state of awareness, such as NIRVANA or SATORI.

DEVELOPMENT, PERSONAL OR SPIRITUAL. Sensitive evolution begins when an individual becomes willing to be impressed by unfolding psychic senses or a contact with one in spirit, to "hear" a bit differently, to improvise. One awakens in one's own fashion to create a personal style—to "march to one's own drummer." That which dwells within is inspired to be heard, to share in the energy of each level. To encourage expressiveness is to encourage the soul to live in one's outer world.

DEVIL. *See* Dweller on the Threshold; Lucifer; Satan.

DHARMA. The way of high character, duty, or purpose; our mission in life; a reason for being; service to the Plan, to God, to PLANETARY LOGOS. Used to denote the positive forces we have earned to help us meet well the experience of life; sometimes erroneously called "good karma."

DHARMA LIGHT. An Eastern term for the outpouring of mind, love, and will of the Creator. The grace of God's light, divine light, poured forth upon creation to hold all things together is essential to both happiness and progress along the spiritual path. The inner mystical light experienced by the soul on its journey through the higher realms. Dharma implies law and is derived from the root *dhri*: to hold, to support, to sustain, or to bear. "Walking in the light" refers to universal ethical conduct or the true, correct, and wisely chosen fulfillment of obligations sometimes considered the duty—religious or moral—of humanity. *See* Cloud of Knowable Things.

DHYANI-CHOHANS. A compound Sanskrit Tibetan term meaning "Lords of Meditation." Great beings devoted to contemplating, unfolding, and fulfilling the divine Plan. Conscious, intelligent powers in nature divinely charged with the supervision of the cosmos. Generally speaking, any celestial being who has advanced to a stage superior to the human kingdom. Frequently a specific planetary spirit acting as regent of a planet or planetary chain. Traditionally, Dhyani-Chohans are divided into three major classes or kingdoms—each of which is subdivided into seven sub-classes. They comprise the collective hosts of spiritual beings—the angels of Christianity, the ELOHIM and "messengers" of Judaism—the means for the manifestation of the divine or universal mind and creative will. Having evolved through the Earth life chain in former world periods, this wondrous group of beings now acts as guides, lords, leaders, and saviors of evolving human and planetary life.

DIANOIA. Greek for the "rational mind," which uses deductive reasoning versus *nons,* the mind that relies on intuition for its knowing.

DIE BEFORE YOU DIE. A reference by MOHAMMED, the prophet of Allah, to those who voluntarily die to ego consciousness in order to know Oneness. Those who turn their lives over to the Oneness allow the One to shine through their eyes, heart, and mind into all activities of life. A famous statement oft quoted by Abd Al-Kader, a Sufi sage.

DIGNIFICATION. In the tradition of ALCHEMY, a term for inner and outer preparation through prayer and meditation to begin one's spiritual work.

DIMENSION, FIFTH. The dimension of soul consciousness in which we realize oneness with others, the collective soul of humanity. Home of the MYSTICAL CHRIST, or ADAM KADMON.

DIMENSION, FOURTH. An awareness of our spiritual self or higher consciousness. Home of the individual point of consciousness we know as soul. We acknowledge when we affirm, "the Christ within me greets the Christ within you," or "Namasté."

DIMENSION, THIRD. Home of personality. The physical, emotional, and mental world of which we are actively aware.

DINA. An acronym for Discipleship in the New Age, a group taught by MASTER DJWHAL KHUL (D.K.) through Alice BAILEY. DINA dictations are largely contained in Bailey's two volumes by the same name, *Discipleship in the New Age.* Members were under disciplines given by D.K., and names were not given publically; a few members were revealed privately, one of whom was Vera Stanley ALDER.

DIONYSOS. Greek god of intoxication; a metaphor for "bliss" in Western mysteries.

DISCARNATE. That part of the human kingdom not embodied in physical form presently but existing in nonphysical dimensions. Human beings who have made their transition from Earth-plane life to dwell for a time in nonphysical realms.

DISCERNMENT. One of the GIFTS OF THE SPIRIT achieved after much interaction between conscious mind and higher consciousness. The awareness of what something is *as it exists in the moment* in order to fully recognize the reality of a situation. Openness to learning and revising is necessary in order to adapt to changing events. This goal of the disciple is realized as the energies of the soul and of the higher mind blend in new awareness.

DISCIPLE. In esoteric tradition, specifically a first- or second-degree initiate. In common usage, a pupil or follower who lives a Master's teachings. Those who follow a particular discipline according to a prescribed pattern but also recognize much free will and understanding. Those subscribing to a consistent habit of spiritual living whose knowledge, capacities, and spiritual abilities are demonstrated in daily life. Today's disciple is often called a WORLD SERVER.

DISCIPLESHIP. The act of striving to fulfill the practices and restraints of a particular way or teacher. The manifestation of spiritual principles and guidelines in one's life qualifies one to be a disciple or to advance his/her discipleship.

In Esoteric Christianity several stages must be attained as an aspirant progresses through the evolutionary process: an individual of ideals; probationary pupil; accepted pupil; son/daughter of the Master; and the initiate. In the Bailey teachings, profiled as candidates, little disciples, growing disciples, accepted disciple, advanced disciple, disciple on the thread, disciple in the aura of the Master, disciple in the heart, adept, Master.

DISCIPLINES, DIETARY. Specific eating practices a disciple observes, such as fasting or regulated eating, or to become a vegetarian, vegan, or fruitarian.

DISCIPLINES, SEXUAL. Spiritual practices to help disciples guide powerful sexual energies into constructive patterns of a lifestyle in keeping with one's choice. The most common sexual practices are *celibacy,* the avoidance of sexual activity; *betrothal,* similar to a modern engagement with public vows on commitment with a plan to move toward marriage (some traditions permit sexual interaction but most do not and see this time as a trial wherein two individuals become better acquainted); *marriage,* two persons in a structured relationship wherein the sexual needs of both are regarded as mutually exclusive; *committed relationship,* wherein two persons commit to an exclusive relationship without benefit of legal status but live together honestly, ethically, and with mutual concern for the needs, sexual and otherwise, of each other; *periodic abstinence,* where by mutual agreement sexual activity is regulated to meet the needs of both parties, usually centered around religions or spiritual concerns; *karessa,* a practice wherein generally both partners' sexual nature is aroused and satisfied by prolonged sexual play without the release of sexual fluids by one or both participants; *tantra,* an Eastern practice of directing the aroused energy from chakra to chakra (of a couple or an individual) while gradually centering and balancing at each point before consciously lifting the energy to the next higher center. The goal is to reach the highest center, experiencing orgasm together or by oneself within the head center rather than in the lower physical center.

DISCIPLINES, SPIRITUAL. Practices come in both additions to and subtractions from our day-to-day lifestyle. The most common beginning practices to expand consciousness and develop love and will are prayer, meditation, contemplation, and adoration. Specific disciplines for those on the spiritual path are: fasting, tithing, silence, and sexual applications (see above). Specific traditions advocate useful additional practices to develop will, that one's choice of self-moderation may be realized. *Discipline* means "the way of the disciple." *Also see* Alms, giving of; Adoration; Contemplation; Disciplines, sexual; Fasting; Meditation; Penance; Prayer; Service; Tithing; Visualization.

DISEASE (OR DIS-EASE). Disharmony between levels of self resulting in a breakdown of health in any of the personality SHEATHS.

DISEMBODIED. Not in physical body.

DISEMPOWER. To free or separate one from the ability to perform; to interfere or break the flow that enables one to express. May be positive or negative.

DISIDENTIFY. To release our identity with the outer in order to develop the true self from within.

DISPASSION. A desired state of consciousness of pure objectivity; neither pain nor pleasure dominates.

DISSOCIATION. A separation or detachment from conscious self that often occurs in trauma, so one part behaves independently of the other, each functioning as a separate unit. Often unaware of the other, such as in abuse; when the painful experience is separated and unacknowledged in order for the personality to continue to function. Such a condition may result in permitting other entities to attach themselves to a host or to gain considerable influence.

DISSOLUTION. In alchemy, the dissipation of the rigid rational structures and established belief systems. Beginning with BAPTISM or an INITIATION rite, one cleanses away the old ideas and habits to begin anew. Water is the symbol of fluidity and freedom to change, to release, and to let go. TERESA OF AVILA stated that perfect dissolution was the key to union with God, an attitude as easily acquired through selfless service to others as through the most devout and self-serving prayer.

DISTANCE HEALING. Healing techniques that may be used without the patient being physically present.

DIVINATION. The art of foretelling future events or revealing hidden knowledge by means of psychic or physical tools. The use of OCCULT, ESOTERIC, or spiritual means to receive information not apparent to the five senses.

DIVINE DESTINY. The implication that the Creator holds a goal for Creation, that there is a SOUL PURPOSE for each incarnation. Divine destiny affirms a reason for the whole of human experience, even when we cannot understand it. Coworking and a greater level of enlightenment are acknowledged as humanity's current goals.

DIVINE DISCONTENT. The irritating impulse that persists after awakening as consciousness begins to sense there is more to life than meets the eye. A restless spirit that irritates personality to sustain its search for deeper understanding.

DIVINE FEMININE. The feminine facet of God, often called the "Mother," delivering qualities of love, sensitivity, and nurturing, concerned with the maturing of the inner nature and the perfection of intuition. An acknowledgment of the soul—"she who dwells within"—that births the Christ-Within.

DIVINE MASCULINE. The masculine aspect of God, usually called "Father," especially concerned with action, intellect, and law. Humanity has over-developed this aspect of its nature to the extent of abuse, so that today major energies have shifted to feminine to bring balance to planetary life. The great HERMETIC principle of GENDER requires all life to express both masculine and feminine qualities.

DIVINE OBSESSION. Used by MASTER DJWHAL KHUL, the Tibetan, to indicate the phenomenon commonly called "WALK-IN" today, though this author prefers "MESSENGER." D.K. maintained that this experience would become increasingly common in the years ahead. *See* Monadic transmutation; Soul exchange.

DIVINE PRINCIPLE. An Agni term meaning "God" or "Creator." This substitute term rose

out of the suppression of religion under communism. The word "God," offensive to the Soviet regime, was prohibited. New terms served to some degree, but the teachings of Agni Yoga were nonetheless kept hidden, veiled in the language of ethics, art, and culture, articulated only in terms of social enrichment.

DIVINE REALIZATION. Moments of revelation merging into synthesis or comprehension.

DJINN. A term used for little people; witches; ghosts; spirit beings, both good and bad. Often considered mischievous as children.

DJWHAL KHUL. *See pp. 170–1,* Masters.

DNA (DEOXYRIBONUCLEIC ACID). An instruction manual for our cells written in code, using an alphabet composed of four letters—A, T, C, and G—which refer to nucleotides that translate into 20 amino acids, the building blocks of protein. The four letters combine to create "words and sentences" that compose the genetic code of each individual. The genetic history, or weaving of physical experiences, is retained in a little-known manner by the DNA. ESOTERICISTS see this information encoded in the ETHERIC BODY and contained in the PERMANENT SEED ATOMS.

Kabalah teaches that human DNA consists of various sequences of genetic letters that combine into a system that creates a human being out of 22 forces of creation that are represented by the 22 Hebrew letters. *Also see* GNA.

DOCTRINES. Religious convictions (taught as facts) to which adherents are expected to pledge allegiance.

DODECAHEDRON. A three-dimensional design in which the lines, angles, and surfaces are equal. Often referred to in sacred geometry.

DOGMA. Specific tenets of a religious sect. Adherents are obligated to accept these as creed to receive grace.

DOGWOOD. The flower that blooms at the Easter season resembling a cross. Each petal's edge bears a mark very like a bloodstain. Its center suggests the crown of thorns. Legend has it that the crucifix was hewn of dogwood. Now the tree grows slight of trunk, not thick enough to support a body.

DOMINIONS. ANGELS of an advanced order who will the PLAN of God and obey the THRONES. They are responsible for the economy of nature and work as agents of supply and demand. They regulate activities and duties of the angels.

DORMITION. The Christian term for the death of Mary, Mother of Jesus, and the lying-in-state stage at the end of her life, prior to the translation of the body into a vehicle of the higher planes and its ASSUMPTION. Corresponds to the ASCENSION of Jesus, the Christ.

DOVE. The descending dove is the most widely used symbol of the Holy Spirit, the third person of the traditional Trinity in Christianity. At Jesus' baptism "the Holy Spirit descended on him, like a dove, and a voice from heaven, saying, You are

my beloved Son; with you I am pleased." (Luke 3.22) Also, the symbol for SOPHIA, the divine feminine.

DOWSING. "Water witching." A nonscientific method of receiving information intuitively through techniques understood by the operator as attunement. Used for locating Earth energy LEYS, underground water, lost articles, and specific answers. The American Dowsers Society, Danville, Vermont 05828, is a recognized authority on this phenomenon. *Also see* Earth energies; Pendulum.

DRAGON. Symbol of the evolutionary energy abiding within human form; the power to be aroused and refined by advancing consciousness. Also called "serpentine," "kundalini," or "fire." "An ancient term for the totality of traces of life-activity deposited in the subtle memory of the Earth. . . . parallel to the psychological idea of the unconscious, and is a powerful force at the basis of the ego's instincts. The terrestrial dragon is another term for the tropical zodiac, . . . [referring] to the zodiac of the Sun or SIDEREAL ZODIAC, the archetypal energy radiating from the stars, as relative to our solar system."[2]

DREAM. A drama presented in an altered state of consciousness to convey meaning to the rational mind. Esotericists consider dreams to be highly significant and worthy of study to uncover concealed messages to the dreamer. Believed by different systems to emanate from a variety of sources: the superconscious, the subconscious, the collective consciousness, or natural, physiological causes. Each symbol and person is considered an aspect of the dreamer—one which s/he is unable to recognize when in the awake state, i.e., the SHADOW. *See* Freud, Sigmund; Jung, Carl.

DREAMING, LUCID. An explicit awareness while in the dream state that we are dreaming. We are not awake, yet often we discover we are able to control the dream, its nature, or its outcome as we desire. This deliberate act of taking control demonstrates the empowerment of the dreamer. Tibetan Masters call it "dreaming true," a level of high spiritual consciousness where wisdom and knowledge are accessible.

DRUID. The intelligentsia of the Celtic tradition. From this group of scholars came the priests, chiefs, judges, and magicians (shamans) to teach the immortality of the soul and reincarnation. In Glastonbury, England, they still believe Jesus studied with the Druids before returning to his homeland to be baptized (by John) and to begin his ministry

Mistletoe, sacred plant of the Druids.

DTAKRESIS. In Greek, a term meaning discernment of spirits, a gift of the holy spirit; refers to the ability to discern between various types of thought, more specifically between ego awareness and transcendent impressions.

DUALISM. The nature of the physical plane is to express in polarity with lines of tension between each perspective reflected by opposites: male and female, good and evil, or expansion and contraction.

DUALITY, WORLD OF. The dense world, physical in nature, known as Assiah in Kabalah, has a nature that exists as polarities. Here,

opposites are the natural state of life. The kabalistic tree symbolizes this with three pillars: masculine, feminine, and a middle column of balance. Polarities are reflected in hot and cold, up and down, good and bad, and the human exists in this world of dichotomies until it integrates awareness and develops the spiritual nature where it can see the oneness of all life.

DUGPAS. Tibetan term for testing agents residing within the ego that resist light and seek to slow those on the path. The symbology of good and bad angels represents challenges presented by devas of light and dugpas—dark elementals of self-service that must become aligned to the soul purpose before one's advancement on the PATH OF INITIATION can occur. Dugpas are often called "evil" because they operate on the path of involution, rather than evolution.

DWELLER ON THE THRESHOLD. The individual, as well as collective, has unfinished business that impedes human spiritual advancement. This negative configuration has been labeled "the devil," as in "the devil made me do it." A symbolic name for the collection of unique imperfections (old selves) with which each of us struggles. The sum of all that personality holds and its defects, potencies (physical, emotional, and mental) that limit expression of the soul. The works of Carl JUNG and Roberto ASSAGIOLI help us become conscious of the SHADOW or unknown parts of ourselves. Both Jungian psychology and Assagioli's PSYCHOSYNTHESIS acknowledge the personality, the spiritual nature of each person, and the need for the various parts of the self to function as a harmonious whole.

DZYAN. A Tibetan word meaning "meditation"; also wisdom, or divine knowledge.

DZYAN, THE BOOK OF. An ancient manuscript, the title meaning "The Book of Wisdom" or ". . . of Divine Knowledge," interpreted by Helena P. BLAVATSKY; also referred to as the *Stanzas of Dzyan,* upon which, it is said, she based her *Secret Doctrine:* "part of the same series of long-concealed manuscript treasures. It will not be found in any European library but is in safe custody in one of the mysterious rock libraries of the Himalayas that house other works thought to be lost to humanity since the burning of the great Library of Alexandria." The book contains "the history of cosmic evolution as understood by the abstract algebraical formula of that evolution."[3]

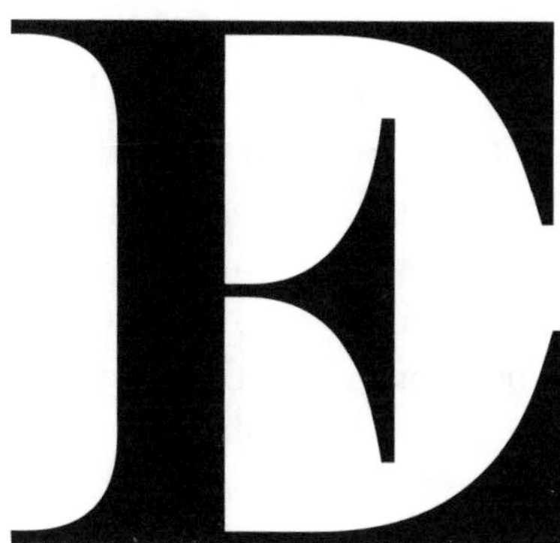

EARTHBORN PARADISES. Places in the astral dimension for those not yet mature enough to enjoy the heavens of the inner world, i.e., playgrounds for young or immature souls unprepared for spiritual training. They will abide there until they reincarnate or evolve to readiness for states of inner life that will offer more opportunities for growth.

EARTHBOUND. Those who, even after death, are so attracted to limited consciousness, they remain in the dense, nonphysical rather than progress into more refined ethers. ADDICTIONS to substances or practices that are only available in the dense world are the principal cause of this condition.

EARTH ENERGIES. Leys, or currents, in the Earth that flow in recognizable patterns to vitalize sites for specific purposes. These are detectable by dowsers or SENSITIVES. The etheric level of the Earth retains the imprint of certain events or energies for some periods of time so blessings or painful energies can linger and blend with Earth energies; some places need to be neutralized through cleansing and healing efforts.

EARTH RELIGION. Any belief system that has as its basic tenet that all life is sacred and connected, honoring nature as the embodiment of Divinity. Its practices seek to bring the individual into harmony with the Earth, its natural cycles, and the rhythms of the universe as sources of spiritual wisdom and experiences of union with the Divine. Such religions oppose the idea that the world is to be subdued and its resources exploited.

EASTER. The celebration of the Resurrection of Jesus, the historical Christ. It is a time full of joy and profound meaning for all Christians. When Jesus reappeared after the entombment, his friends knew death was not final. A movable Christian celebration set by a religious formula: In the Roman Catholic Church, Easter is the first Sunday after the full moon following spring equinox. In the Byzantine tradition, Easter is calculated differently and often follows the Easter Sunday of the Western tradition. One of three major spiritual festivals of the year, the Aries full moon is a time of welcoming the new annual cycle—a true Easter festival of renewal, resurrection, and reconstruction. The cross of the Risen Christ will be the symbol of the forthcoming era. Each springtime, nature demonstrates how beautiful new life can spring from something that seems to have died.

EASTERN ORTHODOXY. The Eastern division of the early church that divided into two factions in A.D. 1054, creating the Roman Catholic Church with headquarters in Rome and the Eastern Byzantine Church with headquarters in Constantinople, collectively known today as the Eastern Orthodox tradition.

ECCLESIASTIC. Literally, a person who is a member of an assembly or church *(ecclesia)* or who takes part in the discussions of a learned group. Also, a cleric.

ECKANKAR. An organization founded by Paul TWITCHELL in 1965 whose major concepts, it asserts, form the basic foundation for all religions, philosophies, and scientific works in our world today; it offers a science of soul travel and total consciousness. The belief that light and sound are the only way the Holy Spirit, called ECK, can be seen or heard by humanity. The twin aspects come together in the form of the Inner Master, the Mahanta. The presence prompts inner awareness and thus provides subtle guidance. Described as a path rather than religion, philosophy, or metaphysics, the three principles of Eckankar are: "[Soul] is always in eternity. It is always in the present NOW. It is always in the heavenly state of God."[1] Eckankar claims it is "closer to being in its original form the science of soul travel than any other paths to God."[2] While the Mahanta is the Inner Master, an individual serves the living ECK as the Outer Master.

ECKHART, MEISTER JOHANNES. b. Hochheim, Thuringia, 1260, d. 1327. Meister means "master" in German. A great German theologian and speculative mystic who founded the school of Rhineland Mystics. Considered to be the ancestor of German Protestantism, Romanticism, Idealism, and Existentialism. Essentially he was a preacher. His doctrine, sometimes obscure, always came from one simple personal mystical experience to which he gave numerous names. His teachings describe four stages of the union of the soul to God: dissimilarity, similarity, identity, and breakthrough. The driving power of this process is detachment. He entered the Dominican Order at 15. He studied in Cologne and was greatly influenced by the teachings of Thomas Aquinas who had died there in the recent past.

ECLECTIC. An approach wherein one selects practices, doctrines, or ideas, and assembles them into a workable personal model.

ECLIPSE. As an astrology term, we learn of two kinds of eclipses—solar and lunar. Lunar eclipse occurs when the Earth passes between the sun and moon depriving the moon of its illumination temporarily; the solar eclipse puts the moon between the Earth and the sun, cutting off the light of the sun from the Earth so that for a time we cannot see the sun. A lunar eclipse can only occur at the time of a full moon; a solar eclipse can occur only at the time of a new moon. The effects of eclipses, when occurring in relationship to a planet in a natal chart, are generally considered challenging.

ECLIPSE, PRE-NATAL. The eclipse (lunar or solar) that occurred just prior to one's birth creates a sensitive reference point to be noted in one's natal chart and remains so during the entire lifetime. The house wherein the eclipse falls will be accentuated during the lifetime.

ECLIPTIC. In astrology, the great circle of a celestial sphere that is the path of the sun or another planet; the pathway or pattern a particular planet travels in its orbit.

ECOBIOLOGY. The study of other forms of energy—organic compounds, basic building blocks—that vibrate outside the wavelength range used in photosynthesis, fundamentally solar-powered, e.g., magnetism.

ECOCIDE. The death of the ecological system of the planet of which humanity is a segment, as well as a perpetrator.

ECOLOGY. The word is derived from "Earth" and "LOGOS." A new understanding of Earth as a living manifestation of divine origin or meaningful life. This new science respects and values nature.

ECONOMICS. From the Greek word *oikonemia* (since 350 B.C.), concerning good management of the household, or right living. Now usually understood as the condition of market values as a system of acquisition.

ECSTASY. A state of rapture; a downpouring or emotional rush that fills the consciousness that can appear to be good or bad—just energy. May occur when one contacts energies of the soul or AGAPE love originating in the higher planes with which humanity occasionally connects. Nonphysical in origin, the highly potent energy lifts one toward ever-higher consciousness or into closer mystical relationship.

ECTOPLASM. The subtle energy of the etheric body of a medium that under certain circumstances can be drawn from the body of a medium; used to cloak discarnates so they can be witnessed in a more or less physical manner, as in the manifestation of an apparition, especially as in seances.

ECUMENICAL. "While the word 'ecumenical' has been related to Christian unity movements, the literal meaning of the Greek word from which it comes, 'oikoumenikos,' would have it relate to the whole of God's family, the whole of the world."[3] In common usage the term often applies more to dialogue and interaction between denominations or sects of a given tradition.

EDUCARE. Latin root word from which "education" derives. Literal meaning "to lead out," as from ignorance or darkness.

EDUCATORS OF THE NEW AGE. World servers who work through integrated head, ajna, and throat CHAKRAS to step down the higher Plan for humanity.

EGO (WITH A LOWER-CASE E). The self-centered, self-satisfied point of consciousness not yet able to release its fascination with the false identity. The personality yet to be prepared or sufficiently trained for spirituality.

EGO (WITH A CAPITAL E). Latin for "I." Individualized self-consciousness; the perfect self that experiences in form and animates the will of human life; the developing, unfolding human soul. This reincarnating self is the lower representative of the monadic vehicle and exists on the plane of abstract intellect, storing the knowledge and experiences of all incarnations. Ego is the divine Self that gathers sheaths about itself as it descends into the world of lower vibration. Also known as the HIGH SELF.

EGOIC LOTUS. The true self, or Christ-Within, that blossoms in the abstract levels of mind, or causal body, coming to birth through interaction of the evolving High Self and the potent charge of the soul. Here, under the influence of the SOLAR ANGEL, higher mind receives the nourishment of the soul (intuitive and atmic currents). This holy aspect unfolds its petals, indicating spiritual maturity. Law, sacrifice, and love are represented by three each of its nine petals. This blossom indicates the one becoming FULLY HUMAN–FULLY DIVINE.

EGO INFLATION. A danger on the spiritual path—when the rewards of expanded consciousness are viewed as accomplishments of the personality (or ego) rather than a natural state of soul awareness and only a point along the path of transcendence.

EGOTISM. A psychology term for excessive self-involvement; a barrier to spiritual growth because the nonself claims the power of identity and denies the true self participation in life experiences; thus, the self is blocked and cannot contribute to self-evolution.

EIGHT-FOLD PATH. BUDDHA's teaching of the way of the middle-road path. These disciplines are to be exercised in specific areas of life to attain release from the WHEEL OF REBIRTH. He summarized the conditions of life in his FOUR NOBLE TRUTHS and taught that the way to escape sorrow is by obedience to the Eight-fold Path: right-belief, right-thought, right-speech, right-action, right-livelihood, right-endeavor, right-remembrance, right-meditation/concentration.

ELDER BROTHERS (BEFORE THE THRONE). A biblical reference to those who, having evolved through human experience, now serve humanity—saints, sages, and holy ones who guide and guard those evolving by the same route, assisting them to become wise and to prepare for tests ahead. We might call their service "divine parenting." These guardians of humanity have inspired the wisdom teachings and designed ancient and contemporary ceremonials to assist all. Sincere aspirants are watched over and may receive aid from humanity's elder brethren, members of the Brotherhood of the Adepts. Serving humanity in many ways, they assure compassion and effective care, especially through periods of darkness in human history. *See* Brotherhood.

Elemental forces. Basic building blocks of earth, air, water, and fire used in the creation and maintenance of the physical world, each with specific roles. They are the forces behind the outer forms facilitating evolution through interplay. Wise Ones guide their work of connecting the inner and the outer. A hierarchy constructed to allow growth at every level permits NATURE SPIRITS to learn how to direct these forces. Nature spirits are watched over by lesser devas who are guided by greater devas, and the pattern evolves up a chain of command to the ARCHANGELS and higher.

Elementals. These essences—earth, air, fire, and water—guided by minute points of consciousness that indwell the elements are known as NATURE SPIRITS, pursue their involutionary experience prior to assuming a physical or material form. Three elemental kingdoms must be passed through before entering the more advanced group of the mineral kingdom. These sub-human forces are on the path of involution, or the downward arc. Although they can be contacted on the emotional (astral) plane, controlled and harnessed through the use of various rites and ceremonies, it is advised they be handled with great care. These intelligences form the link between the parts and the consciousness of the unit, energy field, or standing wave patterns. They can be acknowledged and brought into coworking relationship through *magick* and SHAMANISM. *See* NATURE SPIRITS.

Elemental world. Patterns of lower evolution are everywhere within personality, waiting to be confronted by the purification process. These energies of body, emotion, and mind are maintained by the combined work of elementals who will be acted upon by one's evolving consciousness. Each conscious act impacts the elementals and assists in training them to new ways of being.

Elements. As metaphysically described by Aristotle: fire was made up of qualities of hot and dry; water was cold and moist; earth was cold and dry; air hot and moist. The psychological function of the four elements as defined by Carl Jung are: Fire represents the thinking function, air the intuition function, water the feeling function, and earth the sensation function. Fire and air are active, masculine elements, and water and earth are the passive, feminine elements within our psyche that balance conscious with unconscious to determine personality, attitude, and natural inclinations.

Elohim. Literal Hebrew translation for "Lord." Indicated as *el* on the end of many holy names, as in ARCHANGELS Raphael, Uriel, Gabriel, and Michael. The Old Testament Hebrew term for the gods (plural) of creation, who proclaimed, "Let us make man in our image, after our likeness." (Gen. 1.26)

Emerald Tablet of Thoth the Atlantean. In it are engraved 13 precepts, comparable to the Ten Commandments. Perhaps one of the earliest alchemical fragments but of unknown source, its origin is lost in legend. These teachings have held great influence since the 13th century, combining mysticism and chemistry of great import to Western ALCHEMY and disguised as given by Hermes. This practical treatise offers an advanced formula for personal transformation and accelerated evolution.[4]

EMOTIONAL BODY. The vehicle, or reflective nature, called "astral" (meaning "starry"), wherein reside unresolved emotions and currents of force awaiting expression. Mental polarization involves taking control of the emotional body and clearing it so it may serve as a purified battery for the personality, empowering it to fulfill the purpose of an incarnation.

EMOTIONAL RESIDUE. Unresolved emotions and feelings carried perhaps through lifetimes; also called "glamours" or "psychic residue." As defined and taught in PSYCHOGRAPHY.

ENCRATISM. Extreme zeal, often leading to martyrdom.

ENERGY. The Greek *energeia,* means "active, vital, that which quickens inert matter." An oft-used, modern term for the forces of life at work throughout creation. As humanity becomes increasingly sensitive to unseen forces and the vibration of the environment, these undifferentiated currents are being collectively labeled "energy." At each level of development we touch in to existing pools of vibrations—good or bad—of emotional sensations and THOUGHTFORMS and respond to them according to our free will. In our ascent to higher realities, we contact what are known as energies, entities, and influences. *See* Prana.

ENERGY BIOCIRCUIT. The interplay of forces and energies circulating through the MERIDIANS, CHAKRAS, and NADIS of the etheric body. Not easy to measure by physical means, but recognized for centuries in natural healing, acupuncture, and acupressure therapies.

ENERGY BLOCKS. The life-giving current that animates forms can become congested or tainted. A release must be achieved for the energy to flow again. After release, the flow must be rebalanced in a constructive way—the goal of chakra work, healing spiral, Reiki, acupuncture, and so on.

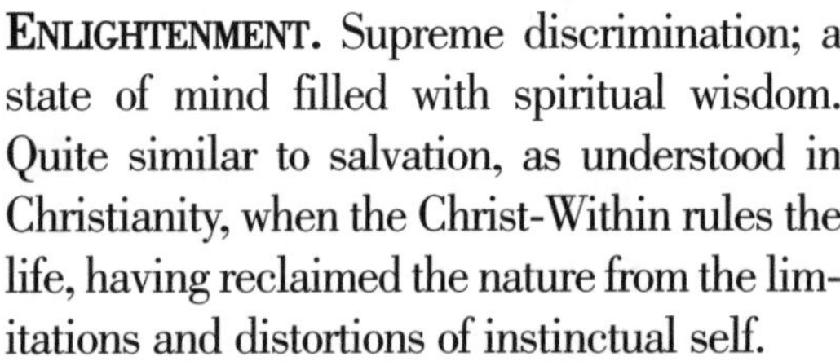

ENLIGHTENMENT. Supreme discrimination; a state of mind filled with spiritual wisdom. Quite similar to salvation, as understood in Christianity, when the Christ-Within rules the life, having reclaimed the nature from the limitations and distortions of instinctual self.

> *Enlightenment, then, is a natural process ruled by biological laws as strict in their operation as the laws governing the continuance of the race. . . . This I believe, is the purpose for which you and I are here—to realize ourselves . . . to bring the soul to a clear realization of its own divine nature.*
>
> —Gopi Krishna

ENLIGHTENMENT, STAGES TO. As defined by John White, an expert in the fields of consciousness research and human development, author of *What Is Enlightenment?* An age-old formula is: from orthonoia (mechanical behavior, or to keep straight) to metanoia (to go beyond or higher than) through paranoia (a state in which the mind is deranged, taken apart, and rearranged) so that a clear

EN

In Greek, the field of the primal source, nameless, undefinable, and from which the following concepts derive:

ENAD. The primal unit of life.

ENADY. The sum total of Enads, or ideal units of the En life.

ENERGY. The one life power of manifestation.

ENONY. The one all existence or all-beingness and nonbeingness, or potential.

ENPOEA. The one life creativity.

ENSOPHIA. The one ageless wisdom, pansophy, or biosophy of omniuniversal life.

ENUNIO. The primal unity, or unity of unities, and the unity of humanity.

From En are derived the three main universes of existence, namely:

ENUNION. The absolute universe or the Poetunion, that is, the intermediate universe that manifests and demanifests the superabsolute and relative universe for the purposes of the ceaseless continuation and re-self-perfection and re-self-beatitude of life and form.

PANENUNION. The universe of mahapralaya, the all-one-union of Enads.

PANUNION. The omniverse or relative universe or multiverse or seven-fold universe, or kosmos.[5]

perception of reality might be experienced. Paranoia is a condition well-understood by mystical and sacred traditions. Spiritual disciplines are designed to ease the passage from a limited state of consciousness to a higher state of awareness. Because metanoia has not been experienced by many, the role of paranoia is not well-understood in our culture. It is seen as an acerbated dead end, rather than a precondition to higher consciousness. The discomfort, confusion, and suffering in paranoia is due largely to the destruction of illusion or ego. Self-realized individuals understand the process and know transformation (all three stages) becomes the pathway to enlightenment.[6]

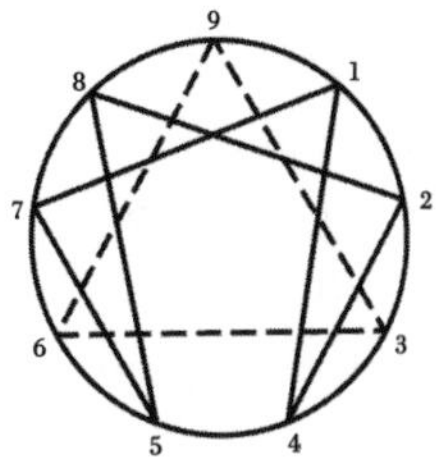

ENNEAGRAM. This ancient metaphysical system popularized by G. Gurdjieff and adapted for modern application defines nine personality types, using a nine-pointed star. It relates to the once-forgotten basis for most systems of numerology; more recently, it has been elaborated upon by Jungian psychologists and found useful in spiritual development. In Greek, *ennea* means "nine" and *grammes* means "points."

ENTHUSIASM. The Agni virtue for Aries. The "fire of Theos" ignites within us to animate our being with higher waves of consciousness. Similarly, enthusiasm kindles others' spirits when it flares and expresses. Those filled with enthusiasm transmit enthusiasm. An old Greek word, *enthousiasmos,* meant "possessed by God."

ENTITY. A discarnate, or spirit being without a physical body, that can be seen or recognized by some, undetectable by others, that continues to live in dimensions other than physical incarnations with some overlap between planes—physical and nonphysical. It is seen or recognized by some and undetectable by others. Its presence may be positive or negative.

ENTITY, ATTACHED. Spirit (discarnate) from past lives or this life that attaches to the aura sphere or human body and needs to be released. Seeking sensations and feelings that cannot be found in the higher planes, it may not know anything about other dimensions or even that it is dead; it is responding to cravings or instincts of an addictive nature or to a limited state of consciousness. PSYCHOGRAPHY or other EXORCISM rites facilitate spirit releasement. *Also see* Discarnate.

ENVISIONING. A technique for consciously bringing into focus the part of the plan or effort we perceive as our own. We begin by accepting as much as we can grasp of the whole design as the overview. We then "zoom in" on our piece and amplify it—energize it, seeing it as rich and as wonderful as we can make it. Next we return this personal segment to the entire plan. In such a way we develop our specific role without minimizing the importance of the whole.

EPHEMERIS. A scientific table of coordinates used to indicate the daily positions of the planets, stars, and celestial bodies as they traverse the heavens.

EPIPHANY. This holy season starts with Epiphany Day, January 6, and continues until Lent. January 6 commemorates the arrival of the Magi, the three wisemen who had been following a great star to find the baby Jesus. The MAGI are believed to have been Persian gentile astrologers/astronomers (synonymous at that point in history). The color for Epiphany Day is white; the rest of the season is green, symbolizing the growth of love among God's people.

E.Q. Emotional Quotient—relates to non-linear thinking. A means of sensing and knowing, opposed to straight, linear, or rational process of thought; usually associated with higher mind, or intuition. E.Q. can be correlated to or as opposed to I.Q.

EQUINOX. Either of two points on the celestial sphere where the ecliptic intersects with the celestial equator. The two times during each year when the sun crosses the celestial equator and the lengths of day and night are approximately equal. The vernal equinox and the autumnal equinox denote the changing of the seasons to spring and fall, respectively. At the spring, or vernal, equinox the sun enters

Aries (the first sign of the zodiac), approximately March 21 annually. Autumn, or fall, equinox occurs approximately Sept. 21 as the sun enters Libra.

Era of Woman. Esoteric teachings refer to the Aquarian Age as a time to balance the nature (masculine-feminine) of humanity through awakening to the values of the feminine influence. *See* Roerich, Helena.

Erks. A planetary center in the etheric located in the province of Cordoba, Argentina.[7] *See pp. 349–55,* Etheric Dimensions.

Eros. In Greek mythology, the God of Love, the son of Aphrodite. The sum of the human instincts of self-preservation—more specifically, love of a sexual or instinctual nature. The aggregate of pleasure-directed life instincts whose energy is derived from the libido. Self-fulfilling love.

Esbat. Monthly meeting of a coven, most often held at full moon (usually 13 each year). Some groups also meet at the dark of the moon.

Eschatology. The theological doctrine that discourses on death and views of the end of the world and human life. Affirms the essential boundary and nature of time, the metaphysical nature of the sovereignty, and its relationship to the world of spirit.

Esoteric. The Greek root *eso* means "within." That which is hidden, unseen, secret, inner, or out-of-sight—the meaning behind the meaning. Obscure but profound to those prepared to receive. In the New Testament, Jesus spoke of mysteries reserved for disciples which he did not offer the public. His public teachings, the parables, while commonly understood, also may contain other, deeper messages.

Esoterica. A body of knowledge describing and exploring hidden influences or laws that underpin outer circumstances, whether understood or not.

Esoteric anatomy. A study of the body beyond its concrete form, especially the organs of the nonphysical body—chakras, etc.—as well as the body in other realms of being, such as etheric, astral, mental.

Esoteric astrology. The study of astrology that recognizes the soul and its work behind the scene of personality and the hidden or inner reasons for life. *See p. 23.*

Esoteric Christianity. The Christian tradition contains both esoteric and exoteric paths of understanding. The esoteric focuses upon developing the Christ-Within and the gifts of the spirit, as referred to in the New Testament; Esoteric, or mystical, Christianity emphasizes keys to transformation of the personality, leading to soul development. Christians often apply four methods of interpreting the Christ message and the Bible in general: 1) traditional, including literal and methodological; 2) allegorical or metaphorical, representing Truth as in mythology; 3) moral or social, emphasizing issues of then and today; and 4) analogical, a Jungian term relating to the psychological, higher mental, or spiritual state, mystical understanding or esoteric meanings. *Ex*oteric Christianity focuses upon doctrine, dogma, and rites, the more familiar practices of traditional churches, while *eso*tericism emphasizes inner awareness and the development of the Christ-Within with its mystical awareness. Principal tools are prayer, meditation, and becoming aware of the nonphysical life of the soul.

ESOTERIC DOCTRINE. A mystical interpretation of perspectives on the evolution of life.

ESOTERICISM. The belief in hidden causes and their effects in the physical realm.

ESOTERICIST. One knowledgeable in and supportive of the concealed wisdom.

ESOTERIC PHILOSOPHY. A perspective emphasizing inner life and practices to enhance understanding of the soul's purpose.

ESOTERIC PSYCHOLOGY. Teachings that emphasize inner knowledge, disciplines, and practices concerning the science and development of the soul. The RAYS are considered significant factors of esoteric psychology.

ESP. *See* Extra-sensory perception.

ESSENCE. Esoterically, the subtle substance that clothes the seed or spark of life. Wrapped in cloak after cloak of matter, the essence protects the divine spark while outer coverings are insensitive to its presence.

ESSENES. One of several sects of Jews living near Jerusalem at the time of Jesus. Popular opinion in metaphysical thought is that Jesus was a practicing Essene.

ET. *See* Extraterrestrial.

ETHERIC ANATOMY. *See* Etheric body.

ETHERIC BODY. The true substantial form, the framework, the "scaffolding" to which the physical body necessarily conforms. Encoded ethers that interface the physical and nonphysical realities to create the physical body and our less dense vehicles of expression. The four ethers are (from lower to higher) chemical, life, light, reflecting. Inherited body types and SEED ATOMS, personal in nature, wait here to be activated, according to time, situations experienced, and energy encountered. Not to be mistaken with the AURA, a much larger emanation. The etheric body is about 1–1 ½ inches larger than the physical body and is often detected as a rather bluish white outline of the body.

ETHERIC PLANE. This region of the physical reality consists of the four ethers of the less dense levels of the physical world and interfacing with the lower three astral frequencies. The physical world is divided into seven sub-planes: the four highest sub-planes comprise the etheric plane, or SUBTLE BODY; the other three become increasingly dense: gases, liquids, and bone. Physical form is modeled or patterned after the etheric model. Similarly, the etheric plane has frequencies penetrating into and beyond Earth's physical atmosphere, linking the physical Earth with the astral plane.

ETHERIC WEB. The fine network of fiery threads that spreads itself over a center and forms an area of fairly large dimensions. It both separates and connects the astral and physical bodies; a similar area will be found in the solar system. The cosmic forces must pass through it to the different planetary schemes.[8] In time the web dissolves, and all become one.

ETHERS. A modern expression of the "water of space." A subtle substance with frequencies that interpenetrate and move more rapidly in vibration than physical matter. The reflective material of our atmosphere less dense than physical matter and through which the spiritual model of life-forms communicates to the physical form. *See* Ectoplasm.

ETHICAL LIVING. *See p. 5,* Agni Yoga.

ETHICS. The code or philosophy we develop and adopt that protects personal integrity, that path of rightness for peace of mind and established harmony between inner and outer. Individual integrity is an imperative for the new era as humanity advances toward spiritual maturity. Blavatsky refers to "divine ethics," Confucius recommends "proper conduct in all things," Agni Yoga teachings are called "ethical living," Buddha refers to "right action," and Jesus teaches, "Blessed are the pure in heart, for they shall see God" and to "love your neighbor as yourself." "Do unto others as you would have them do unto you" is a universal statement of ethics.

EUCHARIST. *See* Communion, Holy.

EURYTHMY. A system of physical movements or dance to move subtle energies into beneficial patterns; not unlike T'AI CH'I, taught by Rudolf STEINER as health-building and healing. Ritualistic in nature, configurations use thoughtforms, words, sounds, and sweeps to create streams of grace and harmony. Often confused with PAN EURYTHMY.

EVAGRIUS PONTICUS. *See pp. 246–51,* Saints.

EVIL. The current or action of life that moves us away from soul's purpose and direction, against the natural current toward evolution and soul-fulfillment. Ancient thoughtforms and emotional charges from the past and, though obsolete, still persist, seeking to prevent progress. That which resists evolutionary forces. The defiant ego that refuses the light of high consciousness, choosing instead to embrace the forces of darkness. *See* Good and evil.

EVOCATION. The manifestation of energy or spirit in response to an invocation. God may evoke a response from us; we may evoke a response from higher or lower spirits or elementals—the response as a result of some action.

EVOLUTION. The progressive, continually accelerating march of all the particles of the universe toward a higher life, universal consciousness, and the complete realization of the Absolute. The natural, unfolding development of latent potential within all life guided by an inherent design. The process of liberation of spirit from the restriction of form. For humanity, the process of awakening to the Plan and purpose of God, expanding in consciousness, and attaining, stage by stage, an ever more inclusive awareness: FULLY HUMAN–FULLY DIVINE. Evolution of the planet is linked uniquely to human evolution as humanity is the *manas,* or mind, for planetary life. Planet Earth evolves as its collective value systems sensitize to purposes of the Logos.

Evolutionary astrology. *See p. 23.*

Evolutionary descent and ascent. The downward movement of a monad projecting soul to personality on its way to experiencing physical life. The development of ego with its many lessons in physical form followed by spiritual maturity frees the point of consciousness known as personality, after which there is no need for incarnation in the lower realm. In the ascent, the spark moves to solar and later cosmic initiations as it returns to the Source.

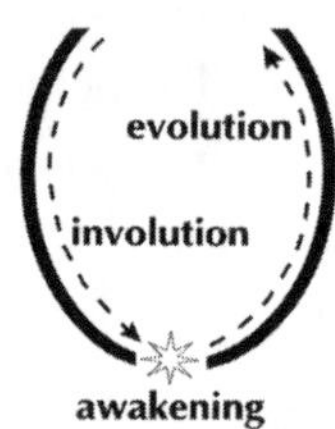

Evolution, planetary. *See* Planetary evolution.

Evolutions, other. Three parallel evolutions are developing through the life of our planet: human, spacial, angelic. Each is centered on a specific plane of existence and evolves into others. For example, humans are centered on the physical and evolve into emotional, mental, and higher dimensions.

Evolution, terrestrial. A family of souls evolving in the subtle planes of Earth that projects its consciousness from the mental plane into the lower frequencies. Called "SPACIAL BEINGS" by many. This evolution has unique qualities of mind and is believed to be able to create beneficial thoughtforms often perceived by certain human beings, i.e., inventions or breakthroughs in thought. *Also see* Evolutions, other; Extraterrestrials; Metaterrestrials.

Evolving life. An entity—anything from a chemical reaction to a society to cosmic life—that becomes unstable (changeable) and self-organizing (capable of structuring and maintaining itself) and experiences anxiety (challenge, stress, damage). By some force, it reorganizes itself, taking into account the perturbing influence and, while maintaining previous talents, adds to them something which contends with the offending irritation. It becomes more clever in order to perpetuate itself.

Existentialism. An attitude or philosophy concerning the fate of humanity and the individual, emphasizing free will and taking responsibility for the consequences of our acts.

Exobiology. A legitimate scientific category addressing issues of UFOLOGY and the development of other forms of energy—organic compounds, basic building blocks—that vibrate outside the wavelength range used in photosynthesis, fundamentally solar-powered, e.g., magnetism, whenever conditions are favorable.

Exorcism. A technique to release a possessing spirit from a human being and advance the possessing entity into the light. *See* Spirit releasement therapy.

Exoteric. From the Greek root *exo,* meaning "outside." The opposite of esoteric, or hidden. Popular religious teachings given openly and publicly. The Christian church has traditionally emphasized the exoteric message of its faith, dogma, and doctrine, while neglecting the mystery side of the Christian teachings. *See* Esoteric Christianity.

Expanded awareness. A state of consciousness in which we sense more than what is readily recognizable through the physical senses or is grasped by the rational mind. The heightened ability to directly perceive and experience subtle truths and realities as they exist in both the subjective and objective worlds. The ability to perceive from the world of causes in which we increasingly identify with divine will.

EXPANDED SENSE PERCEPTION. The utilization of the astral senses in gathering impressions or information, i.e., clairsentience, clairaudience, and clairvoyance. (Also known as ESP, or Extrasensory Perception.)

EXPANDING VEHICLES. Vehicles of consciousness serve as a means of gathering and containing information on each plane of being. As these unfold and develop, we call them "expanding." As we master abilities in each body, that body is brought under more control, tested, and found more reliable to the evolving soul. Existing abilities extend to ever-broader expression.

EXPANSION OF CONSCIOUSNESS. A progression of awareness from one level to another as our recognition of personal and planetary purpose increases. Ability to function effectively on more advanced planes of being or from higher states of consciousness. The registration and assimilation of energies that allow us to build new relationships and to extend our fields of perception and activity.

As an Agni term, the capacity to perceive from a higher and broader perspective, realizing we can free ourselves from a limited point of identity by moving to a wider perspective. The ability to perceive from a number of perspectives instead of being locked into one identity, i.e., the ego, or nonself.

EXPERIENTIAL. A means of teaching and learning by doing; hands-on.

EXTERNALIZATION OF THE HIERARCHY. Name given by MASTER DJWHAL KHUL through Alice A. BAILEY for the return of the disciples and MASTERS, as well as the Christ, to the world of denser vibration and a new round of incarnations by teachers and saints, whereby they will work closely with humanity to prepare for collective initiations and the planetary initiation. This return is imminent.

EXTRABIBLICAL TRADITION OF LEGENDS. Tales that have persisted through time that make claims about biblical personages—Jesus, Mary, Abraham, and so on—that cannot be proved by hard evidence but are accepted as important for their contribution to the belief system, e.g., *The Lost Years of Jesus* and Mary's House at Ephesus, Turkey.

EXTRASENSORY PERCEPTION (ESP). The nonphysical senses that may be developed and used to gather information in nontraditional ways. Also called "extended sense awareness."

EXTRATERRESTRIAL (ET). Those spacial intelligences that transfer to planet Earth to share with and learn from the human evolution. Some observe and others incarnate in human form to complete their path on their kingdom and the human initiations. In *God Hypothesis,* Joe Lewels acknowledges the role of extraterrestrials in the early life of the planet and humanity. Also known as aliens, travelers, brothers, space beings, councils, and a variety of other names. *Also see* Meta-terrestrials.

EXTRATERRESTRIAL MATERIALISM. A disturbed state of mind, according to consciousness researcher John White, exhibited by those who make idols out of UFOs and extraterrestrial life: false gods from outer space. This belief still relies on some rescue from outside rather than recognizing the divinity within that awaits discovery.[9]

EYE OF HORUS. An Egyptian symbol representing the spiritual eye of the illumined. In the Egyptian mystery tradition the Utchat, the all-seeing eye, refers to the Pole Star and to illumination; the eye of the mind. The eye of Horus may be associated with the moon and its phases. An image of the eye of God was buried with the dead to symbolize God accompanying the spirit of the deceased on the dark journey through the underworld.

EYE OF TAURUS. A symbol representing the spiritual eye of the illumined—of pre-Egyptian origin and associated with the Age of Taurus. Literally, the great star Aldebran shining forth as the eye of the Bull; the great light considered to be the source of the intuitional, or buddhic, plane within the constellation of Taurus, the Bull. Also symbolic of the energy of the enlightened one, the great Lord Buddha, rushing into manifestation with great light and power. This energy radiates for a moment from the soul of the disciple who enters into the awareness of the buddhic plane characterized by pure reason, understanding, and enlightenment.

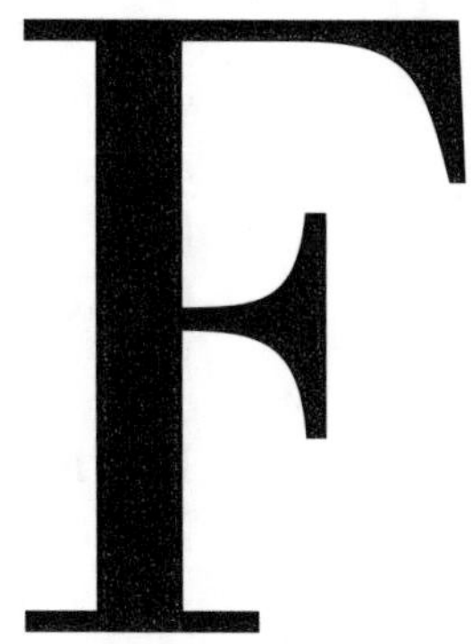

Facilitated apparition. Vivid visionary encounters with the deceased produced through the use of mirrors, as coined by Raymond Moody.[1]

Fairies. *See* Nature spirits.

Fairy-ring. A creation of nature that appears on the ground in a circular design wherein little else will grow. This open circle serves as a cleansing place, a drain for heavy energies, negativity, or pain drawn from a neighborhood or area. An unhealthy place for a dwelling to be built for it tends to block natural clearing processes and to affect inhabitants in unhealthy ways.

Faith. The firm expectancy placed in oneself or another or in one's belief system. A stage of growth wherein one believes with dedication; a later stage is that of *knowing*. Belief is associated with the astral nature, while knowing is associated with the mental.

Fakir. In eastern India a practitioner of yogic schools of thought, particularly associated with those who demonstrate skills in phenomena.

Fall of humanity. This biblical phrase is understood in esoteric teachings as the recorded experience of the human race descending from the astral or etheric reality into the physical dimension, known as the expulsion from the Garden of Eden, where all desire was fulfilled.

Familial love. From the Greek *philia*, meaning family or brotherly love. The bonds of emotion, loyalty, and self-interest that link two or more people through blood ties, tribal bonds, or nationalism.

FASTING. As a SPIRITUAL DISCIPLINE, a limited or regulated diet for the purpose of purification or building will. Often practiced in preparation for holy days or seasons—cleansing the body that the spirit nature might be experienced more clearly.

FATE. Destiny or divine design set into motion with little chance of change. A situation or circumstance to be met.

FATHER. A common perception of God that comes from KABALAH and the action of KETHER sending forth with active (masculine) energy the creation of Chokmah; Binah represents the feminine nature of Kether, thus God. The bearded side-view face of God developed by Western religion symbolizes God as the Father, rather than of an androgynous nature. In esoteric language it sometimes serves as a blind for the MONAD.

FATHER-MOTHER GOD. An address preferred by esotericists to express the Creator's androgynous state of being.

FATIMA. A location in Portugal where Our Lady appeared in 1916 and gave prophesies and warnings to the world. Fatima has been recognized by the Catholic Church as a holy site and approved for pilgrimage. Also, the given name of the wife and first disciple of the prophet MOHAMMED.

FEAR. A serious obstacle to spiritual growth, indicating lack of trust and belief in the goodness of the higher PLAN. Fear, a major destructive component of the DWELLER ON THE THRESHOLD, is said to be the "glue" that holds the Dweller together.

FEARLESSNESS. Agni virtue for Capricorn. Since fear blocks, this virtue is designed to support the energy of life as it moves through creation. Courage is essential for the spiritual aspirant who dares to interact with unknown forces. Fearlessness results as we identify with the highest and release our identity with the false.

FEATHERED SERPENT. An archetype of MesoAmerican traditions, acknowledging spirit imprisoned in matter (crawling upon the Earth) may be uplifted to higher consciousness to ascend. The snake itself symbolizes timeless time, or life eternally inching forward, containing wisdom, consciously or unconsciously. The feathers symbolize the flight to higher levels. Just as the snake travels on the earth and knows the ways of earth, feathered ones can fly high into the other worlds. *See* Ouroborus; Quetzalcoatl.

FEMININE MYSTERIES. *See* Mysteries, feminine.

FEMININE PRINCIPLE. The feminine aspect of God embodied in human form, known as KUNDALINI, SHAKTI, SHEKINAH, or a variety of names for "she who dwells within." Creative energy is hidden within all matter; as it stirs, it gradually evolves all planetary life. Currently, this principle is rapidly awakening to bring increased intuition and realization to humanity.

FENG SHUI. Known as the "art of placement," this classic Chinese form of GEOMANCY demonstrates overt and obscure ways the physical ambience of home and workplace, environment and landscape can spark and nurture the natural potential to be more alive, receptive, and focused. Similarly, clearing can occur of chaotic, unhealthy, or obstructive energies. This technique concerns itself with moving energy, or *ch'i*, directing it to affect the environment by balancing YIN/YANG in a harmonious flow according to the purpose to which a space is dedicated.

FESTIVAL OF HUMANITY, OR FESTIVAL OF THE CHRIST. One of three major spiritual festivals of the year. A celebration at Gemini full moon recognizing the Christed being within humanity. This festival celebrates the human spirit aspiring toward God, seeking alignment with divine will according to the Christ pattern, and dedicated to right human relations. Also known as the Festival of Goodwill and World Invocation Day.

FIERY IMPULSE. An Agni term. The impelling force within that motivates us to strive for oneness toward the primary Source. These forces, natural to the ascent of consciousness, are to be guarded and valued. Without honoring these saturations, we lose our vitality. Each fiery impulse is respected and appreciated because it empowers the spirit in its quest.

FIERY WORLD. In Agni Yoga, the world of FOHAT, higher vibration where the "fire" of God is more pronounced, more intense.

FIFTH KINGDOM (OF SOULS). A new state of collective consciousness currently forming in the fourth and fifth dimensions but not yet manifested on the physical. The model has been created as divine potential by Master Jesus and other MASTERS. When enough humans can sustain the collective energy, the initiation will be granted and a leap forward in consciousness will be achieved by many now in preparation. Corresponds to the Kingdom of God in the New Testament. (The other four kingdoms are the mineral, the plant, the animal, the human.)

FINANCIERS AND ECONOMISTS. A category of WORLD SERVERS working through integrated head, heart, throat, and sacral chakras to step down the higher PLAN for humanity.

FINDHORN. A spiritual, NEW AGE community in northern Scotland founded in 1962 by Peter and Eileen Caddy and Dorothy McLean, which became known for its work with the nature spirits, or DEVAS, resulting in over-sized vegetables. In the '80s, its attention moved more to "growing people" than fruits, vegetables, and flowers. As a young man, David Spangler lived there and his writings made Findhorn well-known and often called the "Vatican of New Age Thought."

FIRE MYSTERIES. An esoteric term for third, fourth, and fifth initiations, symbolized by the Easter mysteries. Intensity builds as we subject ourselves to the fire of purification, being tempered and tried so that all that is not of the higher is burned away.

FIREWALK. A phenomenon wherein a person, in an altered state of consciousness, actually and physically walks barefooted, without harm, on a bed of hot coals. This practice is found throughout the world in a variety of cultures, but within the last 20 years has been introduced to middle-class America as proof of and exposure to the power of altered states of mind.

Fire

Esoterically, three manifestations underlie creation: fire by friction—animated atoms of matter; electric fire—electricity demonstrating as vitality and the will-to-be; solar fire—the fire of matter, and the fire of mind blend, resulting in cosmic mental fire. This solar fire is represented by the six-pointed star of light. Antoine-Joseph Pernety, a Benedictine monk, presented a four-part expression (each one subtler than the previous): 1) elementary, the fire of our stoves; 2) secret fire, external to matter, the fire stolen by Prometheus from heaven, higher consciousness (thought from above); 3) central fire, the fire within matter that engenders and enlightens without burning, digesting, and maturing; and 4) celestial fire, pure and clear, the fiery will of God.

Fire by friction. Electricity stimulating the atoms of matter so as to cause the spheroidal form of all manifestation. The latent heat within the spheres produces differentiation between atoms.[2]

Fire, electric. Fohat, the cosmic fire of creation out of which all is differentiated; as referenced by "My God is a fiery God"—as in "For our God is a consuming fire" (Heb. 12.29) and "Understand, therefore, this day, that the Lord thy God is he who goeth over before thee; as a consuming fire . . . . (Deut. 9.3) Electricity demonstrating as vitality or the will-to-be of some entity manifesting as "Abstract Being, Darkness and Unity." *Also see* Fiery world.

Fires of Space. An Agni term. Cosmic blending of the fusion of sparks precipitated by the Cosmic Magnet. The power of cohesion rests in the fiery seeds of each atom. When the intensified force of the creative magnet is acting, the fire of the seed fuses with the impulsion of the Cosmic Magnet. The manifested fire breathes the impulse of fire into each atom; thus the spirit of creativity is enlivened.

Fire, solar. Cosmic mental fire, the totality of mind either in a mental body, a group, or evolving units. Dual in nature, it is the fire of matter and mind blended.

First Matter. *Prima materia,* often depicted as a square stone or eight-pointed star or luminous spheres as found in the One Thing, out of which all comes forth. *The Lexicon of Alchemy* (originally published 1612) translated by A. E. Waite lists 84 synonyms for First Matter. Most significant are: Philosopher's Stone, Water of Life, Heart of the Sun, Rainbow, Son of Sun and Moon, Sacrificial Lamb, Menstruum, Bride, et al.

Fixed design. These words, from the "I Am the Soul" mantra, refer to the parts of us that are established on the time/space level, e.g., our parentage, race, birth date and place, sex, culture—as compared to those evolutionary potentials of personality, heart, and mind. When we voice, "I am fixed design," we affirm, "I am situated at a specific place of growth or experience, and I accept that. I can do it!"

FLAME. Symbolically represents the HOLY SPIRIT, martyrdom, religious fervor, or "fire of purification." Also, the symbol for AGNI, or "FIRE."

FOHAT. An Agni term. A Sanskrit word for the subtlest fiery energy (currently known) of creation, also called "atomic energy," a reference to the atmic plane. In some writings, "actually omnipresent fire"; in *Letters of Helena Roerich* the term "psychic energy" is used. Fire and energy often are equated in these writings, somewhat as in Kabalah. Fohat is referred to as "primary energy" and "cosmic prana" as well—always respectfully addressed as the beginning of attraction and the electric power of affinity and sympathy, as manifested in pure spirit. Fohat then is the *prima materia* cosmic substance out of which all is initiated into manifestation. Striving prepares us for contact with fohat. The fiery spirit called "Father" would be fohat, which corresponds to CHOKMAH on the kabalistic Tree. Said H. P. BLAVATSKY, "Fohat is the steed, and thought is the rider."

FOHAT/*MATERIA LUCIDA*. A combined Agni term. Fohat as the energy aspect of primal energy-matter and MATERIA LUCIDA as luminous matter are contrasted beautifully in the following quote from *Agni Yoga* (144). "Nurturing the psychic energy, Fohat paves the way to the far-off worlds. Whereas, *Materia Lucida* weaves the strengthening of the consciousness. One strengthens, the other forces one into the depthless pit of perfectionment."[3]

FOOL AND THE TRICKSTER, THE. Usually refers to characters in a story of a ruler with several sons, the younger of whom is simple and kind—beloved by the ruler and despised by the brothers. The ruler of the kingdom is threatened, and the sons are asked for help. The older brothers fail, while the younger son, who has matured from the challenges of his experience, comes to the rescue. The emphasis is on child-like innocence and guilelessness, which provide protection for the "heart-wise." The "fool" is open to all possibilities.

FORNICATION. A word used in the Bible referring to the misapplication of spiritual power or violation of right action. While associated with unlicensed sexual activity, the term is not limited to sexuality.

FORTUNE, DION. b. Wales, 1890, d. 1946. Author, teacher, and founder of the Society of the Inner Light dedicated to the study of the Western esoteric traditions, particularly meditation and personal regeneration. *The Training and Work of an Initiate,* 1930; *Esoteric Philosophy of Love and Marriage,* 4th edition, 1967; *The Cosmic Doctrine,* 1966; biography by Janine Chapman: *Quest for Dion Fortune,* 1993.

FORTUNE, PART OF. A sensitive astrological point helpful in understanding our own nature. A particular formula (sun, moon, ascendant) is used to calculate. Since this point operates on a subconscious or deep level, the native usually responds or copes unconsciously. Not a planet, the Part of Fortune results in connecting all planets involved; if it makes an ASPECT to sun, moon, or ascendant, it shows an ability to integrate all three.

FOUR NOBLE TRUTHS. Part of the principal teachings of Lord Gautama, the BUDDHA, who lived about 500 years before Jesus, the Christ. The Four Noble Truths are: all life is suffering; the cause of sorrow is desire (addictions); escape from sorrow comes when all selfish thought ceases; and the way to escape sorrow is obedience to the EIGHT-FOLD PATH.

FRANCIS OF ASSISI. *See pp. 246–51,* Saints.

FRANKINCENSE. *See* Gold, frankincense, and myrrh.

FREEDOM. An Agni theme. A discipline realized when our consciousness guides, leads, and directs the life, rather than instinct, urges, glamour, or illusion. Freedom to be the true self—clear and clean—is the goal; change and constant adjustment become the way. Advancement and self-discipline clear the way so we may be all that we can be. Correlates to the energy and influence of the number 5. As an Agni term: A state of being in which we constantly move toward a greater and greater overcoming of RINGS-PASS-NOT of consciousness, overcoming all sense of limitation, that oneness with COSMIC CONSCIOUSNESS may be realized. *See* Numerology.

FREEMASONS. Originally a guild of master craftsmen involved with architecture, which defined God as chief architect. An international secret fraternity, the Free and Accepted Masons revitalized in medieval England. Outlawed by Fascism, the Nazis burned their libraries. Its ritualistic elements, such as initiations, derived from the mystery religions. *Also see* Hyksos; Great Seal of the United States.

FREE WILL. The power of individualized consciousness to choose to comply, rebel, create, move or not move, and so on. The will aspect is considered a quality of humanity distributed by the Creator, freely given whereby humanity is empowered to exercise choice. As we evolve, we learn to perceive Higher Will and to adjust our lives to accommodate it.

FREUD, SIGMUND. b. Moravia, 1856, d. 1939. Austrian physician and neurologist whose analytic work with Joseph Breuer led him to the belief that symptoms with no physiological basis could be alleviated by hypnosis and thus had a psychogenic basis. His *Studies in Hysteria* marked the beginning of the psychoanalysis movement. He conceived the tripartite division of the unconscious mind as id, ego, superego and postulated that dreams, like neuroses, are disguised manifestations of repressed desires and the "royal road to the unconscious." In later life, recognizing the limitations of traditional psychotherapies, he expressed interest in Transcendental Meditation as a technique for relieving psychic suffering. *The Interpretation of Dreams,* 1900; *The Ego and the Id,* 1923; *The Future of an Illusion,* 1927.

FULL MOON. The phase of the moon when fully illuminated, reflecting most powerfully the light of the sun.

FULL MOON MEDITATION. A ritual, meditation, or celebration wherein participants choose to receive the blessings of the CELESTIAL HIERARCHY associated with a given sun sign period. Those gathered respond consciously to the unique opportunity for expansion in awareness provided by the hierarchical influence of the ruling constellation during the full moon period as the time of peak exposure to the sun's light. Some call these full moon meditations "SUN SIGN festivals," placing the emphasis upon the brightest outpouring of the particular sun cycle in which the full moon is occurring.

FULLY HUMAN–FULLY DIVINE. A biblical phrase, *Remember ye are Gods* (Psalm 82.6 and John 10.34), holds for humanity the great goal to know oneself fully actualized in human potential provides value for the human experience, as well as affirming the divinity of which we also are a part.

FUNDAMENTALISM. A term used to describe the philosophy of those who affirm the fundamental truths of a religious approach. The term has come to denote a narrow literal translation, not the truer meaning of a parable, or teaching.

FUTURE. An Agni theme. The aim of any true school is to assist one to catch a glimpse of one's future possibility. When we are "on the cutting edge," we are ever forming the guiding influence. We must recognize, each today is the foundation for tomorrow. Correlates to the energy and influence of the number 4. *See* Numerology.

FUTURE MEMORY. The ability to "prelive" or experience future time while still active and functional in the present, to fully live a given event or sequence of events in subjective reality before living that same episode in objective reality. Usually forgotten, to be remembered later when triggered by some "signal." "[A]ctually lived and physically, emotionally, and sensorially experienced, not merely watched (clairvoyance), heard (clairaudience), predicted (prophesied), or known (precognition); and that living is so thorough, there is no way to distinguish it from everyday reality" as it occurs. "(Unlike DÉJÀ VU, the incident clearly addresses 'future' not 'past.')"[4]

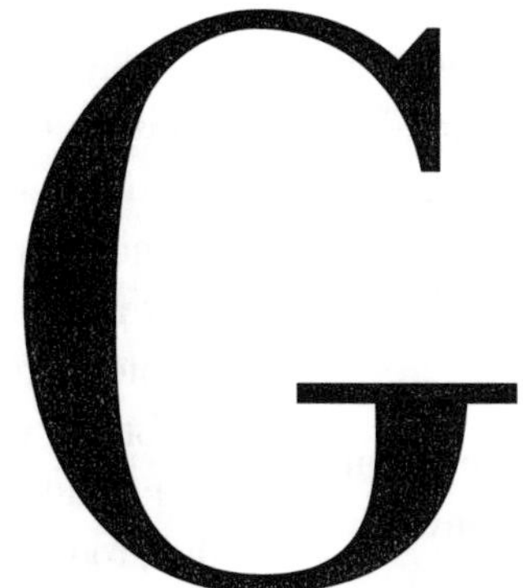

GABRIEL. *See* Archangels.

GAIA. In Greek mythology the goddess of the Earth, who sprang from primordial Chaos and produced Uranus, by whom she was the mother of the Cyclopes and Titans.[1] The Greek name for the goddess Terra, the uninitiated Earth.

GAIA HYPOTHESIS. A modern grasp of planetary life as one entity wherein all species are coordinated and interacting for the well-being of the whole, the living planet, a single organism. This effective system is becoming clearer with more contemporary scientific tracking now possible to see how systemic are the functions of the planet—water, winds, pollution, all kingdoms.

GANDHI, MOHANDAS, MAHATMA. Great Soul. b. Porbandar, India, 1869, d. 1948. Eminent moral teacher and reformer—not only of his homeland but of the world. The embodiment of the principle of *ahimsa,* harmlessness, he became "the almost mystical incarnation of nationhood . . . and exemplar of soul-force to achieve righteous ends by non-violent civil disobedience." He said that underlying all that is ever-changing, ever-dying is "a Living Power that is changeless, that holds all together, that creates, dissolves, and recreates. That informing Power or Spirit is God." Gandhi believed that only in times of true silence was one capable of experiencing Gods mercy.

GARDEN OF EDEN. Esoterically speaking, in the mystery teachings, the Garden is the beauty of the ASTRAL PLANE, where all of humanity's needs were met and when interaction with the Divine was natural. Being expelled from the Garden is the descent from unconscious to a conscious state. Now we must travel through humanity's PATH OF INITIATION to regain entrance to the higher world.

GARGOYLE. Originally functioning as a rain spout on medieval cathedrals, these grotesque figures represent emotions that range from fearsome to humorous and are most often related to the rawness of nature in humans and in the world of nature spirits.

GEBURAH. The fifth sephirah on the kabalistic Tree, most often designated as "severity."

GEMATRIA. The conversion of the letters of a word into numeral equivalents to determine a total, giving the word added meaning. Substituting another word of the same total expands the message of the phrase or context in which the word was used. Sometimes used as a blind to hide esoteric knowledge until one is able to comprehend the true essence.

GENDER (HERMETIC PRINCIPLE OF). "All things have gender": masculine and feminine at work to balance, rejuvenate, or be made whole. Respect for gender is necessary for generation; lack of respect brings about degeneration. *See* Hermetic Principles.

GENE POOL. A collection of genetic possibilities that can exist individually for one person or collectively for humanity, as well as other species.

GENERAL GOOD. An Agni term denoting the higher Plan that benefits the collective of humanity.

GENIUS. Latin, literally meaning "the inmost guiding spirit, talent, or inclination that governs one's ultimate destiny." A quality hard to define.

GENUINE. Not fake or counterfeit; original, sincere, real.

GEOMANCY. An ancient study of right-relationship between sacred structures, the sites upon which they sit, lines of magnetism, LEYS, running invisibly over the whole surface of Earth with certain topographical and astronomical factors. In Western history, the word "geomancy" described a system of divination using patterns created by pieces of soil cast on the ground. From China, the term FENG SHUI describes a successful, intact geomantic system which is becoming popular in the West today. Ultimately, geomancy has to do with the movement of spiritual energy throughout the Earth and between the Earth and this universe. This movement is basically calculated according to the harmonies of sacred geometry. The science of EARTH ENERGIES: e.g., LEYS, DOWSING, grids. Geomancy means "Earth measurement."

GERMAIN, COMTE DE ST. *See pp. 170–1,* Masters.

GESTALT THERAPY. A didactic therapy in which one enacts the role of self, other characters, and/or symbols because they contain "the whole"—the meaning of the German word *gestalt.* As a therapy, the movement of the mind that occurs as new insights and breakthroughs in awareness are realized as one perceives from various perspectives. Frederick "Fritz" Perls, considered the primary developer of Gestalt, one of the most powerful psychotherapies to be developed in the 20th century, wrote:

I do my thing, and you do your thing.
I am not in this world to live up to your expectations.
You are not in this world to live up to mine.
You are you and I am I,
And if by chance we find each other, it's beautiful.
If not, it can't be helped.

Ghost. The nonphysical, or etheric, body of an entity that lingers in the dense world after death, especially when attracted.

Gifts of the Spirit. Paul named nine gifts of the spirit after Pentecost. (1 Cor. 12.8–10) Older terms and their more modern interpretations are:

Wisdom — insight, inner knowing
Knowledge — telepathy with divine mind, piercing the veil
Faith — inner knowing
Healing — of body, emotion, or mind
Working of miracles — use of natural laws beyond our understanding (psychokinesis/telekinesis)
Prophecy — foretelling, in the awake state and in dreams
Discerning of spirits — in spirit communication, discriminating between astral and spiritual dimensions
Divers tongues — speaking from altered states
Interpretation of tongues — understanding what is channeled

Glamour. ILLUSION on the astral plane intensified by desire. A false picture that, when held in the mind and charged with emotional energy, becomes a forceful, dominating factor, blinding and misleading us in order to secure satisfaction and survival. Groups and individuals create, maintain, and energize glamours, e.g., "Everyone who finishes college has it made." A glamour functions by arousing the emotional desire that produces or charges the false picture or belief. Through this process we eventually learn the lessons of life and dissolve the desires that hold us in bondage to personality. *Also see* Maya.

Glory body. A biblical term for the LIGHT BODY.

Glossolalia. The proper term for the mediumship of "speaking in tongues." from the Greek *glossa* ("tongue") and the Italian verb for "to talk."

Glyph. A character that demonstrates its meaning symbolically—as in ASTROLOGY, to represent the twelve signs of the zodiac and the planets.

GNA. The new genetic code being introduced into approximately 10 percent of human beings—incarnate or not—at the turn of the millennium. The physical bodies will become more subtle according to particular spiritual laws. In the past, hereditary traits, height, skin color, physical features and defects, and some psychological tendencies have passed from parent to offspring by DNA. This is what is beginning to change. The DNA is of animal origin and can only take humanity to a certain level. The new genetic code, the GNA, will make possible greater integration into inner realities. Those receiving the GNA release the old structure of heredity and karma as it is of stellar and immaterial origin. Therefore, individuals are not conditioned by the heritage of their species.[2] *Also see* DNA.

Gnome. *See* Nature spirits.

GNOSIS. Greek for "knowledge." Direct experiential knowledge of divine things, intuitive spiritual insight that transcends cognitive reason. Nondualistic awareness versus theoretical ego knowledge. Rather than faith or good moral behavior, most Gnostics regarded this intuitive perception as the true path to God. Mystical knowledge held in the CLOUD OF KNOWABLE THINGS and available to those who make themselves capable. Inner knowing by intuition, the truth of the inner reality that guides us into harmony with the One Great PLAN. Uncapitalized, means simply "mystic" or one gifted with spiritual insight. Also called DAATH, SOPHIA, WISDOM.

GNOSTIC GOSPELS. Collections of truth teachings pertaining to a belief system. The Gnostics were persecuted and went into hiding in the early centuries of Christianity. All Gnostics were not Christians, but all were in touch with inner wisdom and belief in other realities.

GNOSTICISM. A variety of spiritual movements around the time of Christ. Gnostics—mystics who worked with inner, revealed knowledge—considered inner knowing to be the way to experience God. The teachings (of Gnosticism) were declared heretical by the Roman church at the Council of Nicaea when the mystery tradition yielded to new doctrines of Christianity, the more mystical to survive underground in hidden form. A major point of contention was that Gnostics believed each soul could go directly to God consciousness, not needing an intermediary or a personal savior (Jesus) as taught by the formalized Church. Today, certain individuals who use mystical practices identify themselves as Gnostic. A faith acknowledging the importance of one's inner wisdom. Some Gnostics were Christians, many were not, but all teach each individual could attain the wisdom.

GNOSTICS. Those who contact inner wisdom (*gnosis,* in Greek). Also, the identity of particular sects.

GNOTHOLOGY. The study of knowing thyself, as revealed through gnosis, inner teachings. From kabalistic and Greek teachings; derived from *gnosis* comes *gnothi seauton,* "know thyself," attributed to Greek philosopher Thales (ca. 624–546 B.C.) and inscribed over the door of the temple of Delphi.

GOAL-FITNESS. An Agni term. The purpose that underlies all comeasurement and is the basis of cause and effect. Purpose particularly denotes Ray 1, first aspect of deity and thus the great ruling law of the universe. Each of us must have purpose to be sent forth and must fulfill that purpose to return. Thus goal-fitness acknowledges the purpose of each atom of creation.

GOD. The creator, the Absolute, the generating power of the universe, the maintainer—and the destroyer when any part of creation has outlived its usefulness.

GODDESSES. *See pp. 180–3,* Mothers and Goddesses of the World.

GODHEAD. An impersonal term for the Source of All, less personal than God. A recognition of the creator of life from which All flows.

GODHOOD. A name given by the Christ to the exalted state that created all life and beckons all humanity to "Remember, ye are Gods." The state of divinity from which our creative nature is derived. "Made in the image and likeness" is our true nature as well.

GOD-IMMANENT. The God within creation. *See* Christ-Within.

GOD IS THE ONLY PHARMACY. This phrase, coined by George Pappas, reminds us the true cure for healing the ills of humanity rests with the Divine.

GODLING. A term coined in contemporary society to represent the concept of humanity evolving into its god-self. Every mortal contains a god seed, or "SPARK OF GOD," and is in the process of developing its divine consciousness.

GOD, THE FATHER. The Absolute, the spirit that goes forth seeking expression.

GOD, THE MOTHER. Matter receives, then responds to the spirit impulse with form-building, giving birth in cooperation with the spirit of creative force, or father influence.

GOD-TRANSCENDENT. The God beyond the world of human affairs. The Supreme Intelligence that was from the beginning and is without end. The ultimate Source from which all life springs and to which all life returns.

GOD-WITHIN. The divine spark confined within matter, which, in time, evolving DISCIPLES realize and honor with total allegiance.

GOETHE, JOHANN WOLFGANG VON. b. Germany, 1749, d. 1832. Poet, novelist, dramatist, considered the founder of modern German literature and leader of the Romantic movement were expressed in He used poetry and symbolic language to express his supernatural tendencies. His most famous work is *Faust,* 1808.

GOLDEN AGE (OF HARMONY). An era, according to spiritual writings, when humanity awakens to its divine nature and demonstrates high consciousness. We read of Golden Ages of the past and of a promised, long-awaited age to emerge now in the AQUARIAN AGE—an age of peace, a time of harmony among all people and all kingdoms on Earth.

GOLDEN CORD. Biblical term for threads of the ANTAHKARANA that connect the soul to the body. *See* Aka cord.

GOLD, FRANKINCENSE, AND MYRRH. The biblical account of the three gifts brought by the MAGI to the newly born Jesus contains significant symbology. *Gold.* Reserved for the rich, for nobility. When one king paid tribute to another, it had to be gold. The common people never touched it but dealt only in copper coins. *Frankincense.* An aromatic gum resin used chiefly in incense, produces a thick, sweet smoke. It is associated with religious rituals, both Jewish and gentile. This symbol means God's presence is perceived. *Myrrh.* A grizzly symbol. Oil of this bitter herb has only two uses: a narcotic drink to kill pain or an ointment for embalming the dead. Throughout the Near East, its significance was nothing other than suffering and death.

GOOD WILL. Humanity's effort to express the god-nature in a loving manner; a Ray 2 love-wisdom aspect.

GOLDEN RULE(S)

Here is important evidence that faiths around the world have a foundational harmony in their underlying principles. As we grow toward high consciousness, we begin to see the sameness of the teachings that guide us to enlightenment.

Brahmanism. This is the sum of duty: Do naught unto others which would cause you pain if done to you. *Mahabharata 5.1517*

Buddhism. Hurt not others in ways that you yourself would find harmful. *Udana-Varga 5.18*

Christianity. Whatever you wish men to do for you, do lidewise also for them; for this is the law and the prophets. *Matt. 7.12*

Confucianism. Surely it is the maxim of loving kindness; Do not unto others what you would not have them do unto you. *Analects 15.23*

Islam. No one of you is a believer until he desires for his brother that which he desires for himself. *Sunnah*

Judaism. What is hateful to you, do not to your fellowman. That is the entire Law; all the rest is commentary. *Talmud, Shabbat 31a*

Taoism. Regard your neighbor's gain as your own gain and your neighbor's loss as your own loss. *T'ai Shang Kan Ying P'ien*

Zoroastrianism. That nature alone is good which refrains from doing unto another whatsoever is not good for itself. *Dadistan-i-dinik 94.5*

GOPI GIRLS. The milkmaids of KRISHNA, a model for and symbol of the soul's intense love of God. The "girls" are the epitome of higher emotions, such as goodness, justice, truth, wisdom, kindness, patience, gentleness, serenity, and peace. Krishna, the one who loves all equally, is complete divine love, never lessened by loving all.

GRACE. An outpouring of spiritual power that frees from restriction and lifts the consciousness into a new state of awareness. We embrace love, freedom, beauty, and joy to invoke grace, a state gifted from the higher world when we realize a shift in consciousness that reveals the underlying and little-understood laws of life at work. Grace brings healing, freedom from restriction—perhaps physical, but not necessarily.

GRAIL, THE HOLY. The legendary cup used by Jesus at the Last Supper (establishing the EUCHARIST) is symbolized in all traditions as the chalice or vase that holds the elixir, the mystery of life. The Grail appears in different forms in different sacred myths as the archetype for the chalice into which higher awareness can flow and a symbol of the process necessary to achieve holy consciousness. By whatever name, it is the holy vessel for which

GOOD AND EVIL

GOOD (capital G). Anything that increases awareness, freedom, responsibility, and the opportunity for creativity. The Good can only be created and experienced by sentient beings who are devoted to what they may become.

EVIL (capital E). Anything that decreases personal awareness, creates dependency, and reduces the possibilities of freedom and growth. The Evil may only be created and experienced by sentient beings who hate the fact of their own existence.

GOOD (small G). Whatever society is attached to as a cultural value. It may be Good or Evil or possessed of no spiritual content.

EVIL (small E). Whatever society fears, rejects, or uses to define itself negatively. It too may be Good or Evil or possessed of no spiritual content.[3]

all initiates quest. *Also see* Ark of the Covenant; Bottomless Cauldron; Jataka; Moon Bowl; Tse-bum.

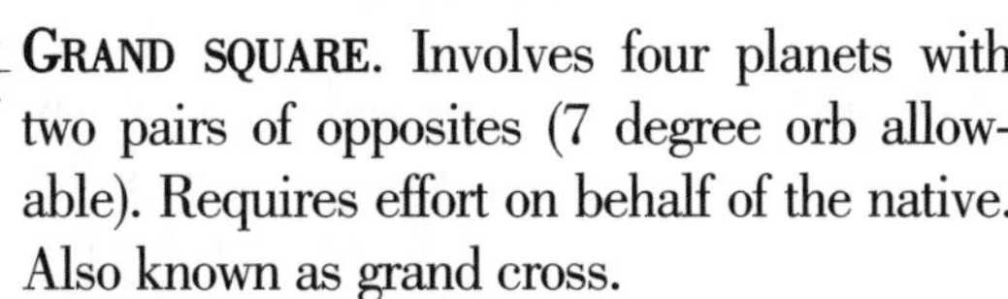

GRAND SQUARE. Involves four planets with two pairs of opposites (7 degree orb allowable). Requires effort on behalf of the native. Also known as grand cross.

GRAND TRINE. Three planets about 120 degrees apart (7 degree orb allowable) with all three in the same element. Favorable influence for the NATIVE.

GRANULATION. An Agni term. Often used in connection to FOHAT to describe the earliest stirring and movement of primary matter, referring to a process far removed from the physical plane, as in the original "at the time of creation" when forms of energy-matter were beginning to differentiate.

GRAPES. Bunches of grapes symbolize the wine of holy Communion. The grape vine or leaf is often used as an emblem of Jesus, the "true vine."

GRAPHOLOGY. The study of character by interpreting nuances of handwriting.

GRAY, MARY. Born in Paris, France (n.d.), Mary (Mrs. Roland) Gray was the daughter of an artist, William Tudor of Boston. Her family's close friends were Ralph Waldo Emerson, William James, Julia Ward Howe, Col. Higginson, and others of the group of liberal minds of New England early in the 20th century. Having basked in such philosophical thought early in life, she grew to contemplate the serious side of life. Educated at Bryn Mawr and Radcliffe, she was an avid student of mysticism and knew many of the leaders of philosophy in the U.S. and Europe, where she was a compelling speaker publicly and on the radio on international issues, oriental philosophy, and Christian mysticism, as well as spiritual law. The mother of several children, she established two schools in California that operated for some years, devoted to her conviction that character building formed the basis of civilization. She wrote five books, including *The Gateway of Liberation,* 1935; *The Temple of Amon Ra,* n.d.; and *Spiritual Laws—Rules of the Evolutionary Arc,* n.d.

GREAT ADVENT. An Agni term. Helena Roerich used this term for the REAPPEARANCE OF THE CHRIST.

GREAT AGE. *See* Age, Great.

GREAT COSMIC MOTHER. The etheric space that holds seeds of all potentialities, nurturing and sustaining life as it seeks expression throughout the planes.

GREAT INDIVIDUALITY, THE. An Agni term. Helena ROERICH used this term for the Christ. Her comment is that the Great Lords take everything into consideration according to the Law of Goal-fitness and that the world is not ready for the Great Individuality to return in physical form. She states the Great Individuality will rule "invisibly visible," equipped with the RAYS of the powerful but invisible Laboratory.

GREAT INVOCATION, THE. *See p. 107.*

GREAT SEAL OF THE UNITED STATES. On the back of the dollar bill close examination reveals 28 sacred Masonic symbols, including the mystical symbol of the GREAT PYRAMID, the Star of David, *Annuit Coeptis,* Latin for "He has blessed our beginning," and *Novus Ordo Seclorum,* "The new order of the Ages."[4] *See* Freemasons.

GREAT WHITE LODGE. One of many names attributed to the spiritual hierarchy of planet Earth, also known as the Great White Brotherhood.

GREAT WORK, THE. The collective soul purpose of humanity—a greater reason for the incarnation of the human kingdom—is to evolve by dissipating all that is inferior within the group mind and to congeal all that is superior. One gradually becomes conscious of this higher reason for being as veils that separate personality and soul are dissolved through meditation, purification of distortions, healing of emotional scars, and inner realizations. The collective goal of humanity is called the "Great Work," while the individual goal is called "SOUL PURPOSE."

GREAT YEAR. Twelve periods, or ages, each approximately 2,150 to 2,250 years in length. Includes all 12 zodiacal signs.

GREEN MAN. Horned nature god worshiped by the peasant class of Europe, representing the power of nature (e.g., PAN). It later became the imagery for the DEVIL by the Christian church. The PENTAGRAM (once used by folk people as a symbol of security but not church-approved) and the Green Man were considered evil.

GRIEF, STAGES OF. Results in deterioration. The stages are:

Shock—denial, numbness, desire to escape

Emotional flooding—intensity, ups and downs, great swings, outbursts

Disorganization—confusion, depression, restlessness, withdrawal, no sense of what we need, loneliness

The Great Invocation

A mantra to be spoken by awakened ones. Given by the Master DJWHAL KHUL through Alice A. BAILEY for the purpose of invoking the Lord Christ to come to the aid of suffering humanity. Three stanzas (1935, 1940, 1945) comprise the Great Invocation, but only the third is known widely and said by large numbers to create the cry of humanity for assistance to the human kingdom and the planet. Used with dedication by WORLD SERVERS.

Stanza One (1935)

Let the Forces of Light
Bring illumination to mankind.
Let the Spirit of Peace be spread abroad.
May men of goodwill everywhere
Meet in a spirit of cooperation.
May forgiveness on the part of all men
Be the keynote at this time.
Let power attend the efforts of the Great Ones.
So let it be, and help us to do our part.

Stanza Two (1940)

Let the Lords of Liberation issue forth.
Let Them bring succour to the sons of men.
Let the Rider from the Secret Place come forth,
And coming, save.
Come forth, O Mighty One.
Let the souls of men awaken to the Light,
And may they stand with massed intent.
Let the fiat of the Lord go forth:
The end of woe has come!
Come forth, O Mighty One.
The hour of service of the Saving Force
Has now arrived.
Let it be spread abroad, O Mighty One.
Let Light and Love and Power and Death
Fulfill the purpose of the Coming One.
The Will to save is here.
The Love to carry forth the work
Is widely spread abroad.
The Active Aid of all who know the truth
Is also here.

Stanza Three (1945)

From the point of Light within the Mind of God
Let light stream forth into the minds of men
Let Light descend on Earth.

From the point of Love within the Heart of God
Let love stream forth into hearts of men.
May Christ return to Earth.

From the center where the Will of God is known
Let purpose guide the little wills of men—
The purpose which the Masters know and serve.

From the center which we call the race of man
Let the Plan of Love and Light work out
And may it seal the door where evil dwells.

Let Light and Love and Power restore the Plan on Earth.

In 2000 Lucis Trust updated the wording of the third stanza due to resistance to some terms. There were no errors in the original form, but more contemporary and universal words provided greater clarification.

Stanza Three (updated)

From the point of Light within the Mind of God
Let light stream forth into human minds.
Let Light descend on Earth.

From the point of Love within the Heart of God
Let love stream forth into human hearts.
May the Coming One return to Earth.

From the center where the Will of God is known
Let purpose guide all little human wills—
The purpose which the Masters know and serve.

From the center which we call the human race
Let the Plan of Love and Light work out
And may it seal the door where evil dwells.

Let Light and Love and Power restore the Plan on Earth.

Reorganization—new hope, new skills, new interests, finding new meaning in life, taking positive actions; recovery is in process

Also see Death and dying, stages of.

Group. The sum of several lives aligned around a specific identity or intention. As it evolves collectively, it develops purpose, personality, and soul. As each member contributes to the unified form, each is entitled to draw upon it as needed.

Group consciousness. A unity of any number of minds around a common denominator.

Group meditation. "Where two or three are gathered in my name . . ." the power of the Christ is invoked and magnified.

Group mind. In wisdom teachings, the mind of the whole of a collective. Often used for the awareness of the whole of humanity, both incarnate and discarnate. In Eastern symbology humanity's shared akashic record, where all collective knowledge is held—past, present, and future. *Also see* Group consciousness.

Group soul. The collection of unique qualities a group creates as it unifies in group action with a purpose or direction or around a goal, a leader, or a central atom.

Guadalupe, Our Lady of. An apparition on Dec. 12, 1531, when Mary appeared to a poor peasant, Juan Diego, on a hillside in Mexico.

The Maya tell the story this way: A Mayan Indian sees a beautiful woman as he is walking by the site of the destroyed Mayan Temple of Tepeyac, dedicated to the Princess Tonantzin-Cihuaco'atl. She instructs him to go tell the bishop she wants a temple built on this site. With much trepidation and hesitation, he does as she asks. The bishop says she must give him a sign.

The Mayan hurries back to deliver the bishop's message to the lady. In response, she points to a rose bush blooming out of season. He picks a cluster of roses, places them under his cactus cape, and rushes to the bishop. In his presence and others', he thrusts open his cape to show the beautiful roses. Seeing their astonishment, he follows their eyes to observe not just the roses but a painting of the Lady on the inside of his cape.

Needless to say, a cathedral is built and dedicated to Our Lady of Guadalupe. The cape, made of cactus fiber and with a life expectancy of about 20 years, continues to exist today and is displayed periodically to the public at the Cathedral of Our Lady of Guadalupe outside of Mexico City.

Guardian angel. A protective presence who may be summoned to strengthen our souls as we meet the challenges of human incarnation. *See* Solar Angel.

Guardian Band of the Planet. Hierarchy of the PLANETARY LOGOS with an emphasis on the service it renders that guiding one, the Christ—teacher of angels and of humanity.

Guardian spirit. A nonphysical caretaker providing care, protection, and guidance to assist its charge to evolve in consciousness. This influence walks with its charge through difficult periods, seeking to provide encouragement and positive energy, as well as "sensed" companionship.

GUCUMATZ. One of three names used in Central and South America for the Feathered Serpent of the Meso- and South Americas; the others are KUKULCAN in the Yucatan and QUETZALCOATL, the most common.

GUIDANCE. Connecting with the inner self that provides a sense of knowing as we attune to a higher dimension of self. Until we connect with guidance from within, we need guidance from an outer mentor, a moral code, or ethical philosophy.

GUIDE. A discarnate spirit entity usually associated with communicating guidance, often thought to be a somewhat advanced friend in spirit with whom we have shared previous lives. A spirit friend who can provide some companionship in a new and spiritual realm.

GUIDED IMAGERY. Visualizations and other uses of image-making mechanisms often guided by another for a purpose such as healing meditations or positive affirmations.

GUIDED MEDITATIONS. A process using imagery and suggestions to move one from the outer beta consciousness to a more inward focus, the alpha or even deeper level; usually used to assist in relaxation or a posture of contact with inner knowing or feeling.

GUNA. A Sanskrit term. The interaction of three electric qualities pervading all levels of creation responsible for the material universe. SATTVA, the positive, dynamic influence, results in mental brightness and elevation. RAJAS, the neutralizing influence of restlessness, is compulsive activity for the sake of motion. TAMAS is the negative influence of sluggishness and inertia. These forces are described, respectively, as action (will), rhythm (harmony), stability (inertia).

GURDJIEFF, GEORGE IVANOVICH. b. Alexandropol, Caucasus region, Russia, ca. 1866, d. 1949. Grew up in a family steeped in traditions of an ancient esoteric culture handed down by oral history. He was given both religious training and a modern scientific education by men who understood his need for essential values. His need to comprehend the meaning of life became so strong, he attracted many learned and remarkable people from various disciplines. They traveled together in large and small groups, covering many countries of the Middle East and central Asia, seeking "the remnants, the descendants or the living presence of human beings who were in contact with an eternal and unchanging core of true wisdom."[5] Esoteric knowledge came to them. Several foundations were started in his lifetime, which continue his teachings today. *All and Everything,* 1950; *Meetings with Remarkable Men,* 1963, *Herald of the Coming Good,* 1933, 1970; *Views from the Real World,* 1973.

GURU. In Sanskrit *gu* means "darkness," and *ru* means "to illuminate." Combined, the word *guru* means "one who illumines the darkness." A spiritual teacher or guide; a master in metaphysical and ethical teachings who is identified with the grace of bestowing spiritual power on a disciple.

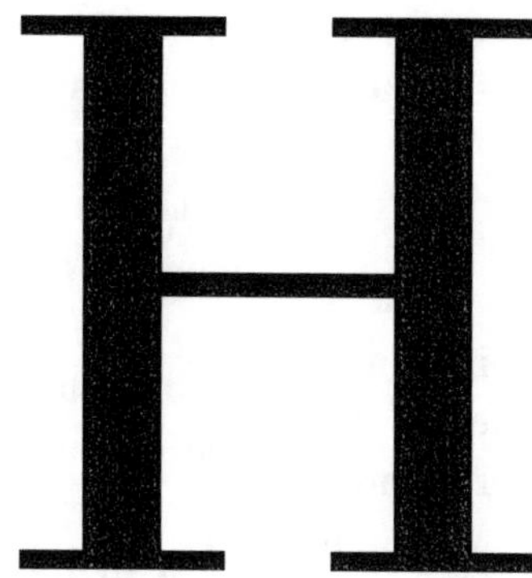

HABITUATION. Conditioning that results from repeated exposure.

HAG. *See* Crone.

HAGIA SOPHIA. A Greek phrase that means "Holy Wisdom" (sometimes called Saint Sophia). A great cathedral dedicated on A.D. Feb. 15, 360, to Holy Sophia (Wisdom). Built at Constantinople to serve as the major church of the Emperor Constantine, it was rebuilt after a serious fire in 404 and again in 537. This last structure is the famous beautiful edifice that served as a Great Christian Cathedral, a mosque, and now a museum.

"The inside appearance is one of great space, height, and richness. The rare and costly building materials were brought from many parts of the Roman Empire. The marble-lined walls have many colors and designs. Mosaics decorate the vaults. These were covered over by the Turks. After the building became a museum, the mosaics were uncovered. Many beautiful pictures were found. Among these are figures of Christ and the Virgin Mary and portraits of rulers and officials.

"The floor plan of Hagia Sophia is oblong. The building is 250 feet (76 meters) from east to west and 235 feet (72 meters) from north to south. Over the center is the great dome, which measures 185 feet (56 meters) high and 107 feet (33 meters) across."[1]

Shortly after the first millennium, the rift between the Eastern and Western Christian branches caused the church to split into two major communities: Roman and Orthodox. Constantinople was the home of Eastern Christian Orthodoxy until the city became Istanbul in 1453 and was ruled by the Ottoman Empire until 1923, when it fell and the government of Turkey was established.

Rome became the home of the Western branch, or Roman Church. Today Istanbul (formerly Constantinople) once again is acknowledged as the cornerstone of Eastern Christian Orthodoxy.

HAIL MARY PRAYER. The formal name of a Christian prayer celebrating the ANNUNCIATION, when the Angel Gabriel appeared to the Virgin Mary and she consented to be the mother of Jesus. The words of Gabriel create the opening salutation, "Hail Mary, full of grace. Blessed art thou among women." (Luke 1)

HAJJ. Pilgrimage to MECCA, birthplace of MOHAMMED in Saudi Arabia, to be undertaken by every Muslim at least once in a lifetime, excusable only by financial or health difficulties. One who has made the journey may take the additional name Hajji. Many pilgrims on Hajj also visit Medina, Mohammed's burial place.

HALL, MANLY PALMER. b. Canada, 1901, d. 1990. Author, lecturer, and minister of an occult/metaphysical group in Los Angeles, the Church of the People. In 1934 he established the Philosophical Research Society, fulfilling a life-long dream of founding a school modeled on the ancient school of PYTHAGORAS to disseminate wisdom teachings throughout the West. *Reincarnation: The Cycle of Necessity,* 1939; *First Principles of Philosophy*, 1942; *Self-Unfoldment by Disciplines of Realization,* 1942; *The Mystical Christ,* 1951; *The Secret Teachings of All Ages,* 1977; *The Rosicrucians and Magister Cristoph Schlegel: Hermetic Roots of America,* 1986.

HALLS OF LEARNING. Three in number, each stands for a particular state of consciousness wherein we make contact with new awareness as we dissolve the veils that create the separate halls.

1) The Hall of Concentration is entered at the third initiation, or TRANSFIGURATION. Here we connect with the inner teacher and receive great instructions and new understanding of the spiritual laws that guide life and each segment of creation.

2) In the Hall of Choice, related to the fourth INITIATION, initiates are prepared to stand on their own, between the Earth and heaven, renounce all they have had and been, and withdraw from the physical side of life.

3) The Hall of Blinded Men is entered at the sixth or seventh initiation. The release of the veil of separation creates a tremendous light that blinds the initiates as they see the "glory of the Lord." This concept is to help us understand that at each initiation we contact greater light, love, and synthesis for ourselves and for the human race in its quest for evolution. *See* Veils, four.

HALLUCINATION. Distorted reality or invalid astral perception.

HALO. From the Greek word *halos,* meaning "luminous ring of white or colored emanation about the head and body of a highly evolved being." The crown of light that surrounds the head of a spiritually vital one.

HAMMURABI. King of Babylon, 1792–50 B.C., frequently called the Great Law Giver; as Sumer's civilization was uncovered, it became clear there were preexistent systems of social order even as early as Urnammu, a ruler of Ur, ca. 2350 B.C. *See pp. 337–47,* Humanity's Genesis.

HANUKKAH. The Jewish eight-day festival of light celebrating the 2nd century victory of the Maccabees and restoration of the Temple. A miracle kept an oil lamp with one day's worth of oil burning eight days, a sign of God's protection over his people.

HARE KRISHNAS. Established in the U.S. by guru Maharishi, a Hindu, the sect grew quite large and introduced many to Lord Krishna. A great deal of effort is invested in publishing and making the U.S. aware of Lord Krishna and the Hindu religion. The group has built a large temple in Muthura, India—the area of the birth and life of Krishna, according to legend. Groups of people in India who worshiped the child Krishna, formed under the Muslim domination of India and continue today. The religious practices of this faith center on contemplation of Krishna's *lilas* or sports. Followers seek to obtain visions of God during private meditations and at religious assemblies.

HARMLESSNESS. Agni virtue for Sagittarius. Building a consciousness that can pass through the currents of the world without becoming destructive becomes the work. The Buddha said, "It is not enough to cease to do evil, it is time to do good." However, not all have built such a consciousness. Harmlessness not only does not set negatives into motion, it creates a positive aura of protection about us. *See* Gandhi.

HARMONIC CONVERGENCE. The initiating of the 25-year transition period, beginning in 1987, of leaving the Piscean Age and entering the AQUARIAN AGE, according to the MAYAN mysteries. These years have been divided into five-year segments comparable to the five stages of dying: 1987–1992, denial; 1992–1997, anger; 1997–2002, bargaining; 2002–2007, depression; 2007–2012, acceptance. The new world begins!

HARMONY. Agni theme. Ugliness in all its aspects is a dangerous malady. For humanity's sake, we must understand its cure and its dissolution. It is time to realize that words should be beautiful and produce exalted thinking. We learn to bring harmony to words, colors, tones, and actions. Holding a place of peace within, we expand this to the world through will and love-wisdom. Correlates to the energy and influence of the number 6. *See* Numerology.

HATHA YOGA. *See* Yoga.

HEALER, SPIRITUAL. One who uses either the art or science of techniques of energy transference designed to recharge or balance the energy system of the etheric body in order to facilitate health and healing.

HEALING. One of the seven SACRAMENTS of Christianity. Formerly called "Last Rites," the anointing of the sick and dying is now known as a sacrament of healing.

HEALING, ABSENTEE, OR REMOTE. Healing energies directed from the source to patient or receiver without touch or immediate contact; may be at a great distance.

HEALING ENERGY. A beneficial psychic force or energy transmitted from one to another with the intent of assisting and supporting the receiver in life experiences.

HEALING, FAITH. Closely related to spiritual healing but with added emphasis on one's trust or belief in a particular deity, approach, or practice.

HEALING, MAGNETIC. A psychic force or energy that flows by the process of osmosis or drawing from the more highly charged to the lesser. A natural process of sharing of one's vitality that can be facilitated by intent. The channel may be aware of decreased energy afterwards.

HEALING, PSYCHIC. The practice of sharing vitality with another.

HEALING RITE. One of seven specific SACRAMENTS of Christianity. Anointing the sick and the dying with holy oil is now referred to as the sacrament of healing. Formerly known as Last Rites, this Christian ritual is felt to bring healing help to those in need—physical or spiritual. The deceased are anointed, which serves as a closing of the chakras in preparation for the journey through the planes. *See* Last Rites.

HEALING, SPIRITUAL. From the Greek word *sozo* meaning "to save" or "to make whole"; the noun *soter* translates "savior" or "healer." From this base comes salvation, healing, wholeness, and holiness. Also, *heal* comes from the Old English 'hal' such as hale and hearty, as does *health.* A means to reach into higher vibrations than the usual consciousness in order to connect with soul energies and channel these to a recipient.

HEART. The heart is a symbol of God's love and the love of humans for one another. Its religious meaning can be found in 1 Sam. 16.7, "I do not see as man sees; for man looks on the outward appearance, but the Lord looks on the heart." The heart is also considered to be the source of wisdom, inner knowing, impersonal love, courage, devotion, and joy. The heart center (chakra) represents the positive emotional center of consciousness, the contact point of the mental nature to "thinketh in the heart."

An Agni word referring to the purified heart, the accumulator that permits passage of the manifestation of the subtle FOHAT, the light (fire) of a special quality to emanate into expression. Heart is often used to mean "soul" or "soul quality."

HEART BEHIND THE HEART. An important concept that the heart center is not the physical organ but the etheric organ of sensitivity activated by lifting the consciousness to a sensitive, caring frequency in harmony with the soul itself. It is this heart that is sensitized to the touch of the soul whereby the attentive one is intuitively prompted and guided.

HEART-CENTERED PATH. A particular style of spiritual leadership and life-styling wherein one is allowed great freedom to weave one's particular way through power of choice and learn through the consequences. Less defined than a solar plexus path and works well for more mature souls ready to exercise self-discipline and discrimination.

HEART MATH™. A recent discovery that the heart has its own nervous system—a "brain" that affects the amygdala, the thalamus, the

the cortex—helps to explain what some psychologists already realized. It was known that the body's nervous system connected the heart with the brain, but it was presumed that the brain made all decisions. Recent research shows the heart responds as if it has its own distinctive logic. The selectivity of the heart's response indicates it does not mechanically react to a signal from the brain; the response depends upon the nature of the task and the type of processing required. More intriguing, research shows the heart appears to send messages to the brain that the brain not only understands but obeys.[2]

HEAVEN AND HELL. Two designated points of experiences in the astral reality. Heaven denotes higher, beauty-filled levels; hell (Sheol or Hades) denotes lower, pain-filled realms. *Also see* Hellfire; Purgatory.

HEAVEN ON EARTH. An aspiration of many religions, saints, and holy ones who tell of such realizations as "restoring the Garden on Earth." Inherent within this goal must be the adaptation of human consciousness to a stage of awareness little realized today. This vision will be fulfilled by the realization by humanity of right relationship between science and technology and morality and the transformation of human consciousness. Each enlightened one becomes a role model for the new and fundamental comprehension of a cosmic wholeness—all parts and all creatures—that must be transcended for the Oneness to be realized from within each. Then will emerge the consciousness necessary to create a higher, holier state on the planet.

HEINDEL, MAX. b. Carl Louis Van Grasshof, Germany, 1865, d. 1919. Student of Rudolf Steiner and founder of the Rosicrucian Fellowship. In 1907 an elder brother of the ancient Rosicrucian Order appeared to him and transmitted the material eventually published as the *Rosicrucian Cosmo-Conception.* His work with the ephemeris—tables showing the daily positions of the planets—led to a new and widespread interest in astrology. *The Rosicrucian Mysteries,* 1911; *Message of the Stars,* 1913; *Simplified Scientific Astrology,* 1928, *Rosicrucian Philosophy in Questions and Answers,* 1922.

HEKHOLATH. Halls or chambers of higher realms, accessible through the contemplative practice of MERKEVAH (chariot) mysticism.

HELINE, CORINNE. b. Georgia, 1882, d. 1975. Author, musician, and healer. A student of Max Heindel, founder of the Rosicrucian Fellowship, in 1922 she received "an inner commission to interpret the Bible in the esoteric tradition," which became a life-long work. The New Age Bible and Philosophy Center in California was established in the 1930s to disseminate her many works. She married Theodore Heline in 1938 and they established the New Age Press. *New Age Bible Interpretation* (seven volumes), including *Mystery of the Christos,* 1961; *The Cosmic Harp,* 1969; *Color and Music in the New Age,* 1964; *Healing and Regeneration Through Colors,* 1943.

HELL. Or Hades (abode of the dead in Greek mythology), or SHEOL, the Hebrew term. An etheric place of restriction, absent of love and light, on the lower astral plane where the old consciousness of humanity awaits the purification of its negatives.

HELLFIRE. Representative of the agony of creation—the presence of divine fire (the MONAD, or SPIRIT) trapped in matter and forced to vibrate in slow matter: "stuck."

HEMISPHERES, RIGHT AND LEFT, OF THE BRAIN. To the right half of the brain is attributed the ability to assist consciousness to connect with others, to bond, and respond sensitively to others. As well, the right hemisphere is considered the sphere that connects us to imagination, intuition, and slower brain wave activity. The left hemisphere is the part of the brain that evaluates, analyzes, and reacts, as well as guides responses to the outer world. Science has discerned the right hemisphere of the brain controls the left side of the body and the left hemisphere operates the right side of the body. *See* Three-brain concept.

HERACLITUS. b. ca. 500 B.C. Greek philosopher whose most famous doctrine is that everything is in a state of flux—you can never step into the same river twice. What appears to be a changeless stability of the world conceals a dynamic tension between opposites controlled by reason, logos, or its physical manifestation, fire; that fire is the ultimate constituent of the world. The fire of the human soul is thus connected to the cosmic fire that virtuous souls will eventually join. *On Nature, Fragments.*

HERBAL MEDICINES. The use of plants or plant parts in a natural state or a derivation for their healing effect, avoiding chemicalization or the more processed form.

HERETIC. By derivation, one who is "able to choose," thus, all who choose to think for themselves rather than blindly believe what they are taught. Many religions persecute members who stray from the principal doctrine, labeling them "heretics," implying "undesirable." They have a noble predecessor in St. Paul who, in his first epistle to the Thessalonians (5.21), counseled, "Prove all things; hold fast to that which is good."

HERMAPHRODITE, MALFORMED. *Monstrum Hermaphroditus,* or the gross blending or melding of opposites to be strengthened and purified. Represented here are intense images invoking primal nature of archetypal copulation that alchemists believe occurs between opposing forces of sulfur (burning stone, masculine qualities) and mercury (quicksilver, feminine) in the bowels of the Earth, producing all metals, including the noblest of all, gold.

HERMES TRISMEGISTUS. "The Thrice Great." The Greek Scribe of the Gods, God of Wisdom, and the Egyptian God Thoth. A legendary Egyptian sage, said to be the author of the tarot, Neo-Platonism, the KABALAH, alchemy, and astrology, he gave rise to Hermeticism, a school of mystical religious thought of significant influence in the Middle Ages and the Renaissance. Based on "The Hermetics," a series of philosophical treatises written by various authors between the 2nd and 4th centuries A.D., the tracts include astrological writings from the Egyptian tradition, Persian secret rites, and interest in regenerative experience and religious ecstasy from Greek sources.

Hermetic Principles

Seven in number, considered the underlying foundation for life in the material world. *See individual definitions;* Universal law.

1. Mentalism	All is mind; creative intelligence flows from divine mind.
2. Correspondence	As above, so below; know thyself if you would know another.
3. Vibration	Everything is in motion; physics has proven matter is merely higher vibration, even as it appears solid.
4. Polarity	Everything is reflected by opposites; poles of duality form a line of tension that keeps each extreme related and reflective.
5. Rhythm	Everything flows in and out; the pendulum swings; rhythm compensates.
6. Cause and Effect	Every action has a related action; or, nothing happens without a reason. Karma is the Sanskrit word for the law of relationship between first cause and outcome.
7. Gender	All things are masculine and feminine energies at work, expressing as creation, generation, regeneration. To be pure, we respect gender; disrespect moves us to self-destruction.

The Precepts of Hermes engraved upon the Emerald Tablets

1. Speak not fictitious things, but that which is certain and true.
2. What is below is like that which is above, and that which is above is like that which is below, to accomplish the miracles of one thing.
3. And as all things were produced by the one word of one Being, so all things were produced from this one thing by adaptation.
4. Its father is the sun, its mother is the moon; the wind carried it in its belly, its nurse is the earth.
5. It is the father of perfection throughout the world.
6. The power is vigorous if it be changed into earth.
7. Separate the earth from fire, the subtle from the gross, acting prudently and with judgement.
8. Ascend with the greatest sagacity from the earth to heaven, and then again, descend to the earth, and unite together the powers of things superior and things inferior. Thus you will obtain the glory of the whole world, and obscurity will fly far away from you.
9. This has more fortitude than fortitude itself, because it conquers every subtle thing and can penetrate every solid.
10. Thus the world was formed.
11. Hence proceed wonders, which are here established.
12. Therefore, I am called Hermes Trismegistus, having three parts of the philosophy of the whole world.
13. That which I had to say concerning the operation of the sun is completed.[3]

Hermetic chain. The hidden influence that creates the ladder of life, or the evolutionary chain, hard at work, pushing consciousness forward. Out of sight, this force brings opportunities to learn and grow, to satisfy unfinished business, and to provide challenges to overcome.

HERMETIC TRADITION. The closely held, hidden traditions of wisdom teachings, usually given an aspirant or disciple under strict circumstances and instruction by a guru or mentor; not necessarily religious in nature. Hermetics and Gnostics are closely related in wisdom teachings, but Hermetic doctrine is not restricted to such traditions, i.e., physical knowledge is "hermetic" (in a sealed vacuum) until discovered, as in the secrets of DNA or the atom.

HERO'S JOURNEY. In *The Hero with a Thousand Faces,*[4] Joseph Campbell identifies three distinct stages to the hero's journey: 1) departure or separation from one's former identity as a hero deserts the old for the new; 2) fulfillment, or initiation into a new consciousness (group, church, or tribal level) where unknown forces, experiences, or realizations are acquired and a decisive new awareness is won; and 3) the return—empowered now to bless and guide others—includes establishment of new parameters or new renditions of old foundations.

HESYCHASM. From the Greek root meaning "to be still." An early Christian mystical path of transcendence that traces its origins to the 4th century DESERT FATHERS, described as a shift from ego-centered to ego-transcendent consciousness through three steps: dispassion, stillness, and union with the Source. The technique—rejected by the Western Church, which discouraged individual experiences of the Divine—survived due to the support of the Orthodox Church for quiet meditation of personal self-mastery.

HESYCHAST. Practitioner of hesychasm, an ancient Christian mystical tradition with a rich body of instructions for transcendence preserved by the Eastern branches of the Church.

HEXAGRAM. A six-pointed star formed by extending each side of a regular hexagram (six sides) into equilateral triangles. As two interlocking triangles, the hexagram symbolizes "as above, so below." This configuration begins as two triangles touch—one descending Earthward, the other pointing upward. The first represents the soul reaching downward and the second is personality re-formed and ready. As they touch, they represent the lower three chakras ready and the top three chakras stirring. When the heart (fourth chakra) opens, the triangles blend into the mark of the disciple, the six-pointed star.

HIERARCHY. The delegated, directive supreme authority and power overseeing planetary life on the higher planes, guiding and teaching initiates and disciples. Also known as the Great White Brotherhood, orders, or brotherhoods of initiated souls, working as a field of intelligence serving the Creator. Holy ones who demonstrate leadership and service, awakening humanity to its greater potential and revealing a path of ascent to higher realities of life for those aware of Hierarchy. Consisting of many departments, different qualifications, branches of the Plan, this inner structure holds the blueprint for humanity as, one by one, personalities come to know themselves as part of the one great soul, the human

HIERARCHY OF NEEDS

The higher needs which appear to arise in man after his basic survival needs are met are the result of an inner pressure toward a fuller expression of being, a self-actualization, in the same naturalistic sense that an acorn may be said to be pressing toward an oak tree.

—Abraham Maslow

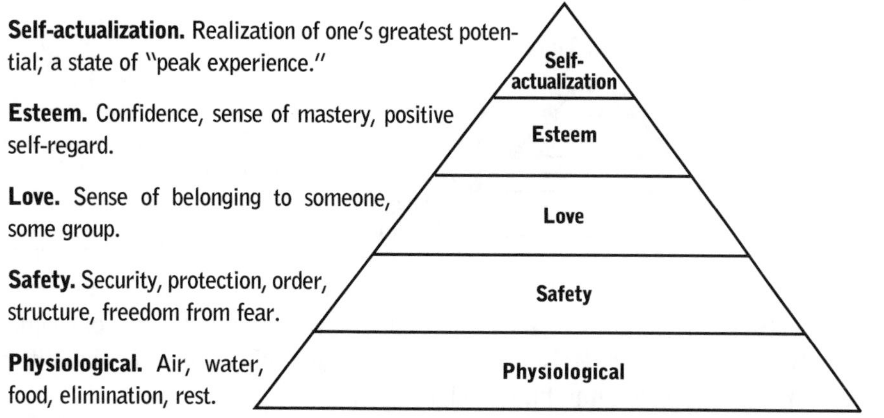

soul incarnated in the world of matter. *See* Brotherhood; Externalization of the Hierarchy.

HIERARCHY OF A CONSTELLATION. The sacred line of power bequeathed by a constellation to affect lesser life in its process of evolution. *See* Celestial hierarchies.

HIERARCHY OF LINEAGES. Seven types or lines of workers (disciples) advancing human consciousness, often unrecognized in the world: contemplatives, healers, mirrors (reflectors), governors, warriors, prophets/sages, and priests. The inner monad leads each to her or his line of service. *See pp. 349–55,* Etheric Dimensions.

HIERARCHY, PLANETARY. *Hier* means "sacred" and *archy* means "to rule." Overseeing planetary life on the higher planes, this delegated, supreme authority directs, guides, and teaches initiates and disciples. Also known as the Great White BROTHERHOOD, these orders or groups of initiated souls work as a field of intelligence serving the Creator, or the Plan of Creation. The sacred line of power that guides all life within a planetary scheme to its particular goal according to a higher Plan. The group of spiritual beings existing on the inner planes of the solar system that is the intelligent and directive force responsible for the evolutionary processes of the Earth. Additionally, advanced ones of twelve CELESTIAL HIERARCHIES influence planetary energies for the benefit of all life. Hierarchy is reflected in the Earth scheme, described by the OCCULTIST as "the occult

HIGHER THIRD

This mediation technique, which comes from Eastern thought, is designed to lessen the sense of loss experienced in compromise. When two opposing points are to be reconciled, each point seeks to lift perspective and move closer to the other, forming a triangle of movement, higher and toward center, until a point of reconciliation is found: the Law of Higher Third.

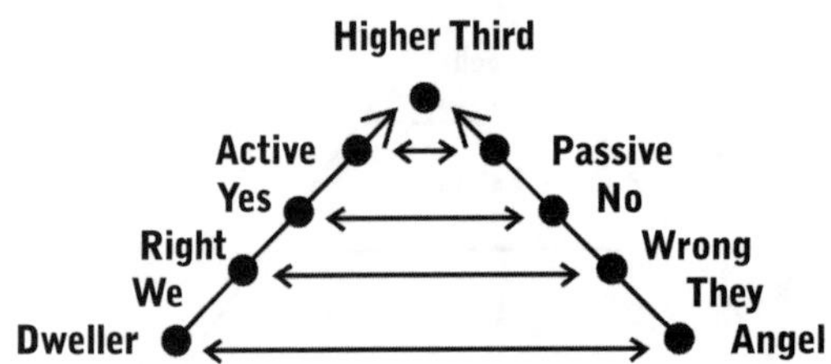

> *In order to settle . . . conflict, a new principle comes in, other and higher than the two conflicting instincts, and aiming both to override and to reconcile them. This third principle is the ethical ideal.*
>
> –Sri Aurobindo

THE HIGHER THIRD—the route of collision versus Higher Third reconciliation. This chart illustrates the opposites we encounter in life. When caught in any of them, we have difficulty making the best decision. If we can lift our consciousness to view the situation from a higher level, we often find a unique solution.

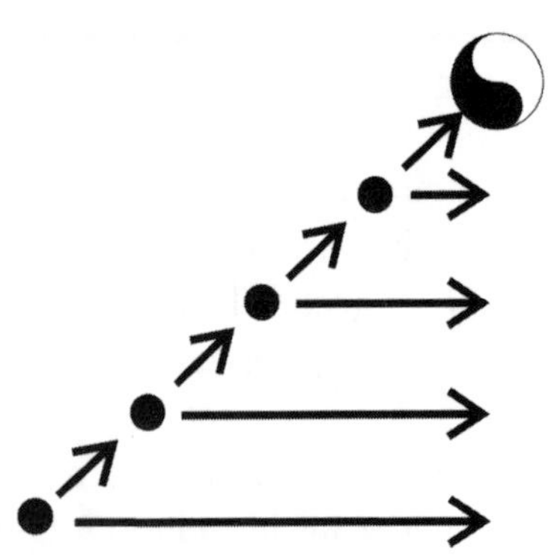

Technique for Using Higher Third Principle

The way to use this technique is to first see the maneuver.

Step 1. Opposite positions arise. Compromise may cause each to feel loss.

Step 2. Life position to higher level and nearer the treasured perspective. Both Will Feel progress is being made. Positions are closer, but without loss. Keep adding positive thought.

Step 3. Continue to focus upon unifying principles, and invoke more subtle perceptions

Step 4. Each position moves to a more elevated perspective that allows for agreement. The new position gains much and suffers no loss. Creative thinking and respect for what each offers are the goals of this concept.

Hierarchy formed of CHOHANS, ADEPTS, and INITIATES working through their DISCIPLES," meaning, "in the world."

HIEROGLYPHS. A system of allegorical drawings, designs, or symbols used to convey meaning, language, or thought. A form of prescript writing developed by earlier cultures to preserve ideas, history, and dates.

HIEROPHANT. The initiator who stands as a representative of the HIERARCHY within the subtler plane or on Earth. In the inner world the great initiator is the Christ—"No one comes unto the Father except by me"—for he is the teacher of angels and of humanity for this planet. On the Earth the person who is chosen by the inner world and who serves by GNOSIS is the lesser initiator. Many copies are GLAMOURS and invalid as far as spiritual worth is concerned.

HIEROS GAMOS. Greek for "sacred marriage" between the masculine and feminine aspects of God. Sophia/Wisdom is portrayed as the feminine partner in this marriage.

HIGH CONSCIOUSNESS. An expanded state of knowing or understanding characterized by increased awareness and sensitivity to seen and unseen realities. Also, the practice of an ethical lifestyle guided by high principles. The consciousness achieved through activation of the higher chakras.

HIGHER AND LOWER MINDS. The two departments of the mental body that vibrate to the personality and to the soul. The midpoint (fourth level of seven, the heart) is a place of decisive development and the home of the High Self and the Christ-potential within humanity. Higher mind is synonymous with and often called "ABSTRACT MIND."

HIGHER FORM OF HUMANITY. Existing and diverse wise ones, as well as a goal of species. Friedrich Wilhelm Nietzsche, Henri Bergson, Pierre Teilhard de Chardin, Sri Aurobindo, Gopi Krishna, Richard Maurice Bucke, L.L. Whyte are but a significant few who have reached this potential.

HIGHER WORLDS. The aggregate of the more subtle planes of existence—home of the soul (the intuitive, atmic) and the monadic divine plane of origin. These higher worlds, commonly called, would generally be the planes above the personality planes: physical, astral, and mental.

HIGHLY SENSITIVE PEOPLE (HSP). This contemporary term refers to high-strung, nervous, timid, overly sensitive or fearful people. Mental health professionals now acknowledge 15 to 20 percent of the population fit this identity. Characteristics they share: highly aroused by new or prolonged stimulation, strongly reactive to noise and light, intolerant of pain, hunger, thirst, caffeine, and medication; susceptible to stress-related and psychosomatic illnesses and to others' moods and emotions. Highly intuitive, able to concentrate deeply, right-brained and less linear than nonHSPs; highly conscientious, especially good at tasks requiring vigilance, accuracy, and speed; excellent at spotting and avoiding errors. "Sensitivity is an inherited trait," says research psychologist and psychotherapist Elaine Aron, "that tends to be a disadvantage at high levels of stimulation." Everything is magnified by HSPs.[5]

HIGH SELF. The ball of wisdom, or sum total of awareness, one collects through personal experiences in this and all previous incarnations. Also called the "lower mental unit," this ball of knowledge serves as a high point in consciousness, guiding personality through the physical, emotional, and mental issues of everyday life.

HILARION. *See* Masters.

HILDEGARD OF BINGEN. *See pp. 246–51,* Saints.

HIMALAYAN CENTERS. In North India, Nepal,and that region these centers have served a long cycle as planetary anchoring points for the masculine energy from the higher realities. This energy is now receding, and the incoming evolutionary force is being delivered through the Andes mountain range of South America. The shift began to be recorded in the 20th century—an early source being *Secrets of the Andes* by Brother Philip,[6] and others have received similar messages. A great deal of research and record-keeping has been done by Trigueirinho in Figueira, Brazil, since the mid-'80s. *Also see pp. 349–55,* Etheric Dimensions.

HINAYANA. This first of three schools of Buddha, the lower path, reveres the path of renunciation; the pursuit of a rigorous purified lifestyle for the sake of spiritual goals (not indulging in SAMSARA or self-delusion); enlightenment for self. *See other two schools:* Mahayana, Vajrayana.

HINDUISM. An Eastern religion of antiquity that gave birth to Buddhism, similar to Judaism generating Christianity. The religion of Brahma, Vishnu, and Shiva. Krishna was considered an incarnation of Vishnu; BABAJI of Herakhan is considered an incarnation of Shiva.

HITTITES. A kingdom of Asia Minor that flourished ca. 1750 B.C., producing an ancient culture that is still imperfectly known and continues to be investigated. Many cuneiform inscriptions are of Hittite and Babylonian origins. Many believe the Hittites created the federations of cities in Cappadocia by 1800 B.C. and began to decline about 500 years later.

HO. The Native American word for affirming "and so it is" or "I agree." A power word when used as a mantra.

HOD. This eighth sephirah on the kabalistic tree is called "splendor"—specifically, the "splendor of the mind."

HODSON, GEOFFREY. b. 1886, d. 1983. A kindly and dignified English gentleman, he became self-illumined in his early adult life and traveled the world three times in his long international lecturing career for the THEOSOPHICAL SOCIETY. Known as an illumined occultist, mystic, yogi, healer, philosopher, and humanitarian, as well as an inspiring speaker, Hodson modestly referred to himself as a student of THEOSOPHY, which, in its purest form, he saw as an important means whereby humanity could save itself from itself. His 200 articles and 50 books embody insights from both angelic and adeptic sources, as well as his own direct clairvoyant and yogic research, wherein he would leave his physical body at will and travel in full awareness to explore nature's hidden realms.[7]

HOLISM. When the aspects of self synthesize. The holism of self leads to whole, wholesome, and holy. Also spelled "wholism."

HOLISTIC. A term affirming the nature of all to be sacred or holy (comes from the root word *sozo,* to save or giving rise to healing and holism); making whole, at one, a synthesis of many parts establishing a greater state when all is unified. *Also see* Healers, spiritual.

HOLLOW EARTH THEORY. This ancient concept that periodically emerges concerns the makeup of planet Earth with human life. A most interesting story is written in the diary of Admiral Richard E. Byrd about his exploration of the North Pole where he was intercepted, taken inside the planet, and given a message by a beautiful race of people to give the American government. Byrd delivered the message and was forbidden to share it with others. After his death his diary was published by a daughter.

HOLY GHOST. An archaic term of the early Christian tradition which later was changed to HOLY SPIRIT. Correctly, the etheric imprint of the overshadowing Holy in the reflective ethers; lower levels hold a vibration (or imprint) of the higher consciousness that expresses when the Divine interacts with either an individual or the collective. This reflection, distorted in the lower planes, will exist until all is drawn back into rest.

HOLY GRAIL, THE. *See* Grail, the Holy.

HOLY OF HOLIES. Biblically, the inner-most, consecrated, small sanctuary of the temple of the Jews, entered only by the High Priest and then only once a year. The term has since been used to refer to the sanctuary of other sacred places, even the HEART BEHIND THE HEART of the disciple.

HOLY ORDERS. A public vow to a life of service to God and to the work of Spirit. A conscious commitment of allegiance with the forces of light to serve and work for humanity regarding enlightenment (SALVATION). Responding to the call of the Soul to live not for ourselves alone but for others and for God. A public vow to serve and to stand for spiritual beliefs. This may be monastic, as a nun or monk, a priest, a minister—lay or ordained. One of the seven SACRAMENTS of Christianity.

HOLY SPIRIT. The third person of the TRINITY; the power of active intelligence in the universe. An aspect of divine consciousness that expresses in the physical realm without physical form through overshadowing those who are receptive to this high frequency or intelligence. The aspect of divine nature that is the vital, form-building energy ensouling all matter. Generally considered to be feminine. The Divine-Within that links creative expression from the world of spirit to the world of form, the MAHAT. Also known as Christ Consciousness, the Comforter, SOPHIA, Holy Breath, and HOLY GHOST.

HOLY WEEK. In the Christian tradition, from Palm Sunday through Easter Sunday. Each day of the week is significant, some bearing special names: Maundy Thursday commemorates the Last Supper (the CHALICE and the wafer are symbols of the wine and bread); on Good Friday, the day of the Crucifixion, black is used to commemorate Jesus' death on the cross and his closure in the physical; on Holy Saturday, the church is dark, the altar stripped, recalling Jesus' time in the tomb; Easter Sunday concludes the week with a celebration of the Resurrection.

HOMO-CHRISTOS. The state of attainment of the divine potential in mortals: fully human and fully divine.

HOMO NOETICUS. The new mind-being in the next stage of evolution of the *homo sapien.* A higher form of humanity emerging on the planet now, characterized not by genetic changes but by noetic (mind) changes. A mystical state of consciousness that is the basis and constant mode of awareness through which all experience is registered, a new breed emerging in humanity psychologically adapted to the altered conditions nature is imposing as it restores balance to human and planetary life, presenting a logic that is multilevel, integrated, simultaneous—not linear, sequential, either-or. Considered an evolutionary thrust. One who fulfills the divine injunction, *Let the mind be in you that was in Christ Jesus."* (Phil. 2.5) Consciousness is the guiding principle by which to define Homo noeticus, says John White, a movement from self-centeredness to God-centeredness characterized by a profound change in consciousness, *MOKSHA*—part of the process of enlightenment. See ChristoSophia; Theosophia, Christ Within.

HOMOSAPIEN. A neutral term used in the context of evolving humankind. Believed to have appeared on Earth as a new kind of "thinking man" appearing about 35,000 years ago, sweeping Neanderthal man from the face of Earth. Because they created lasting cave art, they were first called "cavemen." *See pp. 337–47,* Humanity's Genesis.

HOOP, SACRED. The symbol of a circle used by most North American native traditions representing the oneness, continuity, and completeness of the human family.

HOPE OF GLORY. Divine potential awaiting expression from within human beings; our inheritance, for we are made in the image and likeness of God. (Gen. 1.27) The Christ in us—the hope of glory. (Col. 1.27)

HORARY ASTROLOGY. *See p. 23.*

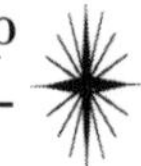

HOROSCOPE. Means "hour pointer"—a map or chart computed by astrological configurations for a person or event to reveal the interplay of planetary influences at work at a specific time and place. Also called the "natal chart." *See* Astrology.

HORUS. The son of Isis in the Egyptian mysteries, known for expressing the holy consciousness in a perfect blending of masculine-feminine qualities. In the mysteries of Isis, she is the veiled DIVINE FEMININE who brings forth the holy child, Horus. The mysteries of Christianity are closely related.

HOUSE. An astrological chart is divided into 12 sections creating a wheel. These sections, or houses, each approximately 30 degrees, signify the relative division of the heavens according to the birthplace and the birth time of an individual or event. Each house represents a basic field of activity or experience, the meaning of which is modified by the planets occupying the house and the sign that rules the house due to its placement on the house cusp.

HOUSE OF THE VIRGIN MARY. At Selçuk, near Ephesus, Turkey, the site is restored and endorsed by the Roman Catholic Church. Here at Ephesus the first church dedicated to Our Lady was built. Also, the Third Ecumenical Council was held in Ephesus in 431 A.D. Four popes have endorsed the discovery of the House of Mary: Benedict XIV (1740–1758), Leo XIII (1878–1903), Pius X (1903–1914), Benedict XV (1914–1922), and Pius XI. Popes John VI and John Paul II have visited the site. *Also see pp. 258–9,* Seven Churches of Asia Minor.

HUBBARD, L. RON. b. Tilden, Nebraska, 1911, d. 1986. The founder of the Church of SCIENTOLOGY in 1953 who developed Dianetics, a process of psychoanalytic clearing of traumas from childhood and past lives.

HUGH OF ST. VICTOR. Christian mystic who taught that we have physical eyes with which to see the material world, a mental eye to perceive ideas and concepts, and a spiritual eye with which to see the will of God. From Ken Wilber in *Eye to Eye:*

> . . . Hugh of St. Victor . . . distinguished between *cogitatio, meditatio,* and *contemplatio. Cogitatio,* or simple empirical cognition, is a seeking for facts of the material world using the eye of flesh. *Meditatio* is a seeking for the truths within the psyche itself (the *imago* of God) using the mind's eye. *Contemplatio* is the knowledge whereby the psyche or soul is united instantly with Godhead in transcendent insight (revealed by the eye of contemplation).
>
> Now that particular wording—eye of flesh, mind, and contemplation—is Christian; but similar ideas can be found in every major school of traditional psychology, philosophy, and religion. The "three eyes" of a human being correspond, in fact, to the three major realms of being described by the perennial philosophy, which are the gross (flesh and material), the subtle (mental and animic), and the causal (transcendent and contemplative). . . .[8]

HUMANISM. A focus on human potential without spiritual component.

HUMANITARIAN LOVE. Latin: *humanus.* The bonds of affection that move a person to nurture and embrace another simply because each is a member of the human family and understands the inherent kinship and unity of all people. Devoted to the welfare of human beings; philanthropic.

HUMANITY. Comprised of those beings in whom the densest substance and the highest spirit are united by intelligence.

Agni theme. We learn to identify as one with all, knowing the work we do is for the well-being of the whole human race, the lifting of group consciousness. As we each make sacred our own nature, burning away distortions, we realize our bond with all of humankind, and compassion results. Correlates to the energy and influence of the number 2. *See* Numerology.

HUMILITY. Agni virtue for Aquarius. Comes from *humus* meaning "earth" or "soil," knowing we come from earth, respect the Earth, and will return to her womb when buried. Surrendering nonself to High Self or personality acquiescing to our true purpose; never an aspect of denigrating ourselves, which would distort the great truth of our being. Minimizing self-importance of ego and expanding the significance of the High Self.

HUMOR. In Latin, *umor* means "to be fluid and flexible," like water. The ancients believed there were four humors upon which temperament and health depend, each playing a part in the temperament of an individual: blood, phlegm, choler, and black bile. Ancient physiology believed the relative proportions determined disposition and health. Humor places us in a playful, amused, or funny state of mind. As it relieves us from a restricted sense of self, we find ourselves unencumbered momentarily. As such a state helps us triumph over adversity, it is credited with healing properties.

HUNA. A Polynesian HERMETIC tradition focused on wholeness with an understanding of how each aspect contributes to the whole. A complex and well-developed science of health and ethical living practiced in the Pacific Islands.

HUNAB K'U. Mayan SOLAR DEITY, known as "Creator of Measure and Movement."

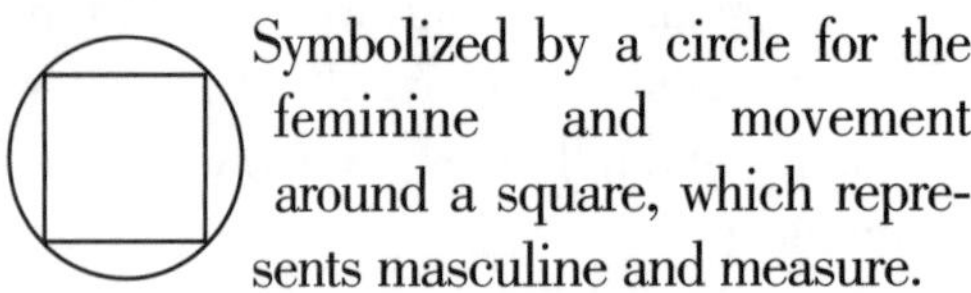

Symbolized by a circle for the feminine and movement around a square, which represents masculine and measure.

HUNDREDTH-MONKEY CONCEPT. Relates to a well-known story about monkeys on a Japanese island who were observed to achieve wisdom and diligence in a new skill which, without physical contact, seemed to leap to monkeys on other islands. (The skill was that of washing sand off before eating sweet potatoes that had been airlifted to the islands' monkey populations.) After becoming accepted as fact, has been denied as scientifically valid, but continues to be understood as the impact a percentage can wield upon the whole.

HYDROMANCY. Divining technique using water as the medium into which one gazes to achieve visions or to contact the deceased or spirits. In Shakespeare's *Macbeth* three witches boil a brew and conjure apparitions from its surface.

HYKSOS. An Egyptian band of "Shepherd Kings" who taught the priesthood of Egypt 6,000 years ago and are said to have constructed the GREAT PYRAMID. Said to be the same teachings of Moses, which Jesus memorized and which 16 U.S. presidents were to have learned—from George Washington to both Roosevelts, Truman, and Ford—all FREEMASONS.[8]

HYPERBOREAN ROOT RACE. *See* Root race.

HYPERSPACES. Other space-time frameworks, dimensions that interpenetrate our own. Located within us even while they seem to be outside, at the same time they are outside the range of the physical body, though we arrive there by going within.

HYPNOTISM. An altered state of consciousness wherein the individual, in a sleep-like condition, is quite responsive to suggestions made by the hypnotist.

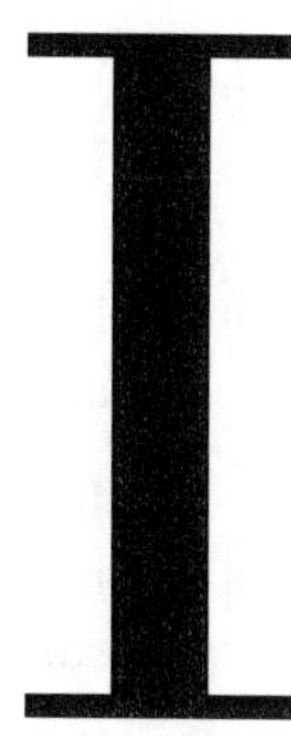

I-Am presence (or consciousness). Derived from the mantra "I am that I am." An affirmation of our identity with the divinity that invokes oneness and spiritual empowerment. Used in the practice of meditation and contemplation to affirm the indwelling and divine Self. An identification with the One God who animates all things and who dwells within.

I am that I am. A meditation SEED THOUGHT excellent for exploring our true nature, claiming relationship of the Self-within to the Self, the whole. Contemplating this phrase helps us realize our true essence and unites us to the universal Oneness. We each learn we are a reflection of the Great I Am.

I Am the Soul. A phrase used as an affirmation to remind our NONSELF of our true identity. We neutralize the belief that we are a personality with a soul and come to know we are a soul having a human experience. The Soul is the true reality, and we are constantly seeking to realize it more deeply. This centuries-old mantra of unknown source is still used today. We affirm:

I am the soul,
and also love am I.
Above all else I am
both will and fixed design.
My will is now to lift
the lower self into the light divine.
That light am I.
Therefore I must descend
to where the lower self awaits,
awaits my coming.
That which desires to lift
and that which cries for lifting
are now at one.
Such is my will.

Iberah. A PLANETARY CENTER (in the etheric) located over the center of Brazil and in the

Provinces of Corrientes and Río Negro, Argentina.[1]

I CHING. *The Book of Changes.* An ancient Chinese book of wisdom and philosophy composed of 64 sections called "hexagrams." Historically, used as a source of divination in conjunction with the tossing of coins or yarrow stalks. The beautifully composed text gives spiritual direction, emphasizing ethical living and right-relationships as understood through the observance of nature and the cycles of the heavens and Earth.

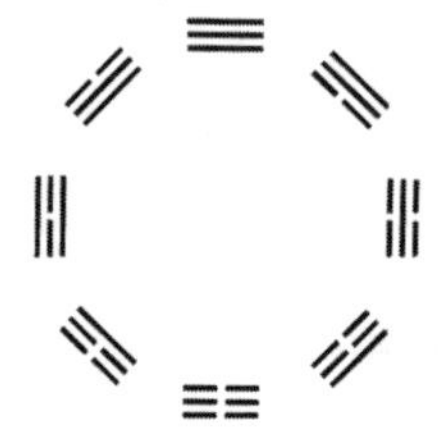

ICHTHUS. This earliest symbol for Christ, *ichthus,* is the Greek word for "fish." The five Greek letters spelling fish, IXOYS, form an anagram for the name and title of Christ: Jesus Christ, Son of God, Savior. Christianity was an underground movement for its first 300 years. The ichthus served the first Christians as a secret sign used to identify themselves as believers, while it remained a mere decoration to outsiders; used frequently in early Christian art and literature. It appears many times in the catacombs of Rome, sometimes alone, sometimes in fishing scenes and in themes relating to the Eucharist.

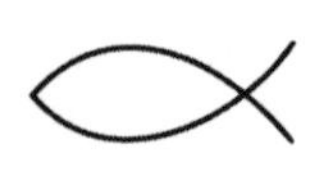

ICON. A precise style of painting identified with Christian orthodox traditions. The method is passed down from skilled artisans (iconologists) to apprentices with little or no variation of firmly established, stringent rules for the depiction of a particular subject or person.

ICONOGRAPHY. The study of icons, their history, and exacting specificity, often includes learning to paint icons in their traditional style and manner.

IDA. One part of a threefold thread or channel in the spinal column. This channel in the subtle body is activated by means of spiritual practices and disciplines under the guidance of a Master or teacher. The current on the left, the Ida or Ira, is associated with the feminine flow- or form-side of the currents of KUNDALINI.

IDEAOPLASM. Name given by John Philip Bessor, a UFO researcher, for the primitive ectoplasmic creature "originating in the stratosphere, capable of materialization and dematerialization," also described as "gelatinous meteors." Bessor's research is similar to Trevor James Constable's in regard to CRITTERS and UFOLOGY.

IF THE EYE BE SINGLE, THE WHOLE BODY SHALL BE FILLED WITH LIGHT. Matt. 6.22 refers to the single focus of mind and soul to be as one in order to guide us in life. Generally accepted as referring to the spiritual eye being opened—the third eye, eye center, or brow chakra. The PESHITTA BIBLE reads, "the eye be bright," meaning "filled with radiance." *Also see* Light body.

IHS. The letters IHCOYC form the name of Jesus in Greek. As Latin became the dominant language in the years following Jesus' death, the Greek C of IHCOYC was changed

to a Latin S. Thus the abbreviation became IHS instead of IHC. The widespread use of this monogram of Christ in ancient times was and today is often incorporated in a Latin cross form.

ILLUMINATE. Enlighten, stimulate, reveal, make comprehensible; charge with light-giving properties.

ILLUMINATI. An international group of intellectuals who claims enlightenment or access to special awareness; believed to have been established over two centuries ago for the purpose of coordinating world power toward beneficial purposes.

ILLUMINATION. As light (perception, understanding, and realization) ignites the mind, concepts are comprehended, and the mysteries of life stand revealed. The light overcomes darkness.

ILLUSION. Distortions within the mental nature that masquerade as truth, claiming our allegiance until we encounter a different perspective—stronger and more convincing. Illusions stand as guideposts of false concepts to direct us in ever-widening spirals until they are confronted. Less emotionally charged than GLAMOURS, they are subtler and more dangerous because they are accepted as "truth": "My way is the only way." Clearing illusions is a great work for those on the PATH OF INITIATION: false interpretations; mirages that exist individually and collectively for humanity ultimately to clear. In occultism everything finite (such as the universe and all in it) is illusion, or MAYA. It is one of the original definitions for "sin."

An illusion is a living thoughtform maintained and energized by personal or group belief. To awaken from illusion, we must change our mental concepts. Every illusion is a hindrance to freedom. Before we can function on higher levels of the mental plane or enjoy the freedom of the intuitional plane, we must clear our illusions through meditation and will. This cleansing process often causes pain in the personal life.

IMAGERY. The use of image-making abilities in particular ways, often for specific reasons; spontaneous imagery is also valid.

IMAGE-MAKING MECHANISM. A level of mind wherein the ability to image is developed—the mind screen—commonly referred to as "imagination." An important step in evolution is achieved when we can visualize, i.e., use the image-making mechanism.

IMAGES. Inner or outer pictures used on the indirect path to act upon consciousness—the purpose of all sacred art: ICONS, TANKAS, statues, even sacred architecture. Aware practitioners use them conceptually to connect the inner and outer realities. Those unconscious of the inner nature are assisted by sacred influences toward an awakening. Three classes of imagery occur in our inner states: MANTIC, PHOSPHORIC, and TELESMATIC.

IMAGINATION. The vital image-making ability of the creative mind used to produce and hold images for a variety of reasons: to etch into place desired programming to use in manifestation or to receive symbols and pictures from either personality-level awareness or soul impressions. This delicate mechanism is of significant importance to bring impressions from higher levels to lesser levels of mind where, vibrating more slowly, they now can manifest. The ancients referred to it as a divine gift hidden within each; also called the Word or Thought of God, the Star in Man, the celestial body.

IMAM. A title of a Muslim religious leader.

IMMANENT. Existing only within; transcendent; nonphysical, such as "God Immanent." (Not to be confused with "imminent," expected presently or soon).

IMMATURITY. This barrier to spiritual growth is acknowledged when we realize we respond from personality rather than from the soul maturity of our nature. Once noted, guidelines can be given to assist the maturing process. Use of love and will, objectivity, and developing other aspects of our nature help the process. Freedom from the selfish ego identity is a major work in the maturing process.

IMMORALITY. Practices inconsistent with the ethics of a moral life.

IMMORTALITY. Without cease; eternal. Unending life that continues beyond the demise of the physical.

IMPERIL. As an Agni term, a crystalline precipitate within the nerve channels of an organism, formed in response to an irritant or negative stimulation. Highly toxic to the organism, it is the most contaminating ingredient of the human condition. It can be dissolved only by high-level, opposing frequencies of truth, beauty, and goodness, together with complete rest.

IMPERSONALITY. Objectivity from a higher level; the withdrawal of ego energy.

IMPRESSION. A subtle awareness of thought or idea touching one's mind, gradually etching itself into consciousness.

IMPRINT. The pattern that lingers in the mind after contact with soul energy or awareness.

IN-BREATHING AND OUT-BREATHING, CONSCIOUS. The deliberate use of breath to derive benefits such as relaxation, recall, stress reduction, or reaching an altered state.

INCARNATION. Any given lifetime or embodiment—usually referenced as on planet Earth; often used in conjunction with rebirth or reincarnation.

INCENSE. A sweet-smelling preparation used to clear the astral level of a given area—often to cleanse and purify a space dedicated to spiritual work to aid in invoking spiritual power or holy influences. Incense may be burned to help neutralize negative energies or to clear the space of unhealthy influences.

INCLUSIVENESS. Movement away from fragmentation and separation toward embracing all facets or aspects of ourselves, of others, and of the greater Oneness.

INCONJUNCT. In astrology, two planets 150 degrees, or five signs, apart (allowable orb 5 degrees). A difficult aspect to reconcile, it demands an adjustment of attitude. Also called a "quincunx."

INCUBATION. The ancient practice of sleeping near relics at a holy site in order to encourage a healing process; considered instrumental as preparation to invoke or receive miraculous healing or guidance at holy shrines. Also, in dream work, to program oneself to dream in response to a specific question or issue.

INCUBUS. Two negative influences of the astral plane sap individuals of sexual energy: incubus (oppresses women) and succubus (attacks men). These intense psychic contacts—considered intentional aggression by ghostly forms convertible in nature (male/female)—attach temporarily to a living person for the action of drawing off sexual energy to which they are addicted.

INDIGO CHILDREN. A new term applied to children currently incarnating with a new perception and sense of self, as well as a new GNA formed or forming in the etheric body. These independent souls seem highly empowered from within. Learning styles differ from the usual, and the temperament is often at variance to "normal." They may be diagnosed and misdiagnosed as ADHD (Attention Deficit with Hyperactivity Disorder) or ADD (Attention Deficit Disorder). Acute sensitivity creates challenges for both themselves and others. All of these are not children, however. It is believed these are the beginning of the sixth SUB-RACE of the fifth ROOT RACE and their temperament offers hope for the future, believing humanity is moving toward a more balanced intuition, rather than being so rationally focused as the fifth sub-race. Excellent resources in this area are *The Indigo Children* by Lee Carroll and Jan Tober and *The Care and Feeling of Indigo Children* by Doreen Virtue, Ph.D. José Trigueirinho also speaks of the "new ones" as those both adult and children who have created the right-sided consciousness. *See pp. 349–55,* Etheric Dimensions.

INDIVIDUALIZATION. The process by which a social individual differentiates from others. One's natural progression from undifferentiated mind to individual awareness and development of the ego mind. The life process strengthens the ego so that further integration is possible.

INDIVIDUATION. Carl Jung coined this term for the journey of consciousness from the ego mind to include an awareness of the influences of the individual unconscious and the collective consciousness of humanity. This leads to greater integration of the personality and readiness for SOUL INFUSION.

INDUCTION. To lead into, introduce, or entice. Induction techniques are used to lead the consciousness of oneself or another in a particular direction.

INERTIA. This barrier to spiritual growth arises from the lowest GUNA. The tendency to not advance, laziness, satisfaction with status quo, dullness.

INFINITY SIGN. *See* Lemniscate.

INFLUENCES. Intelligences such as devas, angels, or spacial beings, as well as individuals. While an influence may be a THOUGHT-FORM or even the will of another by manipulation, attraction, or KARMA, it may be a part of us—a memory or programming that has slipped below our level of consciousness, or at the suggestion of another (often society), we may confuse as our own. In our ascent to higher reality we contact what are known as energies, entities, and influences.

INITIATES. From the Latin root meaning "first principals of any science." Those dedicated to the study and mastery of the mysteries of the science of self, the One Self in all selves, and have made themselves ready for the Path of Initiation. Most Western systems divide initiations into five steps. On the esoteric Christian path, these steps are modeled by the life of Jesus, THE CHRIST. Before the first initiation, we are aspirants or candidates on the probationary path. Common terms are "disciple" for first and second degree, "initiate" for third degree, "adept" for fourth degree, and "Master" at the fifth initiation.

INITIATION. Admission into sacred teachings or the spiritual life. The order of the initiation process is: struggle for capability; call for the test; take the test itself; pass the test; transfer of energy, title, or recognition; then instability while learning to function in the new position. Also, admission into the sacred teachings or organizations of an esoteric or occult discipline. *Also see* Cosmic initiation; Solar initiation.

INITIATION, PLANETARY. The testing of the collective of all life forms existing upon and within a planetary body to see if it can vibrate to a more intense love frequency. Each initiation lifts the frequency of the planet and benefits the entire solar system. Earth is not yet a SACRED PLANET.

INITIATION—THE ESOTERIC CHRISTIAN PATH. A process of awakening to our true identity and using soul energy in service to humanity; a developing process of understanding or expansion of consciousness. Esoteric Christianity depicts seven major events (the first five are taken in connection with humanity, the last two usually not):

1. Birth of the Christ-Within
2. Baptism
3. Transfiguration
4. Crucifixion
5. Revelation
6. Decision
7. Resurrection

INNER ALIGNMENT. The establishment of right-working relationship between levels of consciousness and levels of being, especially as the term is used to create an awareness of inner resources in order to know our inner nature.

INNER CHILD. The modern term for the level of inner self or basic self, imprinted by energies and experiences of our formative years programmed unconsciously. *See* Child-within.

INNER GUIDANCE. A sense of caring and direction provided from within by the GUARDIAN SPIRIT, the wise inner teacher, one's higher consciousness, or the soul.

INNER KNOWER. The wise level of self that remains connected to the BALL OF KNOWLEDGE or soul awareness that perceives past, present, and probable future, and what one is ready to bring to consciousness. Often thought of as the soul, High Self, guide, or teacher. As defined and taught in PSYCHOGRAPHY.

INNER PLANES. Higher or hidden frequencies of each plane not recognized while conscious in the physical, awakened state, i.e., an inner-plane experience refers to an event occurring out of sight, most often behind the veil of sleep and revealed in a rather dreamlike manner. Not a product of the subconscious; nor is it a dream, but an experience of another dimension imprinted on the memory in a delicate, gossamer awareness, sometimes recognized and recalled by conscious mind.

INNER-PLANES CLASSES. Gatherings behind the veil of sleep to which aspirants can be called, during slumber and out-of-body, to assist and hasten evolution of consciousness. Also called HALLS OF LEARNING, where ideas and concepts are introduced, or CHAPELS OF SILENCE, where energies, forces, or influences are rendered. Gatherings are called "classes," regardless of the type of exposure that takes place.

INNER PRESENCE. A divine point of consciousness hidden deep within the personality of which we usually are unaware. At a given point of spiritual achievement, we awaken to this new identity, sometimes known as the QUIESCENT SELF.

INNER REALITY. A different consciousness guides the spiritual nature than rules the personality. As we comprehend this, the task becomes to "know thyself" and bring the outer into alignment with the inner in order to perceive this dimension of the self.

INNER SELF. The spiritual nature, often hidden even from ourselves.

INNER TEACHER. The guide of our inner and outer lives though not always recognized, who assists us at each level of experience. Some know this one as a guide, while others will perceive the one as a MASTER or teacher. Varies with the development of the aspirant or disciple.

INNER WORLD. A realm of nonphysical reality not recognized by the analytical, outer mental state. In esoteric teachings, creation is described as seven PLANES—six of which are inner; only one, the physical, manifests as materiality.

INQUISITION. A period of organized religious persecution initiated by Pope Gregory IX in 1233 to eradicate ideas alien to approved church dogma and doctrine. Untold numbers were imprisoned, tortured, and/or put to death by burning—mostly women—in Spain, Italy, France, and the Holy Roman Empire, and later in North America. Lasted approximately 300 years.

INRI. An abbreviation using the four initials of the Latin inscription nailed above Jesus' head at the CRUCIFIXION; stands for *Jesus Nazarenus Rex Judaeorum,* meaning "Jesus of Nazareth, King of the Jews."

INSTINCTUAL MIND. The intelligence that abides beneath the surface of intellect and that governs our body through its survival senses.

INSTINCTUAL THINKING. The unconscious mental process that creates form; a perceptual structure forged from the animal nature humanity brought forth as it evolved from kingdom to kingdom.

INTEGRAL YOGA. *See* Yoga.

INTEGRATED PERSONALITY. One who is ready for a deeper awareness of his or her subtler nature and the inner worlds; the physical, emotional, and mental bodies are coordinated and ready for soul contact.

INTELLIGENCES, DEMONIC. Points of consciousness—though rarely encountered—that have never incarnated at the human level; usually negative or detrimental to the life of the evolving human; often labeled as the influence of the devil or Satan but usually are on the path of INVOLUTION or foreign to the human dimension.

INTENTION. A fixed point held as a dedicated focus toward which to strive.

INTENTIONAL COMMUNITY. A group of individuals united around an intent or keynote with a specific purpose or reason for being, usually in a common location.

INTER-DIMENSIONAL. Between planes, realities, or worlds.

INTER-DIMENSIONAL PASSAGEWAYS. Used to transfer beings from various kingdoms (of Earth) to subtle realms. Persons may go through these entrances when pure of heart and intention and when guided by the Inner Self.

INTERFAITH. An approach of respect for beliefs other than one's own. Example: An interfaith Christian would identify with the Christian approach while fully appreciating the wisdom and practices of other religions as valid. Interfaith practitioners see all pathways as the interaction of God with humanity throughout history. An interfaith approach honors the ways others come to the Source and does not sanction proselytizing.

INTERPENETRATING. When energies blend and infuse with each other, creating a vibrational field somewhat like a mist.

INTER-SOLAR GROUP. Cosmic forces helping the evolution of the PLANETARY LOGOS and playing a role in balancing the advancement toward the goal of the greater whole.

IN THE WORLD AND NOT OF IT. This biblical phrase refers to one in physical body who is involved with the material dimension but has expanded in spiritual awareness beyond its limited understanding.

INTRA-OCEANIC. Within the ocean—a center or reference to a bubble of consciousness that works from below or within the ocean; related to PLANETARY CENTERS.[2]

INTRA-TERRESTRIAL. *Intra* meaning "within," *terrestrial* meaning "Earth"—a center of consciousness within the planet itself that reflects and expresses the planetary being. More highly evolved beings currently assist humanity (without recognition, except by a growing number of individuals) as it advances. Within their subtle bodies, some human beings visit these dimensions. *See* Intra-oceanic; Planetary centers.[3]

INTROVERSION. Turning one's attention inward for the purpose of self-awareness or self-study.

INTUITION. Literally, "inner teachings." A wisdom of the heart. Direct or spiritual perception, a subjective sense belonging to the soul. Spiritual intellect; insight provided by the intellect of the soul from the mind of Reality itself, beyond the domain of pure reason. A knowing or awareness existing at a level of mind or consciousness beyond mental reasoning or normal intellectual comprehension.

INTUITIVE CONSCIOUSNESS. This level of mind, also known as Christ consciousness or Buddhic consciousness, is the plane of soul awareness that interpenetrates the mental nature so its impress can be recorded and recognized.

INTUITIVES. Those who are sensitive to higher reality and can receive information from areas beyond the personality's dimension.

INVISIBLE WORLDS. Realities subtler than the physical senses can detect, therefore, not visible to the physical eye but detectable by other than physical senses.

INVOCATION. A prayer or statement used to call forth a higher power.

INVOKE. To petition for support; to call forth through prayer, incantation, concentration, projection, or visualization, e.g., "Lord, heal my son." To request assistance of higher forces to act upon the lower worlds. A manner of summoning power, influence, or action from an unseen force, level, or source. To petition a desired power or energy to influence the physical world in a specific manner.

INVOLUTION (PERIOD OF). A stage or process in which spirit or life descends into matter, called a "path of descent." Often referred to biblically as the "FALL"—the result of souls wanting to experience the power of choice and the secrets of life. Involution of spirit into matter happens so that form may be built, enabling EVOLUTION. The human involutionary period is characterized by the specialization of the form side of human life through which the senses mature and the astral apparatus is perfected by the Self for the utilization of matter. A model that describes this process is the concept of the MONAD from which flows a stream of energy into denser PHYSICAL PLANES. This monadic current—which, as a SPARK OF GOD, is immortal and One with the Absolute—forms a point of consciousness, the soul, which in turn projects part of itself to form a personality in the physical world. The projection of the monad, the soul in human form, is unconscious on the physical plane and expresses through personality to acquire experience and awareness. In time, it will develop a creator consciousness in the dense world and reunite with the original Source through the process of evolution.

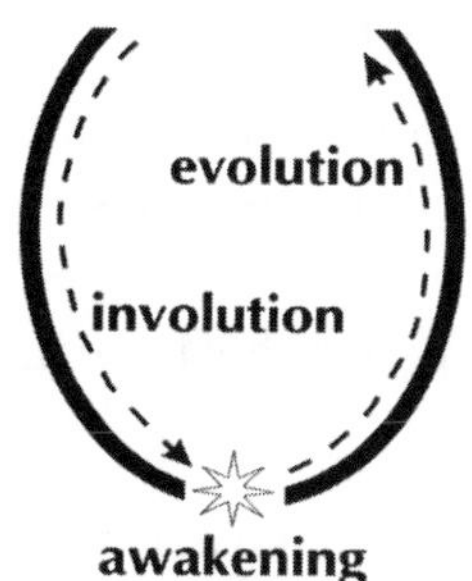

Involution is the descent
of spirit into matter;
evolution is the
return of matter to spirit.

INVOLUTIONARY PERIOD (PLANETARY). A stage or process preceding evolution in which a greater deity (incarnated as a planet) descends deeper and deeper into matter—the "path of descent." Involution of spirit into matter happens so that form may be built and experiences met to facilitate evolution. Descent into matter is typically represented by a series of planets in which the least physical form is a mental globe (a thoughtform in the mind of God); then an astral form (made of the feeling or reflective ethers); then an etheric model denser than the previous form; lastly the physical model that vibrates as matter, the most densely concentrated form, before the ascent reverses the pattern, shedding denseness at each progressive step. *See* Initiation, planetary; Sacred planets.

IPSISSIMUS. Latin for "he who is most himSELF." One who is Self-realized, or SOUL-INFUSED. Guided by the holy consciousness, this one has transformed personality to be the vessel of the Most High.

IRDIN. Inner communication taking form; a cosmic language or vibration now being sensed. All languages on Earth have one or more words in Irdin say the teachers of MIRNA JAD.[4]

IRIDOLOGY. The science of the study of the eye's iris. This diagnostic system reads current and past health conditions from the appearance of the physical eyes.

ISHVARA. The center point equivalent to the cosmic spirit within our being; the moment manifestation begins; a point of manifestation, as though held in the bosom of God. Also, the name of the family home where Nicholas ROERICH lived as a child in Russia, about 100 miles from St. Petersburg.

ISIS. *See pp. 180–3,* Mothers and Goddesses of the World.

ISLAM. A world religion established by MOHAMMED approximately 700 years after the life of Jesus and the beginning of Christianity. A RAY 6 religion of great passion and devotion. Islam considers Mecca its holy city and Jesus a great prophet. It claims a relationship to both Judaism and Christianity and is the fastest growing religion in the world today. *Islam* means "submission" (to God). A principal emphasis of Islam is how to live a holy life, with strict rules for daily life, as presented in its holy book, the KORAN. SUFISM is to Islam as KABALAH is to Judaism—the ESOTERIC message emphasized, rather than doctrines and dogma.

Jacob's Ladder. In Kabalah, the overlay of the four worlds from the densest to the least dense when the appropriate sephiroth overlay each other, thereby creating a stairway from the lowest point (Malkuth on Assiah) to the highest (Kether in Atziluth). Also, in the Old Testament, Jacob's dream experience when he saw the angels descending and ascending the planes of creation, between heaven and Earth. (Gen. 28.12) The esoteric implication is that each soul descended into matter to experience and learn. To reach higher reality, we must build a point of consciousness on each plane, advancing level by level, expressing that awareness wisely in order to ascend.

Jainism. Considered an unorthodox East Indian religion, for it rejects the authority of the Vedas. Jains do not believe in God but that divinity dwells within every soul and perfect souls are venerated as the supreme spirit. The practice of noninjury is particularly stressed. Its founder, Mahavira, was a contemporary of Buddha and the last of 24 teachers who were referred to as Jinas, the conquerors.

Japa. The continuous saying of a mantra or the practice of repetitious praying on beads in the Hindu tradition.

Jataka. The legend of the origin of the Chalice of Buddha, the Tse-bum. From four lands came Four Guardians of the World who offered chalices made of sapphire.[1]

Jehovah. The modernization of Yahweh created from YHVH (Yod Hey Vau Hey), the written form of the tetragrammaton, the holy name of God. Never used by the Hebrew people and, according to Aramaic scholars, an error perpetuated by Christianity.

JESUS. Master of RAY 6 (devotion) and wayshower of the Christian religion. The life of MASTER JESUS is used as the example for the human PATH OF INITIATION in ESOTERIC CHRISTIANITY. *See* Christ, historical.

JESUS PRAYER, THE. "Lord Jesus Christ, Son of God, have mercy on me." A familiar mental prayer taught specifically to still the mind and provide a focus. While often said aloud, many Christian mystics traditionally count its recitations on beads or focus upon it with the breath to hold the mind fixed upon the Christ.

JEWEL IN THE LOTUS. An ancient name given in Eastern spiritual traditions to the soul as that point of consciousness that steps down the energies of the MONAD to the personality and acts as a guiding light. Also referred to as the True Self, the I-Am Presence, the highest aspect of monadic manifestation, the central nucleus or inner flame, the focal point of energy in the SPIRITUAL TRIAD, or the liberated Self who is attuned to God- or Creator-Consciousness. This point of life contains within itself all possibilities, all potentialities, all experiences, and vibratory activities. It embodies the will-to-be, the quality of magnetic attraction, and the active intelligence of its inner Self. *See also* Egoic Self.

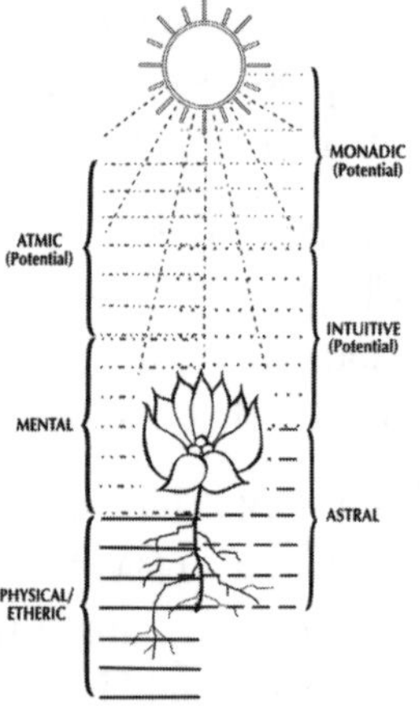

JIHAD. A holy war justified by Muslims against nonbelievers.

JINA. "Conqueror," one who has achieved an exemplary spiritual victory over the afflictions and conditions of life.

JIVA. "A Hindu term for individual soul. Literally, a 'unit of life'."[2]

JIVANMUKTA. One who is a liberated mortal, the perfected human beings who are the Great Ones who model for all the divine possibility. These are the Masters, the Mahatmas, the Adepts, the elder brothers of the human race.

JNANA YOGA. *See pp. 326–9,* Yoga.

JOACHIM OF FLORA. b. Italy, ca. 1132, d. 1202. Christian mystic, Cistercian abbot and mystic, who stated, "The reign of the Father is past; the reign of the Son is passing; the reign of the Spirit is at hand"[3]—now being interpreted as the forthcoming era of the DIVINE FEMININE. While on a pilgrimage to the Holy Land, he was converted by the sight of some great calamity, perhaps an outbreak of pestilence. He spent all of Lent in contemplation and is said to have received celestial illumination for the work of his life. Ordained priest in 1168, he applied himself to biblical study, especially to hidden, or esoteric, meanings. Though never officially beatified, he is venerated as a *beatus.* Dante declared Joachim "endowed with prophetic spirit," but he disclaimed the title. "The mystical basis of his teaching is the doctrine of the 'Eternal Gospel'," in which there are "three states of the world. . . . In the first age the Father ruled, representing power and inspiring fear, to which the Old Testament dispensation corresponds; then the wisdom hidden through the ages was revealed in the Son, and we have the Catholic Church of the New Testament; a third period will come, the Kingdom of the Holy Spirit, a new dispensation of universal love which will proceed from the Gospel of Christ, but transcend the letter of it."[4] He founded an independent and very strict order, the Florians, that flourished briefly.

JOAN OF ARC. *See pp. 246–51,* Saints.

JOHANNINE. A reference to the Church of John wherein inner development or sensitivity is emphasized; John the Beloved is considered the titular head. The Church of Peter is considered the outer, formal development of the church in the world, with St. Peter the founder and the Pope in Rome the titular head.

JOHN THE DIVINE. *See pp. 246–51,* Saints.

JOSEPH OF ARIMATHEA. *See pp. 246–51,* Saints.

JOURNALING. Privately recording freely expressed thoughts in writing; open sharing of thoughts and impressions on paper. Frequently the free-flow triggers latent knowledge and thoughts to be recognized by conscious mind. May precipitate an expanded awareness or experience from the right hemisphere of the brain.

JOY. Agni virtue for Pisces. First we must discern the difference between happiness and joy. Happiness fluctuates by the actions of the outer world; joy is that which sustains us, even while happiness rises and falls. When one touches the energy of the soul, the charge that floods us is joy, also called SAMADHI, the peace that passes understanding.

JUDAISM. The Hebrew religion of the Jewish people. A RAY 5 religion with strict rules for spiritual living, considered the religion of the Aries Age, the "tree" from which Christianity blossomed and grew. Abraham is considered the father of Judaism, Christianity, and Islam. Master Jesus, the Great Initiate and Wayshower of Christianity, came from this tradition and was perceived by some as the expected MESSIAH. Thus, this life and teaching initiated the new religion to become Christianity.

JUDGMENT. In *The Way of God* Rabbi Moshe LUZZATO taught that the main reward is in the world to come and sought to help clarify life and its events. This world, he taught, rewards the wicked with prosperity for their few virtues, while the righteous are punished with suffering for their few faults.

JUDGMENT DAY. Esoterically, the time after death when we review our life and see for ourselves the errors, lacks, or foolishness of our Earth plane experience, generally awakening a resolve to learn or do better at our next opportunity. In some religions a fearful time of judgment by God (or another); however, in esoteric thought, one "judges," or evaluates, oneself to see where one has fallen short of the mark.

JULIAN OF NORWICH. *See pp. 246–51,* Saints.

JUNG, CARL GUSTAV. b. Switzerland, 1875, d. 1961. Psychiatrist and collaborator with Sigmund Freud until their parting over differences concerning the role of sexuality in neuroses. From his research into fantasies and dreams, he affirmed that these arise from the collective unconscious, a "reservoir of memories in each person that precedes historical memory." He saw the archetype as an instinctive pattern, a basic universal image in the dream life of people of many unrelated cultures, and dream symbols as indications of religious intuition and revelation. He found among many religious traditions the symbols of quaternity, trinity, and duality. The animus-anima, or male-female, components together, he believed, expressed the interaction and wholeness that belong to being human. He saw the MANDALA as an archetypal image of the psyche, a symbolic expression of the soul's feeling of total completeness—unity with nature, unity with humanity, and unity with God. He thought the goal of psychic development to be the Self. *Psychic Energy,* 1928; *Psychology and Religion,* 1937; *The Undiscovered Self,* 1957; Autobiography: *Memories, Dreams, Reflections,* 1962; *Man and His Symbols,* 1964.

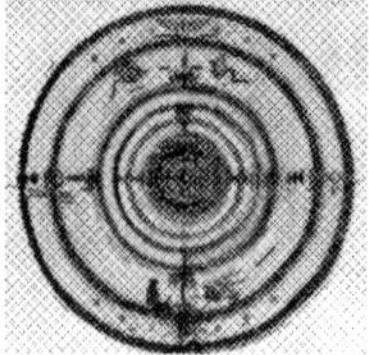

Mandala

As far as we can discern, the sole purpose of human existence is to kindle a light in the darkness of mere being.

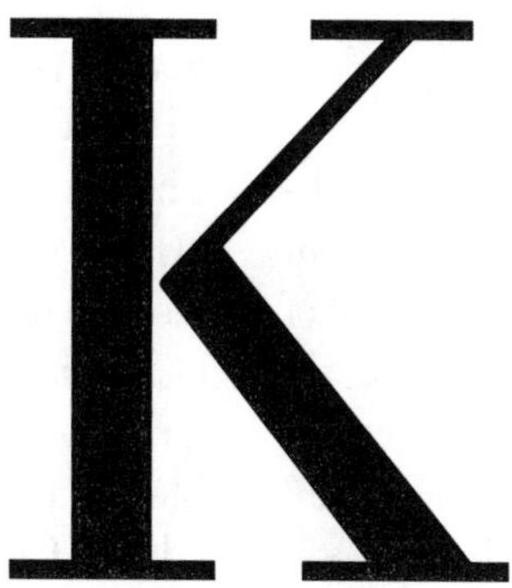

 **KABALAH** (also Kabbala, Kabbalah, Cabala, Qabbalah, et al.). The philosophy of Judaism based on an esoteric interpretation of the Hebrew scriptures and passed down as a secret doctrine to the initiated. Regarded as a primary school of thought, the Kabalah is the "spirit" of Judaism, its mystical part, as opposed to the "letter" of its law, or exoteric Judaism. This hidden wisdom, or theosophy, of Judaism, basically the unity of God and creation, purportedly had its basis in the archaic Chaldean secret doctrine. Kabalah's principal ways are action, devotion, and contemplation which integrate body, heart, and head. The word itself was derived from the Hebrew root, QBL, meaning "to receive," and refers to the practice of relaying esoteric knowledge by word of mouth. By some accounts, this system of theosophy is of celestial origin and was given to early patriarchs through the ministry of angels. Others claim the Kabalah was given to Moses at Mt. Sinai. King David and King Solomon are said to have been initiated into the Kabalah. Rabbi Simeon Ben Jochai was to have written down a portion of these mystical teachings at the time of the destruction of the second temple. His son, Rabbi Eleazar, his secretary, and his disciples gathered his treatises and from them composed the Zohar, meaning "splendor," which is the literary source of kabalism. It is said that at the time of the Dispersion, the Kabalah was preserved through the symbology of the tarot cards.

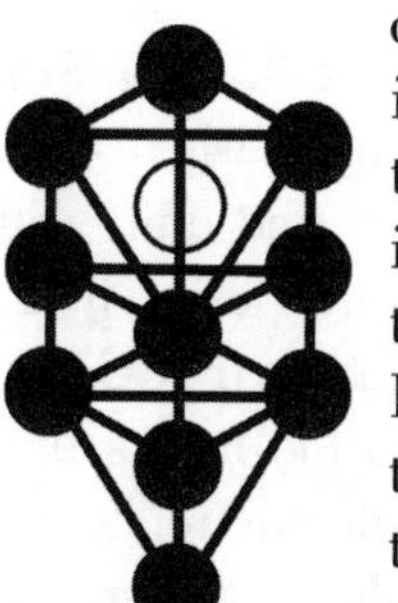

Kabalistic wisdom is divided into two orders. The first draws from above (heaven) and descends to this world—

the linking of various worlds and their emanations. The second begins in this world and travels upward—the levels of prophecy and divine inspiration (entrance to the ZOHAR).

KABALAH, CHRISTIAN. Kabalists believe without question Jesus of Nazareth taught wisdom from the mystical line of Judaism; Paul, Saul of Tarsus, also was acquainted with the Kabalah. Two significant factors influenced the development of the Christian version of Kabalah: knowledgeable Jews became Christians—often under duress—and in Europe Kabalah became fashionable among the intelligentsia as material for theological debate.

KABALISTS. Those who study and practice the Hebrew mystery teachings, the Kabalah, and interpret the hidden meaning of the scriptures.

KADMON. *See* Adam Kadmon.

KAHUNAS. Priests and priestesses of the HUNA tradition, literally "keepers of the secret," originally from Hawaii and the South Pacific. As his lifetime effort, Max Freedom LONG studied, observed, and wrote five volumes, classic texts on the Huna tradition, its philosophy, ideology, and healing concepts.

KAIROS. Higher consciousness. From the Greek, meaning "for a moment when God's will is fulfilled." A response and unity with the source of life and creative force. It has nothing to do with desire to be used by God as much as surrendering unto the holy source and will to which we are already related. A trusting openness establishes a means by which we may accept the fact that spirit can move through each of us, in time coming to acknowledge that the same great identity exists in the other.

KALI. Associated with Agni, the god of fire who had seven flickering tongues of flame. The seventh, Kali, was the most ruinous—a symbol of dissolution and destruction. Kali is also the name of the divine Mother, the consort of Shiva, patron of transformation who destroys ignorance and maintains world order. Kali blesses and frees those who strive for knowledge of God. Bengal, India, is the seat of most of her devotees.

KALI-YUGA. In Eastern teachings, the period of destruction and planetary purification now in progress and from which our world is emerging. *Kali* means "iron" and reminds us of the many challenges the Industrial Age presents.

KAMA. Emotion, desire.

KAMA MANAS. The lower mind or animal nature of a lower or reincarnating ego. This mind is colored by personal desire (ambition/personal love, masculine/feminine—equally selfish).

KARESSA. *See* Disciplines, sexual.

KARMA. Means "to act"; literally, "action, deed, or work." The inevitable order of cause and effect that governs existence at all levels. Influences from current and past lives bring learning experiences and relationships into the present life. The spiritual law, *reaping what we sow,* refers to cause and subsequent effect. Karma may be positive or negative, but—whether reward or retribution—it is always just and trustworthy. As consciousness evolves, karma requires adjustment and/or compensation for all pluses and minuses: individual, group, and planetary.

KARMA-FREE ACTION. Opportunities to express ignorance without penalty, usually in response to a command or instruction given from a being of higher comprehension; we earn merit for obedience even if actions are not wise. For example, if a chela obeys a teachers' erroneous instructions, the teacher receives the karma; the chela receives credit for obedience.

KARMA, LAW OF. Also known as the Law of Cause and Effect. One of seven ever-just universal principles that guide all life in its evolving consciousness: the HERMETIC PRINCIPLES, or Hermetic laws, of 1) mentalism, 2) correspondence, 3) vibration, 4) polarity, 5) rhythm, 6) cause and effect, 7) gender. These collective influences maintain and support life through its processes of creation, orderliness, and destruction. Within the framework of this structure, numerous operations of cause and effect are defined: the presentation of an opportunity to change; the Law of Retribution; physical action; the Law of Forms; the sum total of our acts, both in the present and preceding births. Karma is not a hard and fast rule; it is changeable according to a person's attitude, desire, and ability to learn from experience. To satisfy karma, one must make a shift of consciousness, gaining understanding in a new way.

KARMA, LORDS OF. The Lords of Karma for our system are under the rule of a greater Lord of Karma on Sirius. We are governed by the Sirian Lord of Karma. *See* Celestial Hierarchies.[1]

KARMA YOGA. *See* Yoga.

KARMIC DEBT. That which is due as a result of previous action(s). Cause initiates effect—as related as two sides of a coin.

KARMIC RELATIONSHIPS. The experience of individuals brought together as a result of cause and effect. Such souls may or may not have prior experience with each other but have need of a related experience for their growth. Relationships provide opportunities for each soul to progress, which does not mean each will. One may satisfy the karmic need while the other may or may not, but their coming together provides the opportunity to satisfy certain lessons. *See* Cosmic relationships; Soulmate; Worthy opponent.

KARMIC SHEET. The record of cause and effect already in place.

KATAPHATIC. An approach to spirituality that employs imagining techniques—the forming of mental images of what is not present, used today in most guided meditation approaches.[2] *See* Spirituality, approaches to Christian.

KATHOLICOS. Greek, meaning "Christian universality." Related to the term from which "Catholic" was derived and the foundation for ecumenicism.

KESTREL. This small falcon, also known as the sparrow hawk, was revered by the ancient Egyptians for its ability to fly vertically, as well as horizontally, symbolizing the ascension of spirit in esoteric teachings.

KETHER. The highest-vibrating (first) sephirah on the TREE in each of the four WORLDS of KABALAH, equated with the crown chakra, the highest of all energy centers on the human body. Also known as SHAMBALLA in Agni Yoga and as the highest heaven in Christianity.

KEYNOTE. A sentence or statement providing an underlying theme, tone, or focus. When used as a SEED THOUGHT, the keynote establishes a vibration or tone to magnetize additional individuals, thoughts, and/or insights to itself. It may refer to a thought used during a full moon period or relating to a specific goal or occasion. The keynote of the lunar cycle focuses more tightly upon transitory energies than the seed thought in order to concentrate the sun-moon impact of the period. Also, our fundamental response to life, determined by RAY and SUB-RAY. This inner-soul tone magnetizes a quality and style, our strengths and weaknesses by its presence, and then we strive to overcome the limitations imposed through this collection.

KEYS. As a religious symbol, keys often represent the direction to higher consciousness. A house key may admit or exclude a person. As a psychic symbol, a key, or tool, is being presented to capture our attention.

KEYS, CROSSED. The symbol of the Pope, one key is silver, the other is gold. The silver is said to unlock the mysteries of Israel, the Kabalah of the Old Testament, and the golden key is to unlock the mysteries of the New Testament.

KHUL, DJWHAL. *See pp. 170–1,* Masters, Djwhal Khul.

KIN. Mayan for "light"—a POWER WORD when spoken as a mantra. Often used as an invocation for healing or wholeness by intoning "Kin" seven times in an elongated manner, as K-I-I-I-N-N-N, vibrating the tones through the personality vehicles.

KINESIOLOGY. A technique using touch to determine information stored at a subtle level beneath the awareness of the rational mind.

KINESTHETIC. Relating to the sense of touch, i.e., acknowledging information obtained through the sense of touch.

KINGDOM. Synonymous with "realm" and "world," in esoteric study. In Christian Kabalah, Malkuth, the Earth, the dense world in which we live, is made up of four kingdoms—mineral, vegetable, animal, and human—evolving to manifest a fifth, the kingdom of souls.

KINGDOM OF SOULS. Modern terminology for the "Kingdom of God," as used in the New Testament. The manifestation of a new kingdom of soul-conscious beings who are to emerge by evolution out of the human kingdom into a new GROUP MIND similar to the manner in which the human kingdom came forth from the animal kingdom to establish its own evolutionary path of progress.

KINGDOMS. Each of five kingdoms contributes to the whole:

1. Mineral kingdom comprises the bulk of the physical body of planet

2. Plant kingdom builds the vascular system and supplies food for both animals and humans
3. Animal kingdom creates the astral/passionate dimension of planet
4. Human kingdom contains the mental dimension of planet
5. Kingdom of Souls will be comprised of soul-infused beings and will build the subtle mechanism for Earth to become a SACRED PLANET; the soul (intuitive and atmic) dimension of planet. The subtle inner planes are now guiding humanity toward this INITIATION

KIRLIAN PHOTOGRAPHY. A technique of measuring the emanations of life force radiated by any physical or etheric body. Developed by Semyon and Valentina Kirlian in Russia in 1939, it was first reported in this country by Sheila Ostrander and Lynn Schroeder in their book, *Psychic Discoveries Behind the Iron Curtain.*

KNIGHTS TEMPLAR. A military order of the Temple of Solomon founded by a Burgundian, Hugues de Payns, and Godeffroi de St. Omer, a French knight, in Jerusalem in 1119 to protect pilgrims journeying into the Holy Land. Soon joined by other knights, a religious chivalry quickly formed around the nucleus. Baldwin I, king of Jerusalem, gave them a portion of his palace for their headquarters, allegedly part of the Temple of Solomon.

The secret organization included a hierarchy and clergy, which were exempt from the jurisdiction of diocesan rule. They began in poverty and accepted charity; even spartan food was scarce. They wore uniforms of white mantles for bachelors, black or brown ones for married knights, both with red crosses.

By mid-12th century, the new order had a foot in most Latin kingdoms of Christendom. As its power grew, it became the greatest commercial agency between East and West, amassing immense wealth. Its success aroused the envy of France's Philip IV, who began a series of attacks upon them. With the election of Pope Clement V, Philip could persecute the order.

Rumors about their secret rites were widely circulated. Templars were brought from around the kingdom when a grand process was opened in 1316 in Paris. At the end of a three-year persecution, King Philip seized the whole treasury of the temple in France. Knights were tortured en masse; under extreme brutality, many confessed to alleged atrocities but later repudiated the charges. There was probably foundation to some of the heresy charges for their intimate connection with the East and their long-established order had possibly rendered their Christianity less traditional than that of western Europe. It seems they were "victims of their own arrogance, commercial success and superstitious ignorance of their own contemporaries."[3]

KNOWER. The impersonal level of awareness created through objectivity (WITNESS CONSCIOUSNESS) and spiritual insight. Saturated by soul awareness, it becomes increasingly active with aspects of soul insight to help the integrated personality in the living of life. Contacted most often by contemplation.

KNOWLEDGE BOOK, THE. This "celestial book" began to be dictated to Bulent Corak of

Istanbul, Turkey, Jan. 11, 1981, was completed in 12 years, and has been translated into English. The unique characteristic of *The Knowledge Book* is that it has been dictated by a technique called "Light-Photon-Cyclon," which the world dimension does not know presently. The technique loads the time energy on the letter and meaningful frequencies into the reader. For this reason, the moment you read the book, it is said, you will understand it; afterwards it is erased from memory, only its rough knowledge remaining. Provided you read the book continuously, you may deduce at least 10 messages from a page by bringing different interpretations to the information within it in proportion with the consciousness you have attained. However, you cannot memorize even one page of the book word by word since its program is dependent on time and since "time is shifting."

The dictation claims the frequencies of the Old Testament, the Psalms of David, the New Testament, the Koran, and the philosophies of the Far East have been united with the energy of the Mighty Energy Focal Point and thus have been loaded on all the letters of the book as a total of the six frequencies. However, this book is not a book to be worshiped. It is a guide book—the reason it has been bestowed on planet Earth as a book for all of humanity.

Designed to habituate humanity gradually to the frequencies of universal dimensions, the book thus provides ways to enter these dimensions easily. During this final transition program, three cosmic ages have been recognized for our planet for the salvation of humanity (each cosmic age referenced is one century). Our planet, which has been taken into a very accelerated evolution program since the year 1900, completed its first cosmic age in the year 2000.

KNOW THYSELF. An ancient injunction inscribed over the Temple of Apollo at Delphi. The teachings hold that to know another, we must first know ourselves. From the root word *gnosis* (Greek) and the expression *gnothi seuton* attributed by many to Greek philosopher and scientist Thales (ca. 624–546 B.C.).

KOANS. Contemplative thoughts in the Zen school of wisdom. Paradoxes; seemingly unsolvable riddles.

KOOT HOOMI. *See pp. 170–1,* Masters.

KORAN. The sacred book of scriptures of the Islamic religion.

KRISHNA. A Hindu deity, considered an incarnation of Vishnu, the most celebrated avatar. The reputed speaker and teacher in the BHAGAVAD GITA. Krishna is India's greatest prophet. His teachings have many similarities to those of Jesus. Many Westerners regard him as an incarnation of Jesus. *Also see* Radha.

KRISHNAMURTI, JIDDU. b. So. India, 1895, d. 1986. Perceived by Charles LEADBEATER and the THEOSOPHICAL SOCIETY as the new world teacher. As a young man, he was prepared for the role of MAITREYA by Annie BESANT, president of the Theosophical Society; however, he renounced the assigned role and pursued his own way as author and teacher. Krishnamurti maintained that organized beliefs are "an impediment to inner liberation." *The World of Peace,* 1985.

KRISHNA YOGA. *See pp. 326–9,* Yoga.

KRIYASHAKTI. A Sanskrit term meaning "made in the image and likeness of God." Associated with the SIDDHIS, the rising of the kundalini by a rush of energy and the resulting phenomenal experiences.

KRIYA YOGA. *See pp. 326–9,* Yoga.

K'U. Mayan for "the energy of the Creator residing within a physical body"; *kundalini* in Hindi. Also, part of HUNAB K'U, Mayan for the Creator. This syllable is also found in the middle of Malkuth and the beginning of Kumara and Kuan Yin—interesting to note. Mayan wisdom teacher Hunbatz Men believes the Maya gave the term "KUNDALINI" to the Hindus. This syllable salutes the "god" energy honored by wisdom traditions of the world.

KUAN YIN. Means "she who hears prayers." This BODHISATTVA OF COMPASSION is a beloved image in the East. *Also see* Mothers and Goddesses of the World.

KUKULCAN. One of three names used in Central and South America for the FEATHERED SERPENT, most common in the Yucatan. The other names are QUETZALCOATL and GUCUMATZ.

KUMARAS. Literally youths, designated Holy Youths; defined as a class of Solar Pitris (lords) who provided direct assistance to humanity. The seven highest self-conscious beings in the solar system; the sum total of intelligence and of wisdom. At the head of our world evolution stands the first kumara (SANAT KUMARA) aided by six other kumaras, three exoteric and three esoteric, who are the focal points for the distribution of the force of the systemic kumaras; guardians of the power of planets; arbiters of nations and continents; judges of GOOD AND EVIL.[4]

KUMARA, SANAT. *See pp. 170–1,* Masters Sanat Kumara.

KUNDALINI. The evolutionary force within humanity. Literally, the "circular power," defined as an electric, fiery, occult, or fohatic power. The primal energy of the universe, some part of which lies coiled in potential form at the base of the human spine. When channeled upward through the body to the brain, it is associated with the state of enlightenment. As this powerful spiritual energy awakens from dormancy, it rises along the spine, activating the CHAKRAS, igniting change, stimulating life activity. The awakening of this mystical force is related closely to the process of spiritual evolution which leads toward final union with the Divine, or God-realization. The transpersonal being-energy lies dormant in

humans, often called serpentine; the evolutionary force is enclosed and at work in matter. The Holy Spirit, or PARACLETE, stimulates the kundalini and facilitates its ascent.

KUNDALINI YOGA. *See pp. 326–9,* Yoga.

KURUKSHETRA. The battleground, burning ground, a point of friction between personality and spirit for transmuting forces and forging new awareness. A second major stage occurs as the ARHAT completes burning ties to the human condition.

KUTHUMI, MASTER. *See pp. 170–1.*

KWANZA. A cultural celebration of African ancestry; a nonreligious, nondenominational, family celebration. Founded by Dr. Maulana Karenga, this American tradition—a seven-day feast, Dec. 26 to Jan. 1—is based on African rituals and an evolving respect for diverse cultures. At its core are seven principles: unity, self-determination, collective work and responsibility, cooperative economics, purpose, creativity, and faith.

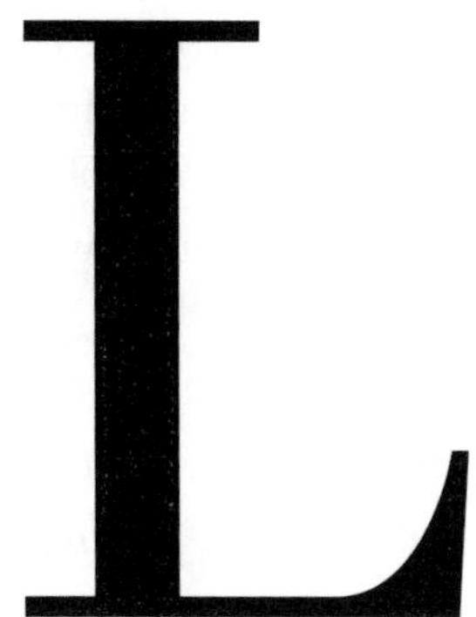

LABORATORY. As an Agni term, a reference to the planes and worlds of creation wherein lessons, expansion of consciousness, learning and growing are perpetual.

LABOURS OF HERCULES. *See p. 150.*

LABYRINTH. An intricate single-path design of a specific number of circuits from the outside to the center and back out (not to be confused with a MAZE, which may have dead-ends or false turns). The classic design calls for seven circuits, but some have only four and a popular modern version has twelve. Evidence of the labyrinth dates to about 3,000 years ago. Often considered a doorway to the higher worlds, at the center of this "invisible temple" is the heart (or goal, or womb, or sun). An excellent tool as a walking meditation for physical, emotional, mental, and spiritual harmony and balance. Often constructed over LEYS. Circuits are frequently associated with the CHAKRA system or the ZODIAC.

LAMA. The title for "teacher" given to monks of a sect of BUDDHISM originating in the Tibetan-Mongolian part of the world.

LAMSA, DR. GEORGE. b. Assyria, 1892, d. 1975. Translator of the PESHITTA BIBLE from Aramaic, the language of Jesus and of Lamsa. "Uniquely fitted for the task to which he devoted the major part of his life. . . . native of ancient Biblical lands, where he lived until World War I. Until that time, isolated from the rest of Christendom, his people retained Biblical customs and Semitic culture which had perished everywhere else. This background, together with his knowledge of the Aramaic (Syriac) language, enabled him to

Labours of Hercules

From Greek mythology, a path of discipleship depicted through Hercules' labours as he astrologically enacted the life history of every aspirant. Hercules means "the incarnated, not-yet-perfect Son of God." Hercules was a son of humanity and of God. The twelve labours are archetypes of zodiacal influences depicted as duties Hercules must perform:

Aries, the capture of the man-eating mares

Taurus, the capture of the Cretan bull

Gemini, gathering the golden apples of the Hesperides

Cancer, capture of the doe or hind

Leo, the slaying of the Nemean lion

Virgo, seizing the girdle of Hippolyte

Libra, the capture of the Erymanthian boar

Scorpio, destroying the Lernaean hydra

Sagittarius, killing the Styphalian birds

Capricorn, the slaying of Cerberus, guardian of Hades

Aquarius, cleansing the Augean stables

Pisces, the capture of the red cattle of Geryon

As each drama's challenges are met, the candidate is rewarded by receiving its strengths or positive character traits. (Based upon the Alice A. Bailey book of the same name; other sources sometimes change the order of the Labours.)

recover much of the meaning that has been lost in other translations of the Scriptures."[1] He also authored several books of commentary on biblical and cultural insights to biblical teachings: *Old Testament Light; New Testament Origin; Gospel Light; More Light on the Gospels; Idioms of the Bible.*

Land of milk and honey. A term used to encourage the quest for the holy. Teachings affirm, all mystics come from the same land and speak the same language. That land (level of consciousness) flows with the milk of understanding and the honey of wisdom. It is the kingdom of heaven and the promised land of all God-realized people.

Lao Tzu. Chinese philosopher, mystic, and sage of 6th century B.C., regarded as the inspiration of Taoism. Lao-Tzu taught how to keep apart from the world, yet to remake it by following the Tao, the Way—the way of harmonious interaction with the environment, of evolution, of life, of reason, of the cosmos. The *Tao Te Ching,* the "Book of the Way and of Virtue" and the bible of Taoism, seems to presage Christian Gospels with admonitions to "Repay evil with good" and "Walk in the Way and you shall find peace."[2]

Tao never does anything,
yet through it,
all things are done.

LAST RITES. Usually thought of as connected to death, last rites are truly an invoking of life force for right action. A blessing to benefit the soul and body assisting the indwelling consciousness to proceed toward right action, which may manifest in renewed health or easy transition. Last rites may include COMMUNION, the use of holy oils, holy water, candles, and prayers to assist in the creation of a sacred atmosphere. One of the seven SACRAMENTS of Christianity. *See* Healing rites.

LATENS DEITAS. The term Thomas Aquinas used for the God-Within or the CHRIST-WITHIN—biblically, the "HOPE OF GLORY."

LAUREL CROWN, OR WREATH. A crown woven of laurel leaves or the equivalent that indicates the initiate's peace of mind when purification of the astral (feeling) and mental natures is achieved. The second of three crowns to be won on the path of initiation. *Also see* Crown of thorns; Lotus crown.

LAYA YOGA. See Yoga.

LAYING-ON-OF-HANDS. Techniques of spiritual healing wherein direct contact is used in transferring energy.

LEADBEATER, CHARLES WEBSTER. b. Cheshire, England, 1854, d. 1934. Author, clairvoyant, student of theosophy, and colleague of Annie BESANT in the early work of the THEOSOPHICAL SOCIETY. In 1893, under spiritual guidance, he began what was to become a life-long investigation into the phenomenon of CLAIRVOYANCE. *The Masters and the Path,* his most important work, describes what Dr. Besant called the "Perfected Men, the Masters, the Men beyond Mankind," and steps to be taken on the spiritual path to reach that eminence, from probation to acceptance as disciples, and beyond. In later work with Besant, the phenomenon of auras was explored, and the authors reproduced in color many different forms they had seen—some evoked by listening to music, some apparent in people experiencing a specific human emotion, some even seen emanating from buildings where crowds had gathered. Both Leadbeater and Besant maintained that Gautama, the BUDDHA, had previously incarnated as other great spiritual teachers: HERMES, ZOROASTER, and Orpheus. Leadbeater is considered to have been a pioneer in the evolution of new thought exploration. *The Masters and the Path,* 1946; *Thought-Forms,* 1911; *The Chakras: A Monograph,* 1972.

LEADERSHIP. Agni virtue for Cancer begins with the concept, "The hand that rocks the cradle rules the world." Then we are told, "We build a lighted house and dwell therein." The third step, we realize "The whole world is our home." Leadership is advancement in these processes, holding the light for the planet.

LEAD TO GOLD. The heavy lead of ignorance must be refined into the diaphanous gold of illumination. Generally associated with ALCHEMY, an old term for TRANSFORMATION.

LEFT HEMISPHERE OF BRAIN. One part of the NEOCORTEX (the third brain). Its unique characteristics are rational thought, the ability to analyze, judge, and evaluate. Relates comfortably to the outer world and its secular standards. The goal of the disciple is to be able to utilize both left and right hemispheres

THE LAWS[5]

A law is but the effect of the continued intelligent activity of the Life aspect as it works in conjunction with Matter. . . . A law is in reality the effect of the life of a greater entity as it encloses a lesser within its living processes.

LAW OF ATTRACTION. Determines the present allegiance, governs the immediate condition of the planetary types, and is concerned with the consciousness or the soul aspect.

LAW OF CORRESPONDENCES. The interpretive law of the system, which explains God to man.

LAW OF DESTINY. . . . affects the Ashram and the Hierarchy as a whole, and neither is under the Law of Karma, as usually understood. This Law of Destiny has been brought into being since the foundation of the Hierarchy on Earth; it is the result of the pledged and united dedication to service which is the outstanding note of the united Ashrams. It is therefore a sevenfold law, for it takes on the seven colours of the seven rays, the seven qualities, modes and methods, techniques and energy expressions of all the seven rays. It is therefore, as far as humanity is concerned, free from all evil, because it is selflessly motivated and is—in a measure—a difficult law to comprehend. Pure destiny, devoid of all evil intent, is an enigma to the average disciple. It appears to contravene other more familiar laws. As the race of men achieves increasing purity in the three worlds, this pure destiny will become correspondingly effective.

LAW OF ECONOMY. Determines the past, conditions the planetary consciousness, and concerns itself with the form or matter aspect.

LAW OF LOVE. In reality but the law of the system in demonstration on all the planes. Love was the impelling motive for manifestation, and love it is that [sic] which keeps all in ordered sequence; love bears all on the path of return to the Father's bosom, and love eventually perfects all that is.

LAW OF MAGNETIC ATTRACTION. Through this law atoms of substance are drawn together, manipulated in a rhythmic manner and held together in form.

LAW OF MAGNETIC CONTROL. Governs the control of the personality by the spiritual nature, via the soul nature. The Law of Magnetic Control holds sway paramountly on the buddhic plane, and in the development of the control of this law lies hid the control of the personality by the Monad via the egoic body.

LAW OF MATERIALIZATION. Sometimes called the Law of Hidden Radiance. This law concerns the Light which is in humanity and the covering of that Light, in time and space, in order to produce its intensification and subsequent radiation so that, through humanity, light may eventually reach all forms of divine expression. Through humanity's achievement, and through the conquest of darkness by light, the light of consciousness in all forms must be brought to a condition of a "shining glory which will irradiate the planet, and shine forth into the world of planets as a testimony to the glory of The One."

LAW OF REBIRTH. Deals with the taking of an outer garment or physical form. Reincarnation.

LAW OF SACRIFICE. This law means the impulse of giving. The whole secret of the doctrines of "the forgiveness of sins" and of the "at-one-ment" lies hid in this simple phrase.

LAW OF SACRIFICE AND DEATH. This law is the controlling factor on the physical plane. The destruction of the form, in order that the evolving life may progress, is one of the fundamental methods in evolution.

LAW OF SERVICE. The third Law of the Soul, which is intended to govern all soul activity. The science of Service is a definite technique of at-one-ment. This Law of Service may not be escaped. Evasion brings its penalties, if that evasion is conscious.

LAW OF SYNTHESIS. Determines the future, certifies the goal, and is concerned with the life or spirit aspect. The law of a coherent will-to-be persisting not only in time and space, but within a still vaster cycle.

LAW OF VIBRATION. The basis of manifestation, starting on the first plane. This is the atomic law of the system, in the same sense that on each of our planes the first subplane is the atomic plane.

and to be able to discern which is appropriate for a needed application. This particular talent is called DISCERNMENT.

LEMNISCATE. A symbol meaning "eternity," looks like the figure 8 on its side; also known as the "infinity sign."

∞

LEMURIA. A mythical land—said to predate Atlantis, located in the Pacific Ocean region—that met with destruction. Some inhabitants are said to have survived by fleeing to other areas. Lemurians are considered a ROOT RACE or GROUP MIND that emerged from the etheric and formed the first physical bodies of humanity especially sensitive to the astral/ feeling nature. This ancient area often is referred to as the Land of Mu.

LEMURIAN ROOT RACE. *See* Root race.

LENT. The term comes from the Middle-English word for spring meaning "lengthening of days" and is a season beginning Ash Wednesday and lasting 40 days, not counting Sundays. Christians spend extra time reviewing their lives, their lessons, and planning how they may return God's love by helping others. The color for Lent is purple, in memory of the heavenly king and to demonstrate repentance for the mistreatment of Jesus.

LET THE DEAD BURY THE DEAD. (Matt. 8.22) Let the unawakened—not physically dead but not alive to higher consciousness—take care of the dead. Those on the same level of consciousness are to care for each other. Let those who are aware care for those similarly awakened to the greater life. Awareness separates people into either dead or alive.

LEVI, ELIPHAS. b. Paris, 1810, d. 1875. A kabalist, often considered a teacher of BLAVATSKY who became well-known in Europe for his OCCULT writings on magic, which some felt were excellent, yet many experts questioned. He was influenced by Francis Barrett and was a part of the OCCULT society of both Paris and London. He was particularly intrigued by MESMERISM (new in his day), the KNIGHTS TEMPLAR, and NECROMANCY. He believed he conjured APOLLONIUS OF TYANA several times.

LEVITATION. A phenomenon of overcoming gravity by the power of an altered state of consciousness. Stories are told of several saints—both Eastern and Western—who experienced spontaneous levitation, e.g., PADRE PIO.

LEYS. Currents of energy flowing within the Earth, invisible to scientific instruments but discernible through attunement. Just as the human body has energy channels (MERIDIANS), so the body of MOTHER EARTH has energy lines. Just as every living being is animated by the life force, so too is the Earth. Ancient stone monuments are sometimes felt to be grand acupuncture needles—gathering, purifying, and increasing these teeming energies. DOWSING and other sensitivity techniques are used to detect, measure, and evaluate leys. (The more common term, "ley lines," is redundant.)

LIBERAL CATHOLIC CHURCH. Dates back to 690 A.D. when St. Willibrord began a mission to North German tribes from Utrecht, Holland, and is tied in its earlier years to the Free Dutch Church, later becoming the Old Catholic Church. James Ingall Wedgwood (of the famous stoneware and pottery family) was the great missionary bishop of the Liberal Catholic Church, an active member of the THEOSOPHICAL SOCIETY, at one time its General Secretary—which complicated matters for the young church. He was elected Presiding Bishop, and in concert with the newly consecrated C. W. LEADBEATER, translated a Latin liturgy into English. "Old Catholic Church" was renamed "Liberal Catholic Church" in 1918 to reflect a growing emphasis on freedom of thought. They emphasize a joyous and uplifting approach to worship.

LIBERATION. A traditional name for God-realization or enlightenment; the discovery of ultimate identity, resolution of all dualities into cosmic unity. To be free from limitation, oppression; or release from false beliefs and negative personal perspectives. Such emancipation allows one to advance toward evolution of human potential. *A peace that passes understanding.*

LIFE ATOM. The individual spark of divinity—the MONAD—that nurtures the unfolding soul.

LIFE IS GOD'S GAME. Respectfully acknowledges our participation in a structure of principles, laws, and goals set into motion by the Creator. This Eastern expression is never used disrespectfully; it is uttered with esteem and awe, recognizing we have no control over the great happenings of the planet and the universe.

LIFE REVIEW. An evaluation of one's existence, whether done while alive or from the spirit perspective after physical death. Events and lessons are recalled and examined in the light of expanded knowing, thus experiences and connections between the present incarnation and others may also be revealed. Also called "death review."

LIGHT. A degree of electrical energy which, when condensed, forms matter. In spiritual terminology, light is a synonym for the cosmic mind-stuff from which all was created, used to designate wisdom, creativity, understanding, insight, and knowing—all of which illuminate.

LIGHT BEING. A spirit of high vibration or holy presence, without form and often without specific identity. Related to near-death experiences and contact with the light and apparitions.

LIGHT BODY. The body created through the transformation of the astral body, lifting desire into aspiration and leading the disciple into TRANSFIGURATION. Transfiguration is achieved as the electric fire of the SPIRITUAL TRIAD pours into personality levels through the processes of advanced meditation and contemplation. The illumination of the spiritual triad acts upon the HIGHER MIND, stimulating the release of the lights of the atoms of the three vehicles (physical, astral, and mental) of personality, producing enlightenment or transfiguration. In this achievement the astral body is cleared of its GLAMOURS, and the ILLUSIONS of the mental body are purified, allowing the individual to stand in the radiance of the spiritual triad. The human soul makes itself ready to wear this "robe of glory." As the light body is woven or built, the astral body, blending into the mental body, disintegrates, and we are able to enter into more direct communication with the intuitional plane, home of the soul. Light, as illumination, produces the ability to mediate with matter, referred to as RAY 3; the color generally attributed to Ray 3 is yellow.

LIGHT, EXPERIENCES OF THE. A variety of occurrences that expose the brain to the light of higher consciousness. Examples are (but not limited to) profound meditation, near-death experiences, apparitions or visitations, out-of-body experiences, and other hard-to-explain mystical phenomena.

LIGHT WORKERS. Those who perceive the light of higher consciousness and seek to both express and amplify that consciousness in harmony with that awareness, working to improve themselves for the good of all.

LIL. A Mayan power word used for purification, healing, and calling in the light—practiced in a series of prolonged tones as L-I-I-I-L-L-L and repeated at least seven times in each cycle, invoking subtler energies to aid in transformation.

LILY. This symbol of virginity, purity, and chastity when portrayed with saints or sages also represents the Virgin Mary and the ANNUNCIATION of Jesus, or at Easter the purity of Christ and the Resurrection, life renewed.

LINEAR. Regarding the rational thinking, left-brain process, that which is analytical, directing, unwavering, straight to the point. Considered a more masculine style of thinking.

LINE OF TENSION. Two points—the soul and the personality—create a line of tension upon which each person (and humanity) evolves. This pull between higher and lower forces choices and consequences, thus learning and evolution occur.

LINGUISTIC BRIDGE. A technique which moves the client in an altered state of consciousness from present to past by way of a phrase, or series of words, a saying, or expression repeated by the subject and charged with thought or emotion. (Move backward, please, to another time when you found yourself saying, "________ ______." What is the situation?) As defined and practiced in PSYCHOGRAPHY.

LIPIKAS. Lofty DEVAS who serve as deities, guiding human beings in working with the forces of nature. A common reference, LORDS OF KARMA, is not quite appropriate, for these are more the points of consciousness in the mighty forces that move as currents through embodied life, allowing individuals to respond to the flow. These devas record the use of energies in each person's higher nature, hence the karmic account to be balanced in the process of evolving toward higher awareness. In the Christian Bible the recording angels; from the Sanskrit *lipi,* meaning "to write" or "scribe."

LIS-FATIMA. A PLANETARY CENTER in the etheric spread over a circle that includes Western Europe and the Iberian Peninsula.[3]

LITURGY. From the Latin *liturgia,* meaning "public service." Usually the minister or priest has a defined role in a service, ritual, or observance offered for participation of a religious congregation.

LIVING ETHICS. This Agni term implies living according to the high standard of spirituality we set for ourselves, i.e., to fulfill the themes and disciplines to which we are committed. The Agni yogi is to live out the teachings in the midst of daily duty and responsibility. AGNI YOGA is often called "Ethical Living."

LIVING IN THE NOW. An expression to encourage staying anchored in the current events of life—one moment at a time, one day at a time—rather than dwelling on the past or exaggerating expectations of the future. Being with the opportunity each moment presents; also known as "being fully present."

THE LORD'S PRAYER

Traditionally believed to be a uniquely Christian prayer, the Lord's Prayer (Matt. 6.9–13) was derived in its entirety from the Talmud, from which Jesus taught his disciples. The following ancient Jewish prayer was divided into ten parts, corresponding to the ten sephiroth of the kabalistic Tree and the four worlds.[4]

> Our father which art in heaven, be gracious to us. O Lord, our God: hallowed be thy name, and let the remembrance of thee be glorified in heaven above, and upon the earth here below. Let thy kingdom reign over us, now and forever. Thy holy men of old saith, Remit and forgive unto all men whatsoever they have done against me. And lead us not into temptation, but deliver us from the evil thing. For thine is the kingdom, and thou shalt reign in glory, forever and forever more.

LODGE. The organized Hierarchy of humanity; also "White Lodge" or BROTHERHOOD.

LOGOIC PLANE. The divine point of Creation from which all arises. The One.

LOGOI, THE SEVEN PLANETARY. Seven great CHOHANS serving the Christ and the Plan, guiding and guarding planetary life and all levels of consciousness evolving within this domain. All religions reference these guiding Wise Ones who serve the SOLAR LOGOS in specific terms, i.e., Christianity, the "ELDER BROTHERS BEFORE THE THRONE"; Buddhism, the Seven Great RISHIS.

LOGOS. The Greek title given to the Creator of All; literally the "Word," reminding us that the Word went forth and set all into motion.

LOKAS. In Hindu and Buddhist thought, the heavenly planes; often reported to be populated by the devas (Hindu) or angels (Jewish, Christian).

LONG, MAX FREEDOM. The best known authority on the Huna tradition of the ancient Polynesians. This teacher and businessman with a background in psychology arrived in Hawaii in 1917 and spent 14 years learning from his native friends. His works also provide personal guidelines for self-improvement and exposed correlations between the Huna faith and religions of today. *The Secret Science Behind Miracles,* 1948; *Secret Science at Work,* 1953; *The Huna Code in Religions,* 1965.

LORD OF CIVILIZATION. The MANU of a ROOT RACE who watches over and directs the forces of evolution in building a civilization while that wave of consciousness is in power; also known as Lord of the World.

LORDS OF COMPASSION. Those tender influences of the higher world assist in time of trials, particularly working with feminine energies under the DIVINE FEMININE influence. The term comes from its correlation with the Bodhisattva of Compassion, Kuan Yin, and the Eastern tradition.

Lords: of Fire, Flame (or Love), Form, Individuality, Karma, Mercury, Mind, Wisdom. *See pp. 43–5,* Celestial Hierarchies.

Lords of the Law. Three guides—the Manu, the Bodhisattva, and the Mahachohan—constitute the spiritual triad of the planet. These beings hold the blueprint for the unfolding Plan.

Lots Of Vital Energy. These words form the acronym LOVE and imply love is much more expansive, much more powerful, much more life-sustaining than readily acknowledged. Love is the energy of the Creator that sustains and evolves all creation: Lots Of Vital Energy. As the heart opens, we become generous and sharing, a conduit for the higher forces of life and empowered to step down this life-giving flow for the benefit of all. It is the nature of the disciple to love and to care.

Lotus. A flower of the East of great beauty, a sacred symbol of Hinduism and Buddhism. It grows in swampy areas with its roots in muck, holding itself above the water and open to the light, a representation of the soul that opens to the illumination in full array of beauty and breaks through into clarity—after personality, with its roots in Earth matter, is nourished by the emotional waters of the astral nature and guided by the structure of the mind. It represents both beauty and achievement.

Lotus crown. A representation of the flowering of the high consciousness of an initiate as the energy of soul and purified personality blend and blossom. Acknowledged also as "the fragrance of the soul," it makes itself known. The third crown to be won on the Path of Initiation. *Also see* Crown of thorns; Lotus crown.

Lotus posture. A specific Hatha Yoga posture used for centuries as a resting or centering point.

Lotus with three pearls. This logo has been adopted by Sancta Sophia Seminary (founded by this author) to symbolize a wholeness of consciousness that can emerge from the integration of three pearls of wisdom: Kabalah, Esoteric Christianity, and Agni Yoga.

Lourdes. Site of an apparition of Mary, who guided Bernadette (d. 1878) to dig in the earth, whereupon a healing spring came forth. In 1858, Our Lady appeared 18 times from Feb. 11 to 16, and miracles continue to this day, still a place of pilgrimage in southwest France.

Love-wisdom. Exemplifies "Thinketh in the heart, feeleth in the mind," a goal for the spiritual aspirant who is integrating the three vehicles (physical, astral, mental) of personality. An appropriate reminder: "Behind emotion lives feeling and behind intellect is knowing." The two points of duality (feeling

LOVE

Five levels of love—EROS, PHILIA, SELF-LOVE, HUMANUS (humanitarian), and AGAPE—correlate closely to the chakras. Since the evolution of love is its principal work, Christianity is often considered a school of BHAKTI YOGA; while closely related, it is not. Bhakti is a RAY 6 approach, Christianity a Ray 2 approach born in a Ray 6 age. We could say Christianity has a Ray 6 personality and a Ray 2 soul.

Love is the Agni virtue for Leo. Not just attraction or emotion but the flow of divine energy that sustains all life. LOTS-OF-VITAL-ENERGY of the soul. A cool stream of unconditional energy emitted to bless all.

The Five Manifestations of Love

EROS. From Greek mythology Eros, the god of love, son of Aphrodite, is a symbol of the sum total of the human instincts of self-preservation—more specifically, love as a sexual or instinctual nature. The aggregate of pleasure-directed life instincts whose energy is derived from the libido, it is self-fulfilling love.

PHILIA. Derived from the Greek, *philos*, this word signifies the love for one's family, group, or friend, personal affection or fondness, or social sympathy. Our brotherly/sisterly bonds include national, religious, or racial identity. Here begins self-love—as self-esteem. Now the quiescent self is nurtured and begins to become conscious of self and the needs of self. In due time, this new awareness—self-love—will choose to "do unto others as we would have others do unto us."

SELF-LOVE. The bridge between the passionate energy of the lower chakras and the higher. We must develop self-love in order to raise the vibration of our being and to open our heart center (in cooperation with others) or prepare ourselves to experience higher love.

HUMANUS. This Latin word means "humanitarian," denoting the bonds of affection that move us to nurture and embrace another simply because we are all members of the one human family. Humanitarian describes those people who are devoted impersonally to the welfare of all human beings, distinguished as the love of soul for soul, and philanthropic (loving humankind). Its true expression is unconditional love.

AGAPE. This Greek word depicts spontaneous, transformative love expressed without calculation of cost or gain to the giver or merit of the receiver. This potent spiritual love expresses the fiery spirit as God's own love for humanity—the love the Holy Spirit pours forth upon and through people of high consciousness, that humanity may experience the divine love nature as it is nourished to become FULLY HUMAN–FULLY DIVINE.

and knowing) must integrate until we love with the mind and know with the heart. Then love-wisdom, RAY 2, results in maintaining that which has been created. Its color is blue.

LOWER BODIES. The three VEHICLES of expression vibrating in the dense world of personality, i.e., physical form, emotional nature, and lower mental body.

LOWER MIND. The three lower levels of the MENTAL BODY where old, instinctual thinking of the species, as well as personal programming, exists, as do the imprints of early unconscious life and the home of the rational processing mind. These lower vibrating frequencies establish the foundation for thinking in personality. Also known as the NONSELF, indicating an identity with personality rather than Creator.

LOWER SELF. *See* Basic self.

LOW SELF-ESTEEM. A BARRIER to soul expression and illumination created by distorted thoughts and feelings regarding the nature of our being. This confused attitude of judgment blocks the light of the soul from penetrating to awareness, misrepresenting the value of our contribution. It is called a GLAMOUR, indicating a highly charged emotional scar that warps our ability to perceive our true value.

LUCID DREAMING. A simultaneous dual state of consciousness: dream-state and awake-state. Awareness of dreaming while asleep and within the dream, often with the ability to control the dream action or content.

LUCIFER. Called a fallen angel in the Bible, a LIGHT BEING who led souls to experience in the denser world in the DESCENT INTO MATTER, or what is commonly known as "the fall."

In Kabalah one of the highest of the archangels. Lucifer refused to submit to Adam—as even Michael, captain of the Hosts, had done. Thus Lucifer, whose name means "bringer of light," was given the title of Samael, God's poisoner. As Samael, he is assigned to Geburah, whence he continues his work. Also known as Satan, the tester, the destructive aspect of divine judgment and leader of the hosts that test creation. Even Lucifer is to be redeemed, according to the Kabalah, at the End of Days in just proportion to his state of submission.[5]

"Dr. John Algeo, president of the Theosophical Society in America, points in 'Lucifer: What's in a Name?' (The Quest, September-October 2001, p. 162-3) that the way 'Lucifer' got to be used as a name for Satan is 'a complicated story.' Isaiah 14:12 reads 'How you are fallen from heaven, O day star, son of the morning! How you have been cut down to the ground—you who laid low the nation' (Dead Sea Scrolls Bible, the oldest known version of the Bible). This actually refers to the King of Babylon, who had the title 'Day-Star,' which is a name for the planet Venus, the first planet or star seen in the morning just before sunrise. Hence the king was also called 'son of the morning.'

"When the Hebrew scriptures were translated into Latin, the word lucifer, meaning 'light bearer,' was used. The reference to falling from heaven, Algeo notes, was Isaiah's sarcastic way of putting the Babylonian king in his place. In effect Isaiah was saying to the king, 'You think you are so high and mighty, but look at you now—you, the so-called Day Star, have fallen from your place in the heavens and have yourself been cut down to the ground.' Early Christian interpreters misunderstood the expression 'fallen from heaven.' Instead of recognizing it as a figure of speech playing on the destruction of the wicked King of Babylon, who called himself the Day Star, they thought it was a literal statement about a fall from heaven and identified the event with the legendary fall of Satan. And thus, Algeo says, 'Lucifer,' a term for the planet Venus, became one of the names of Satan. It was a mistake caused by misunderstanding figurative language as a literal statement."[5]

LUMINOUS. Emitting light, especially self-generated light.

LUNAR BODY. A physical form in which the history of human EVOLUTION is stored in its PERMANENT SEED ATOMS. The moon is the celestial "lunar body"; however, the human ASTRAL BODY is also referred to as the "starry" or "lunar body."

LUNAR INITIATION. A period during the involutionary process in which the development of humanity's astral senses was emphasized. Progress was achieved by an evolving humanity becoming aware of the Plan through unfolding astral senses so that humanity could develop feeling and learn to guide personal emotion rather than be ruled by the instinctual nature. Those who achieved INITIATION became the forerunners for mass consciousness, as with every level of evolution.

LUNAR MYSTERIES. The ARCANA or unseen patterns, powers, and factors that ruled the planet throughout the INVOLUTIONARY PERIOD. Through these great laws and forces, humanity and all the kingdoms were guided and stimulated in such a way that all life was pulled into the denser desire nature. The unconscious, passionate, instinctual nature empowered in this lunar phase still vigorously affects all life, primarily on the subconscious level.

LUNAR MYSTERY TRAINING. Taught workers to set aside the conscious mind and to subject one's unconscious nature to the use of another, usually a discarnate. In earlier stages of human evolution, trance work was an important tool to secure guidance from higher realities. The medium would vacate her or his physical form by withdrawing to the astral plane and a discarnate could enter from that plane and speak or act through the physical body.

LUNATIC. From the Latin word *luna,* meaning "moon," indicative of the belief that fluctuations of sanity relate to phases of the moon. One so affected by lunar forces that the rational mind suffers from a loss of control and from imbalance.

LUZ. Mayan for "light," as in enlightenment, the light of high consciousness—an awareness that comes as the blessings of a golden age. Mayan WISDOMKEEPERS often speak with reverence about the Aquarian Age as the "time of Luz" or the "Age of Flowers."

LUZZATO, RABBI MOSHE. b. 1707, d. 1746. An Italian kabalist said to have possessed one of the most brilliant minds of several centuries and the most profound understanding that any mortal could attain.

LYCANTHROPY. The belief that certain people can change into animals, such as wolves, seals, cats, as related in myths, sagas, and fairy tales. Also includes the ability of birds to change into women. This concept appears in Asia, the Middle East, Europe, and in the Americas, particularly by the Inuit of the far north. *Also see* Shape-shifting.

Macrocosm. The great universe, or cosmos; the big picture or magnificent view of life from an all-inclusive perspective. A system that reflects one of its components on a large scale, e.g., the cosmos reflects the life of humanity; humanity reflects the life of a single person; a single person represents the life of a single cell, only functioning on a larger scale. Macrocosm/MICROCOSM reflects the law of AS ABOVE, SO BELOW.

Maggid. Hebrew for "inner teacher."

Magi. Wise ones who practiced ancient wisdom, astrology, and so on. The root word from which *magic* is derived. *Magician* denotes one who could control his or her consciousness and experience altered states of consciousness. An old term for transformation of consciousness, the term *magick* was replaced by *alchemy.*

Magic. The art and practice of shifting consciousness at will. The conscious direction of mind and resolve to accomplish a particular goal. The old alchemy term, spelled *magick,* meant "transformation of consciousness." *Black magic* is the manipulation by a disciple of spiritual training and talent to one's selfish desires or purposes. *White magic* is the disciple's use of talents and training to serve all and for the uplifting of consciousness. One may personally benefit as well, but the purpose must go beyond one's own advantage.

Magical virtue. A reference to the energy of mystical teachings that correlates to LOVE—Lots Of Vital Energy. Also, the excellence held as divine potential within each of us—the power of the soul that awaits awakening.

Magnetic healers. A category of WORLD SERVERS integrating the forces of head, heart, and ajna (brow center) to promote health and wholeness. One's personal psychic, or magnetic, energy from the etheric body is used, rather than drawing subtler energies of higher frequencies, as in spiritual healing.

MAGNETIZED CONSCIOUSNESS. When charged with aspiration and a passionate desire to know, we can focus, by an act of will, on a word or phrase (i.e., a SEED THOUGHT) that becomes the nucleus of all attention. Being so charged, this word or phrase begins to draw to itself additional thoughts and ideas of the same essence, or vibration, like a magnet. Variations of this practice can be used by those in spiritual training to build virtues within the nature, to signal one's desire to be taught by the inner teacher, or to gain conscious awareness of contents from the CLOUD OF KNOWABLE THINGS.

MAGNUM OPUS. Latin for a "great work"—one's most notable achievement, soul purpose, or goal. Referred to in spiritual teachings as freedom from the WHEEL OF REBIRTH for individuals and as the release of the whole of humanity for the collective. The greatest work is for the whole, and we each seek our part in it.

MAHA. Sanskrit for "great."

MAHABHARATA. The great epic of Hindu scriptures of which the BHAGAVAD GITA is only a part.

MAHACHOHAN. The Great CHOHAN, the Lord of Civilization, the head of all ADEPTS, and the lord of RAY 3 of active intelligence, the intelligence aspect of deity. As head of the third great department of the PLANETARY HIERARCHY, he presides over the activities of the four minor Rays, their MASTERS, and the synthesizing Ray. This Great Being—responsible for manifestation of the principle of intelligence for an entire world period—assumes the duty of developing a great civilization. Also, the embodiment for the planet of the third aspect of deity: intelligence.

MAHA KUMBHA MELA. An age-old Hindu festival (earliest recorded date, 500 A.D.) held at the confluence of the Ganges, Yamuna, and Sarasvati rivers in India every 12 years with a special emphasis on every twelfth gathering, or every 144 years. In January 2001, the largest-ever Mela occurred with multitudes worshiping, meditating, and sharing generally with the intention of creating a collective consciousness to revitalize nature and for individuals to cleanse their impurities to become better people.

MAHAMUDRA. In Buddhism, a series of practices and movements that leads to a state of enlightenment. *Also see* Mudra.

MAHASAMADHI. The great rest or sleep; the great peace, death, or higher reality. *Maha,* "large" or "great"; *samadhi,* "peace."

MAHAT. HOLY SPIRIT (feminine); that spiritual power residing in matter that responds to the charge of FOHAT (masculine) and results in creative activity.

MAHATMA. An Eastern title of great respect, meaning "Great Soul," acknowledging an enlightened MASTER, proclaimed generally by the followers of the wise and holy one, e.g., GANDHI.

MAHAYANA. The second of three schools of Buddhism uses two classes of scriptures: the Sutras for its ethical teachings and the Tantras, in which are given the practices of YOGA, meaning "union." Teaches the rejection of DUALITY; seeks merit and enlightenment for the sake of all sentient beings. *See other two schools:* Hinayana; Vajrayana.

MAITREYA, LORD. A visible proxy on Earth of the invisible deity; often a symbol of mind or thought, especially divine mind. In Eastern spiritual traditions the guiding consciousness that permeates humanity with an awakening of the God-Within. Specifically, the anticipated incarnation of the BUDDHA to restore DHARMA, expected to occur some 2,500 years after Buddha's passing. The time given for the reappearance is at the beginning of the AQUARIAN AGE. This WORLD TEACHER, head of HIERARCHY, is also known as BODHISATTVA, Imam Mahdi, and Prince of Peace, as well as in ESOTERIC Christianity, the Christ—teacher of angels and of humanity.

MALA BEADS. A set of uniform beads used in the Eastern tradition upon which prayers are counted.

MALEVOLENT BEINGS. Inhabitants of other planes that are not all sweetness and light (just as on the physical plane) but seek to penetrate human psyches in order to stop our evolutionary progress and enslave us to their will. These beings are said to appear in enticing ways to tempt us from the evolutionary spiritual path.

MALKUTH. The tenth SEPHIRAH on the kabalistic TREE equates to the dense world of form (lowest vibration on the Tree) called the "kingdom," comprising the CHALICE into which the energy of the higher world descends, finally arriving in the densest form of each of the four WORLDS.

MAMMALIAN BRAIN. A specific area of the BRAIN that relates one thing to another and that develops social responses and bonding. *See* Neocortex; Reptilian brain; Three-brain concept.

MAN. This English word is derived from the Sanskrit *manas*, "to think." Thus, the "race of man"— denoting the thinking, evolving kingdom—is not a reference to the male gender but to the mind being. Each human is a combination of masculine and feminine energies and, under the guidance of mind (manas), learns how to use these forces to benefit all kingdoms evolving on planet Earth.

MANA. Hawaiian term for PSI energy.

MANAS. Sanskrit, meaning "to think." Refers to the mind-principle becoming dual in the human condition—divided into higher manas (ABSTRACT MIND) and lower manas (rational, CONCRETE MIND). Emanations from the mental plane distinguish the human from the lower kingdoms: reasoning faculty, intelligence, understanding, individual mind, and powers of attention and choice. Humanity is to evolve the mind for the planet. *Kama manas* refers to LOWER MIND, the Sanskrit *kama* meaning "desire," while *manas* refers to HIGHER MIND.

MANASADEVAS. These high-ranking DEVAS—also known as agnishvattas or SOLAR ANGELS—embody the will or purpose of the Logos and are the cosmic prototypes of solar angels, working in the higher realms. These messengers, it is suspected, could be from the mental plane. Since the term is ancient, the question is raised: Are they the inhabitants of the mental plane that we recognize today as the META-TERRESTRIALS (SPACIALS) of our planet? Although not proven, it is easy to make a case for this proposition.

MANASAPUTRAS. *Manas* meaning "mind" and *putras* meaning "sons" translate literally as the Sons of Mind; also termed the Solar Pitris (Fathers). These great benefactors of the human race stimulated the dormant mind-principle during the Lemurian ROOT RACE. The Sanskrit name given to the SOLAR ANGEL, in its own body on the abstract levels of the mental plane.[1]

MANDALA. A diagram, imagined or actually depicted; typically a circle or square containing a central symbol. A symmetrical design used for meditation and contemplation, intended to balance and attune one's energies to a higher influence. Representing the enclosure of sacred space and penetration to the divine center, it assists the integration of cosmic intelligence. Both a pattern of existence and a system upon which meditative visualization is based.

MANIFESTATION. Bringing forth a concept, thing, or event into a readily perceived form, moving from the invisible to the visible, from abstract to concrete. Similarly, a form in which someone or something, e.g., individual, divine being, or idea, is revealed on the denser planes as apparition or dense body. Also, the action of materializing the realities of subtler planes.

MANSER, ANN. b. Montana, 1896, d. 1977. Spiritualist teacher, artist, and co-author of the *Pages of Shustah* lessons and the *Pages of Shustah Card Book* with Cecil North. Widely known for her AURASCOPES—written, detailed analyses of individual force fields surrounding both human beings and animals. With no information other than the name, sex, and, if animal, the species, Ms. Manser was able to determine the health, karmic involvements, problems, degree of spiritual development, evolutionary status, past conditioning, and future indications insofar as they are impressed upon the auric field of the personality under investigation. Her entire adult life was dedicated to studying the areas of auras, color, force fields, evolutions of the kingdoms, and the Kabalah. She became the first private teacher of this author from late 1965 to 1974, and of others as well. Ms. Manser was an active supporter of the Temple of the Living God in St. Petersburg, FL, an interfaith, nonsectarian religious and educational church-center, researching metaphysics and philosophy, with emphasis upon uniting religion and science.

MANTIC IMAGES. Symbols or pictures drawn from the subconscious, commonly used in dream work and psychoanalysis; often prophetic. Particularly useful with past experiences, signs of internal health and healing, products of personal experience, distorted prejudices. *Also see* Images; Phosphoric images; Telesmatic images.

MANTRA. A word or phrase arranged rhythmically to generate certain vibrations when sounded—spoken or sung. The sound itself is understood to express and be one with the divinity invoked by POWER WORDS. The mantra, repeatedly spoken to the subconscious—aloud or silently, in prayer, incantation, or meditation—focuses heart and mind upon a guiding principle to program new awareness. Mantras associated with a specific energy, teacher, or group are intoned to receive spiritual guidance and strength, e.g., *OM MANI PADME HUM* or *OM NAMAH SHIVAYA.*

MANTRA YOGA. *See* Yoga.

MANU. Also known as Lord of the World or Lord of Civilization. The office in the PLANETARY HIERARCHY filled by a great one who serves as founder and ruler of a holy PLAN and builder of a human ROOT RACE, continents, flora, civilizations, and nations. Guides the work of the BODHISATTVA and the MAHACHOHAN for a particular period, destroying and rebuilding forms through which SPIRIT is to evolve. The Manu represents and embodies one of three aspects of divine manifestation, the RAY 1 aspect of creative will. The three great guides of the human race are the Mahachohan (Ray 3 aspect), the Bodhisattva (Ray 2 aspect), and the Manu.

MANVANTARA. The Creator's out-breath, or a period of cosmic activity, as opposed to the Creator's in-breath, or PRALAYA, a period of dissolution. The rhythm and cycle of manifestation and dissolution.

MANY ARE CALLED, BUT FEW ARE CHOSEN. Tibetan saying that—similar to this quote from Matt. 22.14, "Many profess religion, but few practice it"—reminds us that we must align to the higher, inner regions, not just be intellectual in our approach or devotion. The Way is realized by carrying out daily that which comes from the divine within in order to bring our Earth life into harmony with the essence of Self. As this is realized, we are admitted to higher states of consciousness. ALL are called to high consciousness, but only a few prepare (make themselves ready) for service.

MARIAN APPARITIONS. Certain visitations of Mother Mary approved and declared by the Vatican to be "valid."

MARIAN YEAR. A year dedicated to Mary for her intercession on behalf of humanity; e.g., 1987 was declared by Pope John Paul as the Marian Year for Peace, as have a number of years historically.

MARIEL. A spiritual healing system developed by Ethel Lombardi of Locksport, IL, in the 1980s, using energies of the divine feminine for hands-on healing. She received the procedure from spirit and taught the approach to many throughout the U.S.

MARRIAGE. One of the seven Christian SACRAMENTS, this holy ceremony is conducted by a minister or priest as God's representative. Two who have prepared spiritually take vows of love and dedication to each other before the community of believers of which they are a part. An intimate relationship, legal and spiritual, wherein each party pledges to both physical and non-physical levels of union. Each commits to support and participate in an agreed-upon lifestyle, allowing the other a degree of control over one's life. Marriage is a discipline referred to in 2 Cor. 6.14 KJV: "Be ye not unequally yoked together with unbelievers." Esoterically, this means the initiated should not be wed to the uninitiated because values and goals are incompatible. *See* Soulmate.

MARTYR. Greek, meaning "witness" or "testimony," "bearing allegiance to the faith to the end of one's life." Often used for one who loses his or her life for a cause or faith.

MARY MAGDALENE. A female disciple of Jesus from the small village of Magdala, which means "strong tower." Modern research often implies Mary Magdalene to be a favorite of Jesus or that a more personal relationship may have existed than is acknowledged in the Bible. Perhaps her role was that of being a "tower of strength."

MARY, MOTHER OF JESUS. Presently very active in both the inner and outer worlds, providing guidance and protection for those who align themselves to the Divine. "Mother Mary" is a Christian term of endearment for the mother of Jesus, who gave her to all of humanity when he was on the cross and commanded of John, "Behold, thy Mother"—translated to mean "humanity, this is your mother." Mary personifies the divine feminine archetype. Also called the Blessed Virgin, Queen of Peace, and Mary of Bethlehem, after the Ascension of Christ, she served the Christ ministry as esoteric head of the tradition until her translation and assumption into heavenly spheres at the close of her Earth life. Action and contemplation are summed up in Mary, the model Hebrew mother—wholly receptive, yet wholly self-giving. This "Queen of Heaven and Earth" is a MASTER OF RAY 7. Proclaimed "THEOTOKOS, Mother of God," at the Third Ecumenical Council in Ephesus (Turkey) in 431. *See pp. 180–3,* Mothers and Goddesses of the World.

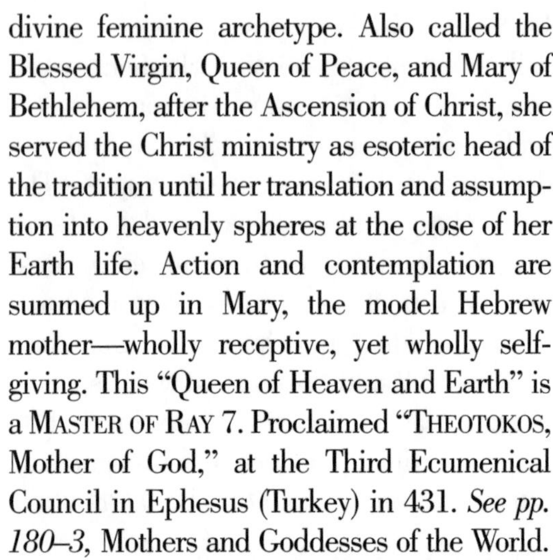

MASCULINE MYSTERIES. *See* Mysteries, masculine.

MASHIAH. A Hebrew word meaning "sacred person" or "legitimate ruler," not identifying one as the Messiah but as a revered rabbi or reb—a sage.

MASLOW, ABRAHAM. b. New York City, 1908, d. 1970. Humanist psychologist who postulated that the higher needs that appear to arise in the human being after basic survival needs are met are the result of an inner pressure toward a fuller expression of being, a self-actualization, in the same natural and predestined sense that an acorn may press toward becoming an oak tree. Maslow and his contemporaries saw the technique of TRANSCENDENTAL MEDITATION as a means of achieving extraordinary human growth, creativity, and fulfillment. Maslow is known for his definitive HIERARCHY OF NEEDS and understanding of the evolving human nature. *Toward a Psychology of Being,* 1968;

Religions, Values, and Peak Experiences, 1970. *See illustration p. 119.*

MASONRY, MASONS. *See* Freemasons.

MASS THINKING. A group mind-set that produces form and acts as programming on the collective until some break free.

MASTERS DJWHAL KHUL, HILARION, JESUS, KUTHUMI, MORYA, ST. GERMAIN, SERAPIS. *See pp. 170–1,* Masters.

MASTERS OF WISDOM. Members of the ADEPT brotherhood who have evolved through the human experience and now act as guides for humanity. Also called ELDER BROTHERS, their names generally are unknown, and they may be women or men. C. W. LEADBEATER says at least 60 Masters of Wisdom are incarnated on Earth at any given time.

MATERIALISM. A belief, or "ism," that asserts nothing of value exists that cannot be explored by the five physical senses, thus denying the nonphysical.

MATERIA LUCIDA. An Agni term. We are introduced to the idea of space, not as empty but as a womb of subtle ethers having received the sparks of FOHAT and nurtured them to high consciousness. Materia Lucida, also called a "curling chaos," is revealed as the matter aspect of the original energy-matter; so all matter originates in primal form, the true nature of which is light, consciousness, and love. In vol. 1 of her *Letters* Helena ROERICH says, "Creative Materia Lucida serves as an embodiment for the high spirit." She reminds us that Materia Lucida is the outer garment or covering for the spirit on all levels of manifestation; form is then a covering over a "seed of psyche-life." The waves of luminous matter contain the consciousness of the RAYS which dawn as enlightenment occurs.

MATERIA MATRIX. An Agni term. Primary matter that does not penetrate to the earthly sphere due to the whirling of infected lower layers. But FOHAT, as granulation of primary matter, can reach the earthly surface in the form of sparks by the outflow of radiant matter, MATERIA LUCIDA. Realized sparks of fohat and streams of Materia Lucida are benevolent, for they imbue the spirit with the urge of evolution.

MATTER. Densified spirit that coagulates into building blocks containing receptive energy or intelligence awaiting ignition.

MATTHIAS. Replaced Judas Iscariot, making the Twelve complete again after the death of Master Jesus.

MAYA. That which does not exist and is therefore illusory, the world of appearance. The GLAMOURS, ILLUSIONS, or DELUSIONS perceived by limited mind. The phenomenal universe; unreality; all that is finite, subject to decay and change; all that is not eternal and unchangeable. The agreed-upon collective hypnosis of a culture, religion, or society that seeks to regulate the guidelines of behavior for its people. In the Hindu tradition, the great cosmic force responsible for the phenomena of material existence.

MAYA (THE CULTURE). An ancient Meso-American high civilization about which little is known. Today many Mayan people have lit-

MASTERS

One who, having mastered the lower levels of self, has developed an individual consciousness or recognition of oneness with God. Called "Master" of high consciousness because he or she accepts students to guide their personal development by sharing energy and wisdom. In the Western esoteric tradition, a fifth degree initiate, one who has achieved self-mastery: the personality vehicle—now reworked and purified—expresses the higher nature. Eastern tradition refers to the third degree initiate as "Master." Many Masters—teachers from both spirit and physical dimensions—stand ready to give guidance to any and all individuals who seek it.

DJWHAL KHUL, MASTER. "The Tibetan." A teaching Master of RAY 2 who has provided humanity with nearly 10,000 pages of teachings through his AMANUENSIS, Alice A. BAILEY, with whom he was in subjective communication from 1919 until she died in 1949. His telepathic dictations conveying esoteric thought were subsequently published in 20 volumes by Lucis Trust, NY.

HILARION, MASTER. Master of Ray 5, science and exactness. He is said to have established spiritualism as a way humanity may perceive and study ongoing life in the nonphysical realms. Believed to have been St. Paul in a previous incarnation; today at work in Egypt. Communicant: David Anrias, *Through the Eyes of the Masters,* 1932.

JESUS, MASTER. The Great Initiate who serves as the wayshower for the Christian tradition and example to all of humanity; a Master on Ray 6 of devotion. Believed to have been Joshua, son of Nun, in a previous incarnation, Jesus of Nazareth surrendered his body to be used by the Christ—teacher of angels and of humanity—thus becoming the historical Christ. Thought to be living today as a Master in Syria. *Also see* Christ.

KUTHUMI, MASTER. A Master on Ray 2, love-wisdom, the Ray on which the Lord Christ vibrates. Love-wisdom is to integrate heart and mind and originates as will-to-unite. PYTHAGORAS in one of his previous incarnations. Resides today at Shigatse, monastery of the Tashi Lama in Tibet, to the best of public knowledge. (Also spelled Koot Humi.)

MORYA, MASTER. The CHOHAN of Ray 1, creative will; *also* known as El Morya. He is said to be the influence encouraging the establishment of mystery schools throughout the world in this period of transition. A Rajput prince believed to have occupied the Mogul Emperor Akbar's body in a previous incarnation. He now resides at Shigatse, according to modern revelations.

ST. GERMAIN, MASTER. Master of Ray 7 of orderliness. Comte de St. Germain, *also* known as Count Radzicki, is said to have appeared first in 1561 and to have subsequently undertaken several incarnations, particularly among THEOSOPHISTS, and is now an ascended Master. Historical research suggests he was, at different times, a European nobleman, an alchemist and mystic, and a leading spirit of the ROSICRUCIANS, early advocates of the doctrines of theosophy and the development of psychic powers. The "I AM" Religious Movement begun by Guy Warren and Edna Ballard is a form of theosophy that envisions the ascended Masters known as the Great WHITE BROTHERHOOD, particularly St. Germain, as guiding the world toward a new, enlightened age. Biography by Isabel Cooper-Oakley: *The Comte de Saint Germain,* 1912.

SERAPIS, MASTER. Master of Ray 4, harmony through conflict, and the painter Paul Veronese in a previous incarnation. He has communicated that in the coming new Age of Enlightenment, "art, once handmaiden of religion but in this materialistic age completely divorced from it, will again fulfill its highest function, that of inspiring reverence in the beholder." Together, The Venetian and Serapis will train the artistic mind of the future.

VENETIAN, THE. Master of Ray 3, active intelligence, now working with the devic evolution. In telepathic communication with author David Anrias, he has said that in the imminent merging of Uranus and Aquarius, "humanity has possibilities of spiritual development so vast and comprehensive as to precipitate a great change in the future of the whole race, when a new religion will be evolved uniting the spiritual and the scientific elements."[2]

Pictures courtesy of David Anrias, *Through the Eyes of the Masters* (New York: Samuel Weiser, Inc., 1971).

tle understanding of their most illustrious past (200 B.C. until A.D. 900); however, it is believed the Mayan culture followed the Olmec with great influence. They calculate their history in a much longer cycle. Developers of a civilization of city-states and specialists in mathematics, time-keeping, and astronomy, they left an array of hieroglyphs, calendars, temples, PYRAMIDS, and cities to be studied. Today the Maya continue to live in the Yucatan, Guatemala, Belize, and Honduras. The term *Maya* means "mother."

MAYAVIRUPA. Hindu term for the illusionary body, such as an apparition, created by a MASTER to use for service when desiring to interact with the physical plane. In English, we would say the ETHERIC or densified LIGHT BODY used to appear on the more material plane. The Taoist tradition calls this form the "diamond body."

MAY THE HOLY ONE BE RESTORED UNTO HIS THRONE. A kabalistic prayer, the inner meaning being, "May the holy consciousness be realized by humanity." We could say, "May the collective consciousness of humanity be Christed." This prayer was taught by Aryeh Kaplan, author of *The Sepher Yetzirah.*[3]

MAZE. A path full of dead ends, barriers, twists, puzzlement, and so on—literally and symbolically. While a LABYRINTH has only one path to be followed, the maze has specific choices to be confronted.

MEANDERING. A creative manner of thinking and living—wandering, free-flowing, indirect.

MEANINGFUL COINCIDENCE. JUNG'S synonym for his created term, "SYNCHRONICITY."

MECCA. The birthplace of the prophet MOHAMMED in Saudi Arabia to which the Muslims pay homage. A pilgrimage to the Great Mosque in the center of Mecca, asked of the faithful of Islam at least once in a lifetime, is called a "hajj." Many Muslims on HAJJ visit Medina also, where the prophet is buried.

MEDICINA CATHOLICA. Latin for the universal medicine that heals all disease.

MEDICINE MAN. Shaman or healer, as called by most indigenous peoples.

MEDICINE WHEEL. A circular sacred design created by North American Natives representing the invisible temple wherein life is experienced. Many believe the circle symbolizes the universe and the center of the Earth. Directions and elements are to be acknowledged as one enters an openness to spirit reality where the inner and outer become one. Shamans usually perform the rituals, although a variety of needs could cause a medicine wheel to be constructed. Usually they are dismantled after rituals are completed.

MEDITATION. A practice resulting in contact with high consciousness; the transfer of the human consciousness into that of soul awareness. A science that helps us attain a direct experience of God, usually through periods of silence in which the work of concentration, contemplation, and gestation brings about soul growth. Techniques vary; however, the goal is to be centered and receptive to spiritual knowledge and insight through contact with the God-Within or high levels of consciousness. The technique of attuning our physical, emotional, and mental bodies to the spiritual source.

MEDITATION, ACTIVE. A form of meditation in which the mind, rather than passive, is poised, alert, and focused upon a thought or word. The practitioner intends to become magnetically charged by a SEED THOUGHT or an ideal in order to attract droplets of divine energy and wisdom or streams of creative ideas, to pierce through veils to the essence and quality of a thought. Specific techniques in which energies are focused bring about a breakthrough of understanding and "knowing." The goal is to penetrate and learn from the CLOUD OF KNOWABLE THINGS, the mind of God, or the higher storehouse of wisdom, including an awareness of spiritual activities, with increased perceptions of the world and our participation in it. Subtle concepts harmonically attuned to the chosen THOUGHT-FORM rush into the mind prepared to receive these energies. Active meditation is particularly helpful to achieve SOUL INFUSION and is advised after developing a receptive consciousness—an open and ready mind—and after mastering passive meditation. Considered an advanced form of meditation.

MEDITATION, PASSIVE. This approach involves a relaxed openness with a gentle surrender toward complete peace and sense of being without much effort and incorporating deep relaxation. The primary work of this gentle, open, and receptive procedure is to build the cup mechanism, often a goal of first practices. Generally used to connect outer consciousness to the brain's RIGHT-HEMISPHERE capabilities. Ultimately this cup develops into the CHALICE into which the droplets received in active meditation can become transformed into conscious comprehension. *See* Meditation, active.

MEDIUM. An individual who allows his or her personality VEHICLE to be receptive to temporary habitation by an intelligence—good or bad—without form. Often confused with "PSYCHIC."

MEDIUMISTIC. A particular sensitivity to ASTRAL energies or influences. People often discover they are easily influenced or take on the feelings or thoughts of others; usually believed to be a result of LUNAR MYSTERY TRAINING or the lack of development of appropriate psychic boundaries. This sensitivity can be the result of past-life service rendered as a medium. Certain bodies tend to be particularly affected by the presence of entities, or DISCARNATES, often destabilizing one's health.

MEDIUMSHIP. The process of cooperating with discarnates, delivering messages, or receiving extrasensory impressions, most often relaying them to others, usually in an unconscious state.

MEDJUGORJE, YUGOSLAVIA. Apparitions of Our Lady Maria began June 24, 1981, when she appeared to six children, ages 10 to 16. Our Lady continues today (2002) to visit young adults and present messages for the public. As of now, the Roman Catholic

Church has declared this to be an APPARITION in question.

MEDULLA OBLONGATA. The conducting medium whereby the spinal cord contacts other portions of the brain; part of the feminine branch and located at the skull's base. The greatest number of the body's nerves are located here, making it a chief depository of nerve force, and therefore, a primal focus for spirit inflow. Streams of nerve force intersect in the medulla, causing it to become the "Golgotha" of the body, the place of crossing. Nearby, however, is the Tree of Life whose ascending spires or branches appear to lift symbolically toward the pineal gland, or crown of the head. Thus we bear within ourselves the way of calvary and the glory of the Resurrection.

MEISTER ECKHART, JOHANNES. *See* Eckhart.

MELCHIZEDEK. Considered an angel of the order of virtues, the priest-king who received a TITHE of spoils of war from Abraham (Gen. 14.17–24). The mysterious being known as King of Peace and Priest of the Most High God who initiated Abraham. Kabalah teaches, he is "without father or mother, knowing neither death nor the end of days." Head of the MYSTERY SCHOOL where Abraham studied. Adam, Melchizedek, and Jesus are said to be of the same lineage. Jesus is designated a priest forever, according to the order of Melchizedek (Heb. 5.10). Legend has it that he had used the GRAIL, the chalice of wine, in his sacred ritual, and Jesus re-enacted the rite.

MENORAH. The seven-candle candelabrum specified by God on Mt. Sinai. Made of pure gold to represent the unified and unchanging divine world of emanation, it is composed of the central axis of grace, right and left arms of Mercy and Severity, 10 plus one sephirah positions, and 22 decorations. Said to represent the exoteric form of the esoteric scheme of existence, it is to be contemplated as well as utilized in worship.[4] In the OCCULT tradition, the menorah reminds us of divine light shining forth in seven RAYS.

A nine-candle menorah (eight candles, one for each day of HANUKKAH, and one to light the others in sacred ritual) used in Jewish homes during Hanukkah—a reminder of God's grace and protection and the salvation of the people by the victory of the Maccabees, who led the struggle for independence against the Syrians, restoring the Temple of Jerusalem to the Hebrew people in the late 6th century B.C.

MENTAL BODY. Layers of mind built of frequencies, each of which contains a record in thought established as the soul evolves. The mental vehicle reworks, synthesizes, and integrates with the BUDDHI as awareness expands.

MENTAL BRIDGE. A REGRESSION technique that moves the client in an altered state of consciousness from present to past or future through use of mental imagery, visualizations,

or symbology; generally used in psychoanalytic therapies. As defined and taught in PSYCHOGRAPHY.

MENTALISM (HERMETIC PRINCIPLE OF). "The ALL is MIND; the Universe is Mental" of *The Kybalion*[5] embodies the belief that all matter is the mental creation of "THE ALL," in whose mind we "live and move and have our being." *See* Hermetic Principles.

MENTAL PLANE. A band or frequency of vibration of mind-stuff that organizes into ranges of knowing from instinctual and subconscious to intellectual and then subtle, abstract, intuitional knowing. The physical, mechanical organs of the brain (REPTILIAN, MAMMALIAN, NEOCORTEX) are developed in humanity to translate the subtle frequencies of mind into various functions. The mental sub-planes (from the highest) are divine contemplative; inspiration and holiness; Cloud of Knowable Things; point of contact for Solar Angel, high self; thoughtforms, personal and others; glamours and illusions; and old karma and inherited patterns of thinking. Also called the mental sheath of an individual. *See* Planes, cosmic.

MENTAL RESIDUE. False concepts, distortions, or ideas no longer of service carried forward from bad programming, teachings, or previous lives. Often called "ILLUSIONS"—false truths masquerading as real.

MENTAL SHEATH. The field of mental energy of an individual (or group, etc.) that expands by attracting MIND-STUFF and organizing it through the efforts of the individual mind of each user, forming both a higher and lower mind of seven levels. The mental sheath contains all developed layers, each of which may be clear, distorted, or some of each.

MENTOR. Guide, teacher, GURU, or confessor. Someone who "knows" and takes another into apprenticeship.

MERIDIANS (OF PHYSICAL BODY). Streams of energy that flow through physical body to maintain the distribution of ch'i, or life force, to all systems, organs, and cells so that the vehicle of matter can relate to inhabiting spirit. If imbalanced or out of harmony, the flow is affected.

MERKEVAH. Means "chariot"—the LIGHT BODY in which one can move freely in non-physical dimensions. Yoredei Merkevah are those who descend in the chariot. Ma'asey Merkevah is the work of the charioteer.

MESMERISM. Recall technique useful for exploring non-rational levels of mind. Rediscovery began with the work of Franz Mesmer (1734–1815), an Austrian physician, and the technique laid the foundation for HYPNOTISM. Wisdom teachings suggest many earlier civilizations used altered states of consciousness and mesmerism/hypnotism in their cultures. The ATLANTEANS are said to have developed it to a high degree.

MESOAMERICAN. The mid-continental area of North and South America, more specifically the Mayan region that links the native traditions of both Americas.

MESOPOTAMIA. Translates "land between the rivers" (Euphrates and Tigris), the biblical land of Shin'ar, where the first cities arose.

(Gen. 11) The olden part, SUMER, is where the oldest urban cities of the world were found—Ur, Nippur, Lagash, Isin, Larsa. Under the kings of Ur, Sumer was the center of an empire that encompassed the whole of the ancient Near East.

MESSENGER. An individual who delivers the word, or message; "word" often refers to a prophet. "Messenger" is the term preferred by this author, rather than "WALK-IN."

MESSIAH. In the Hebrew tradition, the Anointed, the long-awaited holy one to be sent to the people by God the Almighty.

METAMORPHOSIS. The process of adaptation one experiences—consciously or not—as awareness and experience change. Ignited from within, the outer form is the last to reflect the transformation and adjust to a rebirth, a new consciousness. Consider the butterfly.

METANOIA. This Greek word, like TOB, means much more than repentance; it refers to a shift from ego-centered to trans-egoic consciousness. Its greater meaning acknowledges a shift in consciousness when one is aware of a higher level—meta, "higher than," and *nova,* "mind"—and becomes sensitive to HIGHER MIND or to the Holy Spirit in traditional settings. In esoteric thought, HIGH SELF, Soul, Transactional Self, or WITNESS CONSCIOUSNESS. *Also see* Enlightenment, stages of.

METAPHYSICS. The study of laws higher than the physical and dealing with universal truths to teach humanity to align with the purpose of life.

META-TERRESTRIALS. Spacials who incarnate in the MENTAL PLANE of Earth and project themselves into denser planes. Truly native to planet Earth, they vibrate at a subtler frequency than devic or human consciousness and are thought to be responsible for much of the UFO phenomena to which humanity is currently awakening. They often transfer into the human evolution to learn compassion and caring. After transferring to humanity, they are obligated to complete both their native evolution and the human INITIATIONS. *Also see* Evolutions; Extraterrestrials; Manasadevas; Spacial beings.

METATRON. *See* Archangels.

METEMPSYCHOSIS. An ancient Egyptian doctrine indicating the immediate passage of the soul at death into another body. Both metempsychosis and TRANSMIGRATION are incorrectly used for the word REINCARNATION. *Also see* Pythagoras.

METHEXIS. "[F]rom a Greek verb meaning 'to share in', the transference of material from one stratus of intelligence to another . . . . when in a state of mental dissociation or DETACHMENT; that is when a part of the mind lacks clear coordination with the rest of the mental system."[6]

METTA. Equality, oneness, wholeness. A PALI word meaning "loving kindness, the capacity to see the goodness in ourselves and others."

MIASMA. The distorted consciousness of one or a collective that must be cleared before higher mind or soul can reflect its knowledge to personality.

MICHAEL. *See* Archangels.

MICHAELMAS. Sept. 29 is the annual Christian date to reflect upon the justice of God and the protection provided by Archangel Michael for those who invoke his aid. At this celebration the earlier part of the year is reviewed to observe what karmic seeds have been sown and what has been gained in soul growth.

MICROCOSM. The little universe manifesting in and through the physical body of the human. Minute bits of consciousness that live, work, and express within this miniature universe. Acknowledgment of the smallest, seemingly microscopic particles in the processes of life and of the roles they play. *Also see* Macrocosm.

MIDDLE-ROAD PATH. Having experienced both great riches and extreme austerity, the BUDDHA pronounced the middle-road path the safest route for most people as they advance to higher states of consciousness.

MIDHEAVEN. In astrology, the highest point of a circular chart, the point between the ninth and tenth houses.

MIKVEH. A ritual bath to remove negative forces.

MILLENNIUM. A period of 1,000 years. Currently, we are in the third millennium of Christianity.

MIND. The registration of knowing for an individual or group, ranging from the lowest point of survival instinct to the subtlest waves of consciousness held in MIND-STUFF. In the human realm, mind extends from instinct to intellect to intuition, expressing itself through various ways of knowing. Brain is mechanism, not mind. *See* Group mind; Mental plane; Three worlds of mind.

MINDFULNESS. A dynamic one-pointedness demanding a broad level of concentration more difficult than narrower types of attention; often associated with meditation. Mindfulness as a goal becomes a state of self-observation that helps us see personality and/or the NONSELF from a higher perspective. Implicit in: *I am not the body, I am not the emotions, I am not the mind; I am the user of the body, the user of the emotions, the user of the mind. I am the soul.* Mindfulness expands the spiritual nature and provides a point of observation from which awakened ones move more energetically toward enlightenment.

MIND IS THE SLAYER OF THE REAL. An expression that denotes the ability of rational mind to block, distort by rigidity, and hold us in bondage—not permitting reality to be expanded or truth perceived—through rejection of the soul's subtler realities: its interlocking impressions, intuition, and gentle touches. When separation rules, rational mind resists inner truth.

MIND, LEVELS OF. The levels of mind are: 7) instinctual, 6) programming, 5) conscious, 4) realm of HIGH SELF and SOLAR ANGEL. Three subtler levels exist wherein the egoic lotus develops in order to utilize the higher energies of the soul. The third and second levels serve the Solar Angel anchored in the highest; here the most subtle abides and shines its light into the denser lower levels. Each level is built within individuals; the collective mind also develops these levels as a sufficient number of humans achieve such.

MIND, NON-LOCAL. A modern term being applied by many, particularly Larry Dossey, M.D.,[7] for that part of one's self that can act at a distance in both time and space in a knowing way. Scientific data supports unexplained body/mind experiences of distance healing, telepathy, precognition, and impressions from a distance. Such research is being presented at some 60 medical schools across the U.S.[8]

MIND OF CHRIST. Divine intelligent love, like the COSMIC CHRIST (the indwelling intelligence). When enlightened, we develop mind: the clarity, balance, and focus that Jesus, the historical Christ, displayed 2,000 years ago. "Let the mind that is in Christ Jesus be also in you." In modern language we might say, "what the Soul knows—that we are one body/mind/soul and one with all others, all else." Another term is CLOUD OF KNOWABLE THINGS.

MIND OF GOD. The omni, all-knowing aspect of the Creator.

MIND SCREEN. The projected point used to visualize pictures within the mind and developed by practice. Once the capability is achieved, the image-making mechanism of personality projects upon it. It is available to higher consciousness, i.e., High Self, Soul, or other intelligences.

MIND-STUFF. Sir James Jeans's term for universal (PSI) energy. The free-floating vibrational matter of the mental plane known as "chitta" in the Vedic tradition or "chi" (electromagnetic life force) by the Taoist, to be drawn together by minds that can enter subtler frequencies and exert a pull toward form reality. These become the mind builders or leaders for the expansion of consciousness for all of humanity and the key to luminous life, whether for individuals, the collective, or the Earth.

MIND, SUBTLE. The higher frequencies of the MENTAL BODY, each more subtle than the preceding. Here the intuitive frequencies blend with mind, that inner knowing can occur. The highest frequencies are the domain of the SOLAR ANGEL who helps us integrate the intuitive frequencies. Here the EGOIC LOTUS unfolds until the fourth INITIATION and the CHALICE breaks, setting the Solar Angel free. These subtle planes acquaint us with the subtle worlds. *See* Path of Initiation, Christian.

MIND, THREE WORLDS OF. Humanity "made in the image and likeness" of divine mind creates the little life it experiences in the planes of lower vibration. Three minds of humanity in its world are identified as physical (brain), astral (desire mind), and the mental mechanism (mind), which ranges from instinctual to higher abstract. Herein exists the impulse that reflects the Creator Source.

MIND WITHOUT HEART IS CRUEL; HEART WITHOUT MIND IS FOOLISH. This saying reminds us that the powerful emotional and mental natures must be brought into balance and integrated for the benefit of the individual and of all; otherwise, misuse of power results.

MIR. The Russian word for "peace." A POWER WORD when spoken as a mantra.

MIRACLE. The use of UNIVERSAL LAWS, beyond mortal comprehension. There is no escaping universal laws; they are neither breakable nor alterable. When experiences cannot be explained, they are labeled "miracles," ostensibly phenomenal.

MIRNA JAD. An etheric PLANETARY CENTER located in a mountain chain in South America. *Also see pp. 349–55,* Etheric Dimensions.

MIRROR GAZING. A common method of divining used in ancient times for psychic information, OUT-OF-BODY travel, diagnosing illness, or summoning spirits.

MISHNAH. The primary oral tradition, or law, used to understand the written Torah.

MISONEISM. "[A]n unreasoning fear and hatred of new ideas . . . a major block to public acceptance of modern psychology. It also opposed Darwin's theories of evolution—as when an American schoolteacher named Scopes was tried in 1925 for teaching evolution."[9]

MITHRAISM. The worship of Mithras—Persian god of light and guardian against evil—flourished in the late Roman Empire, rivaling Christianity. Its central theme is that of Mithras killing the primordial bull, the first act of creation. In the West, the cult became a mystery religion with strong emphasis on blood atonement, fellowship, strict moral discipline, and a distinctive dualism. Mithraism taught that the soul ascended through several realms and that there was personal salvation after death for the faithful and punishment for the wicked.

MIZ TLI TLAN. A PLANETARY CENTER in the etheric located high over the Peruvian Andes. *Also see pp. 349–55,* Etheric Dimensions.

MOHAMMED. Born in Mecca on the Arabian peninsula ca. 570, d. ca. 632. Reluctant prophet and founder of the Islamic faith. When the archangel Gabriel delivered to him his purpose in life, Mohammed hesitated, then picked up the work and lived a courageous life as a spiritual teacher. He said the Koran was revealed to him by God, later to be recorded by his followers. His flight from persecution to Medina in 622 became the beginning of the Islamic era. Known as "the Prophet" by the Muslims.

MOKSHA. A radical change of consciousness "that provides a stable platform for the outworking of itself in *all* aspects of our activities" within the grand design of human evolution—even "the conversion of the body *itself,* the body and the mind, which are *junior* to the spirit.[10]

MONAD. An indivisible and divine life-atom. The immortal self within each living successive incarnation and progressing to the stature of the ADEPT beyond which extends unlimited EVOLUTION. The spark of Divinity invested in the constitution of human beings. The innermost self, the source of life and light that nurtures the unfolding soul. This true Self, a breath of the Absolute, is in no way influenced by conditional, finite personality. The immortal and eternal principle within us, an indivisible part of the integral whole, the universal spirit from which it emanates and into which it will be absorbed upon its return to the GODHEAD. Any self-contained system of

MOTHERS AND GODDESSES OF THE WORLD

The DIVINE FEMININE, or veiled mother, is represented similarly but differently from culture to culture. Known as Mother Nature, Mother Matter in her earthiest form, she is Sophia in her most restricted expression, innate wisdom. She is considered veiled because wisdom—or the mystery of life—is never readily available but must be pursued to be realized. The divine feminine guards her mysteries, usually considered six or so, gradually leading seekers inward. The process of her guardianship is often described as "brooding," as she watches over the world until her time nears. Sophia, her esoteric name, is better known today as our respect for innate knowing, or gnosis, expands. Usually portrayed as the virgin (purity), the mother (life-giving), or the crone (wisdom), her many aspects are revealed in her personifications in different traditions:

In most ancient cultures, the goddess or mother was the mysterious being who guarded the secrets of birth, death, and creation. On the continents of Europe, Africa, North and South America, and Asia, the deity was Woman. In Egypt, the Goddess was She Who Makes the Universe Spin Round. In Greece, she was the Great Mother, the Prophetess. In Polynesia, she was Creator and Destroyer. In South America, she was the Oneness That Contained All Dualities.

Mother of the World sculpture by Mary Martha Butler, given to and on display at Light of Christ Community Church, Sparrow Hawk Village

APHRODITE. Greek goddess of love, mother of EROS.

ARTEMIS. This popular goddess in the Mediterranean area prior to Christianity, depicted with a chest of eggs or breasts, symbolizes the self-sufficient woman. The goddess enables women to seek their own goals and a life of their choosing. Ephesus, with its great temple, was a major place of initiation for Artemis.

GODDESS, DARK, OR DARK MOTHER. Called by the Greeks, the "darkness in the midst of which shines the light of power." The term has been applied to the Black Ishtar, Black Diana of Ephesus, the Black Virgin of early Christianity. She is the hidden mother, the black Isis, SOPHIA, Mother of Mysteries.

GODDESS, TRIPLE. Sacred day, May 24, annually honoring the goddess who exhibits herself as maiden, matron, and hag, or CRONE. HERMES shares the triple form with lunar goddesses. Considered androgynous and called "trice greatest," Hermes also shares the same feast day.

HERA. The beautiful goddess Hera is the Roman symbol of strength and power. Both

Greek (Juno) and Roman traditions taught that the great goddess brought peace and harmony upon those to whom she bestows her blessings. Wife of Zeus, Hera was originally worshiped as Queen of the Sky. She expresses the active divinity of Woman, presiding over all phases of feminine existence. She is a reflection of the eternal light, untarnished mirror of God's active power, image of goodness. Hera unchanging makes all things new. She deploys her strength from one end of the Earth to the other, ordering all things for good.

ISHTAR. Lady of the Battlefield, aided the HITTITES in battle. It is said, she came down from the skies to smite hostile countries.

ISIS. The Egyptian archetype and deity, consort of Osiris and mother of Horus, for the divine FEMININE PRINCIPLE of the universe and a major personification of the divine Mother prior to Christianity, bringer-forth of the perfect indwelling self. *I am she who is the goddess of women. I have instructed humanity in the mysteries. I, Isis, am all that has been, that is, or shall be; no mortal has ever me unveiled.* The mysteries of the Self and the mysteries of the universe, which are but one and the same, go on forever. There is no end to seeking, no end to learning, no end to wisdom, no end to challenge and growth. Isis, the feminine nature, conceals her mysteries well, deep within her womb. The Virgin (the purified self) gives birth to the Self-within and reveals her innermost secrets. It is believed the cult of Mary (portrayed with the child Jesus) absorbed the energy of Isis and her mysteries into its new form. The mysteries of Isis contain wisdom of mother and child, faithful wife, and courageous seeker for the aspects of her scattered ANIMUS.

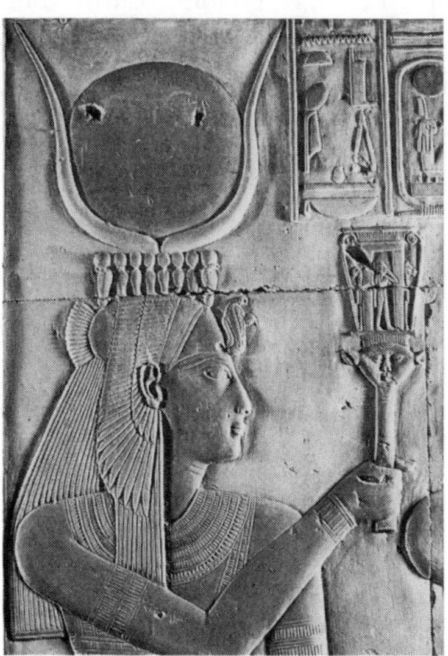

KALI MA. Appearing with long, flowing hair and a dark complexion, in one hand Kali Ma holds a symbolic sword with which she destroys evil. She is universal Mother in the aspect of the consumer of negativity, the lower human nature. High on a large platform stands Kali, the divine Mother of the Hindu tradition. Here, the gentleness and the terror of the fierce Mother meet, creating a strong desire for peace and for a life of divine love. She is the imageless, formless silence, full-blown in loving, full-blown in frightening. The erotic, expansive, many-armed goddess is usually pictured brandishing weapons in frenzied movement with her dancing arms.

KUAN YIN. This ancient Chinese symbol of the BODHISATTVA OF COMPASSION is the grandmother aspect of the goddess. Known for her mercy, an embodiment of beauty and purity, when her form and divine qualities are contemplated, they resolve into delicate musical sounds, imparting peace and harmony. As the wise woman, this healer, teacher, and sage represents the three aspects of holding strength in restraint, unity, and love. Her skills with herbs and healing, wise counsel, and gentle caring make her a mainstay of matriarchy. Her hands deliver daughters and ease pain. With vast understanding of the past, she commits her knowledge to the ever present.

LILITH. First wife of Adam, according to Hebrew tradition. This form of the goddess is considered vengeful, hostile to childbirth, and demanding human sacrifice. LILITH, meaning "night monster," was sometimes characterized as a dark demon or phantom who personified evil and ignorance. In the magical tradition of the Hermetic Order of the Golden Dawn, Lilith is described as "Queen of the Night and of Demons" and is one of the goddesses of Quilphoth, a negative reflection of Malkuth of Kabalah. Lilith's main "flaw" was independence and lack of sustenance of Adam. Choosing freedom, rather than obedience to him, she fled.

MARY OF BETHLEHEM. The divine mother of the patriarchal period glows with a radiant human personality. Just as man, woman mirrors two aspects of life—activity and contemplation united in one soul. When perfectly harmonized, she is an image of God, in whom masculine and feminine are synthesized and transcended. She is Rachel and Leah, Martha and Mary—at one moment surrendering to love, at another laboring to give when she feels nothing. The contemplative side is full of faith and confidence. Knowing life is God's choice, she cooperates continually. She receives in order to encourage life; she is the garden of the Lord, image of beauty, wisdom, and holiness. As receptive ground, she blossoms with a rich variety of flowers and plants. She is truly the archetypal "handmaiden of the Lord" for the Christian tradition. *Also see* Mary, Mother of Jesus.

MOTHER EARTH. Native Americans so named the feminine creative principle at work for planetary life. As mother of the planet, she utilizes the elements as the source of supply for the preservation of physical life. All needs are met from the bosom of Mother Earth; therefore, Earth must be treated with respect, honored as the life-giver by all who dwell thereon. She is mother matter, watching over humanity, transmitting the message of far-off worlds, leading humanity into the labors of Earth life.

MOTHER GOD. The divine feminine principle, receptive in nature, also known as SOPHIA, a balance to the masculine father force. Better known in Eastern Christian orthodoxy than in Western approaches to Christianity. Little understood, veiled in matter but always responsive to divine will.

NEFERTITI. "The beautiful one has come" has often been short-changed by those who stressed only her physical attributes. She was addressed by her people as "Ruler of the Nile," "Daughter of the Gods." As wife of the Pharaoh, she held religious power; her carvings dominated the temple. She was the only queen addressed in prayer and accorded divinity while her husband was still alive. She was praised in an Egyptian hymn as "youthful forever and ever." United from the beginning with her Creator, she is the perfect model of balance and achievement.

SOPHIA. The literal translation in Greek is "wisdom." When graced with her beautiful presence, she bestows many blessings. Originally worshiped as the celestial virgin and wisdom of inspiration, she presides over all levels of inner knowing. Biblical writings call Wisdom the "companion of the Creator." (See Proverbs in the Holy Bible, and in the Apocrypha see the Book of Wisdom and the Wisdom of Solomon.) She whispers intuitive prompts at the edge of mind and encourages abandon. The mysterious shadow embraces loving play. Sophia reveals the great unknown—the male the shadow of female, and the female the shadow of male. She exists as the mysterious knower within movement and measure, the space in which consciousness lives, veiled by form. In Sophia, intellect and love are wed, becoming intuition, inner knowing, and thus wisdom. Better known in Eastern Christian orthodoxy than in Western approaches to Christianity, her daughters are said to be Faith, Hope, and Charity.

YEMEN-YAH. The divine black Mother with her beautiful ebony face and exquisitely chiseled features is the personification of the divine feminine. Seven rays swirl from her head; strands of seven different metals form her collar. Rays flow to Earth from her heart and from her hands, unceasingly blessing all children of the Earth. Yemen-Yah, the universal Mother, speaks: *I show myself to my people as they can perceive. To those who need form, I am the mother of the peoples of the plains, the forests, rivers, mountains, deserts—of the nomads. To those who need no form, I am the dark light from which all form proceeds.* Woman, the basic symbol of the surrendered soul, is timeless, at the root of all life, the womb. In her receptivity, she is bride and mother, available for the experience of deepest love.

any size that, if divided, ceases to exist as such; whereas, if absorbed into a larger system, it becomes part of the greater.

MONADIC PLANE. The highest plane of creation is the LOGOIC, or Divine—the Oneness. From there the individual spark, or monad, journeys to its home, the monadic plane, on its way toward denser planes. *Also see* Planes, cosmic.

MONADIC TRANSMUTATION. A term introduced by Trigueirinho. *Also see pp. 349–55,* Etheric Dimensions; Walk-in.

MONEY. Concretized energy, its value to be used with DISCERNMENT.

MONOTHEISM. The belief in the One God above all gods arose with the pharaoh Akhenaton in Egypt about 2000 B.C. Judaism, Islam, and Christianity are modern monotheistic religions.

MONTGOMERY, RUTH. d. 2001. Author of 13 books, most about metaphysics, Ruth Montgomery began her career as a journalist, covering the White House for Hearst newspapers. Her many best-sellers astonished the nation with the accuracy of their predictions of things to come, as well as her revelations about after-death and REINCARNATION. She was the first to tell the world of the existence of WALK-INS (including this author), coining the phrase and describing these "harbingers of a new order that will bring peace on earth in the 21st century" in *Strangers Among Us* and *Threshold to Tomorrow.*

MOON BOWL. The name of the Holy GRAIL from the lost ATLANTIS.

MOON SIGN. The astrological position calculated with a specific formula revealing the constellation in which the moon was located at the time of one's birth. One of the three most important personal placements in an individual's chart, i.e., sun, moon, and ascendant.

MORPHOGENETIC FIELD. A term coined by Rupert Sheldrake of Great Britain as he studied the life field that exists around every living form. The concept is focused on etheric reality; major examinations and research are now being conducted by physicists as they venture into realms formerly known as MYSTICISM or METAPHYSICS.

MORYA, EL. *See* Amhaj, the; Masters.

MOSQUE. Muslim temple.

MOTA. Aramaic for "DEATH," explained by Dr. George LAMSA to mean "not present, but somewhere."

MOTHER EARTH. A title for this planet, showing respect and love for the service she renders to matter and for her life-giving properties. Earth is considered feminine in the mystery tradition because she is receptive to other intelligences evolving through her created form. Among Native Americans, she is the creative principle and source of supply for preservation of life. All needs are met from the bosom of Mother Earth; therefore, planet Earth must be treated with respect and honored as the life-giver by all who dwell thereon. The WORLD MOTHER of many traditions is "a virgin pure as the snow on the mountains, as beautiful as the most colorful lilies, and as wise as Mother Earth." It is her mission to sustain the brotherhood of men and the sisterhood of women all over the world. Known as Malkuth in Kabalah.

MOTHER MATTER. An acknowledgment of the nurturing care the physical reality renders to the sparks of life that are entrusted to her care.

MOTHER PRINCIPLE. The feminine precept in creation often known as Sophia, wisdom; the Mother aspect of the deity; that receptive part that accepts the spirit aspect in order to manifest in matter. A cosmic force that leavens and nurtures.

MOTHERS OF THE WORLD. A reference to the DIVINE FEMININE. Particularly prevalent in Agni Yoga writings, many systems of thought honor this concept.

MOTHER TERESA. *See* Teresa, Mother, of Calcutta.

"MOTHER, THE." *See* Richards, Mira.

MOTIVATION. The drive to excel. The energy one uses to strive toward a particular goal.

MOUNT KAILAS. A mountain in Tibet sacred to the Hindus and considered the home of Lord Shiva, patron of transformation. Includes the general area in India to which BABAJI HERAKHAN returns time and again. It is said he always reincarnates in sight of Kailas, called the "crown of the world" in Hindu and Buddhist cosmology and geographically centered near Mount Kailas in Tibet and the northern border of India.

MOVEMENT. Four styles of movement define personalities and assist us to understand the kind of physical energy we carry: racer, dancer, stroller, and trekker.

MOVEMENT AND MEASURE, ALL IS. A Mayan reference to their great deity, Hunab K'U, who is called the "Creator of Movement and Measure."

M'SHEKHA. Aramaic for the Greek word "Christ" from which we get the word "messiah." A title conventionally translated "anointed" but really means "perfected" or "enlightened," the ideal form of humanity.

MU. The historical name for the Pacific tectonic plate ascribed recently as the huge submerged continent of LEMURIA where a "golden age" was to have existed. Called by ancient wisdom "Motherland" or "Pacifica," the race that developed there was called Lemurians.

MUDRA. A SANSKRIT word referring to certain positions of the fingers and hands used in devotional YOGA or in exoteric religious worship to convey emotions and blessings. These positions are considered by oriental mystics to have particular esoteric significance and are found both in Buddhist and Hindu religious art throughout India and Northern Asia.

Mudras are used in a psycho-physical process in various YOGAS in order to seal the energy and attention of the practitioner.

MUMMER. Means "masker." Mumming was often an important feature of Christmas festivities. The custom, perhaps traceable to the ancient Roman Saturnalia, began with men and women exchanging their clothing and going from house to house thus disguised. In its Christian context the "stranger" is welcomed in the name of the Christ-child. Since there were few strangers in ancient times, the disguise concealed identity. Thus Christmas became a time of "open house," when all were invited in to share.

Mumming also related to the visit of the Magi to Bethlehem. In 1377 Londoners—as elaborately disguised "Mummers"—paid homage to the young Prince Richard, son of the Black Prince. Elegantly dressed and on fine horses, they reenacted the Magi honoring the baby Jesus. Some blackened their faces to

MUSES, THE NINE

In Greek mythology, the daughters of Zeus and Mnemosyne (goddess of memory), angelic beings of sacred knowledge, the embodiment of inspired creativity, representing the perfection of learning and action. The cultivation of the Muses within humanity holds the hope of understanding, true peace, justice, and ecological harmony and recreates intellectual, spiritual, and social unity. Plato's school, the Academy, was dedicated to the Nine Muses, according to Thomas Daffern.[11] Many consider Wisdom, or Sophia, to be the mother of virtues, the Muses:

Calliope	politics, economics, development	Polyhymnia	religion, philosophy, spirituality
Clio	history, education, scholarship	Terpsichore	musicology, dance, drama
Erato	psychology, love, sexology	Thalia	literature, humanities, language
Euterpe	art, architecture, design	Urania	natural sciences, ecology, medicine
Melpomene	conflict, justice, global security		

signify all races honored the King, demonstrating that all humanity would kneel, all were to pay homage.

MUSIC OF THE SPHERES. The tones of the creative currents flowing from the cosmic song, or silent sound. Commonly thought of as emanating from heaven or the higher astral, becoming audible as the tones densify. Heavenly voices or songs heard in mystical moments.

MUSLIM. The common name for followers of Islam; literally, "one who surrenders to God."

MY GOD IS A FIERY GOD. An oft-repeated phrase from the biblical teachings of Heb. 12.29. "Our God is a consuming fire." Another, "goeth over before thee, as a consuming fire," is from Deut. 9.3. In KABALAH this references the World of ATZILUTH, which is the realm of fiery archetypes, the world of the MONAD.

MYRRH. *See* Gold, frankincense, and myrrh.

MYSTERIES. Truths that cannot be realized simply by the telling. While they are not secrets, they must be pondered in order for the Great TRUTH to be revealed. Truths are unveiled from within or not at all; the outer consciousness prepares itself through meditation and contemplation for the revelation of the "mysteries of life."

MYSTERIES, FEMININE. Hidden, ARCANE areas of human life—sexuality, birth, death, healing, intuition, and play—are the focus of the divine feminine. Truths, tests, and challenges for humanity emerge as the wisdom within these realms is gleaned. When the pendulum swings too far, the masculine mysteries will once again regain prominence. *Also see* Mysteries, masculine.

MYSTERIES, FIRE AND WATER. "These two pathways are called fire and water. Hence it is written (Berachot 22a; Mechilta Pesikta Zutrati, Yitro 20b) that the Torah (Bible) is likened to fire as [is] said, 'Is not my word like a fire?' It is also likened to water, in the secret of 'Ho, everyone that thirst, come to the water.' Yet water and fire are two complete opposites, and one destroys the other. Water extinguishes fire, and fire dries the water. In the physical world, what does one who has cold water do when he is thirsty and cannot drink the water because it is cold, yet he has a fire and he cannot put the water directly on the fire because it would extinguish the fire? He puts the water inside a vessel and places the vessel with the water upon the fire, and in that manner the vigor of the fire goes into the water. Now he drinks hot water that is composed of fire and water. Thus the vessel reconciled the fire and the water. He now enjoys both of them together. . . . The same applies in spirituality and to those two paths that . . . contradict each other and have been likened to fire and water. Both aspects are called right and left, namely faith and knowledge, because they contradict each other. He who follows the Torah [Bible] of Moses becomes as this vessel that reconciles . . ."[12] *Also see* Fire mysteries; Water mysteries.

MYSTERIES, MASCULINE. Usually enumerated as adventurous (seeking the unknown), courageous, the victor, the conqueror, physically strong, the achiever, competitive, oriented to the mind, loyal, determined, willful. In the 20th century, masculine force reached its detriment and began to relinquish control, allowing the feminine mysteries to emerge to bring about an era of restored harmony. A long-promised golden age, an era of balance, is prophesied by WISDOM TEACHINGS. *Also see* Mysteries, feminine.

MYSTERIES OF ISIS. Secret teachings of Ancient Egypt concerning the mother of Horus. The deity considered to be the mother of humanity in pre-Christian eras.

MYSTERIES, THE GREATER. Higher teachings available to prepare one to understand the part one plays in affecting the greater whole of life. Lesser teachings, or mysteries, pertain to the individual's evolution, the greater to the evolution of humanity, planetary life, or cosmos. Certain lesser realities must be integrated (not just intellectually comprehended) before one can be admitted to the inner Halls of Learning and the greater work—similar to Initiate.

MYSTERIES, THE LESSER. The first levels of study and practices for spiritual growth leading toward the SOUL PURPOSE for the CHELA or DISCIPLE, initiating an apprenticeship for the GREAT WORK.

MYSTERIUM MAGNUM. Latin for the One Reality.

MYSTERY. Esoterically, a spiritual reality that transcends normal reasoning and must be repeatedly contemplated for its essence to be grasped.

Mystery religions. Traditions that concealed their teachings and practices until after a period of testing, probation, and INITIATION, requiring adherence to stringent rules. Many veils cloaked the true understanding as taught to those accepted, while most had some outer forms of identification, i.e., the THERAPEUTAE of Egypt and Greece were identified by their white robes and healing work, as were the ESSENES. Early Christians were instructed to add love and generosity to their practices.

Mystery school. An institution where practical teachings and techniques prepare individuals for inner development. No outer structure can assure inner success, but such an environment is constructed and assistance rendered to facilitate progress in expansion of consciousness and an awareness of the hidden life beyond human consciousness.

Mystery teachings. *See* Ancient wisdom teachings.

Mystic. A person with an awareness of a multidimensional reality who, seeking to have a personal relationship with God, witnesses to expanded life, stepping down her/his insight or understanding as best it can be for the benefit of others. The mystic is considered a blend of the ORPHIC and the OCCULTIST.

Mystical body of Christ. The second Person of the Trinity, the Logos who gives form to life by descending into matter. Through the sacrifice inherent in assuming the limitations of matter, the Logos is the "heavenly being" in whom all forms exist and of whose body all forms are a part. ADAM KADMON is the corresponding term in KABALAH.

Mystical experience. A transient occurrence in which, without the exercise of will, one has a direct and immediate confrontation with what one believes to be the Ultimate, a sharing of divine heart and divine presence felt as a form of divine love.

Mystic Christian. An individual who seeks to know oneness with the Christ through personal experience and communication, rather than through dogma and commandment. The consciousness becomes attuned to the essence of the way and is nurtured by inner contact with the Christ and the arcane body of oneness.

Mysticism. Comes from *mystos,* meaning "to keep silence," or *myen,* "to be closed," i.e., the eyes or lips; something unspeakable. Usually associated with the practice of union with the Divine, to facilitate direct contact with the eternal and invisible higher worlds. Mystics pursue these experiences through love and devotion.

Mystic marriage. The state of consciousness that unites the heart and mind of an initiate, transforming the nature of both.

Mystic way. A path of devotion and service to the cause of God as made known to the individual through an inner connection to the Divine.

Myth. A parable or legend told to preserve an understanding of truth. Since it is often esoteric or difficult to grasp, it is best shared or disguised by being cloaked within a story; thus the message is protected and preserved until its hearers can detect its meaning. Teaching myths have guided the minds of humanity throughout all cultures for thousands of years. Does not mean "untruthful," though sometimes translated so.

MY WILL TO HIGHER WILL. A phrase used to affirm the willingness to surrender the personality to the soul, a great goal for the spiritual seeker. A practice often included in on-going life as the surrender and acceptance of direction believed to come from a higher source.

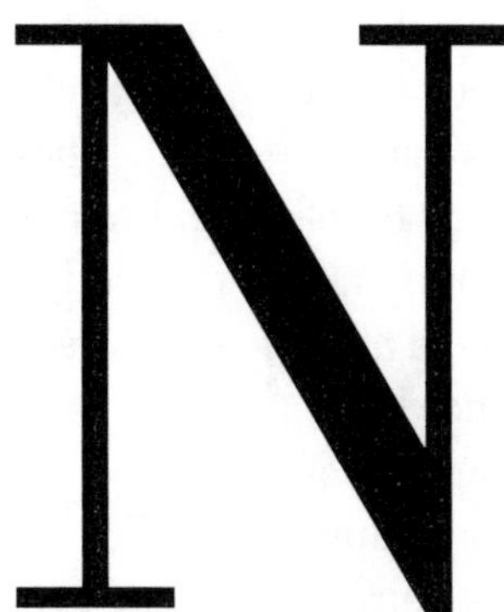

Nadi. One of numerous points created by the crossing of lines of energy in the etheric (nonphysical) human and planetary bodies—the circuitry connecting the chakras. According to the wisdom of the East, each body has numerous nadis, which can be used as energy pressure points to help maintain good circulation and balance.

Nadir. In astrology, the lowest point of a circular chart, between the 3rd and 4th houses.

Nag Hammadi Scrolls. Codices dating back to the 4th century, named for the site of their discovery near the Egyptian village of Al-Qasar in 1945. Buried in a storage jar beneath a large boulder were 13 leather-bound books written in Coptic, reflecting Gnostic and early Christian elements. They are now housed in the library of the Coptic museum in old Cairo. *Also see* Dead Sea Scrolls.

Nails. Because of their use in the Crucifixion, nails appearing in religious symbology represent the physical suffering of Jesus.

Namasté. An ancient Sanskrit term and common Hindu blessing meaning "The Self (divinity) in me greets the Self (divinity) in you" or its equivalent, truly affirming, when we greet each other from the sacred place of love, light, and spirituality, there is only oneness.

Nanak, Guru. Founder of the East Indian religious sect, the Sikhs; a 16th century saint.

Narcissism. Excessive love of oneself.

Natal chart. *See* Horoscope.

Native. Astrologically, a reference to one's sun sign type and designation, e.g., one is a native of Aries.

NATURE SPIRITS. Lesser devas who may be detected at times. These less evolved beings direct the efforts of ELEMENTALS and are guided by more advanced devas. They dwell in the etheric and project themselves into the physical elements at times. Four types of nature spirits, one for each of the ELEMENTAL FORCES, are each assigned a name and a task. Most religions and cultures acknowledge these little-comprehended components of nature in some way. *Gnomes* are the nature spirits of Earth—the elves, brownies, fairies, little people. *Undines,* the water sprites, show themselves as images, faces in sparkling water or rapids. *Sylphs* are air spirits who work with winds and clouds. *Salamanders* cloak themselves in fire and dance in flames. Since humanity is on the path of EVOLUTION and the elementals on the path of INVOLUTION, it is considered an error for us to disrupt their efforts for purposes of our own. Lesser devas are the directors of ELEMENTALS, guiding them as their area of service. We are permitted to invoke the assistance of nature spirits and required to honor their contributions. Humanity may address the lesser devas and nature spirits but not the elementals themselves.

NAZCA LINES. Giant designs on the plains of Nazca, Peru, were etched before the time of Christ. They cannot be detected standing on the ground; one needs to be roughly 1,000 feet above the Earth to see the patterns. These unique hieroglyphs—peacock, spider, whale, hummingbird, fish, monkey, astronomical lines (the longest, 5 miles; presumed to indicate summer solstice for planting purposes), and so on—encourage many to believe humanity has experienced air travel in the distant past. These mysterious and wondrous markings currently are being compared to CROP CIRCLES.

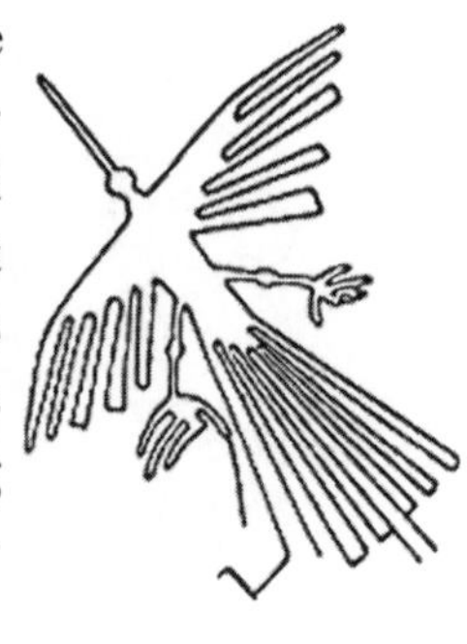

NDE. *See* Near-death experience.

NEAR-DEATH EXPERIENCE (NDE). A self-explanatory term used when an individual has moved to and beyond the brink of dying but returns to outer consciousness, often aware of a new dimension of life. This so-called death experience awakens the awareness of life's continuity, and new values of a subtler nature register upon the experiencer, to be integrated into the personality life upon return. A scientific study in the 1970s brought these profound happenings to public awareness as a result of Dr. Raymond Moody's *Life After Life.* It was estimated by Gallop Poll in 1993 that about 13.5 million people in the United States have had such an experience.

NEAR–NEAR-DEATH EXPERIENCE. A term coined by P.M.H. Atwater[1] in her research of the effects of LIGHT EXPERIENCES upon the consciousness. She points out that any number of events quite similar to the NDE have occurred spontaneously. OUT-OF-BODY experiences will come immediately to mind, but other "experiences of the light"—as in profound meditations, phenomena hard to explain or identify, as well as moments of COSMIC CONSCIOUSNESS—are included. Each registers upon the brain mechanism, and research is affirming how major shifts in perception result.

NECROMANCY. From the Greek word *nekros* meaning "dead," and *manteia* meaning "divination," indicating conscious contact with DISCARNATES to receive information or assistance. Some consider the revitalization of a corpse itself an act of necromancy, while most see it only as the conjuring of the spirit of the corpse.

NEFILIM. "Astronauts" descending to Earth from the heavens, according to Sumerian, Babylonian, Assyrian, Hittite, and Canaanite histories and languages. Writing extensively on these cosmic travelers, Zecharia Sitchin says the Old Testament refers to them as those "cast down upon earth." (Gen. 6.4) Interpreted "giants" earlier, modern translators have begun to leave it in this form, exercising more speculation about its true message. *See pp. 337–47,* Humanity's Genesis.

NEMESIS. Goddess of vengeance and anger, in Greek mythology.

NEOCORTEX. The latest stage of development in the physical BRAIN consists of two hemispheres capable of communication and coworking. The right hemisphere relates to the whole of life, while the left analyzes and evaluates. This level of brain activity produces measurable intelligence quotient (I.Q.). *Also see* Hemispheres, right and left, of the brain; Three-brain concept.

NEOMAMMALIAN. The midbrain between the REPTILIAN BRAIN and the neocortex whose function is to bond humans one to another through the feeling nature and caring relationship to the whole of life, while the neocortex develops an awareness of separation and individual differentiation. Also referred to as Old Mammalian. *Also see* Hemispheres, right and left, of the brain; Three-brain concept.

NEO-PAGANISM. A modern Earth religion that borrows and adapts from pre-Christian pagan religions, sometimes with additions from contemporary religious thinkers.

NEO-PENTECOSTAL. A modern term referring to current interest in the phenomena of the GIFTS OF THE SPIRIT (which were demonstrated at Pentecost), as expressed in psychic abilities and MYSTICISM.

NEOPLATONISM. School of philosophy founded in Alexandria in 3rd century A.D. that combined doctrines of Plato and other Greek philosophers' ethical concepts with Judaism, Christianity, and mysticism of the Near East. This perspective greatly influenced the Mediterranean and early church, teaching that in the ultimate One that lies behind all experience, dualism between thought and reality is overcome; also that the One can be known only by the method of abstraction. One must gradually divest the experience of all that is specifically human so that in the end, when all attributes have been removed, only the Source is left. They maintained that the Absolute, which "has its centre everywhere but its circumference nowhere" (Plotinus), could only be reached by mystical experience.[2]

NEPHESCH. One of three souls defined in KABALAH, Nephesch is known as the animal 

or vital soul. This soul maintains the body and its functions, its instincts and cravings that are remnants of the animal kingdom. *Also see* Neschamah; Ruach.

NESCHAMAH. The highest of three souls as defined in Kabalah. Relating to the supernal TRIAD, from which BINAH emanates the whole plan of Creation, Neschamah is the highest soul residing across the ABYSS with the supernal triad and is unknown until DAATH constructs the bridge of consciousness and begins to gather higher awareness. *Also see* Nephesch; Ruach.

NESTORIANISM. A doctrine that taught that human and divine beings remained separate in the incarnate Christ; ascribed to Nestorius (d. 437), patriarch of Constantinople, whose followers survived as the Assyrian church, chiefly in Asia Minor. The doctrine was ecclesiastically condemned in 431, after which the church separated from Byzantine Christianity.[3]

NETZACH. The seventh sephirah on the kabalistic Tree denotes victory; considered the home of passion, the drive for life.

NEW ADAM. Born of the emerging divine-within through the overshadowing of the HOLY SPIRIT. Often this title denotes the emerging, new, more-aware human on the path of EVOLUTION back to the Source, as is given in the New Testament. The CHRIST modeled a new human being with a consciousness humanity is now considered capable of attaining.

NEW GROUP OF WORLD SERVERS. This terminology was given to the world by the MASTER DJWHAL KHUL in the BAILEY materials (Lucis Trust). Recently (1990) advised to drop the "new" since adequate numbers of WORLD SERVERS have identified themselves over a measurable period of time to anchor the will, dedication, and service necessary to do the work of the HIERARCHY.

NEW JERUSALEM. A prototype city in the ethers said to be the home of spiritual beings. In Eastern teachings, SHAMBALLA.

NEW MOON. A phase of the physical moon when lunar influences assist in rapid new growth, releasing the past and beginning anew. A time for planting new thoughts and being receptive to changes in one's life. When a new moon occurs, the sun sign and the moon are in the same ZODIAC.

NEW PARADIGM. A fresh prototype, idea, or awareness; a revelation in formation; a possibility in process of being realized, e.g., the immanent potential of humanity coming into form.

NIGHTLY REVIEW. In this exercise practiced before sleep, we review the day backward to capture situations needing repair or resolution. Considered an important discipline for serious students, this practice copes with mishandled situations daily rather than permitting an accumulation to be confronted after death.

NIGHT OF BRAHMA. *See* Pralaya.

NIGODA. Among living creatures, the smallest, simplest form. Nigodas are understood to have only one sense perception, namely touch, according to the Jain tradition.

NIPSIS. Greek, a state of concentration in which the object of attention is the thought of

NEW AGE

Refers less to a time period than to a state of consciousness. The new, awakening consciousness expressed through thoughts and actions reflecting an awareness of the divinity and oneness of humanity and all of life. A shift in consciousness characterized by a global perspective and attention to universal questions and challenges. Unity, synthesis, intellectual development, scientific discovery, and ethical and spiritual living are keynotes of the present new era. Often specifically refers to the AGE OF AQUARIUS presently upon us, but indeed Master Jesus was "New Age" when he stood as a model of the new way he deemed possible. Many different opinions exist regarding the exact beginning of the Aquarian Age (see below).

The New Age and the Aquarian Age

The New Age is underway now, during the last part of the Age of Pisces, especially since the start of the New Age in 1899.

"Rudolf STEINER was the first person to coin the term 'New Age'—and for him, it had a very specific meaning, drawn from the Hindu chronology of *yugas*. Hindu teaching concerning the yugas describes four past world ages *(yugas)*: the Golden Age in the far-distant past which lasted 20,000 years, followed by the Silver Age, which extended over a period of 15,000 years; then the Bronze Age, which was 10,000 years long; followed in turn by the Iron Age, which lasted 5,000 years. The Iron Age (Hindu: *Kali Yuga)* is also referred to as the Dark Age. Hindu chronology dates the beginning of the Dark Age to February 17/18, 3102 B.C. (=3101 astronomically). Lasting five thousand years, it came to an end in 1899. According to research presented in my book, *Chronicle of the Living Christ, Kali Yuga* ended on September 10, 1899. The New Age (Hindu: *Satya Yuga)* is the Age of Light, lasting 2,500 years, or half the length of *Kali Yuga.* In view of the Hindu chronology of yugas, evolution is evidently accelerating, with each yuga being correspondingly shorter than the preceding one. With the beginning of the 20th century, humanity entered the New Age, which will last until the year 4399."[4]

the intellect—somewhat like SEED-THOUGHT MEDITATION. As focus is held, the mind magnifies and detaches into expanded awareness.

NIRMANAKAYA. Literally, "without body." Advanced entities working with all evolving life, within karmic boundaries, from spirit rather than form side of life; related to wisdom, energies, and influences behind the manifested side of life.

NIRVANA. The ultimate goal of the Buddhist path: cessation of suffering. Liberation; conscious absorption in the one divine life of the cosmos. The ultimate and absolute existence or state of consciousness attained by those who have achieved supreme perfection and holiness through the destruction of the limitations that prohibit recognition of the real Self. The annihilation of separative thoughts, intentions, and motives. Those who have attained this stage of absorption in pure Cosmic Being have progressed through evolution so far along the Path that the personality has become thoroughly impersonalized without loss of consciousness—more specifically, personal and individual absorption or identification with the true and divine Self, perfect peace. The state of freedom from karma, and the extinction of desire, passion, illusion, and the empirical self. Enlightenment.

NIRVIKALPA. A state of intuitive consciousness where great insight is realized as expanded and unlimited awareness dawns upon the experiencer. The impact is quite similar to a near–near-death experience.

NIRVIKALPA SAMADHI. Quite similar to a near–near-death experience wherein one experiences expanded consciousness and momentary enlightenment without suffering any biological threat to the physical life.

NODES. In astrology, the nodes are in celestial longitude where the moon crosses the ECLIPTIC. Interpretations of moon points represent a personal path from the past (southnode) to the future (north node). These components are always directly opposite each other in a natal chart. The movement—from south node, an area of comfort, to north node, area of new experience—represents the journey to which the soul has committed itself prior to incarnation. One of three definitive routes EVOLUTIONARY ASTROLOGY uses to study soul purpose in a specific incarnation.

South Node

North Node

NOETIC. Pertaining to or originating in the intellect; from the Greek word *noesis*, meaning "understanding."

NONATTACHMENT. Freedom from restraint or manipulation; the ability to release physical or emotional possessions or restrictive obsessions, yet capable of responding wisely and compassionately from higher levels.

NON-LINEAR THINKING. A means of sensing and knowing, contrary to the straight, linear, or rational process of thought; usually associated with HIGHER MIND, or intuition. Can be correlated to E.Q., as opposed to I.Q.—emotional quotient vs. intelligence quotient.

NONRELEASE. This barrier to illumination is also known as attachment, with additional nuances; also, unforgivingness.

NONSELF. The EGO, personality; the unreal, misguided, false self.

NONSENSE. The mischief we set into motion when we allow the senses of the NONSELF, or personality, to guide us in life experiences, though we often learn through them.

NOSTRADAMUS, MICHEL DE. b. St. Remy, 1503, d. 1566. French astrologer, seer, and physician to Charles IX and Catherine de

Medici. A collection of his apocalyptic prophecies in two volumes of rhymed quatrains (1555–1558), though often enigmatic, appear to foretell events: French Revolution, the two world wars, struggles in the Mideast, Kennedy assassinations, fall of communism in Russia, and emergence of the ANTICHRIST. The "King of Terror" was prophesied to appear in the seventh lunar cycle of 1999, heralding the end of the world as we know it. *The True Centuries,* 1558.

NUMEROLOGY

The study and spiritual understanding of the vibration of numbers, rhythms, and cycles. A science of self-discovery that helps us comprehend the uniqueness of life, keys to personal karma, and how to identify talents and purposes. Characteristics of numbers are:

Number	In the Human Experience	In Cosmology
0	Potential, choice.	The Absolute. Undifferentiated Oneness.
1	Leadership, independence.	The Divine Spark still at-one with the Solar Logos (not the Absolute).
2	Balance, cooperation, diplomacy.	The fall of man. Soul awareness begins to awaken.
3.	Creativity, and self-expression.	Division of consciousness into male and female forms to bring forth new life.
4	Organization, order; bringing ideas and plans into concrete form.	Earth and form. The human stands upright with the germ of the divine self within.
5	Freedom, versatility, change, resourcefulness.	The consciousness of the senses and mind. The number of man, free will, experience.
6	Responsibility and service within family, home, community.	Man begins to "look up." Realizes there may be a purpose to life and begins to take responsibility for actions
7	Silence—where spirit and matter meet.	Male-female energies are in harmonious flow of intuitive receptivity and assertive reaction.
8	Cause and effect (karma), gaining mastery on all levels and planes.	Higher law prevails in all aspects of the life.
9	Universal or brotherly love. Completion of a cycle within the life.	The Divine Man on Earth. Completion of a cosmic cycle of experience.

NOTARIKON. Used two ways in Kabalah, both aimed at abbreviation: 1) the forming of one word by taking the first and final letters of another word; 2) taking the letters of one name as being the first or final letters of each word in a sentence.

NO-THING, NO THING. The Creator that set manifestation into motion. That which cannot be defined or "about which naught can be said." The Source that created all that ever has existed and ever will exist. The unmanifest. Most often related to Kabalah but not restricted to that source. Synonymous with the ONE THING.

NOVENA. Means "ninefold." A series of nine consecutive days of prayer, usually for a specific intention. Both Christian and Eastern religions encourage novenas.

NUMEN. A spirit inhabiting natural phenomena, places, or objects. Also, creative genius.

NUMINOUS. Charged with an indwelling light incapable of being described or comprehended, not necessarily noticeable from without. Pertaining to the supernatural or spiritually elevated nature.

N'UN. A name given by African tribes for the resting spirit within that is awakened by a sacred form of "heated" dance.

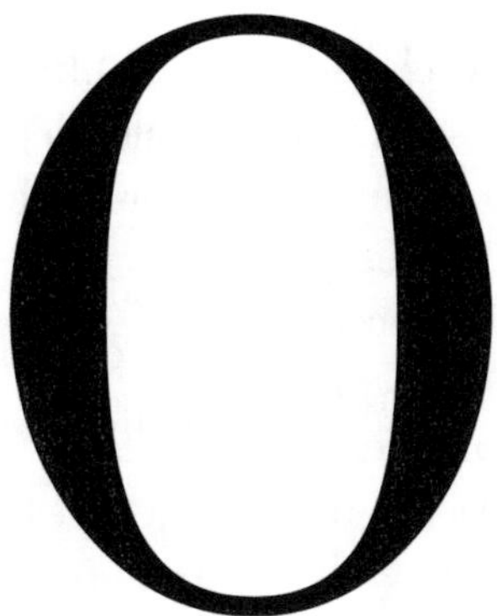

OBE. *See* Out-of-body experience.

Obedience, vow of. Taken by a subordinate in spiritual life in return for INITIATION or admittance to a desired tradition, this pledge is binding upon the CHELA and the initiator until both agree to dissolve the oath or when spiritual development of the "younger" has developed to a degree that both realize through guidance or high consciousness the time for release has come. Many continue to love and obey long after the formal need for allegiance has passed. The initiator carries the spiritual responsibility for the chela's development and answers to the inner world while the vow is intact. The wiser is charged by the law of KARMA for errors, while the compliant chela remains free from error.

Objectivity. The ability to view a situation from an impersonal, detached perspective in order to achieve a broad, holistic awareness.

Observer. One who practices WITNESS CONSCIOUSNESS, created through objectivity and spiritual insight; also called the KNOWER.

Observing self, the. Arthur J. Deikman, M.D., psychologist, introduced this term, similar to "WITNESS CONSCIOUSNESS." In this state, we learn to see with objectivity what is reflected to us or what is reflected upon. The observing self bridges ordinary consciousness and the higher realm of thought, thus creating a link between her or his mind and divine mind, retaining power of choice and free will in light of this higher perception.

Obstacles on the Path. The four greatest impediments to seekers of high consciousness are enumerated as MAYA, GLAMOURS, ILLU-

SIONS, and the DWELLER ON THE THRESHOLD. *See individual entries.*

OCCULT. That which is hidden, or occluded, and must be studied to be understood. In Latin, "to conceal," formed with the prefix *oc* meaning "reversely, inversely, opposite, against," thus the opposite of "cult." In occult philosophy each is taught to do her or his own thinking. The word may be used to correlate to the study of universal phenomena, but the true study of occultism seeks to penetrate the causal mysteries of being.

OCCULTISM. The science of life or universal nature; the need to realize an inner orientation to God. Occult studies are those hidden from or not known to most of humanity. An occult science not only includes the physical, psychic, mental, and spiritual part of the human being but also studies the structure, operation, origin, and destiny of the cosmos—also called the HERMETIC PRINCIPLES or ESOTERIC sciences. The occult is known as the KABALAH in the West and MYSTICISM, MAGIC, and yogic philosophy in the East. Studies also include ESOTERIC PSYCHOLOGY and magic (both black and white); contacting human MASTERS and inner teachers, SPACIAL BEINGS and DEVAS; and trance work, including mediumship. Those on the PATH are expected to strive for dedication, purification, discipline, teaching, and service. As a precaution, these teachings were hidden from the selfish—educated and uneducated—so the divine sciences would not be misused or turned into black magic. Occult traditions include the mystery schools of Egypt, Greece, Rome, and others, as well as the initiatory traditions of secret societies such as the ROSICRUCIANS and FREEMASONRY.

OCCULTIST. One who studies the mysteries (concealed, esoteric) of life, seeking greater knowledge of the hidden and ageless wisdom.

OCCULT MEMORY. That which is held in the subconscious—out of sight and out of mind—of an individual or group, i.e., humanity.

OCCULT PATH. A way of embracing inner awareness, not readily revealed; intense purification of the nature.

OCCULT TRUTHS. Realities that lie behind the apparent and are comprehended only gradually as we continue to perceive the cause side of life.

OCTAHEDRON. A solid figure having eight faces. One of five three-dimensional shapes that has equal lines, angles, and surfaces; associated with sacred geometry; the other four are the cube, pyramid, pentagon, and sphere.

OFFICIALS OF THE SEVEN RAYS. The CHOHANS and MASTERS who exemplify the qualities of the RAYS and guide the seven streams of divine energy flowing from the GODHEAD.

OIKOUMENIKOS. The Greek word from which "ecumenical" derives; literally relates to the whole of God's family, the whole of the world.

OLCOTT, COLONEL HENRY STEEL. b. Orange, NJ, 1832, d. 1907. A lawyer, agricultural expert, and journalist who covered Spiritualist phenomena. In 1874 he began a lifelong friendship with Madame Helena Petrovna BLAVATSKY (HPB) when the BROTHERHOOD sent her "to America to search for Colonel Olcott, the comrade who would supply what was lacking in herself—the power of organization and of speaking to men and gathering them round him and shaping them into a movement in the outer world—and how the Society was founded in New York, and later had its Headquarters moved to India."[1] They cofounded the THEOSOPHICAL SOCIETY in 1875 and *The Theosophist* magazine in 1879. The Colonel spoke of having seen and met Masters Morya and Kuthumi in their physical bodies. "Colonel Olcott wrote the first catechism of Buddhism intending it for the use of children, but he made his answers difficult even for grown-up people to understand," according to C. W. Leadbeater; however, it was " . . . a splendid work."[2] "In 1882 [they] moved the Society's headquarters from Bombay to an old British summer estate in Adyar, near Madras, where it remains today"[3] and where Olcott died. *The Buddhist Catechism; Golden Rules of Buddhism;* and *Old Diary Leaves,* six volumes, containing many of his conversations with Blavatsky.

OLD-OLDS. A newly coined term pertaining to those of extended longevity, past the usual senior citizen age and needing specialized care. This category begins in the 80s (individuals make it difficult to be exact) and extends to over 100. As new ways of caring for and understanding elders are being defined, many are coming to believe severe difficulties, e.g., dementia, can be avoided if we better understand the psyche and unfinished business or suppressed anxiety.

OLIVE BRANCH. This universal symbol of peace represents God's reconciliation with humanity through Noah. During the flood, Noah sent a dove from the ark to determine whether the waters had receded. "And the dove came back to him in the evening; and, lo, in her mouth was an olive leaf plucked off; so Noah knew that the waters had subsided from off the earth." (Gen. 8.11)

OM. The creative word deemed to be the original sound, the generative first word or tone that vibrated through the receptive void, shaping and continuing to maintain creation. Also considered the great primordial sound, the sound current, or silent sound—the sound of all sounds together. Pronounced home, without the h and usually prolonged, Om is the first and foremost syllable of the ancient, sophisticated SANSKRIT language. Used as a power tone, the Om invokes divine interaction. According to Torkom SARAYDARIAN, "the O is the spirit and the M is the reflection, . . . or the human soul."[4] Sometimes spelled and pronounced *Aum*, the Om of the VEDAS comes to us in the sacred word *Hum* of the Tibetans, the *Amin* of the Muslims, and the *Amen* of the Egyptians, Greeks, Romans, and Jews. In Hebrew it means "sure and faithful." *Amen*, as used by Christians, usually is translated "so it is" or "so be it." A more esoteric translation is "and so I affirm" in active proclamation, not passive agreement.

OMEN. An indicator used to divine or to demonstrate favor or disfavor of the gods; a future event foretold.

Om mani padme hum. A Buddhist chant, literally, "Hail, jewel in the lotus within. Amen." *Mani padme* represents the "jewel" of the LOTUS, the essential wisdom lying at the heart of Buddhist doctrine, the divine essence. *Hum,* the limitless reality embodied within the limits of the individual being, unites the individual with all life of the universe.

Om Namah Shivaya. Literally, "I take refuge in Lord SHIVA." Also translated, "In the name of Shiva" or "Lord, you are my very refuge." One of many mantras uttering god names. Any god or goddess name may be used: Allah, Brahma, Kali, Diana—whatever deity one would invoke for assistance or protection.

Omnipotent. All-powerful; having unlimited or universal power, authority, or force.

Omnipresent. Being existent everywhere, with no limitation. The prefix is from the Latin *omnis,* meaning "all."

Omniscient. All-knowing, such as the mind of God.

Om tat sat. Hindu adage affirming "I am that," similar to "I am that I am."

One becomes three. The truth held as part of right formation, that the one divine and only reality divides into male and female for manifestation in the outer world to occur. Kabalistically speaking, KETHER (the One) expresses itself through CHOKMAH (first sephirah on male PILLAR) and BINAH (first sephirah on female pillar). *Also see* Seven becomes twelve; Three becomes seven.

One Mind. The supreme being or divine mind, as used in the perennial wisdom. In HERMETIC texts often symbolized as the sun. The name of God is the name of the ONE THING or NO THING. All of these terms are basically indescribable and can only be perceived.

Oneness. The GROUP SOUL of humanity; confirmed at the fifth dimensional consciousness where we can truly realize we are all one. The spiritual state that affirms all are united in ADAM KADMON.

One Thing. As used in perennial wisdom (especially in the EMERALD TABLET), the supreme force which cannot be seen, with no form until it is "grounded" in material reality by the action or thought of the mind of the supreme being. Called "It" and pictured as a chaotic mass, full of churning primordial energy, preexisting, completely autonomous and dependent upon nothing for its existence; a morphic field. In HERMETIC texts the moon often is used as a symbol for the One Thing. Described by Chinese sage LAO TSU 2,500 years ago: "There is a Thing confusedly formed, born before sky and earth. In the silence and the void, standing alone and unchanging, ever present and in motion, it is capable of being the mother of all," chapter 25, *Tao Te Ching* by Lao Tsu. *See* Materia Lucida.

Opposition. In astrology, two planets located 180 degrees, or six signs, apart (allowable ORB 7 degrees). Such signs become hidden helpers to one another when the two influences come to appreciate the perspective of each.

Opus Magnum. The "Great Work" of the alchemist who seeks to build the Philosopher's Stone within oneself.

Oracle. Prophet, seer, or visionary through whom an authority of some type may be speaking.

Oracle of Delphi. Located on the slopes of Mt. Parnassus above the Corinthian Gulf, regarded as the central point of the whole Earth, Delphi was called the "Navel of the Earth."

"The most famous ORACLE was that of Apollo at Delphi. Traditionally the oracle first belonged to Mother Earth, but later it was given to (or stolen by) Apollo. The medium, a woman over 50 known as Pythia, lived apart from her husband and dressed in maiden's clothing. The Oracle's fame became Panhellenic between the 7th and 6th centuries B.C. when Apollo's advice or sanction was sought by lawmakers, colonists, and founders of cults. Pythia's counsel was most often in demand to forecast the outcome of projected wars and political actions. Consultations were normally restricted to the 7th of the Delphic month, Apollo's birthday. They were banned during the three winter months when Apollo was believed to be visiting the Hyperboreans in the north land. According to the usual procedure, sponsors were necessary, as well as the provision of ritual cakes, *pelanos,* and a sacrificial feast that conformed to rigid physical standards. The ritual of the Delphi Oracle included bathing in the Castalian Spring built above a volcanic chasm, drinking from the sacred spring Cassotis, and then entering the temple. She descended into a basement which was placed above the gaseous vapors rising from the chasm, mounted a sacred tripod, and chewed laurel leaves (Apollo's sacred tree). Pythia would speak intelligibly or otherwise, and priests would interpret her words to the inquirer in what was often highly ambiguous verse."[5]

Oral tradition. The manner in which ancient wisdom was passed down through the spoken word—distributed through stories, music, poetry and drama, allegory and myth. Only recently have "the teachings" begun to appear in written form.

Orb. In astrology, the term for the number of degrees significant or allowed for aspects to be valid.

Order of World Guardians. An organization established and maintained by Vera Stanley Alder for many years. She authored a newsletter of the same name from the '40s until her death in 1984, inspiring many to become WORLD SERVERS.

Ordination. A sacrament of the Christian tradition wherein the devotee vows obedience to God and the Christ. This ordained one serves as a spiritual guide and teacher for the church, the community of believers, and the world.

Organs of higher perception. The evolving sensory organs that change how humanity understands life and its unfolding as they mature, both individually as chakras develop and collectively as a new consciousness is built.

ORGONE. Term for PSI (life) energy, coined by Wilhelm Reich (1897–1957), Austrian psychoanalyst taught by Sigmund Freud.

ORIGEN. b. Egypt, ca. A.D. 185, d. 254. Alexandrian theologian, teacher, and spiritual writer of early Christianity who led a life of strict asceticism, demanding severe fasting, vigils, and poverty. He believed the soul existed with God prior to the creation of the physical body, that the Genesis stories of Creation and the fall of man were allegorical, not factual accounts. He taught that all things have a double aspect: corporeal and sensible, accessible to all, and spiritual and mystical, discerned only by the enlightened. He believed that suffering and pain are part of God's redemptive PLAN and that there is spiritual resurrection for fallen souls. Imprisoned and persecuted during his lifetime, he was eventually condemned as a heretic. Though often misunderstood or altered, his teachings stood for 500 years before being anathematized and are now reemerging. Origen's influence on Christianity is considered to be monumental. *Hexapla; De Principiis.*

ORMAZD. *See* Ahura Mazda.

ORPHIC. Derived from *Orpheus*, the poet and musician of Greek mythology who is symbolic of the most important mystery religions. A person who seeks experiences of God through the senses, as in nature, music, art, drama, feeling. PANTHEISM is considered an orphic approach to spirituality.

ORTHONOIA. *See* Enlightenment, stages of.

ORTHOPRAXY. Correct practice, or right action, or right endeavor, as we say in our prayers—*ortho* meaning "right" or "straight"; *praxein* meaning "practice."

OSIRIS. The male god of Egyptian mysteries, husband to ISIS and father of HORUS. Just as Mary was overshadowed and conceived Jesus, so the Egyptian tradition taught Isis the mother was overshadowed by Osiris, the god being, and conceived Horus, the son—represented by the small falcon, the current SPARROW HAWK.

OUIJA BOARD. A divining board painted with letters and numbers used to communicate with discarnates. The planchet, or pointer, easily manipulated, moves from letter to letter to spell answers to questions. Because it takes no wisdom to operate and contact with ignorant or distrustful spirits may occur, one is usually advised to avoid this particular physical device. Believed to operate by ectoplasm and the astral force of personalities present, both incarnate and discarnate, thus considered a reckless method of attempting communication.

OUROBORUS. This cosmic serpent, depicted with its tail in its mouth, is the symbol of the manifested universe in its cyclic aspect of completeness. The feathered serpent of the Western wisdom tradition symbolizes the primordial unity that encloses all time and space. The snake on various headdresses suggests an alert and focused spiritual/inner mechanism. The serpent encircling the all represents wisdom contained. In in-depth psychology, it typifies the Earth, the Great Mother against whom evolving consciousness (in myth, the hero fighting the dragon or serpent) must struggle in order to individuate. In

The Power of Myth, Joseph Campbell writes, "Life sheds one generation after another, to be BORN AGAIN. The serpent represents immortal energy and consciousness engaged in the field of time, constantly throwing off death and being born again." Also the symbol of the RING-PASS-NOT and of the PLEROMA.

OUTER PLANES. The so-called physical, astral (emotional), and mental planes of personality.

OUT-OF-BODY EXPERIENCE (OBE). A specific incident of discovery when one becomes aware of self when the consciousness is focused in the astral vehicle rather than the physical. Experiencers realize that awareness exists even when not attached to the physical body—an awareness that feels, senses, and continues to recognize and know. This ASTRAL TRAVEL/projection relieves a great deal of anxiety concerning life's continuance after bodily DEATH. *See* Immortality.

OVERLIGHTING. A method of the higher world to provide strength and awareness to a worker in the dense world. Overlighting fortifies the worker, who may or may not be aware of the spiritual help being received.

OVERSELF. "A term Paul Brunton [1898–1981] coined for the higher self or soul. Overself is the meeting point of the human and the divine. It is a fragment or particle of the divine, a 'ray shining from' the divine, but not the Sun itself. In one sense the Overself is the core of an individual, and in another sense the individual is held by the Overself."[6]

OVERSHADOWING. An influence of the higher world coming into or over the receptive, sensitive disciple for the purpose of higher reality. Done in such a way as to dignify humanity and serve the Christ (called by whatever name), overshadowing delivers energy, a message, or an influence of the Holy to humanity. Three ways are being exerted at this time to stimulate the flow of the CHRIST CONSCIOUSNESS to humanity:

1) overshadowing currently incarnated disciples and initiates;
2) pouring the Christ life or consciousness upon the masses;
3) the Christ reappearing within humanity, whether in a physical form or etheric, through human hearts.

OVERSOUL. The blended group of souls working as one in consciousness, occurring as the same individuals participate regularly in an action, i.e., family, group, team. Often indicates a group of souls connected through many past lives together.

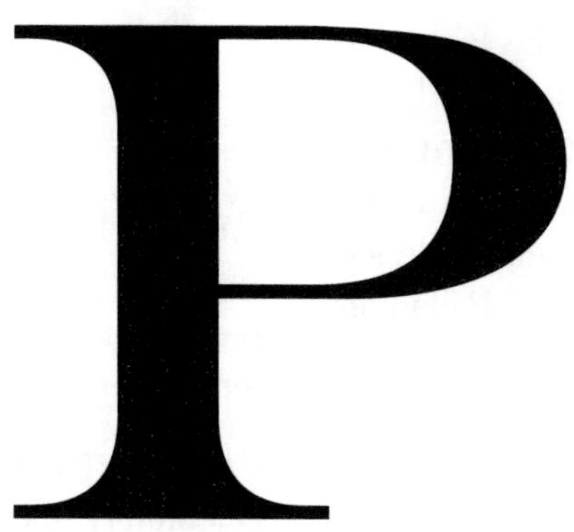

P. In the ancient Greek alphabet, symbolized the integrated person in control of the personality vehicles—physical, emotional, and mental.

Padre Pio. *See pp. 246–51,* Saints.

Pagan. From the Latin *paganus,* meaning "country dweller." In today's vernacular a practitioner of an Earth religion who is attuned to nature and its mystical wonder.

Pali. The language of a number of ancient Buddhist texts used especially within the framework of Theravada Buddhism.

Palladium. A Sophianic symbol in the form of a wooden statue of Pallas Athena, three cubits high with a meteor at its center that was believed to have fallen from the heavens. This meteoric component was buried in the depths of Troy and guarded by vestal virgins. It was said to confer invulnerability to the possessor, for it was considered the power of Troy. Odysseus, disguised as a beggar, secretly entered the city and recaptured it, leading to the destruction of the city.

Buried in the depths below the city of Troy, guarded by vestal virgins, the Palladium was believed to be the source of power. The Trojan priest Aeneas rescued the Palladium from the flames and thus prevented it from falling into Greek hands. It came to rest in Rome, where, as in Troy, a special temple was built for it beneath the city, guarded by vestal virgins. This underground temple gave Rome its power over the whole of the ancient world.

In the 4th century, the emperor Constantine the Great heard the prophecy that Rome would collapse and its power would be lost. In an attempt to secure the future of the Empire, he decided to transfer the capital from Rome to Constantinople, with the idea of creating an even greater empire embracing the East and West. Constantine transferred the Palladium to Constantinople, where it was placed once again in an underground temple guarded by vestal virgins. Recall it was given to Ilia, the founder of Troy, by Athena, Greek goddess of wisdom. Through the power of the Palladium we have a sun symbol, a burning light of wisdom beneath the Earth that confers power upon its possessor. The light of wisdom now radiated from Constantinople.

A few centuries later, the statue of Constantine placed atop the pillar; it was struck by lightening and half the pillar destroyed. It is said the Palladium is still buried beneath this pillar. The world waits with great interest for any clues to the future destiny of the Palladium. Early in the 20th century followers of Rudolf STEINER went to Istanbul and began excavations there to locate the Palladium but without success. *See pp. 268–77,* Sophia Teachings.

PALMISTRY. A study of the unique map contained in every hand, a divine design showing influences at work and traits carried by the incarnated one. An analysis may disclose many insights into one's life, ascertaining intelligence, general disposition, and tendencies by the shape of the hands, fingers, and nails. Past, current, and future events are revealed by the lines and markings on the hand and fingers.

PAN. The "god of nature," considered demonic by some but generally accepted as

instinctual vitality of life, drive, and sexuality. Energy correlates with the sephirah NETZACH on the kabalistic TREE. *See* Pantheism.

PANDIT. Hindi for "learned man," similar to a sage; one who does not choose to have disciples as a guru but shares his or her knowledge for the benefit it can bring.

PAN EURYTHMY. A cheerful, upbeat system of celebratory movement developed by Peter DEUNOV in Bulgaria and unknown to most of the world until the end of the communist era. A sacred exercise designed to be danced daily between spring and autumn equinoxes.

A living circle of beauty, harmony, and unity, giving inspiration to the world. Spread to Western Europe and the U.S. by devotees. Usually danced outdoors in a circle to acknowledge the joy of nature, life, and awakened consciousness.

PANTHEISM. The belief that God, nature, and the universe are the same.

PARA. Beyond.

PARABLES. Simple analogies and teaching examples used by Master JESUS and other wise ones because they can be easily understood by everyone.

PARACELSUS. b. Germany (now Switzerland), 1493, d. 1541. Alchemist. Paracelsus was named Philippus Aureolus Theophrastus Bombast Von Hohenheim. (The adjective "bombastic" was derived from his surname.) Considered one of the most extraordinary and outrageous men of the Renaissance, he was known as the medical Luther to his enemies, which were many. After receiving a doctorate from the University of Ferrara in 1516 (1516 records are missing, so some question whether he was a graduate), Paracelsus began using the name derived from the renowned 1st century Roman physician, Celsus; but considering himself above Celsus, he added "Para."

"Knowledge is experience," he stated. In 1527, a noted physician and lecturer in medicine at the University of Basel, he burned the books of Avicenna, Arab Prince of Physicians, and those of Greek physician Galen. His fame at Basel lasted less than a year as he viciously attacked many medical malpractices of the times. He fled for his life after he had enraged doctors, apothecaries, and magistrates. Within eight years, after traveling leisurely and writing prodigiously, he made a triumphant comeback and enjoyed the rest of his life in wealth and much favor with royalty. While under appointment by Prince-Archbishop Duke Ernst of Bavaria, Paracelsus died under mysterious circumstances at the White Horse Inn, Salzburg, at the age of 48.

Carl JUNG wrote of him, "We see in Paracelsus not only a pioneer in the domains of chemical medicine but also in those of an empirical psychological healing science."[1]

PARACLETE. Holy Spirit, giver of life, of the New Testament—the advocate who responds to calls for a closer relationship to God. From the Greek word *parakletos,* meaning "call to aid," or "call upon."

PARADIGM. An outstanding example or pattern that presents a comprehensive view or overview, providing a guiding explanation or emerging archetype to express a clearer perspective.

PARANOIA. *See* Enlightenment, stages of.

PARANORMAL. Describing experiences or perceptions beyond what is usually understood as beta (rational or outer) consciousness.

PARAPSYCHOLOGY. The emerging scientific study of PSI, ESP, and psychic realities in order to more rationally understand the phenomena of altered states and little-understood dimensions—often either feared or revered. This broad field of investigation ranges from the diversity of dreams to DISCARNATES, REINCARNATION, TELEKINESIS, and much more. *Para* means "beyond" or "above."

PARASPIRITUAL. Describing experiences or states of consciousness beyond the usual or comfortable range of religious practices, of value to those who accept them as spiritually enriching or transformational.

PAREIDOLIA. Seeing faces in clouds, on walls, on rocks or trees. The illusion or impression is defined by an external stimulus. Once one sees the image, it can be seen by others.

PARSI, OR PARSEE. A member of the ZOROASTRIAN sect in India and the Middle East, descended from Persians.

PARVATI. Wife of Shiva, acknowledged for her beauty and resourcefulness.

Passive-aggressive personality. A temperament that suppresses emotions, rather than responding in a timely and direct manner. The result is a delayed over-reaction hard to associate with the true cause.

Passive meditation. *See* Meditation, passive; Meditation, active.

Passover (Pesach). An eight-day celebration when Jewish families gather to recount the story of the Israelites' exodus from Egyptian bondage and to eat the symbolic SEDER meal.

Past life. Previous incarnation in the physical dimension.

Past-life regression. Technique to bring about differing states of consciousness wherein one can be guided to review, study, and/or heal through recalling or re-experiencing past events. In order to help release trauma experienced in the past that continues to present obstacles to growth and wholeness, one can access and address the trauma. *See* Psychography.

Patanjali. (A.D. 400) Indian founder of the RAJA YOGA system of Hindu philosophy, who defined the purpose of yoga as knowledge of the true self. His four books of *Yoga Sutras* set forth moral and physical disciplines necessary to attain *moksha*—absolute freedom of self—as a result of acquiring COSMIC CONSCIOUSNESS. *How to Know God: The Yoga Aphorisms of Patanjali,* trans. 1953.

Pater of Alcantara. *See pp. 246–51,* Saints.

Path, left-hand. Building personality and its attachments (versus right-hand, mystical ascent) that leads to stronger ego and more experience on the outer—physical and material—to free us of KARMA or to dissolve the barriers within the NONSELF. *See* Evolution; Path, right-hand.

Path of Initiation. The avenue taken by those seeking knowledge of the divine mysteries of life; the process of enlightenment through dedicated service and self-mastery, and the steps or stages delineated by various esoteric systems. As distinguished from the PROBATIONARY PATH, a higher stage of spiritual evolution. Entrance upon the Path of Initiation is marked by simplification of the life, increased self-mastery, and conscious service to the divine Plan. Stages of development in which the center of consciousness transfers from purely human awareness to progressive stages of spiritual awareness. Also called Path of Conscious Return and the Path of Holiness.

Path of Initiation, Christian. The pattern of advancement in Christianity on the Path of Initiation comprises seven great steps common to humanity. Five are usually taken as an incarnated being. The fifth may not be in the body but working closely with humanity. Two more advanced steps occur after physical life. Modeled by the life of Jesus as: birth, baptism, transfiguration, Crucifixion, revelation, decision, and Resurrection, each step symbolizes a test we must pass and strengths we must embody to advance.

First initiation. The birth of the Christ within.

Second initiation. A stage of purification of the astral body.

THIRD INITIATION. A powerful point of merging personality and soul—soul infusion.

FOURTH INITIATION. Crucifixion, realized *by giving one's life* for something—not necessarily dying; sometimes successfully completed by living a dedicated life for a specific cause.

FIFTH INITIATION. Revelation that there is no death; at this point, one is considered a Master. The sixth and seventh occur out of sight in the subtle planes and are little understood.

SIXTH INITIATION. The decision to return to serve humanity or to move through other doorways into the solar system.

SEVENTH INITIATION. Resurrection.

PATH OF OCCULTISM. "Taking heaven by storm" and intent, rather than comfortably awaiting advancement by evolution with one's peers.

PATH, RIGHT-HAND. The mystical ascent upon the path, which leads back to God. *See* Evolution; Path, left-hand.

PATH, SPIRITUAL. "The way" of direct experience and learning by which one progresses through life lessons. Each experience builds part of the CREATIVE THREAD, thus no two individuals' paths are the same. Not just faith.

PATI. Lord.

PATRIARCH. The most elevated male position in the hierarchy of Orthodox churches.

PAX. Latin for "peace."

PEACOCK. In the East the peacock is a symbol of the MASTER, the one who has experienced many lessons and lives through which to view the world (each feather contains an eye). In medieval Christianity the peacock represented the Christ. At the cathedral in Wells, England, a peacock with flowing tail sits as the Christ upon a large cross, a symbol similar to the PHOENIX rising from the ashes, representing the emergence of holy consciousness.

The peacock was the favorite bird of noble ladies and, as an emblem of beauty and glory, it appeared not only in their gardens but also on a Roman coin. In some Eastern countries its feather is still a mark of honor. The eyes forming the beautiful pattern of its wings are the stars and planets of the Hindu universe and a symbol of the "all-seeing" powers of the Christian Church. As a symbol of immortality, the peacock was adopted by Christians through some confusion with the phoenix. As attributed to St. Barbara of Heliopolis, the peacock's feather became the emblem of the city of her birth. Heliopolis was thought to be where the fabulous phoenix practiced its art of resurrection; since the bird was unknown in the West, the peacock took its place. It was believed that its flesh never decayed, like the incorruptible Christian soul.

"The peacock is a symbol of beauty and immortality. It has been said that the eye of the peacock feather holds the secrets of eternity. The design on the peacock's fanned tail is created by intersecting spirals. These same spirals are found at the center of many flowers, like the sunflower and daisy. When sensing rain, the peacock does a geometric dance related to the spiral. In all of nature, minerals, plants, animals and humans, there is divine patterning."[2]

Pearl of Great Price. Confected in the pineal gland by the spirit fire of the active kundalini—a significant goal in ALCHEMY. "Alchemists had an excellent image for the transformation of symptom and suffering into a value of soul," according to James Hillman. "The pearl begins as a bit of grit, a neurotic symptom or complaint, a bothersome irritant in one's secret inside flesh, which has no defensive shell. This is coated over, worked at day in day out, until the grit one day is a pearl; yet it still must be fished up from the depths and pried loose. Then when the grit is redeemed, it is worn. It must be worn on the warm skin to keep its luster: the redeemed complex which once caused suffering is exposed to public view as a virtue. The esoteric treasure gained through occult work becomes an exoteric splendor. To get rid of the symptom means to get rid of the chance to gain what may one day be of greatest value, even if at first it is an unbearable irritant, lowly and disguised." Also known as the "wish-fulfilling jewel" by the Buddhist or as the PHILOSOPHER'S STONE.

Pegasus. A winged horse that came from the blood of the Gorgon Medusa, according to Greek mythology. With just a blow from his hoof, he created the Hippocrene, a fountain where poets gathered to receive inspiration. Its source is a spring on Mt. Helicon in Greece, which remains today.

Penance. Any practice or special action chosen by a disciple or assigned by another to atone for regretful behavior.

Pendulum. A tool used for divining. As a symbol, the shape of the swinging pendulum is a TRIANGLE, the two extreme ends coming to rest at center, held steady by a higher position (or view). *Also see* Dowsing.

Pentagram. *See* Star, five-pointed.

Pentateuch. The first five books of the Bible (also known as the TORAH) given as a foundation for the establishment of humanity—commandment and wisdom, instruction and law, God's revealed will.

Pentecost. A festival of the Christian church commemorating the descent of the HOLY SPIRIT upon the apostles of Jesus, the Christ. Pentecost is the seventh Sunday after Easter, but the season extends to the last Sunday in August. The miraculous phenomena fulfilled Christ's promise not to leave unattended those he had left behind. The early disciples became connected and guided by the holy consciousness, thus preparing them for their work to begin the effort toward establishing the KINGDOM OF SOULS on Earth. The color for Pentecost Sunday is red for the blood of Christian martyrs and for the fire of the Holy Spirit. The second Sunday of the season, Trinity Sunday, commemorates God as the Creator (Father-Mother), God the Son, and God the Holy Spirit; its color is white. The remainder of the season is red.

From Acts 2 we learn about the tongues of fire in the symbol. The descending dove—Sophia/Wisdom—is also used as a symbol of Pentecost.

Pentecostal. In Christianity, particular denominations emphasizing the Gifts of the Spirit that manifested to the apostles on Pentecost Sunday. These denominations generally believe we must manifest one or more of the gifts as a sign of personal salvation. *Also see* Neo-Pentecostal.

Perceiving. A more appropriate way of expressing what we usually call "seeing." Because we say we see, meaning with the mind's eye, we are attempting to relay we comprehend a picture, meaning, or message—that we "got it!" Perception is not limited to seeing as in picture consciousness.

Perennial wisdom. *See* Ancient wisdom teachings.

Perfected human. The Master who has completed the five human initiations and continues on the evolutionary path without the need for incarnation—symbolized as Adam Kadmon by kabalists and as a Christed One by Christians. In a perfected human, energy flows through well-coordinated chakras. *Perfected human* does not mean "perfect," which is a judgment, but the state of excellence toward which we strive. "Perfect," as a judgment, measures one against a thoughtform built over the ages by societies of mostly unawakened ones. A perfected human has mastered him- or herself and flawlessly reflects soul qualities.

Periodic abstinence. The practice of sexual self-discipline by choosing periods of abstinence from sexual activity for the purpose of self-control and lifting the focus of a relationship to a spiritual nature of interaction, rather than allowing the relationship to be maintained on the personality level. Most spiritual teachers recommend some practices of sexual control, and periodic abstinence is a discipline useful to most chelas.

Periodicity, principle of. The precept that undetermined time periods of rhythms and cycles ebb and flow in numerous ways to comprise the evolution of each individual life spark—human or other kingdoms. *Also see p. 117,* Hermetic Principles, Rhythm.

Permanent seed atom. A reservoir of data encoded to preserve information to be used in the evolutionary pattern of an individual on a specific level of expression. These atoms, or small force centers, form the bodies of the personality—physical, emotional, mental, and spiritual—each of which distributes a certain type of force and is able to respond to a particular vibration.

Persona. Jungian term referring to the personality or outer part of oneself readily revealed or displayed to the public.

Personality. The physical, emotional, and lower-mental vehicles projected by the soul into the denser planes through which it experiences life in the slower-vibrating realities for the purpose of learning and maturing. *Also see* Integrated personality.

Person of ideals. Once a soul resolves to maintain its ideals at any cost, a spiritually evolved being enters to help guide it; this may or may not be a physical person.

PESACH. *See* Passover.

PESHITTA BIBLE. The Authorized Bible of the Church of the East. *Peshitta* means "straight, simple, sincere, and true," i.e., "the original." The name was given to this ancient and authoritative text to distinguish it from other Bible revisions and translations introduced into some of the Churches of the East (Monophysites) after the division at Ephesus and Chalcedon in A.D. 431 and 451, respectively. Because this text was in use 400 years before the Christian Church was divided into several sects, it remains the only authoritative text of the Old and New Testaments of all Eastern Christians in the Near East and India, the Church of the East, the Roman Catholic Church in the East, the Monophysites, and Indian Christians. Since all Christians, and even the Muslims in the Middle East, accept and revere the Peshitta text, it proves beyond a doubt that it was in use many centuries before the division of the Church.[3]

PHARAOH. The title given an Egyptian ruler or king. In ancient times this one was required to be prepared by mystery teachings for the role. In the Bible and other historical writings, it was used as a proper name.

PHENOMENA. Experiences or events not definable or demonstrable by laws of established physical science. When the mysteries of UNIVERSAL LAWS are understood, however, these happenings are recognized as natural occurrences.

PHILIA. The Greek word for friendship, personal affection, or fondness; LOVE of friends or our fellow beings; familial love of tribe or family. Social sympathy, but not unconditional, as is empathy.

PHILOKALIA. Greek, meaning "love of the beautiful, the exalted, the excellent"; understood as the transcendent source of life and the revelation of Truth. *The Philokalia* is a collection of texts from between the 4th and 15th centuries by spiritual masters of the Orthodox Christian tradition.

PHILOSOPHER'S STONE. Sometimes known as the "Seed of the Sun" and portrayed as a flaming disc. An energy, concept, or realization synthesized and concretized by those on the path of rapid ascent and used to evaluate life experiences. Finding this stone or substance was the goal of ALCHEMY practiced in the Middle Ages. It was believed that a small tincture of it would transmute large amounts of base metals into gold, heal deadly wounds, and completely transform the body and soul of the alchemist who achieved its manufacture. The stone is thought to be an allegorical interpretation of the highest states of mystical enlightenment attained by alchemists as they projected their own personal TRANSMUTATION process onto their chemical experiments or procedures. Although the actual relationship between consciousness and matter is still a scientific uncertainty, in esoteric and mystical circles it is generally accepted that matter is just a lower vibration of spiritual modalities, therefore subject to transmutation. *Also see* Pearl of Great Price.

PHILOSOPHY. Love of wisdom.

PHOBOSOPHY. Fear of deep thought (as opposed to *philosophy*), as coined by Thomas Daffern, D.Sc., International Institute of Peace Studies and Global Philosophy, London.

PHOENIX. This mythological bird of Egypt, symbolizing resurrection and rebirth, is said to rise from its own ashes every 500 years, to re-form more refined and beautiful, epitomizing truth and hope for civilizations and particular faiths.

PHOSPHORIC IMAGES. Occurring when a carefully built TELESMATIC IMAGE, rich with energy, connects to the spiritual reality for which it is the symbol. We cannot force this image; it occurs as a state of GRACE. It emanates and provides us growth and a sign of progress. *Also see* Images; Mantic images.

PHOTON BELT. A band of electromagnetic energy through which our planet passes approximately every 13,000 years as Earth travels in her orbit around the Sun. According to wisdom teachings—and scientists—we are rapidly approaching the outer influence of this shower. *Photon,* meaning "light," is a quantum of both particle and wave behavior, with no mass or charge, possessing momentum; the energy of light, x-rays, or gamma rays, etc., is carried by photons. Concern is often raised as to how our electronic technology will function as we enter this "belt." Spiritually, it is believed, it will expand the point of light within each cell in our bodies and in the etheric, thus facilitating the building of the LIGHT BODY.

PHRENOLOGY. Reading the shape, knots, and bumps on a person's face and skull to denote intelligence, tenderness, general disposition, and character.

PHYLACTERY. Two small leather boxes containing strips of parchment inscribed with quotations from the Hebrew scriptures, worn on the forehead and left arm by Jewish men during morning prayers. It invokes physical action, repetitive prayer, and the holding of thoughts in contemplation or meditation.

PHYSICAL PLANE. The world of densest manifestation with its etheric/astral counterpart; in Agni Yoga, the lower realms. Most systems designate this world as the "matter" part of creation, that which is known by the five physical senses. The physical sub-planes (from the highest) are: reflecting ether, memory of nature; light ether, medium of sense perception; life ether, medium of growth, propagation; chemical ether, affecting assimilation and excretion; solids; gases; and liquids. *Also see* Planes, cosmic.

PHYSICAL RESIDUE. Body markings or symptoms resulting from past-life imprints. Birthmarks, pains, or phobias are believed to be the result of memories held in the etheric. As defined and taught in Psychography.

PIERCE THE VEIL. To break through the boundaries of rational thought and penetrate higher collective wisdom, often called the CLOUD OF KNOWABLE THINGS or MIND OF GOD.

PILGRIM. Anyone taking a journey toward greater experience, awareness, and maturity.

PILGRIMAGE. A journey—inner or outer—that draws experiences to facilitate expansion of consciousness. While often considered religious or spiritual in nature, this is not so. The journey has to do with maturity.

PILLAR. The kabalistic TREE contains three pillars: the side pillars represent force (masculine) on the right and form (feminine) on the left. This is the TREE OF KNOWLEDGE OF GOOD AND EVIL from Genesis. Only the central pillar is considered real; the others represent the duality of the world and are useful for experience and learning.

PILLARS, THE SEVEN. "Wisdom has built her house; she has set up in it seven pillars" (Prov. 9.1): mentalism, correspondence, vibration, polarity, rhythm, cause and effect, gender. *See* Hermetic Principles.

PILPUL. Literally, "hair-splitting"; dialectics and debate in the Jewish tradition.

PINEAL GLAND. Believed to be the endocrine gland into which the energy of the brow center flows; in effect, home of the THIRD EYE and where SOLAR ANGEL is anchored. The Mercury center, representing the PHILOSOPHER'S STONE, sometimes called the "Seed of the Sun," in sacred art is often portrayed as a flaming disk or as a pine cone.

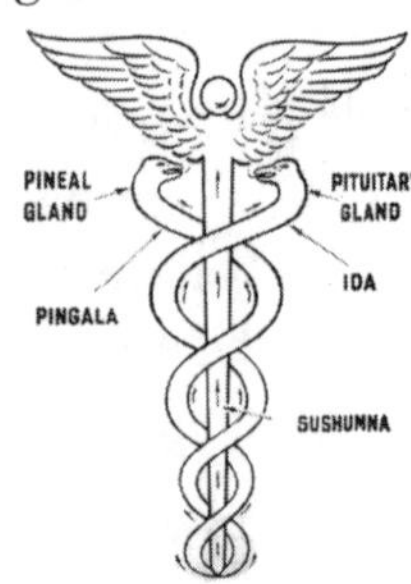

PINGALA. One part of a threefold current or channel through which the KUNDALINI rises along the spinal column from the base of the spine to the crown center. The pingala current, on the right, is associated with the masculine stream of energy, or the force side, of this three-part body mechanism. *Also see* Sushumna; Ida.

PISCEAN AGE. A cycle of time wherein the Earth received the influence of the constellation Pisces for approximately 2,200 years. The primary influence of this cycle, emotional in nature, facilitated sensitivity and refinement, especially by developing devotion within humanity. The Piscean era was ruled by RAY 6 with the specific duty of teaching single-mindedness of purpose.

PISTIS SOPHIA. A "GNOSTIC miscellany" book with excerpts about Jesus' teachings explaining sin and the feminine aspect of God, SOPHIA. Belongs to class of literature such as the *Book of Enoch.* Much about Mary, Mary Magdalene, and Salome. Contains six books.

PITRIS. Fathers. Beings superior to the human kingdom, divided into two classes: the lunar pitris and solar pitris. The lunar pitris supplied the forms for humans of the first ROOT RACE. The solar pitris assisted the human race by awakening the latent mind-principle during the third, or Lemurian, root race.[4]

PITUITARY GLAND. Believed to be the endocrine gland into which the energy of the crown CHAKRA flows; in effect, the point of contact for the soul wherein it is anchored into the physical, mechanical form.

Plan. The concept or blueprint of evolution that exists in subtler realities, as made known through the Elder Brothers of humanity. The Plan represents a divine design for humanity, for the planet, and for all life. Knowledge of this Plan will guide humanity back to the Source of life and enable us to become conscious coworkers. A mandala of action projected to humanity to aid us in finding our way home. A manifestation of divine law; the order and purpose that prevail throughout all existence. In order to participate, awakened humanity seeks to perceive its role individually and as a group.

Plane. As used in the mystery teachings, a well-defined, stabilized frequency wherein life unfolds, i.e., physical, astral, mental.

Planes, cosmic. From the highest to the lowest of the planes of our universe are these seven major planes: logoic, monadic, atmic, buddhic (or intuitional), manasic (or mental), astral, and physical. All of the planes serve as bridges between the individual and the universe.

Planes, seven: physical, emotional, mental, intuitional, atmic, monadic, divine. A gathering of similar vibrations and natures into defined frequencies. Life-forms, both individually and collectively, experience action and reaction herein. Each plane consists of seven levels and is gradually delineated as denser frequencies form a layer and the less dense build upon it until seven substrata are formed.

Planetary body. Humanity, as a group of cells within planet Earth. Spiritual teachings suggest humanity forms the cerebrospinal (brain and nerves) nature of our planet. Simplified, humanity is the mental body of the planet.

Planetary centers. *See pp. 349–55,* Etheric Dimensions.

Planetary chain. The lives of a planet linked in a series. Seven incarnations exist in a chain—descending: mental, astral, etheric, physical; ascending: etheric, astral, mental.

Planetary Christ. *See* Christ, planetary.

Planetary evolution. The planet itself experiences progression. All life forms on the planet are on their own evolutionary path and part of the greater life's maturation as well.

Planetary hierarchy. *See* Hierarchy, planetary.

Planetary initiation. *See* Initiation, planetary.

Planetary Logos. The indwelling high consciousness that forms the physical body of the planet for the purpose of evolving consciousness, both its own and that of the little lives on it and in it.

Planetary spirit. The vital essence (not form) energizing the life of the Earth.

Planetary workers. Those whose allegiance is pledged to the advancement of the goals of the planet collectively and in obedience to the planetary Logos.

Planets and Their Astrological Impact

Since early times, spiritual sciences have recognized that planets bequeath streams of energies known as Ray influences, a relationship emerging even more clearly today. While the study of planetary influences is quite ancient, Ray study was an obscure science found more in Western arcana than Eastern through the contributions of Kabalah, Madame Blavatsky, the Bailey materials, et al.

Earth. Our home planet, considered nonsacred, is in process of transformation, preparing for an initiation. Located in the horoscope directly across from the sun, we write the Earth into our charts and study its influence somewhat with the aid of esoteric astrology. It is considered to be Ray 2 in nature; however, humanity is expressing collectively on Ray 4, which helps the blending of personality and soul. *See* Tiamat.

Jupiter. The placement of this planet indicates areas of good fortune, growth, and expansion in life. Known as a benevolent planet, Jupiter often signals areas of spiritual expression or fervor. The ruler of the sign of Sagittarius, it is considered a sacred planet and Ray 2 in nature.

Mars. The planet that symbolizes the type and amount of physical strength and stamina we have by birthright. This planet asserts the masculine side of our nature and where we will expend physical effort. The ruler of Aries, it is considered a nonsacred planet and Ray 6 in nature.

Mercury. The planet of communication and mental capabilities. Aspects to Mercury help us understand our mental makeup, how our minds work, and what we enjoy studying or contemplating. The ruler of the signs of Gemini and Virgo, it is considered a sacred planet and Ray 4 in nature.

Moon. Represents the astral nature and subconscious pattern held within the subtler part of our natures and revealed through our emotions. Placement of the moon determines areas of great attachment or passion, so success here is very satisfying. The importance of the moon in interpreting a personal horoscope is second only to the sun. The moon rules the sign of Cancer and is considered a nonsacred planet and Ray 4 in nature.

Neptune. The planet that indicates spiritual expression. Its placement in a horoscope reveals where we must face illusion or delusion. A well-aspected Neptune can help us with active creativity and imagination, usually after we have elevated our spiritual understanding. Ruler of Pisces, it is considered sacred and Ray 6 in nature.

PLUTO. This planet is the indicator of rejuvenation and power. Its location becomes a place of challenge for our use of will and personal power. A recent discovery (1930), Pluto often indicates where we could be secretive or less comfortable being direct about matters. Often seen as the planet of the underworld or subconscious. Ruler of Scorpio, it is considered nonsacred and Ray 1 in nature.

SATURN. The planet of discipline, structure, and responsibility, Saturn's placement indicates areas of restriction, self-induced or otherwise. Known as the teacher, or angel of discipline, Saturn conveys the lessons of life; here we make progress as we earn it, usually slowly. Ruler of Capricorn, it is considered a sacred planet and Ray 3 in nature.

SUN. The major focus of the personal horoscope representing our life force, will, and inner life. Its location indicates the character being developed and refined, as well as the life thrust. The sun governs the physical heart and stamina. The sun rules the sign of Leo and is considered a nonsacred planet and Ray 2 in nature.

URANUS. The planet of rapid change and great daring, the placement of Uranus in a horoscope suggests where we might be revolutionary or futuristic in our thinking or behavior. Here freedom is experienced, and creativity runs high. Ruler of the sign of Aquarius, it is considered Ray 7 in nature and sacred.

VENUS. The planet of beauty and love. In a horoscope the aspects to Venus are important indications of the manner in which we express our passion for life, and the placement will reveal the kinds of things we will love. Venus represents the feminine, nurturing nature as well. The ruler of the signs of Taurus and Libra, it is considered a sacred planet and Ray 5 in nature.

VULCAN. A sacred planet that astronomers have not yet positively identified. Vulcan is believed by esoteric astrologers to orbit 8 to 9 degrees away from the sun whose bright light veils it from us and will continue to do so until humanity can handle Vulcan's powerful energies. In the horoscope of an awakened one, aspects to Vulcan are important as they reveal the nature of the spiritual will, its detachment from the form life, and the spiritualizing of matter through creativity. (Vulcan, after all, was a blacksmith.) Ray 1 in nature, Vulcan is thought to link humanity with the Plan

PLANETS. *See pp. 218–19.*

PLASMOIDS. Living organisms, invisible biological AEROFORMS, named "CRITTERS" by their discoverer.

PLATFORM READING. A public demonstration initiated by SPIRITUALISM, to be an awakening experience for the audience to bring greater understanding of spiritual and psychic capabilities and sensitivity. Messages and impressions from the spirit world are given by trained spiritual workers.

PLATO. b. Athens, 428 B.C., d. 347. Described as one of the greatest thinkers of all time, Plato significantly influenced the advancement of esoteric and mystical thought. He did not see the world of the senses as real but believed the world of ideas, in fact, was the real world. The world of experience held only copies of the world of ideas or forms that have always existed in perfection. Matter, being imperfect, distorts the idea.

Born to a distinguished family, he was surrounded by learned people. His early ambitions were political, but after Socrates' death, he was convinced that a man of conscience had no place in the world of politics. He founded The Academy as an institute for the systematic pursuit of philosophical and scientific research, over which he presided the rest of his life. It became the recognized authority in mathematics and jurisprudence.

Plato taught that anyone studying the SPIRITUAL SCIENCES needed also to study mathematics or physical anatomy to remain balanced and grounded.

PLEIADES. A configuration of stars often called the "seven sisters" or "weeping sisters," the daughters of Atlas in Greek mythology. It is said that many spacial beings on the planet at this time are from Pleiades and here to learn human lessons.

PLEROMA. In Greek, "fullness." The supreme divinity in GNOSTICISM. The perfect world, abode of the invisible gods, the universal soul.

PMCD. An acronym for "post-mortem contact with the dead," as framed by Raymond Moody in his research of DISCARNATES; he created a setting in which discarnates could be called and might respond to the one who calls.[5]

PNEUMA. Greek for "breath."

PODVIG. An Agni term, not translatable from Russian, but implying a great or heroic deed—spiritual achievement that unites the soul in greater expression in life.

POLARITY, EXPRESSING AS GENDER COLLECTIVELY. Patriarchy is based on the principle that end results have superior value; matriarchy is based on the principle of relationship. Herein they differ. Polarities desire to unite, and the call for the DIVINE FEMININE today is the result of a cry from a deep need within the human heart. While patriarchy ruled, SOPHIA was rejected and withdrew; thus Earth, or nature, suffered. She returns, however, when even one calls her name, according to Prov. 3.13, 7.4, 14.33.

POLARITY (HERMETIC PRINCIPLE OF). The belief that everything is reflected by opposites; poles of opposites hold the LINE OF TENSION upon which all life advances in the dual world. Polarities range from black and white, female and male, give and receive, express and stifle, fire and water, inhale and exhale, empty and full, and create and destroy. *See* Hermetic Principles.

POLARITY THERAPY. A specific healing technique used to balance points in the ETHERIC BODY. These points, in opposition to one another, are balanced to restore health, a fresh flow or revitalization to the body.

POLITICAL ORGANIZERS. WORLD SERVERS who work through integrated head, heart, and root CHAKRAS to step down the higher PLAN for humanity.

POLITICS. The art of people living and working together for the fulfillment of group needs.

POLTERGEIST. A German word meaning "noisy spirit." Known scientifically as recurrent spontaneous PSYCHOKINESIS, these ostensibly paranormal disturbances include throwing, lifting, and breaking objects. This immature, mischievous, trouble-making spirit demands attention. Such an entity often will be located in a household of sexually active adolescents.

POLYCARP. *See pp. 246–51,* Saints.

POPOL VOL. The MAYAN book of sacred wisdom.

PORTAL OF INITIATION. Doorway to, or facing, the test at each stage of attainment. As one approaches a next level of true spiritual empowerment, there is a great test; with success, the incoming energy of that INITIATION is received from behind the VEIL—most often without the knowledge of the recipient.

POSSESSION. In spiritual thought a negative condition in which the soul that has created a personality is blocked by a possessing entity, which, having taken command, blocks the creator's goals and substitutes its own. SPIRIT RELEASEMENT can return the personality life to order. *Also see* Discarnates.

POVERTY. A vow often taken by a subordinate of a religious order in return for INITIATION or admittance into a particular tradition. The idea is twofold: that all that one has belongs equally to all others (in the order and/or in the world) and that all one truly owns is what is contained in the soul. Such reasoning is to teach that outer things are for right use, and in the truest sense they do not belong in the real world but are only the trappings of the material plane.

POWER ANIMAL. In shamanism, an identity established between oneself and an animal consciousness. A TOTEM. The power animal personifies an aspect of oneself seeking identification and expression.

POWERS. ANGELS of an advanced order who work under the LORDS OF KARMA to balance GOOD AND EVIL in human lives and in planetary systems. Powers deal with the UNIVERSAL LAW of CAUSE AND EFFECT and work to transmute evil to good through strength, severity, fortitude, and justice.

POWER WORDS. Words carrying a particularly high charge of energy into and/or through the consciousness of the speaker for a personal or group purpose. Selected for their effect, such words are used by knowledgeable ones to direct energy for specific reasons. Common and beneficial power words are AMEN, HO, KIN, MIR, OM, SHALOM, SHANTI.

PRACTITIONER. One knowledgeable in practices designed to carry oneself or another toward a desired goal. Specifically, at Sancta Sophia Seminary located at the intentional spiritual community of Sparrow Hawk Village, Tahlequah, Oklahoma, one who has completed foundational academic work and personal growth and demonstrated integrity to earn the endorsement of the religious society—a designated, qualified lay minister.

PRAJNA. "'Wisdom.' Prajna consciousness is often referred to as the causal or deep-sleep state of awareness, in which NOETIC awareness occurs without an appearance of objective content."[6]

PRALAYA. A period of unmanifest when the second (the Son) and third (the Holy Spirit) aspects of the Christian TRINITY rest in the first (the Father) before a renewed cycle begins. A Sanskrit word meaning "period of dissolution or destruction." In Hindu philosophy, the end of the world; also called "Night of BRAHMA" or the inbreath.

PRANA. Hindi and yogic term for "PSI energy" and SANSKRIT for "breath," without which living beings cannot exist. The psycho-electrical field that manifests in the individual as vitality. Also known as *ki* or *ch'i,* prana is the cosmic life-force on all planes of being; the "breath of life." This notion is also known as mana to Polynesians and Hawaiians, as baruka to the Sufis, as Yesod to kabalists; the Iroquois call it orenda, the Ituri pygmies call it megbe, Chinese know it as qi or chi; ki in Japanese. This type of energy comes from the physical sun and works actively upon the vital bodies of every form in the natural world, including the physical form of humanity itself. The nearest name identified through science has been "orgone" by Wilhelm Reich, his perspective being orgone is the all-pervasive ocean of life energy—primordial, massless, and preatomic—from which all other forms of energy are derived. Also related are animal magnetism and odic force. Today in science some studies are calling it X-energy. *Also see* Etheric body; Etheric plane; Physical plane.

PRANIC HEALING. Yogic term for "MAGNETIC HEALING."

PRASAD. A Hindu ritual. A bit of fruit, sweets, or food is blessed in a ritual and offered to deity, then distributed to be eaten by those present as a sacred sharing, similar in nature to Christian communion.

PRATYEKA-BUDDHA. Those who have passed beyond the WHEEL OF REBIRTH and the material world and returned to the divine SOURCE. Their emphasis is not upon service or compassion, but upon a personal goal. The path of the Pratyeka-Buddha leads to immediate realization of the goal (bliss)—the "open path" called "Buddhahood for self alone."

PRAXIS. Greek for the practice or practical implementation of one's chosen discipline—action or spiritual practice.

PRAYER. Coming from the same root word as PRANA (breath), prayer reminds us to breathe the Source in to ourselves, thereby accessing the energy field of God, *in whom we live and move and have our being.* The deliberate attempt to center ourselves in conversation with our deity of choice; the concentration of heart and mind that brings about that communion. The message sent to the Creator through conscious and unconscious wishes, thoughts, and aspirations, representing our search to fulfill our needs and to stretch beyond ourselves to a greater identity and a clear awareness of God's presence in our lives. Often simplified as "talking to God," while meditation represents "listening for God." When public, the person praying, the audience, and God join in communication—a triangulation of communication with purpose.

PRAYER, MONOLOGISTIC. One word, thought, or symbol is focused on to the exclusion of most others. The JESUS PRAYER is an example of a favorite monologistic prayer and used much like a mantra. An important image of the ANCHORITE is the ladder—an image often found in writings of the DESERT FATHERS and mothers, whose history is recorded in the PHILOKALIA.

PRAYER WHEEL. A spiritual tool of the Buddhist tradition wherein a container with many prayers in it is spun as the spinner is in a prayerful state of mind, activating the prayers within for a time and for the intention of the one praying.

PREBIRTH RESIDUE. Imprints or conditions impacting one before birth or in a previous life, as defined and taught in PSYCHOGRAPHY.

PRECESSION OF THE EQUINOXES. Due to small periodic motion of the celestial pole of the Earth with respect to the ECLIPTIC pole, the point at which the sun passes the intersection of the ecliptic and the celestial equator is seen each year in a slightly different position against the stars. The signs, which are measured from the equinox, gradually move away from the constellations whose names they bear, providing the unmoving sphere against which the vernal point shifts slowly backward—a RETROGRADE movement.

PRECIPITATION. In a certain state of meditation, droplets of thought that fall into the opened mind and impact it as impressions or creativity. Similar to densified droplets from a rain cloud, these drops rain down from a reservoir of higher thought, often called the CLOUD OF KNOWABLE THINGS or the rain cloud of thought.

PRECOGNITION. Knowledge of a future event that could not have been predicted or inferred by normal means.

PRECOGNITIVE DREAM. An impression from the dream state of an event that has not yet occurred but has registered within the consciousness of the receiver.

PREDESTINATION. The belief that our physical life, as well as the universe, is planned before

Prayers for Peace

All major religions and cultures call for world peace through prayer.

The Baha'i Prayer for Peace

Be generous in prosperity, and thankful in adversity. Be fair in thy judgment, and guarded in thy speech. Be a lamp unto those who walk in darkness and a home for the stranger. Be eyes to the blind, and guiding light unto the feet of the erring. Be a breath of life to the body of humankind, a dew to the soil of the human heart, and a fruit upon the tree of humility.

The Buddhist Prayer for Peace

May all beings everywhere plagued with sufferings of body and mind quickly be freed from their illnesses. May those frightened cease to be afraid, and may those bound be free. May the powerless find power, and may people think of befriending one another. May those who find themselves in trackless, fearful wildernesses—the children, the aged, the unprotected—be guarded by beneficent celestials. And may they swiftly attain Buddhahood.

The Christian Prayer for Peace

Blessed are the Peacemakers, for they shall be known as the children of God." "But I say to you that hear, love your enemies, do good to those who hate you, bless those who curse you, pray for those who abuse you. To those who strike you on the cheek, offer the other also; and from those who take away your cloak do not withhold your coat as well. Give to everyone who begs from you; and of those who take away your goods, do not ask them again. And as you wish that others would do to you, do so to them.

The Hindu Prayer for Peace

O God, lead us from the unreal to the Real.
O God, lead us from darkness to light.
O God, lead us from death to immortality.
Shanti, shanti, shanti unto all.

O Lord God Almighty, may there be peace in celestial regions. May there be peace on Earth. May the waters be appeasing. May herbs be wholesome, and may trees and plants being peace to all. May all beneficent beings bring peace to us. May thy Vedic Law propagate peace all through the world. May all things be a source of peace to us, and let thy peace itself bestow peace on all and may that peace come to me also.

The Jainist Prayer for Peace

Peace and universal brotherhood is the essence of the Gospel preached by all the enlightened ones. The Lord has preached that equanimity is the dharma. Forgive do I creatures all, and let all creatures forgive me. Unto all have I amity, and unto none enmity.

Know that violence is the root cause of all miseries in the world. Violence, in fact is the knot of bondage. "Do not injure any living being." This is the eternal, perennial, and unalterable way of (spiritual) life. A weapon, howsoever powerful it may be, can always be superseded by a superior one; but no weapon can, however, be superior to non-violence.

The Jewish Prayer for Peace

Come let us go up to the mountain of the Lord, that we may walk the paths of the Most High, and we shall beat our swords into plowshares, and our spears into pruning hooks; nation shall not lift up sword against nation, neither shall we learn war any more. And none shall be afraid, for the mouth of the Lord of Hosts has spoken.

The Muslim Prayer for Peace

In the name of God, the mercy-giving, the merciful, praise be to the Lord of the universe who has created us and made us into tribes and nations, that we may know each other, not that we may despise each other. If the enemy inclines toward peace, do thou also incline toward peace, and trust in God; for the Lord is the one that heareth and knoweth all things. And the servants of God, Most Gracious are those who walk on the Earth in Humility, and when we address them, we say, "Peace."

Native African Prayer for Peace

Almighty God, the Great Thumb we cannot evade to tie any knot; the Roaring Thunder that splits mighty trees; the all-seeing Lord on high who sees even the footprints of an antelope on a rock mass here on Earth: You are the one who does not hesitate to respond to our call. You are the cornerstone of peace.

The Native American Prayer for Peace

O Great Spirit of my Fathers, I raise my pipe to you, to your messengers the four winds, and to Mother Earth, who provides for your children. Give us the wisdom to teach our children to love, to respect, and to be kind to each other, so that they may grow with peace in mind. Let us learn to share all the good things that you provide for us on this Earth.

Shinto Prayer for Peace

Although the people living across the ocean surrounding us, I believe, are all our brothers and sisters, why are there constant troubles in this world? Why do winds and waves rise in the ocean surrounding us? I only earnestly wish that the wind will soon puff away all the clouds which are hanging over the tops of the mountains.

Sikh Prayer for Peace

God adjudges us according to our deeds, not the coat that we wear; the truth is above everything, but higher still is truthful living. Know that we attain God when we love, and only that victory endures in consequence of which no one is defeated.

Zoroastrian Prayer for Peace

We pray to God to eradicate all the misery in the world: that understanding triumph over ignorance, that generosity triumph over indifference, that trust triumph over contempt, and that truth triumph over falsehood.

Chief Seattle's Prayer

Teach your children what we have taught our children—that the Earth is our mother. Whatever befalls the Earth befalls the sons and daughters of the Earth. If men spit upon the ground, they spit upon themselves. This we know: The Earth does not belong to us; we belong to the Earth. This we know: All things are connected like the blood which unites one family. All things are connected. Whatever befalls the Earth befalls the sons and daughters of the Earth. We did not weave the web of life; we are merely a strand in it. Whatever we do to the web, we do to ourselves.

Earth Day Prayer

Let every individual and institution now think and act as a responsible trustee of Earth, seeking choices in ecology, economics, and ethics that will provide a sustainable future, eliminate pollution, poverty, and violence, awaken the wonder of life, and foster peaceful progress in the human adventure.

> *Like the bee, gathering honey from different flowers, the wise person accepts the essence of different scriptures and sees only the good in all religions.*
>
> —Mahatma Gandhi

incarnation and we are held closely to the design, merely acting out responses from which we learn as experiences occur. Free will is limited in this approach; creativity is negated, and we are relegated to either salvation or damnation. The topics of KARMA, PREDESTINATION, and FREE WILL are often used to explain life situations and the part they play in this present life. Each term is easily misunderstood.

PREDICTION. The perceptive reading of an impression (literal or symbolic) received about the yet-to-manifest future—changeable if will, direction, or action shifts. *Also see* Prophecy.

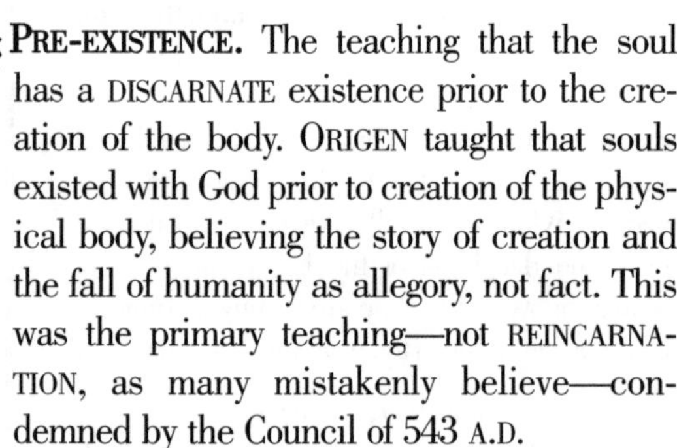

PRE-EXISTENCE. The teaching that the soul has a DISCARNATE existence prior to the creation of the body. ORIGEN taught that souls existed with God prior to creation of the physical body, believing the story of creation and the fall of humanity as allegory, not fact. This was the primary teaching—not REINCARNATION, as many mistakenly believe—condemned by the Council of 543 A.D.

PREFRONTAL LOBE. The emerging new brain, or fourth brain, just beginning to develop from the NEOCORTEX. Sometimes called the "BUDDHA BUMP," it is believed to be an instrument of intuition and sensitivity that is currently becoming part of the physical mechanism. *See* Three-brain concept.

PREMONITION. A sensing or perception of a future event without logic to explain its rational outworking.

PRESTER JOHN. Legendary priest *(prester),* Christian monarch of a vast, wealthy empire in Asia or Africa. The legend appeared in the 12th century and may have been based on Ethiopia or some NESTORIAN kingdom.

PRIMA MATERIA. An Agni term; also used by others to mean the basic building blocks of the world of matter. *See* Chaos; Fohat; One Thing.

PRIMORDIAL. From the beginning of time, existing in its original form.

PRINCIPALITIES. ANGELS of an advanced order who are in charge of the GROUP MIND and nations. Serving as the angelic guides for nations of the world, they are associated with firmness and victory. Also known as Princedoms.

PRINCIPLE OF DIRECTED PURPOSE. Humanity is directed by the NIRMANAKAYAS and the Group of WORLD SERVERS to learn to relate to one another. Through 1) synthesis, 2) focused intention, and 3) right use of will, they 4) direct energy to one another, thereby strengthening life within form.

PROBATIONARY PATH. A time before acceptance into the initiatory process when we are closely guided, tested, and evaluated for eligibility for conscious EVOLUTION.

PROBATIONARY PUPIL. An early stage of DISCIPLESHIP wherein one must prove dedication to the path and earn the acceptance of a wiser one who will aid the process.

PROGRESSED CHART. In astrology, a chart recording the movement of planetary bodies from the birth (natal) chart to a later point in time. Each planet is repositioned and recorded in its position at the later date and anew design is made with reference as to how the progressed influences are impacting the native. The progressed chart is often compared to the natal chart. *See* Horoscope.

Prometheus. A Titan in Greek mythology, a friend to humanity who survived the fall of Atlantis. Chosen to arbitrate apportionment of a slaughtered bull, Prometheus tricked Zeus into taking the bones and fat (which thereafter always remained the god's portion) and leaving the meat for humanity. An angered Zeus withheld fire from humanity so that the meat would have to be eaten raw. When Prometheus, aided by Athene, stole fire from the chariot of the sun and gave it to humanity, Zeus punished him by chaining him to a pillar in the Caucasian Mountains. Each day a vulture came and ate out his liver, and each night the liver (organ of purification) grew back, only to be eaten again. Prometheus is a symbol of the consequences incurred when humanity evolved into Self-consciousness (the fire of the Gods emits the light of consciousness). No longer in blissful preconscious slumber, humanity—now chained (by its own awareness) to the rock of materiality—must constantly undergo pains of purification in order to remain worthy of the inner fiery presence.

Prophecy. The foretelling of a possible occurrence or the reading of a projected outcome. Prophecies are taken as warnings and adjustments to be made to life. A GIFT OF THE SPIRIT, prophecy can be the telling of forthcoming events or an admonition to encourage change. Some consider prophecies as unalterable PREDICTIONS. Example: Appearing at Medjugorje, Our Lady asks the people to pray and fast, to return to the practices of the Church, and to say the rosary to lighten the wrath of God. God tells Abraham he is going to destroy Sodom and Gomorrah (Gen. 18) unless 50 righteous men are found; then he will spare the whole country. Abraham bargains with God, and by the end of the chapter God says he will not destroy them for the sake of ten. This parable is often used to show prophecy can be changed. Some suggest the role of the prophet is to dialogue with God—both informing and interceding to inspire humanity to change its actions.

Prophet. A seer, visionary, or oracle who utters divine messages or predicts future events.

Prophetic vagueness. A subtle touch of spirit—usually obscure—perceived by SENSITIVES in any number of ways: sense of presence, impressions of happenings, symbols clairvoyantly perceptible, or inner hearing. These psychic qualities are guides to prophets and visionaries but not rationally explained. Imprecision seems to be part of the natural process of prophets.

Psi. The entire field of phenomena generally known as PARAPSYCHOLOGY, specifically extrasensory perception and extrasensory-motor activity.

Psi phenomenon. An occurrence resulting from the operation of ESP or PSYCHOKINESIS.

Psyche. The spirit, or soul, as distinguished from the physical form, epitomizing the goal of humanity to achieve divinity: *Remember ye are gods.* The Greek word *psyche* means "soul," "self," or "mind."

PSYCHIC ART. Renderings guided by psychic attunement, usually to one's soul or AURA, symbolically.

PSYCHIC DEVELOPMENT. The enhancing of natural abilities of perception and extended sense awareness through practice and opening the mind to new understanding.

PSYCHIC READING. Using intuitive senses, an attunement is made to an individual or situation for the purpose of receiving and gathering impressions from basic nature or the collective consciousness. The higher form involves the use of the intuitive awareness. Contacts may be initiated by numerous means, e.g., the sound of the voice, holding hands, or reading an aura.

PSYCHIC RESIDUE. An Agni Yoga term. That which the psyche carries from imprints of experience, e.g., child abuse, traumatic divorce, a fire—even after the experience has been evaluated and its lesson reaped. The remnants must be purified in the light of the soul, even by intent.

PSYCHIC SENSES. The nonphysical extra-sensory mechanism of the nonphysical nature, also known as extended sense awareness, GIFTS OF THE SPIRIT, and by specific names, i.e., CLAIRVOYANCE, CLAIRSENTIENCE, CLAIRAUDIENCE.

PSYCHIC SERVICE. As defined by Torkom SARAYDARIAN:

1. Cultivating the potentials of the human soul
2. Helping people meet their High Self and realize the Oneness of all
3. Helping people see their potential to help humanity
4. Helping people bring forth the latent divinity within
5. Helping people process and find solutions to their problems[7]

PSYCHIC SURGERY. A phenomenon little understood but of great interest as to how a practitioner can use energy as a tool to penetrate the body's skin and in some unknown way alter, correct, and/or remove physical difficulties.

PSYCHISM. Extrasensory perception; sensitivity to nonphysical or unseen forces, allowing for heightened image and understanding. A capacity of the mind—or soul—to deliver impressions apart from an individual's physical and psychological aspects; a natural ability that allows conscious awareness of the realities and activities of subtler planes. This may be positive or negative, according to purpose and intent or level of consciousness. Ethical use of psychism does not intrude upon or violate the freedom or will of others.

PSYCHISM, NEGATIVE. The use of extrasensory awareness in a materialistic manner, working from the lower chakras or self-interest.

PSYCHISM, POSITIVE. The appropriate use of spiritual senses to assist an awareness of the nature of life and in service to humanity and the higher Plan.

PSYCHOGRAPHY. A technique used to bring about an altered state of consciousness to heal memories; developed by Dr. Franklin Loehr to identify and map forces of the soul—past, present, and future lives—affecting the present life and personality.

PSYCHOKINESIS (PK). The direct influence of mind on matter. Moving physical articles by the power of mind; the use of mind power by paranormal abilities. Uri Geller and a few others have demonstrated such abilities in the 20th century under the scrutiny of trained observers.

PSYCHOLOGIST. WORLD SERVERS who work through integrated head, heart, solar plexus, and throat chakras to step down the higher PLAN for humanity. In WISDOM TEACHINGS a recognized professional involved with interfacing personality and soul, knowledgeable in esoteric psychology or psycho-spiritual awareness.

PSYCHOMANTEUM. A term originally applicable to a temple where the oracle of the dead was located on the River Acheron. This institution was located at Ephyra in Epirus, an area in western Greece. A Greek archaeologist, Satiris Dakaris, rediscovered this site in the late '50s where remnants of an enormous bronze cauldron were found. Raymond Moody, psychiatrist and researcher specializing in the study of death and dying and author of *Life After Death,* suggests such polished basins were rendered effective in a manner similar to MIRROR GAZING for the purpose of visiting with the deceased.

PSYCHOMETRY. A technique of holding an object and attuning to a previous owner or using the object as a point of focus for gathering information through the psychic senses, primarily that of touch.

PSYCHOSOMATIC. The condition or influence of the inner nature, or subconscious, or the energy of the psyche upon the *soma,* or body, and its expression.

PSYCHOSPIRITUAL. The mental effort made to prepare the mind and mental body to embrace the spiritual level (soul) in preparation for soul infusion.

PSYCHOSYNTHESIS. A counseling technique developed by Roberto ASSAGIOLI to assist spiritual growth through acknowledging the soul and developing will and wisdom.

PURGATORY. This term refers to the purging of distortions that must be experienced on the journey to high consciousness. In *Opening to Inner Light,* author Ralph Metzner wisely says: HEAVEN is the wonderful experience wherein we know we are one with all life, purgatory is the journey of the soul through life lessons and purification to maturity, and HELL is when we get stuck.

PURIFICATION. Cleansing and clearing distortions and impurities. Meditation and spiritual techniques can heal, mend, or cleanse our astral and mental ethers of psychic residue that obscures higher consciousness. Spiritual DISCIPLINES and psychological techniques that dissolve barriers to awareness are for this purpose.

PURIM. Children dress in costume for days before Purim; pious Jews read the Scroll of Esther to remember the valiant Jewish queen who prevented the massacre of her people in ancient Persia in 473 B.C.

PURITY. Agni virtue for Virgo. A state of mind, purity may be understood as "clarity." Level by level we cleanse the personality of its dis-

tortions, glamours, and illusions. Purity of heart and clarity of mind are achieved by persistent observation and holding oneself in the light of the soul.

PURPOSE. The intentional nature of all activity—cosmic, planetary, human, microscopic. The fire of divine impulse that permeates and motivates all forms toward certain action and achievement; the originating cause. The operating and intelligent will guiding every living thing along its path.

PYRAMID. Means "fire within." One of the shapes of SACRED GEOMETRY. Four triangular sides fit together. The number 4 symbolizes the material foundation and the triangle represents the TRINITY. Together they create 4x3=12, a number that reduces to 3, returning us to the trinity—at work as the number of perfected order made manifest. Part of the formula of creation: ONE BECOMES THREE BECOMES SEVEN BECOMES TWELVE, reflecting the inner Plan for the Earth plane. *See* Numerology; Rays.

PYRAMID, THE GREAT. Egyptologists teach this structure was built at Giza near Cairo by hundreds of thousands of slaves as a tomb for the mummy of Pharaoh Khufu (Greek name, Cheops) who reigned for 23 years ca. 2600 B.C. Today, scientists disagree with this history and suggest we will discover more about humanity's past as we unlock long-held secrets of the Great Pyramid.

PYRAMIDS, WESTERN. The world's largest pyramid in ground area (990 ft. base, 195 ft. high) is in the New World, built near Mexico City remnants of the ancient Mexican and Peruvian civilizations. At Mayan centers, such as Palenque, enormous pyramids are found, often as integral parts of ancient elaborate cities.

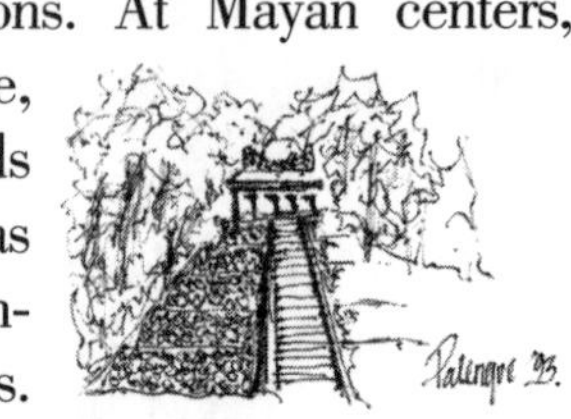

PYTHAGORAS. b. Samos, 580 B.C., d. 497. Greek philosopher, sage, and mathematician. He established a religious community in southern Italy of which little is known. He wrote nothing, and his whole life is cloaked in myth and legend. Pythagoreanism was a way of life (rather than a philosophy) based on asceticism and purification, the relatedness of all living things, rules of abstinence, and beliefs about the understanding and representation of the world of nature through numbers. It propounded that number is the essence of all things and the principle of rational order in the universe. Its leading theological doctrine was METEMPSYCHOSIS, the doctrine that souls migrate from one body to another until complete purification is achieved. Pythagoras believed all spiritual students trained to live lives of profound service must also study either mathematics or physical science to maintain balanced consciousness as they expand their awareness into other dimensions.

QUANTUM ENERGETICS. This healing modality, which includes etheric and nutritional healing methods, is a combination of physiology and anatomy from the scientific community.

QUATREFOIL. This design consisting of four lobes, or foils, of equal size represents the evangelists: Matthew, Mark, Luke, and John. Now sometimes used to symbolize the cornerstone of church unity: scriptures, creed, sacraments, and orders.

QUEST. The search for spiritual realizations to answer the great questions personality naturally asks in its efforts to align itself to the energy of the SOUL.

QUETZALCOATL. Best-known name for the feathered serpent in the MesoAmerican traditions (other names are *Kukulcan* in the Yucatan and *Gucumatz* in the more southern countries). The *quetzal,* a rare, brilliantly colored green bird, is found only in the highlands of South America; *coatl* means "serpent"—thus, "feathered serpent." Also, *co* (serpent) is combined with *atl* (water) to mean literally "feathered serpent of the water." Thus we have the serpent (wisdom) that has evolved out of the water of life (the COLLECTIVE UNCONSCIOUS) and evolved to fly (high consciousness, the feathers of the crown CHAKRA unfolded). *Also see* Ouroborus.

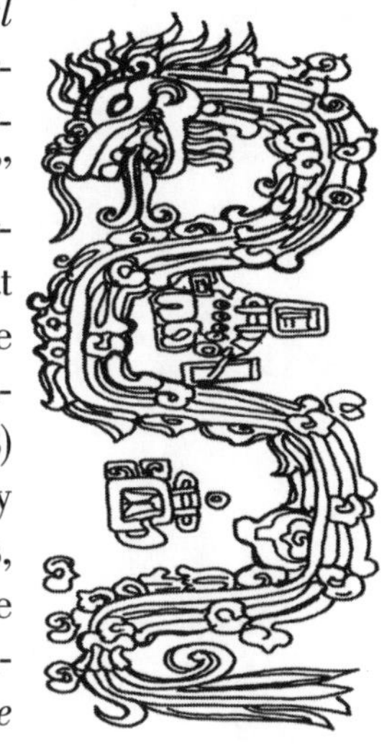

QUIESCENT SELF. The human seed or soul, the quiet self deep within (located at the solar plexus) that contains the slowly vibrating connection to the soul. When we become centered and balanced, we can detect behind the scanning, restless survival mind (ego) another self, a quiet point—the true, or quiescent, self—to be magnified as we balance our survival nature with the evolving consciousness of the subtle self. In time, we truly become FULLY HUMAN–FULLY DIVINE.

QUIET. A spiritual discipline of SILENCE for the purpose of increased awareness of the inner nature. As one becomes accustomed to inner serenity, the chatter of mind gradually abates and connection with the silent sound—the word or flow of soul—is realized. Both Eastern and Western traditions value this method of attuning to the life-line of creation.

QUILPHOTH. In Kabalah, the reflective astral world that contains surplus energies brought into manifestation by human consciousness. The negative reflection of MALKUTH, usually defined as the excesses created by humanity when its desire nature expresses unchecked. This reservoir of negativity (also known as HELL or Hades) is to be neutralized by an awakened humanity. Here exists the energetic pull of "EVIL" that would hold humanity in limitation, drawing it off its evolutionary ascent. It is addressed in the GREAT INVOCATION as "the door where evil dwells."

QUINCUNX. *See* Inconjunct.

QUMRAN. The location near the Dead Sea in Israel of some of the discoveries referred to as the DEAD SEA SCROLLS.

RA. A powerful god of ancient Egypt.

RABBI. Hebrew term for teacher or master of Jewish law; the spiritual leader of a Jewish congregation.

RACE OF MAN. "Man"—derived from *manas,* a SANSKRIT term meaning "to think"—refers to the kingdom of humanity that evolved from the animal kingdom to become the mind-beings whose thought capacity was to build the MENTAL PLANE for the planet and to supply the mechanism whose thoughts or focus would create the circumstances to manifest in planetary life. Ultimately the mind of humanity is to harmonize with the Mind of God and thus resolve disharmony.

RADHA. Consort of Lord KRISHNA, Hindu deity. Many references exist in the great literature of Hinduism about the great love and adventures of Krishna and Radha. To the Hindu, Radha's love for Krishna typifies the passionate love of the human soul for the divine Spirit.

RADIESTHESIA. "The art and science of the PENDULUM." In an intuitive mode the operator links with subtle, complex wave patterns in the fields of life forms, often using a DOWSING device, such as a pendulum, and RADIONICS instruments—as an interface and then as a harmonizer.

RADIONICS. An intuitive healing method facilitated by an instrument or device using the ESP faculty. A trained, capable practitioner can discover causes of disease—human, animal, plant, soil—through a series of questions and answers believed to use the extra intelligence of the collective that each has touched. Usually a technique for working at a distance. Albert Abrams, M.D. (1863–1922), father of radionics, often detected disease before any physical symptoms appeared and diagnosed at a distance with no visible link with the patient.

Rainbow bridge. A common name for the ANTAHKARANA. Also associated with a specific technique to hasten the development of the antahkarana through spiritual focus.

Rainbow Tribe. A modern designation for the blending of people of all races and beliefs into a common focus, usually regarding acceptance and respect for the similarities and differences of traditions and the desire to heal the past and to construct a peaceful future.

Rajas. The central of three GUNAS, electric forces influencing all of life. The neutralizing influence of restlessness, rajas is compulsive—activity for the sake of motion. *Also see* Sattva; Tamas.

Raja Yoga. *See* Yoga.

Rama. The incarnation of Vishnu, second person, or Son, of Hinduism, considered an example of virtue and morality.

Ramadan. The ninth month in the Muslim calendar year, throughout which a daytime fast is observed; the Koran is to be read in commemoration of the Night of Power when MOHAMMED, it is believed, received his first revelations from the angel Gabriel.

Ramakrishna. b. 1834, d. 1886. A Bengali spiritual leader worshiped today by many Hindus as an avatar. In 1856, he became a priest at the Kali temple of Daksineshvara. For 12 years, under the guidance of various gurus, he studied the spiritual practices of various religious systems, including Christianity and Islam. Each tradition led him to illumination so that he could declare on the basis of personal experience that the followers of all religions could realize the ultimate reality if their surrender to God was sufficiently intense. Ramakrishna was described as being "God intoxicated," having deep and broad understanding of the essential harmony of all religions and the spiritual foundation of the universe.[1]

Ram, Lord. A holy being believed to be a manifestation of God on Earth who incarnated prior to Lord Krishna. Sita was his consort. One of the great epics of Hindu literature, *The Ramayana,* contains the story of his life.

Raphael. *See* Archangels.

Rapture. Usually understood esoterically as the state of being lifted into an altered state of consciousness or a less dense dimension by GRACE or a holy vibration, at which time the soul can perceive a higher PLAN, purpose, or way to participate in higher realities. In ESOTERICA this is symbolic of opening to COSMIC CONSCIOUSNESS, no longer belonging to the denser planes. Such an experience reveals the limitations of the physical and sets one free. In some traditional, exoteric Christian approaches, a state of high emotionalism or a teaching (1 Thess. 4.16–17) that Christians will be suddenly caught up into the sky at a certain time, i.e., disappear from the Earth.

Rays, the seven. *See p. 236.*

Reality, field of. The energy matrix, space, or aura of the soul, including the physical body, from which one gives and receives, interacting with other individuals, environments, or entities. We expand our personal consciousness from this private space.

Realization. A profound mystical or dramatic experience of insight (realism). New awareness or perception dawns upon the mind as a deeper sense of knowing, a comprehension to be savored. Its importance is illustrated by the fact that some systems give full attention to it as a path to illumination that begins with mindfulness and proceeds through insight and wisdom.

Reappearance of the Christ. The re-emergence of the Christ is the fulfilling of a commitment to humanity: "Lo, I will be with you even until the end." The Christ is not returning, for he has not left humanity; he or she is expected to reappear in the near future, but no one knows the day or the hour. In esoteric thought many believe the "second coming" will be when some number of mortals develops a CHRIST CONSCIOUSNESS, and this collection (critical mass) of individuals will live in holy consciousness on the material plane. *See* Return of the Christ.

Rebirth. A new beginning, a renewal—"BORN AGAIN" to a new concept, experience, or incarnation.

Rebirthing. A gentle breathing process that releases accumulated negativity—from the present back to and including the birth process. Unwanted behavior patterns are uncovered and released, opening the heart center to more love, peace, and abundance. A powerful healing tool.

Recapitulation. To recall, repeat, or re-experience. In each life the human species is said to recapitulate the evolution of humanity from frog level to fetus to baby. In spiritual thought we recapitulate our experiences of previous incarnations to reach a level of knowing more quickly so that we can again advance on a path of new learning. Recapitulation moves rapidly compared to new growth, which proceeds more deliberately.

Redemption. *Redeem* means "to buy back." The process of restoring balance to an individual or situation with the Source of all creation to become all we have truly been from the beginning. The return of all aspects of life into harmonious union with God through awakening the divine SPARK OF GOD, or spiritual aspect, latent within matter. In the deliverance of humanity from the world of appearances, spirituality realigns us to the world of spirit from a condition of distortion, enabling our recognition of our divine nature.

Reflected world. A mirror image of higher reality cast upon the dense ethers—appearing as authentic, though actually illusory. Contains impressions of the meaning of nature and the thoughts and acts of humanity. A temporary reality, not eternal. The world of MAYA.

Reflection. Pondering or discerning the meaning of words or ideas by revisiting them, not just accepting immediate impressions, and understanding that higher awareness is mirrored in the lower plane as well.

Reflective ethers. The subtle ethers of less dense planes that easily absorb impressions.

Rays, the Seven

Seven streams of force, or emanations, from the Logos express individualized attributes of divine nature. Each bequeaths its quality, color, and sound as it impacts consciousness. The seven Rays are divided into three major Rays of aspect and four minor Rays of attribute. The Rulers, or CHOHANS, of the Rays are also known as Seven Spirits, ELDER BROTHERS BEFORE THE THRONE, MASTERS, or (in Eastern thought) Seven Great RISHIS.

Rays of Aspect

Ray 1 Will, or Power

Each Age is ushered in with a flood of Ray 1 energy, which relates to politicians, those learning to use will, the science of true statesmanship/government, and those mastering techniques of manifesting power. The strong influence of Ray 1 creates the initiator with leadership abilities. Its color is red; its chohan is Morya.

Ray 2 Love-Wisdom

Relates to the sciences of meditation, social evolution, psychology—all sciences of INITIATION, which produce the true psychic. The strong influence of Ray 2 creates an intuitive, maintainer with teaching and healing abilities. Its color is blue; its chohan is Kuthumi.

Ray 3 Active Intelligence, Adaptability

Relates to the history of EVOLUTION, laws governing humanity, OCCULT use of money, the science of communication with the CLOUD OF KNOWABLE THINGS. The strong influence of Ray 3 creates a mediator with a philosophical nature. Its color is yellow; its chohan is The Venetian.

Rays of Attribute

Ray 4 Harmony through Conflict

Relates to the science of color and sound, study of ETHERIC BODY, science of crisis, tension, and new emergence. The true artist surfaces. Its color is green; its chohan is Serapis. It is said, this is the personality Ray of most of humanity today.

Ray 5 Concrete Knowledge, Exactness

Relates to the study of life and space, specific awareness of energies, laws of the cosmos, and hidden chemistry, the science of the soul, meditation, and right use of mind. Unlocking science of electricity and esoteric healing. Its color is orange; its chohan is Hilarion.

Ray 6 Devotion

Relates to the science of approaches to the Higher, the mysteries of INITIATION, the science of service, worship, and devotion to duty. New awareness of the unseen world emerges. Its color is indigo or rose; its chohan is Jesus.

Ray 7 Economy, Orderliness, Ceremony

Relates to the science of cycles; soul and personality; orderliness; divine simplicity; ceremonial magic; and finance. Its color, purple; its chohan, St. Germaine.

Such ethers exist in the etheric level of the physical body and plane, as well as the astral. Here a history of experience is chronicled as a living story called the AKASHIC RECORDS.

REFLEXOLOGY. This spiritual healing technique applies pressure upon specific points of the feet (or hands) of a patient to balance and distribute energy throughout the physical body. The organs and systems of the human body have reference points in the feet, the hands, the ears, and the face.

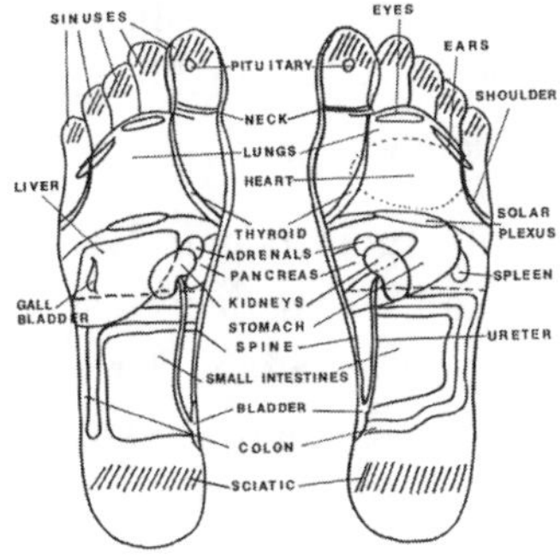

REGRESSION. Exploration of the past; movement backward in time to an earlier point of awareness. Techniques useful to recalling and re-experiencing this life or previous lives may disclose information for healing the present. *Also see* Psychography; Past-life regression.

REIKI THERAPY. *Reiki* is the Japanese word for "universal life energy." *Rei* describes the universal part of the energy—the spirit, or soul, which is continually creating; *ki* is actually a part of that *rei* force, indicating the energy that flows through all living things. "Reiki," as it is commonly used, refers to the Usui System of Natural Healing. After a practitioner has been opened to become a reiki channel, the energy force flows through the hands when they are placed upon oneself, another person, an animal, plant, or anything. Through the use of ancient symbols, it can flow anywhere. The energy seems to have an intelligence of its own, for when the therapist is working with another, the reiki energy will flow to the area where it is needed most, no matter where the hands are placed. Rediscovered by Dr. Mikao Usui late in the 19th century, and brought to the U.S. by Mrs. Hawayo Takote in the 1970s.

REINCARNATION. Based upon the combination of the doctrine of perfectibility of humanity and the principle of PERIODICITY. The human, essentially of a spiritual nature, comes as a seed of Deity into the super-physical and physical worlds to evolve into a perfected human being. As such achievement is rarely possible in one Earth-life, for neither time nor opportunity exists to refine every human power, the principle of periodicity—ebb and flow, going forth and returning—provides each human with opportunities and activities to enter the dense world to experience variations of race, gender, caste, environment, and death. On the ascending spiral path (EVOLUTION) by which we reach our goal of adeptship, each cycle consists of a descent of a portion of the power, life, and consciousness of the EGO into physical incarnation and a subsequent return to the non-physical through which the soul matures toward wisdom. *See p. 117,* Hermetic Principles.

RELIGION. In Latin *religio* means "supernatural constraint." A system of dogma and creeds used to guide belief in a supernatural power. A specific pattern or doctrine teaches the way to experience, give, receive, and live—usually initiated by prophets or inspired ones and followed by others to aid in their spiritual growth.

I have come to the conclusion that whether or not a person is a religious believer does not matter much. Far more important is that they be a good human being.

—The Dalai Lama

Remember to remember. A Mayan expression of great importance in this time of transition between ages, particularly 1987 through 2012, as inner awareness and outer knowledge reconnect. *See* Harmonic Convergence.

Remember ye are Gods. A challenge to humanity as it matures into FULLY HUMAN–FULLY DIVINE. To be understood as right use of the creative power that dwells within, activated to cocreate with Divine Intent.

Remote viewing. Projecting the mind upon a point of focus not in the vicinity of the worker for the purpose of gathering impressions.

REM sleep. Stages of sleep when rapid eye movement (beneath closed lids) indicates brain and/or dream activity.

Renunciation. A state of consciousness wherein one chooses to release all attachments, usually an on-going practice progressing from level to level and to subtler forms of attachments—attention, expectations, recognition, as well as people or belongings. *See* Detachment.

Repentance. A state of contrition whereby one retraces thoughts and actions to make adjustments or amends in order to be set free of regret, karma, or guilt and begin again with renewed dedication.

Reptilian brain. The earliest developed portion of the human brain that forms the mechanical know-how of the physical form and exists to serve, correct, and heal the body itself.

Resist not evil. In Matt. 5.39 Jesus teaches it is better not to engage your energy with acts against evil for it may be the necessary challenge to maintain the flow of evolution. Save your strength for the positive. In the same verse "turn the other cheek" exemplifies nonresistance and nonviolence.

Responsibility. An Agni theme. We are charged to respond to the experiences of life according to our highest level of understanding and spirituality. We are empowered for the purpose of creating an APPROPRIATE RESPONSE to the lessons we draw. Correlates to the energy and influence of 8. *See* Numerology.

Resurrection. Not limited to physical death but also the passage from the death of selfishness and individualism into a life of light, unity, and unselfish love—altogether identified with God. The realization of the divine whole of which each of us is a part and through which each is born into life eternal. Also, the seventh of the human INITIATIONS.

Retrocognition. The extrasensory perception from a past life or earlier within this life of another person or of one who is close to that person, such as a family member or friend.

Retrograde. In astrology, a movement when a planet seemingly travels backward in motion from its usual direction for a calculated period of time. *Retro* means "back," *grade* means "degree."

RETURN OF THE CHRIST. Biblically, a reference to the reappearance of Christ on Earth. Esoterically, believed to be an era of humanity's evolution when CHRIST CONSCIOUSNESS is realized by a critical mass, bringing about an era of approximately 1,000 years of peace, at which time the divinity within each person will fulfill the prophecy of the return.

REVELATION. A message from the Divine revealing new realities (spiritual or human), including DREAMS, visitations, precognitive and psychic experiences.

REVERENCE. Agni virtue for Libra. A more contemporary term for solemnity. Respect and appreciation of all life and an inner awareness of self-worth, valuing each aspect of life, granting dignity and awe to every revelation of the holy.

REVERSE SPECTRUM PHOTOGRAPHY TECHNIQUE. A method of photographing the CRITTERS (sky creatures who live in the etheric realm invisibly) using Ektachrome Super 8mm movie film and an 18A (ultraviolet) filter to objectify the spectrum. With this method UFOs appear in color out of a black background in full daylight. Instructions for this technique are provided in the abridged edition of Trevor James Constable's book re-entitled *Sky Creatures: Living UFOs.* Other verifying photography has been done.

RHAPSODOMANCY. The first sentence to get one's attention upon the random opening of a book of wisdom, such as the Bible—as in BIBLIOMANCY.

RHYTHM (HERMETIC PRINCIPLE OF). "Everything flows out and in; everything has its tides; all things rise and fall; the pendulum-swing manifests in everything; the measure of the swing to the right is the measure of the swing to the left; rhythm compensates."[2] *See* Hermetic Principles.

RICHARDS, MIRA. b. France, 1878, d. 1973. Colleague of AUROBINDO, whom he called "The Mother." She helped establish AUROVILLE Ashram in Pondicherry, India, based on his concepts, which was to be a model of planetary consciousness—where human beings of good will could live freely as citizens and obey the single authority of Truth; a place of peace, accord, and harmony where all the fighting instincts of humanity would be used exclusively to conquer the cause of suffering and misery. Auroville remains in existence today.

RIGHT-ACTION. A spiritual term used to denote alignment with purpose.

RIGHT HEMISPHERE OF BRAIN. One part of the NEOCORTEX (the third brain) with unique characteristics, such as relating to the whole of life, bonding, accessing altered states and mammalian brain capabilities. *See* Left hemisphere of brain; Three-brain concept.

RIGHT-RELATIONSHIP. Self-explanatory but oft-used term in spiritual teachings for harmony between individuals, kingdoms, and perspectives, in accord with the higher purpose of life. An outmoded usage would be "righteousness."

RIG VEDA. The most ancient of sacred verse, or teachings, of the Hindu tradition.

RING-PASS-NOT. The limiting boundaries of one's own consciousness serve as the barrier between each plane of existence preventing ascent. The periphery of the sphere of influence of any life force from the tiny atom of matter to the great atom of a solar system. The limit of the field of activity of any center of positive life. While this confining barrier separates a living system from that which is outside that system, it is not a hindrance or limitation as we progress in evolution and consciousness expands. As consciousness is freed of restriction and vibrates to high realities, we pass easily through the former ring into the next dimension to, in turn, create a new sphere of activity. Until that which cannot vibrate faster or higher is released, consciousness cannot continue its ascent.

RINPOCHE. A Tibetan Buddhist term meaning "precious one," used when addressing a lama.

RISEN CHRIST. Jesus, the historical CHRIST of Easter morning, who demonstrated mastery over death.

RISHI. A Buddhist term for a wise or holy one, a saint or sage.

RITE OF PASSAGE. A formal acknowledgment of one's advancement from stage to stage. A ritual can bestow empowerment and respect to the individual and role s/he is to fulfill.

RITUAL. A prescribed form or order of conducting sacred ceremonies or formulas used to invoke or evoke energies or emotions to empower life. With the RAY 7 influence increasing in the AQUARIAN AGE, we will see a return of orderliness and less wasted emotion, energy, and effort. Rituals, formulas, and ceremonies serve us daily with little recognition. Daily rituals can easily slip below the level of consciousness and assist and empower individuals without recognition. In the new era we will apply these formulas with greater understanding of their purpose and benefit.

ROBE OF GLORY. *See* Light body.

ROERICH, HELENA. b. Russia, 1879, d. 1955. Feminist, educator, spiritualist, writer, and student of THEOSOPHY whose books are today read throughout the world. As a frail and sickly child, she was frequently visited by MASTER MORYA who started dictating the ANCIENT WISDOM TEACHINGS to her in 1924, particularly AGNI YOGA, the yoga of fire, in 13 volumes. She predicted in her writings that the new epoch "under the Rays of Uranus will bring a renaissance of women; the Epoch of Maitreya is the Epoch of the Mother of the World." *Letters of Helena Roerich,* vols. 1 and 2; *On Eastern Crossroads; Foundations of Buddhism. Also see p. 5,* Agni Yoga.

ROERICH, NICHOLAS. b. Russia, 1874, d. 1947. Renowned visionary, author, artist (over 7,000 paintings), and New Age cultural leader; husband of spiritualist writer Helena Roerich. His paintings have been called "unparalleled fiery, luminous, incandescent embodiments of the teachings of the Far East." Psychics said of him that, though old and white-bearded, he seemed to have "an aura of rosy, golden light about him." Nominated for the Nobel Peace Prize for his design of and efforts with the "Roerich Pact and Banner of Peace," which Pres. Franklin D. Roosevelt signed into law in April 1935.

Writing, painting, and teaching in the early 20th century, the Roerichs believed humanity was entering a new era of human advancement when science, philosophy, religion, and culture would be taught as one, giving rise to an enlightened society resting upon the "cornerstone of knowledge and beauty." He foresaw in the new era an artistic return to ethical themes since the dominant essence of an ancient culture was expressed in its religion. He taught that the art of all nations must be protected and used as a transforming agent in our lives. Master Morya, Helena Roerich's spiritual mentor, said of Nicholas, "He is the true Agni Yogi. The fiery man stands for unity, for one humanity, linking the vision of the ages with the labor of daily life." *Shamballa,* 1930; *Realm of Light,* 1931; *Fiery Stronghold,* 1933. *Also see p. 5,* Agni Yoga.

ROLFING. A body-work technique developed by Ida Rolf in the 1970s wherein she proved that by freeing the fascia of the muscles the body could be manipulated and rebalanced in such a way that psychological shifts would follow. She addressed the memories held in the cells and set into motion a new wave of understanding concerning the body and its relationship to the psychological self.

ROSARY, THE. A Christian tradition of prayers said while fingering strands of beads as specifically designated. Other traditions use beads for similar purposes. In the East they are called MALA BEADS. The three sets of mysteries of the Rosary are Joyful, relating to Ray 1, will; Sorrowful, Ray 2, love-wisdom; and Glorious, Ray 3, active intelligence.

ROSE. In Western wisdom teachings the rose often represents prophecy and the chakras, since Old Testament times and more so since the 13th century. "The desert shall rejoice and blossom as a rose." (Isa. 35.1) Often placed upon a cross as in Rosicrucian or esoteric Christian traditions, the rose is to the West as the lotus to the East, symbol of the soul. Mary, mother of Jesus, is often called a Rose of Sharon or Mystical Rose as a title of devotion.

ROSENKREUTZ, CHRISTIAN. Founder of ROSICRUCIANISM. Said to be the 14th century personality of Comte de St. Germain, 18th century (aka Rakoczi), believed by many to be of great significance as Ray 7—ceremonial magic and order—comes to power. *Also see* Dee, John; Master St. Germain.

ROSH HASHANAH. The start of the Jewish New Year (first new moon after autumn EQUINOX) and the following day, YOM KIPPUR (Day of Atonement), known as High Holy Days, begin a 10-day period of reverent introspection and repentance. Known as the "Days of Awe," during which, according to tradition, all the people of the Earth pass before the Lord and are marked in "The Book of Life" or "The Book of Death."

ROSICRUCIANISM. A philosophy of esoteric thought attributed to Christian ROSENKREUTZ ("rosy cross"), probably an adopted name but allegedly a writer living around 1460. A combination of Esoteric Christianity and mystery school teachings from which emerged FREEMASONRY and early THEOSOPHY; a protestant response to the Jesuits. The name itself comes from books published in 1614 and 1615. Several societies associated with the

Root race

In esoteric terminology seven stages of humanity, a series of GROUP MINDS, develop during the cycle of planetary existence. As Earth's humanity passes through these seven root races, the human lifestream evolves. These progressive epochs of dominant cultural complexes, or peoples, are centered in geographic areas where the stream of divine sparks converges into expression: a root race. According to esoteric tradition, the seven primary groups in order are Adamic, Hyperborean (the first two groups, or races, did not take physical form), Lemurian, Atlantean, Aryan—the American-European group mind is the fifth SUB-RACE, or the fifth part of the fifth root race in esoteric determination. Two are yet to emerge (the sixth has been named Aurorean; the seventh is yet unnamed).

Each root race contains seven sub-races, which are like waves coming upon a shore, each evolving toward the goal of the root race in its cycle. Divided into seven sub-periods, or sub-races, each root race attains to a climax of achievement about its midpoint, the 4th sub-race. Here a racial cataclysm begins. Both a new race and the next sub-race are born of the fifth sub-race of the root race as it declines. The new root race then evolves parallel to the latter half of the preceding mother race. The sixth and seventh sub-races continue to perfect the goal of the root race. The intent of the term specifies humanity as a race of peoples evolving and achieving specific evolutionary purposes for the whole of humanity, not in the sense of distinct ethnicities within the whole. *Also see* Sub-race.

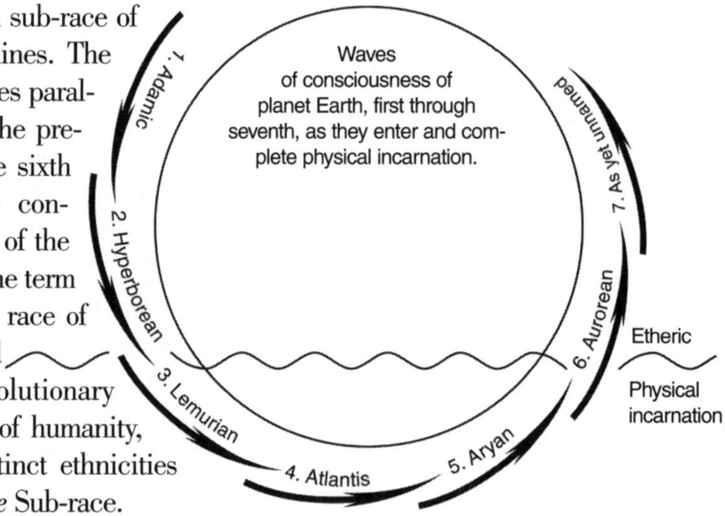

Adamic root race. The first human wave of CONSCIOUSNESS to exist in the subtle world did not take physical form. This seed of humanity began to build the nonphysical form, or model.

Hyperborean. The second human wave of consciousness existed in the subtle world but did not take physical form. Its efforts were directed to the development of the etheric form.

Lemurian. The third wave of human consciousness was the first manifestation of humanity in physical body form. Often considered aboriginal—instinctual and astral; can also represent one who demonstrates a particular mindset attributed to this collective.

ATLANTEAN. The fourth root race, or wave of consciousness, in human evolution. A former inhabitant of ATLANTIS, or one who demonstrates a particular mindset attributed to this collective.

ARYAN. The fifth wave of consciousness in human EVOLUTION, as determined in esotericism; from *Aryavarta* (thus "Aryan"), ancient name of north-central India. The Indo-European-American group mind is its fifth SUB-RACE

AUROREAN. The sixth wave of consciousness said to be appearing about A.D. 2400 in southern California and at the edge of Mexico. The TEACHINGS say the current fifth sub-race of the fifth root race will give birth to this sixth. The contributions of the Slavic people are considered significant to this emerging next wave of consciousness, yet it will be a mixture of all ethnicities.

SEVENTH ROOT RACE. Too far in the future, approximately 5,000 years, to have been named as yet. Believed by most to be of a much subtler form, not in physical bodies such as we know now—perhaps etheric in nature, with a different means of reproduction.

OCCULT and founded in Europe and the U.S. claim to be successors, such as the Rosicrucian Fraternity (1614 in Germany, 1861 in the U.S.).

ROSWELL INCIDENT. Persistent rumors of a UFO crash and recovery in New Mexico in 1947 by the U.S. Air Force, after which bodies of its occupants were spirited away, and the event denied.

ROUND TABLE, THE. Generally associated with Camelot (ascribed to the 6th century) mythology; part of Guinivere's dowry upon her marriage to King Arthur. According to esoteric tradition, the table was built from a template from the wisdom temples of ATLANTIS by the magician Merlin. The archetype was said to have been brought from Sirius and reinforced by placing the glyph of the constellations upon its rim. A replica of the Round Table is on display at Winchester, England.

RUACH. One of three souls defined in Kabalah, Ruach is the intellectual or moral soul. Here exist the mind and reasoning powers—lower and higher levels—influencing each SEPHIRAH surrounding TIPHARETH, which becomes a working unit known as Solomon's Seat. *Also see* Nephesch; Neschaman.

RUNES. Stones engraved with symbols and used by the Vikings for divination. Many similar belief systems use stones in random techniques to guide the consciousness of a seer.

SABBAT. One of the seasonal festivals equally spaced during the year, celebrated by most neo-PAGANS and COVENS of WITCHES.

SABIAN SYMBOLS. A set of 360 symbols associated with a specific degree of astrological designation, created by Marc Edmund Jones through the ATTUNEMENT of Elsie Wheeler in 1925. Each degree has a specific picture or symbol assigned as a power point to be contemplated. Sabian was the name of Jones's school. The concept of a symbol per degree was not new to Jones. It is believed the Egyptians and the Chinese may have used the concept in an earlier period.

SACRAMENTS. Sacred rituals or rites used to invoke spiritual force or power into individual lives and situations. Used as an energy of renewal, revitalization, or resurrection to the life, lifting it in potency and awareness. The seven sacraments of Christianity are 1) Baptism; 2) Confession; 3) Confirmation; 4) Marriage; 5) Holy Orders; 6) Eucharist, or Communion; 7) Healing, formerly called "Last Rites," anointing the sick and dying. *See individual listings.*

SACRED GEOMETRY. The way the essential creative mystery of God is rendered visible; the most cogent expression of the divine Plan known to humanity. A combination of ratios and proportions is the metaphysical pattern or blueprint underlying all manifested forms, e.g., from realms of thought, to universes, to solar systems, to human beings, to atoms. This repeating pattern of harmonic ratios and pro-

SAINTS

Those who have realized a high degree of spirituality, who hunger and thirst for God. Also those acknowledged and so designated by the Christian (Catholic) church through formal recognition.

ANTONY OF EGYPT. b. Egypt, 251, d. 356. A DESERT FATHER, who lived in the wilderness to pursue a life of prayerful austerity. His ascetic disciplines were extreme: hunger, thirst, and lack of sleep; the dangers of lions, crocodiles, snakes, and scorpions. Famous are his vivid accounts of psychological and spiritual ordeals he confronted—demons, both hideous and alluring.[2]

AQUINAS, THOMAS. b. Aquino, Italy, 1225, d. 1274. Highly influential theologian and Doctor of the Church who entered the Dominican Order in 1245, devoting his life to the study of the fundamental questions of creation and purpose, mind and matter, will, the soul, human conduct, habits, grace, faith, the unity of the intellect, and the eternity of the world. His writings—pronounced heretical in his time because they reflected the Aristotelian philosophy that matter has always existed and thus all souls, "active intellects," are one—are today considered fundamental to Catholic thinking and papally approved. One day in 1273, during Mass, he is said to have experienced a profound mystical insight. The glory of divine knowledge so overwhelmed him, from that time forward he took no interest in intellectuality. *Summa Theologica,* completed 1272; biography by G. K. Chesterton: *Saint Thomas Aquinas,* 1956.

AUGUSTINE. b. Tagaste, N. Africa, 354, d. 430. Perhaps the most influential theologian in the entire history of Western Christianity. After his dissolute, irresponsible youth, Augustine became a Christian and retired from the world to a monastic community devoted to prayer and contemplation. His studies resulted in prolific and profound writings on doctrines of grace and predestination and the incorporeality of the soul. He was a significant early theologian who wrote about SOPHIA.

He thought of evil as the deprivation of good; that before the Fall, humans were free both to sin and not to sin, but in the fallen condition are free only to sin. It is the grace of Christ that restores the freedom not to sin; within its limits in each of our various stages as human beings, our will is free to determine itself. He taught that we achieve salvation by doing good works aided by divine grace. *City of God,* 426. *Also see pp. 268–77,* Introducing the Sophia Teachings.

BONAVENTURE. This admired philosopher of Western mystics taught (in the tradition of HUGH OF ST. VICTOR) of the three "eyes" used to gather knowledge: the eye of contemplation, through which we learn of divine realities; the eye of reason, for logic; and the eye of flesh for physical observation.

EVAGRIUS PONTICUS. b. present-day Turkey, 345, d. 399. A friend and disciple of the three great "Cappadocian fathers": Basil the Great, Gregory Nazianzen, and Gregory of Nyssa. A DESERT FATHER, unusual for his learning and literary gifts.

FRANCIS OF ASSISI. b. Francis Bernadone, Umbria, Italy, ca. 1182, d. 1226. An extravagant, profligate youth who was to become the founder of the Franciscan Order of the Catholic Church. After a vision at Spoleto in 1206, he began a life of devotion to the poor and the sick and to the restoration of churches. Denounced and disinherited by his father as a madman, he retired to a little chapel at Portiuncula where he established rules of simplicity, humility, and poverty for his followers, many of them wealthy and influential men. (It is said he fashioned the first nativity at the Hermitage in Grecchio, a custom that endures to this day.) In 1224, he retired to a cell on Mt. Alvena where he received the STIGMATA.

During his lifetime, he had numerous supernatural experiences and influenced thousands by his dedication to poverty, his gentleness and compassion, and his delight in animals and in the works of God as revealed in nature. He was canonized in 1228.

The first Sunday of October is designated a time to remember this patron saint of the ecology movement who demonstrated a life of sensitivity to the younger kingdoms.

GREGORY OF NYSSA. b. Cappadocia ca. 330, d. ca. 395. Not only his parents, Peter and Macrina, but three siblings—Basil the Great, Peter of Sebastea, and Macrina—were canonized. Regarded as one of the great "Cappadocian fathers," Gregory was largely responsible for the formulation of orthodox teaching on the Trinity and on the identity of the Christ as God and human. His many mystical theological texts included the theme of the soul's journey to union with God.

HILDEGARD OF BINGEN. b. 1098, d. 1179. Prolific writer and prophetess, known as the "Sibyl of the Rhine," subject to supernatural religious experiences, many referencing SOPHIA. Cloistered at an early age, she was expected to live a sheltered existence. In 1136 she was made Abbess of Rupertsberg near Bingen, later at Eibingen, and began recording her visions. She was widely influential among kings and prelates and esteemed for her mysticism, especially by the Holy Roman Emperor, Frederick Barbarossa. Her most noted work is *Scivia,* in which she recorded 26 mystical experiences and prophesied great disasters. Her writings—extensive and utterly remarkable—include natural history, medicine, cosmology, theology, music, and poetry. "Her written work surpassed most of those of her male counterparts and outshone them in visionary beauty and intellectual power. As an author, she stood virtually alone among women of her time."[3] *Also see pp. 268–77,* Introducing the Sophia Teachings.

JOAN OF ARC. b. 1412, burned at the stake in 1431 for witchcraft and heresy. A series of visions and guardian voices inspired her "divine mission" to eject the English from France. She led the armies of France to remarkable victories. She was canonized in 1920.

JOHN THE DIVINE. Also known as St. John the Theologian and St. John of Patmos, who received the book of Revelation, or Apocalypse (the last book of the Bible and in all probability the most difficult due to its symbolic language) and author of the Gospel of John. John is said to have lived in Turkey to the age of 120—outliving the other disciples. When the "beloved disciple" was told by Christ his time was near, he dug his grave in the form of a cross and lay down in it. The disciples who stood by were blinded by a great light, and when their sight was restored, they were astonished to find St. John's body no longer there, but a sweet odor arose from manna in the tomb. The ruins of a basilica named for St. John the Divine still exist at Sulçuk, Turkey, near Ephesus, where visitors are welcome. "John escaped martyrdom and was sent into exile on the island of Patmos. Later he retired to Ephesus, where he presided over the local church until the end of his days. . . . known for delivering the same short sermon, regardless of the occasion . . . : 'Brothers and sisters, love one another.' When members of his congregation asked whether they couldn't, sometime, hear a different message, he answered: 'When you have mastered this lesson we can move on to another.'"[4]

JOSEPH OF ARIMATHEA. This righteous member of the Sanhedrin, a wealthy Hebrew, was a secret follower of Jesus. He asked Pontius Pilate for and received the body of Jesus for burial in his own tomb. Some scholars believe this was not the family tomb in his village of origin but newly purchased for the special circumstance of the death of Jesus. Legend has it that after the Crucifixion, he and a number of disciples left the Holy Land and went to the Glastonbury area of the British Isles to live. Wonderful stories about Joseph bringing the Holy GRAIL to the Isles exist in such books as *St. Joseph of Arimathea at Glastonbury* by Lionel Smithett Lewis.

JULIAN OF NORWICH. b. England, ca. 1342, d. ca. 1416. Little is known about "one of the most complex spiritual thinkers and advanced writers of her time." She possibly was a Benedictine and became an ANCHORESS. On her deathbed, only 30 years old, she received revelations from Christ and the Virgin Mary and was cured of her illness. In 1403 she wrote an account of her vision, *The Revelation of Divine Love,* which stresses the importance of the love of God and discusses religious concepts never before contemplated, e.g., the "motherhood of God, 'Mother Jesus,' and the belief that most people and all good people go to heaven. . . . Today, many scholars believe Julian to be the best female British author prior to the great novelists, such as Jane Austen and the Bronte sisters. A brilliant writer, a shrewd thinker, she even rivals her greatest contemporary, Geoffrey Chaucer."[5]

MACRINA THE YOUNGER. b. Caesarea, 327, d. 379. The eldest of nine siblings, three others became canonized, along with her parents, Peter the Elder and Macrina, her brothers, St. Basil the Great Peter of Sebastea, and her sister, St. Emmelia. According to a touching memoir by her brother St. GREGORY OF NYSSA, after the death of her father, she saw to the education of her siblings, especially St. Basil, St. Gregory, and St. Peter of Sebastea. When Basil, an eminent bishop of Caesarea, died in 379, Gregory returned home to find Macrina sick and lying on the two boards she used for a bed. They discussed at length death and the after-life, and Gregory, an outstanding theologian, was amazed at his sister's profound insight into the mysteries of the faith. He wrote, "She was uplifted as she discoursed on the nature of the soul and explained the reason of life in the flesh, and why man was made, and how he was mortal, and the origin of death and the nature of the journey from death to life again. . . . All this seemed to me more than human," he noted, as she continued with her discourse until her last breath.[6]

PADRE PIO DA PIETRELCINA. b. 1887, d. 1968. In 1997, Pope John Paul II officially recognized this Italian Capuchin monk for his "heroic virtues," though he was investigated several times for alleged immorality. It is said that he had supernatural powers, such as BILOCATION and LEVITATION, that he miraculously cured many, and that he bore the STIGMATA. Examined hundreds of times, medical doctors and scientists found no explanation for these events. He was "sought out by believers, including, in 1947, a Polish priest named Karol Wojtyla, who reportedly was told he'd someday be Pope. . . . Wojtyla asked Padre Pio to pray for a friend with cancer; she recovered, and is still [1999] alive. In 1983 the Pontiff put him on the path to

sainthood, and the final step of canonization could come within the next decade."[7] On May 2, 1999, Padre Pio was beatified by Pope John Paul.

Peter of Alcántara. b. Alca'ntara, Spain, 1499, d. 1562. Became a Franciscan in the convent of the Stricter Observance at Manxaretes in 1515. Ordained priest in 1524, he began preaching with much success. His sermons, seeming to "breathe the tenderest human sympathy," often were directed to the poor. Peter's love of God "frequently rapt him into ecstasy. The poverty he practiced . . . was as cheerful as it was real . . . . God worked numerous miracles through his intercession and by his very presence." He was beatified in 1622 and canonized in 1669.[8] Peter wrote many letters of spiritual subjects to St. Teresa of Avila and encouraged her to found her first monastery. Much of what is known about him comes from her autobiography.

Polycarp. b. A.D. 70, d. 155. Bishop of Smyrna, Turkey. One of the most revered of the Apostolic Fathers—the generation of bishops who received their faith from the original apostles. According to tradition, Polycarp was a disciple of St. John the Evangelist, for whom the great cathedral outside Ephesus was named. *Also see* Seven churches of Asia Minor.

Symeon the New Theologian. b. Asia Minor, 949 B.C., d. 1022. A Byzantine mystic associated with Mount Athos, a Greek peninsula and large community of about 2,000 monks—Greek, Russian, Serbian, Bulgarian, Rumanian, and others—who continue a lineage of dedication to transcendence. Through his spiritual experiences and writings, Symeon prepared the way for Hesychast mysticism, a 14th century Eastern movement in contemplative prayer. The central theme of his mystical theology is that by applying classical methods of mental prayer, one experiences a contemplative "vision of light," denoting intuitional illumination the mystic realizes in his encounter with the Divine Unknown. Symeon emphasized that such experience is attainable by all who earnestly immerse themselves in the life of prayer and is essential to interpreting sacred Scripture.[9]

Teresa of Avila. b. Castile, Spain, 1515, d. 1582. Carmelite nun and founder of convents for women wishing to lead a more spiritual life than possible under the disregard for rules then prevalent. She established practices of strict enclosure, silence, austerity, coarse clothing and sandals, and perpetual abstinence. The first was the Monastery of the Discalced (unshod) Carmelites. She gave to Saint John of the Cross—whose *Dark Night of the Soul* recounts his own mystical visions—the task of establishing such refuges for men, while she traveled tirelessly throughout Spain preaching reform despite severe opposition. After suffering much spiritual desolation, she met St. Peter of Alcantara, who declared her supernatural experiences to be of divine origin. By order of her confessor, she recorded them. She is today considered the first known to suggest SEED THOUGHT meditation through her inner spiritual connection, calling her system *oracion de quietud*, or prayer of quietude—called mental prayer by some. *Autobiography*, 1565; *Way of Perfection*, 1573; *Interior Castle*, 1577.

portions is the esoteric structure that links MICROCOSMS to MACROCOSMS and allows OCCULT manifestation, in accordance with the HERMETIC Law of Correspondence, *AS ABOVE, SO BELOW.*

SACRED MYSTERIES. *See* Ancient wisdom teachings.

SACRED PLANET. Any planet whose guiding consciousness has realized the first three COSMIC INITIATIONS. The seven sacred planets—Vulcan, Mercury, Venus, Jupiter, Saturn, Neptune, and Uranus—are more advanced on their paths of ascent than Earth, for they have awakened to their purpose in the PLAN. Nonsacred planets are Mars, Earth, Pluto, Moon, the Sun. *See* Initiation, planetary.

SACRED SPACE. An area properly prepared, constructed, and dedicated to spiritual work or purpose, often following a designated formula.[1] A sacred place is a safe place, dedicated and set apart.

SACRIFICE. Making sacred every aspect of life; sanctification brought about by the fire of purification as it consumes all that is not of the true self. From the Latin word *sacer*, meaning "sacred," and *facere*, meaning "to make."

SADHANA. A religious practice; one's own spiritual path or the truth of one's practice.

SAI BABA. A revered man of India, considered by his people to be an AVATAR, believed to have reincarnated twice in this century. Eccentric and flamboyant in his last incarnation (d. 1918), he is said to sometimes have a wild manner in this lifetime also. He offers many teachings to edify and enlighten—particularly that divine knowledge is to be realized, not taught; that the "unlearned state" that Taoism extols means not mere ignorance but simplicity and inner knowing. At the time of this printing, a controversy on the Internet about Sai Baba's ethics is yet unsettled.

SALAAM. Muslim greeting meaning "peace."

SALAMANDER. ROSICRUCIAN name for the elementals of fire. *See* Nature spirits.

SALVATION. Enlightenment. Mastery of one's lesser self and the realization of one's Christhood or Godhood. The Self-within illumines life with the light of spirit (MONAD). The saving or rescuing of oneself from the power of the nonself. From the Latin word *salvus,* meaning "safe."

SAMADHI. A Sanskrit word meaning "putting together." Deep and profound meditation or absorption in the spirit. Also, the final stage in yogic practice in which the self becomes one with the object of MEDITATION—releasing separative consciousness, entering a state of super-awareness and profound peace, and merging into the One-with-All. A state of immense joy, or bliss.

SAMSARA. Self-delusionary view of the world. Beginninglessness and endlessness of the WHEEL OF REBIRTH.

SANAT KUMARA. The PLANETARY LOGOS, or AVATAR, who in ancient days came from Venus with a number of KUMARAS to assist humanity to anchor its MANAS—MIND-STUFF—and who continues to dwell in SHAMBALLA. THEOSOPHICAL SOCIETY and BAILEY materials support this concept.

SANSKRIT. Ancient Indic language of Hinduism and the Vedas; the classical literary language of India and the BRAHMINS, not spoken as a living language but used as a bridge to the wisdom of the past. Oldest of the Indo-European group of languages. When studying the Hindu culture, high-caste characters in dramas speak Sanskrit, while the lower caste speaks in a more simplified form, akin to Pali, the parent of modern Hindi. The relationship to Sanskrit as the recording, preserving language of the East is similar to Latin as the preserving language of the West.

"The Sanskrit language, whatever may be its antiquity, is of wonderful structure; more perfect than the Greek, more copious than the Latin, and more exquisitely refined than either; yet bearing to both of them a stronger affinity, both in the roots of verbs and in the forms of grammar, than could have been produced by accident; so strong that no philologer could examine the three without believing them to have sprung from some common source, which, perhaps, no longer exists. There is a similar reason, though not quite as forcible, for supposing that both the Gothic and Celtic, though blended with a different idiom, had the same origin with the Sanskrit, and the old Persian might be added to the same family."[10]

SANYASA. In Sanskrit, renunciation of the world, detaching the mind from the world in order to attach it to God, union (yoga) with God as a synthesis of life; wholeness; uniting inner and outer.

SARASVATI. In Hinduism, the four-armed goddess of wisdom, most often pictured holding a musical instrument and other objects in four arms, indicating full use of both intellect and intuition. "The graceful Sarasvati, goddess of poetry and music. Once a river deity, she was associated with rites performed on her banks and became goddess of speech and inventor of Sanskrit. Mother of the Vedas, she executes what BRAHMA conceives."[11]

SARAYDARIAN, TORKOM. b. an Armenian Christian in Turkey, 1916, d. 1997, Sedona, AZ. This well-known teacher and author founded the Aquarian Educational Group in 1961, with centers in Agoura, CA, and Sedona. Even as a child, he was obsessed with the mystery of humanity. He was taught from an early age the value of the principles of beauty, goodness, righteousness, joy, and freedom. He visited monasteries, ancient temples, and mystery schools as a seeker and lived with Sufis, dervishes, Christian mystics, and masters of temple music and dance. He came to the U.S. as an Armenian Orthodox priest with a personal drive to share the AGELESS WISDOM. Meditation was a daily part of his life, and service was a natural expression of his soul.

A prolific author, his over 500 books in 13 languages are read by students around the world. Over 100 of his manuscripts remain unpublished. An accomplished musician and composer with numerous recordings, he mastered piano, violin, cello, and guitar, among others. He lived his life in service to others so they might live their lives more abundantly. *The Science of Becoming Oneself,* 1969; *Christ, the Avatar of Sacrificial Love,* 1974; *Challenges of Discipleship,* 1986.

SATAN. The biblical name esoterically understood as the tester of humanity; derived from "Saturn," the planet of testing and reward for lessons learned. Also known as LUCIFER, a great ARCHANGEL who refused to bow to Adam. This ruler of the lower world of selfish desire, self-centeredness, and abuse of others is rarely understood as the one who delivers tests to mortals to see if they have overcome egotism, selfishness, and disrespect of others. *Also see* Lucifer; Planets, Saturn.

SAT GURU. Sanskrit, meaning "true dispeller of darkness."

SATORI. Merging into the Oneness through meditation.

SATSANG. A gathering of company with truth teachings. Often associated with ceremony, devotional practices, singing, chanting.

SATTVA. The highest of the three GUNAS, electric qualities influencing all of life. Positive, dynamic mental brilliance, elevating consciousness. Also known as action (will). *Also see* Rajas; Tamas.

SATURN RETURN. In astrology, a point where the progressed Saturn returns to the position of the natal Saturn, a slightly variable cycle, with the first Saturn return occurring approximately 28 to 30 years of age and quite significant to outer life—usually creating a major shift in consciousness or change in personality. Soul impacts the life, seeking to lift it into a clearer realization of one's purpose or spiritual reason for incarnation. A second Saturn return occurs around age 56; for the longer life, there is one more return around age 84.

SAVE, TO. "To save" or "to heal" comes from the Greek verb *sozo,* also meaning "to make whole." The noun *soter* translates as "savior" or "healer." In German the word *heilen* means "to save, to heal, to make whole." This understanding adds weight to the true message of theologies: SALVATION, healing, and wholeness for body, mind, and spirit.

SCARAB. Symbol of resurrection or renewal of life, this Egyptian beetle lays its eggs in a dung ball. As they hatch and come to life, we are reminded that what appears as dead or of little value can spring forth with new life.

SCHOFIELD, RUSSELL PAUL. Writer, poet, and spiritual teacher who established a number of Schools of ACTUALISM in the U.S. He developed the teachings of AGNI YOGA over a period of 25 years, which "have been extensively tested. He worked with several clairvoyants and sensitives in making comparative observations and experiments on different states and levels of consciousness."[12] *Imprint Unmistakable,* 1969.

SCHOPENHAUER, ARTHUR. b. Germany, 1788, d. 1860. The first Western philosopher to have access to both Vedic and Buddhist philosophical material, by which he was profoundly affected. He was "unique in intellectual history for being *both* an atheist *and* sympathetic to Christianity."[13] Carl JUNG said, "He was the first to speak of the suffering of the world . . . of confusion, passion, evil . . . . Here at last was a philosopher who had the courage to see that all was not for the best in the fundaments of the universe."[14] *The World as Will and Representation,* 1818, English trans., Dover Publications, 1966.

SCIENCE. From *scire,* "to know," science can be defined as "accumulated knowledge systematized and formulated with reference to the discovery of general truths or operational laws, as such knowledge relates to the physical world." According to John White, "The essence of science is its method, not its data."[15]

SCIENTIFIC SERVERS. WORLD SERVERS who work through synthesized head, throat, and sacral chakras to step down the higher PLAN to humanity.

SCIENTOLOGY, CHURCH OF. An organization established by L. Ron HUBBARD in 1954 with an orientation toward a philosophy of mind clearing, positive thinking, and building a clear consciousness. The organization has applied for and received legal status as a church in the U.S. Its practices have been under scrutiny for several years for brainwashing and other CULT practices. Legal difficulties have plagued its reputation, as has its rigidity and its exorbitant financial fees, restrictive schemes, and internal legal battles. *Also see* Occult.

SCREEN MEMORY. A psychological distortion that occurs when recollecting a traumatic experience, the purpose of which is to distract the consciousness from painfully negative events by coating it with a lovely or different picture—a kind of psychological denial.

SCRYING. *See* Skrying.

SEANCE. A prepared circle or gathering under the direction of one or more SENSITIVES for the purpose of contacting entities, energies, or influences from the subtler planes.

SECOND SIGHT. Celtic term for ostensible paranormal ability, particularly clairvoyance.

SECRET DOCTRINE, THE. A major work of Helena BLAVATSKY. Also a term used for the perennial wisdom that operates out of sight—ESOTERICA—awaiting discovery by one who seeks to know.

SEDER. A Jewish service featuring a symbolic and festive ceremonial meal served the first two days of PASSOVER to commemorate the exodus from slavery in Egypt. The Last

SELF-ACTUALIZATION (SELF-REALIZATION)

The process of understanding and fulfilling the self, activating awareness of the high nature to express freely through personality, allowing for greater self-determination. *See* Maslow, Abraham.

18 CHARACTERISTICS OF SELF-ACTUALIZED INDIVIDUALS AS DEFINED BY MASLOW

1. They avoid publicity, fame, glory, honors, popularity, celebrity, or at least do not seek it. It seems to be not awfully important one way or another.

2. They do not need to be loved by everyone.

3. They generally pick out their own causes, which are apt to be few in number, rather than responding to advertising, to campaigns, or to others' exhortations.

4. Their fighting is not an excuse for hostility, paranoia, grandiosity, authority, rebellion, etc., but for the sake of getting things right. It is problem-centered.

5. They manage somehow simultaneously to love the world as it is and to try to improve it.

6. They respond to the challenge in a job. A chance to improve the situation or the operation is a big reward.

7. They do not need, seek, or even enjoy much flattery, applause, popularity, status, prestige, money, honors, etc.

8. Expressions of gratitude, or at least of awareness of their good fortune, are common.

9. They tend to be attracted by mystery, unsolved problems, by the unknown and the challenging, rather than to be frightened by them.

10. They enjoy bringing about law and order in the chaotic situation, in the messy or confused situation, or in the dirty and unclean situation.

11. They try to free themselves from illusions, to look at the facts courageously, to take away the blindfold.

12. They feel it is a pity for talent to be wasted.

13. They tend to feel that every person should have an opportunity to develop to the highest potential, to have a fair chance, to have equal opportunity.

14. They like to do well what needs doing, to bring about good workmanship.

15. They get great pleasure from knowing admirable people (courageous, honest, effective, direct, "big," creative, saintly, etc.). "My work brings me in contact with many fine people."

16. They enjoy taking on responsibilities they can handle well and certainly do not fear or evade their duties. They respond to responsibility.

17. They uniformly consider their work to be worthwhile, important, even essential.

18. They enjoy greater efficiency, making an operation neater, simpler, faster, more compact, less expensive—turning out a better product, doing with fewer parts, a smaller number of operations, less clumsiness, less effort, more foolproof, safer, more "elegant," less laborious.[16]

Supper celebrated by Master Jesus was a Passover seder.

SEED ATOM. *See* Permanent seed atom.

SEED THOUGHT. A word, phrase, or sentence used as a focal point in ACTIVE MEDITATION to unfold consciousness and increase contact with the inner and higher worlds. We meditate upon these "dehydrated thoughts" to reconstitute the greater meaning.

SEED-THOUGHT MEDITATION. A method of meditation wherein the practitioner takes a posture to pierce the VEIL that separates lower mind from HIGHER MIND. The seed thought may be examined from four viewpoints—form, quality, purpose, and cause—to penetrate beyond the obscure or rational meaning and to perceive the deeper insight available in higher mind.

SEER. A prophet, oracle, or visionary. One who perceives information from the nonphysical reality.

SELF. Written with a lower-case s, designates the personality.

SELF. Written with a capital S, denotes the divine EGO or higher Self.

SELF-ESTEEM. Recognizing the value and divinity of oneself, maintaining a position of respect and appreciation.

SELF-HYPNOSIS. A technique wherein an individual directs the self (reprogramming in a matter of choice) from an altered state of consciousness.

SELF-IMAGE. The picture of oneself held in consciousness—positive or not, conscious or unconscious, and recognized or not.

SELF-INFLICTED NONSENSE (SIN). Beliefs held in the NONSELF that draw personality into false identities; challenges that provide learning experiences. In due time, we awaken to the Self-within and learn to resist the pull of the nonself. In such a way, we begin to see the lessons self-inflicted by false identity and how the nonself holds power through the instinctual and self-serving aspects of our own nature. *Also see its acronym,* SIN.

SELF-LOVE. The capacity to love and respect the courage one must possess to use the human condition as a path to wholeness/holiness. Self-love—the bridge between eros and philia and humanitus and agape—creates the means by which one moves from self-centeredness to be able to access impersonal and unconditional love capabilities. Part of the Great Commandment of the Christian tradition. *Also see* Love.

THE GREAT COMMANDMENT

. . . Love the Lord your God with all your heart and with all your soul and with all your might and with all your mind. This is the greatest and the first commandment. And the second is like to it, Love your neighbor as yourself.

—Matt. 22.37–39

SELF-MASTERY. Overcoming the nonself by developing qualities of the real Self. The first work is to KNOW THYSELF. We proceed to discover the Self and bring its qualities into fullness. The subsequent injunction is to "forget self" and simply be available to the oneness, moment to moment.

SELF-SACRIFICE. An Agni theme. SACRIFICE means "to make sacred"; so in the practice of self-sacrifice, we purify and bless our life so the self-within can express its nature. High creativity and becoming the vessel for the soul result as the self is made sacred. Allowing the self to flow through and into the outer form is the work. Numerologically correlates to the energy and influence of the number 3. *See* Numerology.

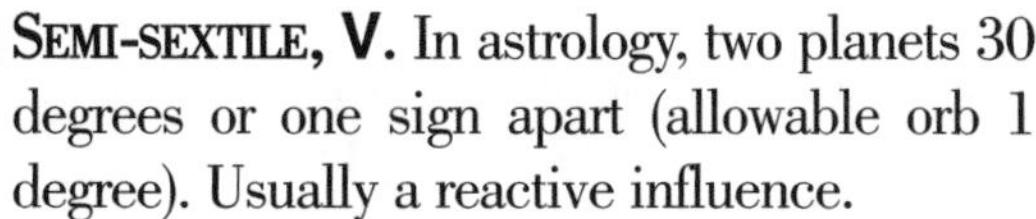

SEMI-SEXTILE, V. In astrology, two planets 30 degrees or one sign apart (allowable orb 1 degree). Usually a reactive influence.

SENSE, SEVENTH. An awareness of intuitive movement or impulse toward movement recognized as a natural impulse that is holistic—integrating mind, body, and spirit. Straight knowing.

SENSE, SIXTH. A common expression for the intuitive sense; spiritually, considered "common sense," while the seventh sense is straight knowing.

SENSITIVES. Those who have an ability—natural or developed—to perceive with extended or astral senses, to receive impressions and information not generally accessible to others. Conscious of the reality beyond the physical through the astral, or feeling, nature, such people may be more acutely aware of thoughts and feelings of others and of occurrences in distant places.

SENTIENT. Capable of feeling; sense perceptive; receptive.

SENZAR. The mysterious language of the MIND that transfers great quantities of insight from the CLOUD OF KNOWABLE THINGS into the mind mechanism in a rapid, non-linear SYMBOLOGY. It then must be transferred to words to be able to articulate the information that has been given.

"Sacred teaching . . . is always given in the universal sacred mystery language. This language was, and is, one which is known of and understood only by Initiates of a certain degree, although identical to those Initiates all over the world and all through history. The name of the language is Senzar. Symbols, numbers and colors play a large part in it. By the time any Initiate has attained a certain mastery of these he will find himself at home with and in touch with this universal secret language," according to Vera Stanley ALDER in *Initiation of the World.*[17]

SEPARATION. In ALCHEMY, the removal of the practicing alchemist from concerns of ordinary reality so one can truly discern what is of greatest value. Psychologically, we must reject old ways, habits, and ideas when confronted with the possibility of a better way of being. The INITIATE is forced to look at her/his life from the highest perspective and objectivity, releasing that which does not serve the deeper purpose of the GREAT LIFE, not just one's own goals.

SEPARATISM. The "me-you" consciousness that holds one's own identity apart from others. Also applies to the alienation of one group from another.

SEPHIROTH (SEPHIRAH, SINGULAR). The ten spheres of the kabalistic Tree: Kether, crown; Chokmah, wisdom; Binah, intelligence, Superior Mother; Chesed, mercy; Geburah,

Seven churches of Asia Minor

A reference to the seven churches—in Ephesus, Smyrna, Pergamum, Thyateira, Sardis, Philadelphia, and Laodicea—to which St. John (the Divine) wrote letters that appear in Rev. 1.11, the last book of the Bible. It is little known that all seven are in Turkey.

Ephesus. Ruins confirm the ecumenical atmosphere of Ephesus at the time of the early Christian church. Near here at Selçuk are the ruins of the Church of St. John the Theologian, the Temple of Artemis, and the House of the Virgin Mary. According to legend, St. John brought Mother Mary here to escape the persecutions in Jerusalem. The Third Ecumenical Council was held in Ephesus (431) in the first church ever dedicated to the Virgin (Church of the Virgin built during the reign of Hadrian, 117–138 A.D.). Early church acceptance of the validity of Mary's presence in Ephesus demonstrates the strength of this tradition. The Roman church affirmed its validity and popes have visited.

Smyrna (Izmir). A modern city today with visible ruins of the early city. St. John appointed Polycarp bishop after he converted to Christianity. St. Polycarp (69–156 A.D.) is believed to have met some of the apostles who knew Christ. As the church of Smyrna was being persecuted, he was subjected to be burned to death, but he did not burn. He was then stabbed. After his death, his body was burned, the ashes collected and buried, a martyr of the Church.

Pergamum. One of the wealthiest cities of Asia Minor as Christianity took root, it attracted a large Christian following. An important center of paganism, its famous temple of the healer-god Asclepius brought people from all over the known world. The caravan route and fine harbor for trade ships attracted travelers, and it became a great Christian center, similar to Ephesus. Many ruins still exist from these early times.

Thyatira. Traces of Christian history are limited here. Built on the plain without natural defenses, the city was invaded and plundered readily. It probably had the richest guilds of artisans in Asia Minor during its Christian era. Its Sheikh Jesus Mosque indicates at least two major religions were present.

Sardis. By the end of the 1st century, the prosperous population is believed to have numbered some 100,000. The mixture of beliefs, however, seems to have worked against the Christians keeping to their faith. Research has located a large church attached to the Temple of Artemis, built to consecrate the pagan temple to Christ. The largest synagogue of its type known to date is also found here.

Philadelphia. This prosperous area, once called "Little Athens," was famous for its grapes and wines. Dionysus and Bacchus had been worshiped here. The Christian community was small and acknowledged as quite loyal. Excepting Smyrna, Philadelphia is the only church in Revelation not reprimanded by St. John.

LAODICEA. Little remains but a marker of this ancient town located on the tributary of the river Menderes (five Laodiceas were founded by Selencid 1Nicator and named after his own mother). This spot was on an important trade and military route from the coast to the interior of ANATOLIA. The Jewish communities founded here were probably those moved by Antiochus III some 200 years earlier. Located not far from Pamukkale. Almost no excavation work has been done. The region is now mostly agricultural, both crops and sheep. This church is accused of being lukewarm—neither as hot as Pamukkale nor as cold as Colossae, neighboring areas.

severity and judgment; Tiphareth, beauty; Netzach, victory; Hod, splendor (of the mind); Yesod, foundation; Malkuth, kingdom. *See* individual sephirah entries.

SEPHIR YETZIRAH. A sacred kabalistic manual that teaches, "MALKUTH (the dense earth) is established upon the throne of BINAH," revealing our planet and life upon it are the dense manifestation of Binah, the Great Mother, out of which comes all potentiality. Binah is the DIVINE FEMININE and home of the HOLY SPIRIT.

SERAPHIM. Angels of an advanced order who act as the cohesive force in the operation of all life. Derived from the Hebrew *seraphs,* the word means "love," and these beings represent universal love and fiery enthusiasm. This celestial hierarchy of Gemini is also known as the Lords of Mercury and brings a RAY 3 influence.

SERPENT. "Be wise as serpents and pure as doves." (Matt. 10.16) The symbol of wisdom and transformation because it grows, sheds its skin, and changes time and again. Joseph

Campbell writes, "Life sheds one generation after another, to be born again. The serpent represents immortal energy and consciousness engaged in the field of time, constantly throwing off death and being born again."[18]

The transformational force is often called "serpentine power" or, in Hindi, KUNDALINI, the sleeping energy of evolution waiting to awaken. Due to the healing power of spiritual force and TRANSFORMATION, the serpent became an integral part of the CADUCEUS, the physician's symbol of two serpents (one black, one white) entwined about a central column and rising to its height. The duality represents spirit and matter in cooperation, the column—EVOLUTION, as well as spinal column—and the top, the highest level of consciousness possible within the world of duality, reconciliation of duality. *See* Ouroborus.

SERVICE. A spiritual discipline particularly related to Christianity as an act of generosity or going "beyond the call of duty" to assist others. To be genuine, service requires an expression not of the personality but of the self-within. Acts can vary; we can give from any level of self, but intent and motivation make a major difference in determining service from ego play. Service is necessary in that we must "pour out" in order to create a space to receive.

As an Agni theme, service is the reason for being. Numerologically, it correlates to the energy of 9. See Numerology.

SETH MATERIALS. Jane Roberts (1924–84), a modern-day AMANUENSIS, received material for about a dozen books from an entity, Seth, who taught through her. *Seth Speaks, The Eternal Validity of the Soul,* 1972; *The Nature of Personal Reality: A Seth Book,* 1974.

SEVEN BECOMES TWELVE. This is the side of evolution journeying back to divine manifestation. Seven planes exist as spirit travels Earthward, but on the ascent side, twelve segments exist. Thus we see twelve disciples surround the Christ, twelve months to the solar year, and so on. The numbers 1+2 equal 3, or return to the TRINITY achieved. *See* One becomes three; Three becomes seven.

SEVEN DEADLY SINS. Pride, greed, anger, envy/covetousness, sloth, gluttony, lust. Antidotes are: oneness heals pride; creativity heals greed; love heals anger; knowing heals envy; power heals sloth; temperance heals gluttony; respectful sexuality heals lust. "The impulse to sin is not sin but to consent to sin, . . . is indeed sin," said Meister ECKHART.

SEVEN GREAT OFFICIALS OF THE RAYS. *See* Chohan.

SEVEN SCIENCES OF ANTIQUITY. Grammar, logic, rhetoric, arithmetic, geometry, music, and astronomy. In Amos 7.7 we find this reference to the antiquity of physical science: "Thus he showed me: and, behold, the Lord was standing upon a wall made of adamant, and a plumbline was in his hand."

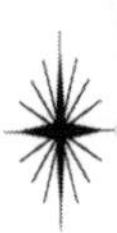

SEXTILE. In astrology, two planets 60 degrees or two signs apart (allowable orb 5 degrees). Sextiles create an ease in understanding and assisting one another.

SHABBAT. Weekly observance of the Jewish Sabbath, or Day of Rest, begins at sundown Friday and ends at nightfall Saturday.

SHADOW. A Jungian term for the incomplete, less refined, and ineptly expressed potential within each of us. Carl JUNG taught that our dreams reveal our shadows—aspects of ourselves we do not recognize in our awakened state, for they are unlived or denied. *See* Dweller on the Threshold.

SHADOWING. Psychic residue identified as attachments of a mental or emotional nature to be dissolved, as well as entities that need to be released to a higher level and replaced with a positive influence, such as the Christ, HIGH SELF, or inner knower.

SHAKTI. This Sanskrit word, meaning "power, strength, might," refers to the energy of the supreme divine Mother. Shakti is the female generative power of energy in the universe; FOHAT is the masculine. Also, the feminine aspect of the spiritual force within each human being called KUNDALINI—one part of the combined force.

SHALOM. Hebrew for "peace," a POWER WORD when spoken as a MANTRA.

SHAMAN. A practitioner of SHAMANISM can deliberately shift levels of consciousness and serve as a guide between realities. Gifted with extraordinary psychic and spiritual abilities, said to be able to leave the body, go into spirit world, discuss with the wise, and bring back helpful information for the purpose of healing the problems of daily life. As healers or prophets (or a combination), they can go out of body at death and/or INITIATION and return. These prophets, healers, mediums, psychics, and spiritual mentors are guides to others concerning spiritual realities. The shaman's gift can be transferred to others, both as energy and as consciousness, and is usually done so by apprenticeship. The term, which comes from the Siberia-Mongolia region, was first applied to persons studied by the anthropologists who witnessed the phenomena. Today, usually refers to the WISDOMKEEPERS or medicine men among indigenous peoples—often with healing capabilities. *See* OBE.

SHAMANISM. Practices that align the self and the world of nature, especially to crystals, plants, and animals. The knowledge and use of such entities for purposes of healing, divination, protection, or greater wisdom.

SHAMBALLA. This sacred island was referred to as White Island or the City of the Gods in ancient mysticism. Headquarters of the Lord of the World, the primary center through which the will of God is imparted for planetary life. There is debate about whether Shamballa is located in a hidden physical setting, perhaps in the Himalayas or in the Gobi Desert area (most accept in the higher ethers of the physical plane over the Gobi). Shamballa is considered the entry point for the masculine energy now receding. *Also see pp. 349–55,* Etheric Dimensions.

SHANTI. Hindi for "peace," in the sense of *shalom* or *mir,* as in the peace that passes understanding, or the peace of God.

SHAPE-SHIFTING. An expression used by indigenous people for the changing of oneself into another form—often as an animal and usually in order to roam about unrecognized.

SHASTRI. A person learned in the Vedas and Puranas, earliest Hindu teachings. One earns this title after many years of study.

SHAVUOT. Celebration of the day when the Torah was given to Moses on Mt. Sinai, seven weeks after Passover. *See other Jewish holidays:* Hanukkah; Passover (Pesach); Purim; Rosh Hashanah; Shabbat; Sukkoth; Yom Kippur.

SHEATHS OF PERSONALITY. The wrappings of body, emotions, and mind through which the EGO functions and with which it often identifies.

SHEKINAH. In the traditions of Judaism and Kabalah, the DIVINE FEMININE that awaits within to activate expressions of wisdom, inner knowing, and protection; a source of grace and blessings, the bearer of divine creativity, the luminous presence of God. A revitalization of this understanding is now happening and enriching Christianity.

SHELL. Often a symbol of BAPTISM since a scallop shell or metal vessel of that shape was used for pouring water over the head of one being baptized.

SHEOL. Hebrew for HELL, the abode of the spiritually dead.

SHINTO. A religion of Japan and Korea marked by the veneration of ancestors and the powers of nature as points of consciousness—similar to MAYAN and Native American beliefs.

SHI'R-YEHOVAH. The unending song of the One Reality.

SHIVA. In HINDUISM, the dissolver or destroyer aspect of God, related to the third person of the Christian TRINITY. The Lord of Yogis, master of the dance, destructor of creation, and third member of the Hindu Trinity.

SHROUD OF TURIN. The burial garment believed to have been wrapped about the body of Jesus after he was taken down from the cross. Extensive examination continues as to its validity. The shroud has been housed in Turin, Italy, since the Middle Ages.

SHU SHU. A Chinese system of DIVINATION.

SHUSTAH. Translates literally "footsteps back to Truth." In Sanskrit *shus* means "returning footpath," and *tah,* "to truth." A school of spiritual thought and specifically designed spiritual symbols for purposes of stimulating the psychic/intuitive senses. Created by Ann MANSER, teacher from St. Petersburg, FL, now deceased. The 70 Shustah cards, five suits of 14 cards, are used for concentration, meditation, and prognostication to reveal secrets of ARCANE wisdom hidden within personality.

SIDDHA. One who has achieved mastery over mind and who manifests the latent faculties of SIDDHIS; a great saint who is the perfection of life.

SIDDHARTHA, GAUTAMA. *See* Buddha.

SIDDHA YOGA. *See* Yoga.

SIDDHIS. Diverse phenomena that result from spiritual disciplines, though not spiritual in their own nature. An example would be meditators who demonstrate abilities such as hopping or flying in particular postures. Considered by the Hindu tradition of southern India to be 18 in number and seen as attributes of perfection or psychic powers acquired through holiness. These powers, according to all great teachers, are not to be sought for their own sake but occur naturally as a disciple works toward enlightenment. *See list below.*

SIDDHIS, THE EIGHTEEN. "In the Vedic tradition, these powers were called *siddhis* (perfections). Eighteen principal siddhis are mentioned. Although these siddhis were normally considered attainable only through the practice of meditation and yoga, in the Vedic alchemical texts it was claimed that all the siddhis were also attainable by either consuming or merely being within the proximity of the alchemically prepared substances.

"The following eighteen principal siddhis are given: (1) the ability to make one's body huge; (2) to make one's body very small; (3) to make one's body very light or very heavy; (4) to experience the Universe through the senses of other beings; (5) to enjoy the pleasures belonging to other worlds; (6) to direct Nature according to one's will; (7) to have no attachment to worldly desires; (8) to continuously enjoy the highest spiritual bliss; (9) to be free from hunger, thirst, and old age; (10 & 11) to see and hear things from a great distance; (12) to move or travel at enormous speeds; (13) to take any form at will; (14) to temporarily leave one's own body and enter into any other body; (15) to permanently leave one's mortal frame at will; (16) to participate in the cosmic activities of the celestial beings; (17) to obtain all desires by mere intention; and (18) to exercise unobstructed authority over all beings." (From Bhagavata Purana, Box X1, discourse 15)[19] Also recorded in *Babaji and the 18 Siddha Kriya Yoga Tradition* by M. Govindan.[20]

SIKHISM. An East Indian religion that follows the teachings of Guru NANAK, 16th century saint. Sikhs believe in one God, immortal creator of the universe who has never been incarnate, and in the equality of all human beings. Their holy book is the *Guru Granth Sahib.*

SILENCE. A major discipline of spiritual traditions practiced for the purpose of inner discovery. Exercises begin with ceasing to talk or responding only when addressed and progress to maintaining a state of inner peace and a quiet mind, leading to ever-deeper experiences of inner calm and serenity to a point of stillness. Layers gradually peel away, and we become attuned to the sound current of silence. *See* Austerity of speech.

SILENCE, SOCIAL. A practice of a number of spiritual traditions wherein one speaks only when necessary, maintaining silence to the greatest degree possible to support the inner experience of CENTERING.

SILENT SOUND. *See* Sound current.

SILENT WATCHER. A title given to the SOLAR ANGEL who watches over the development of the immature human soul until it reaches the fourth initiation.

SILENT WATCHERS BEFORE THE THRONE. Particular types of archangels (guardians of angelic ranks and initiations) known as the Seraphim, Cherubim, and Thrones. The *Seraphim* are fiery ones who stir enthusiasm; the title comes from the Hebrew "seraphs" meaning love. *Cherubim* emanate wisdom and intone truth, supervising the elementals holding the higher will and form for the PLAN. The *Thrones* support the "force of God" through administering laws and judgment for the Lords of Karma. Also called Cloud of Silent Watchers.

SILVA MIND CONTROL.™ An incorporated training technique designed to provide sensitivity training and a rather scientific exposure to those ready to explore human potential, meditation, healing arts, and relaxation.

SILVER CORD. The cord of consciousness, invisible to physical reality, that allows us to leave the physical body, yet remain linked to the physical body while in ASTRAL TRAVEL or projection. Often noted in the OUT-OF-BODY EXPERIENCE (OBE) or NEAR-DEATH EXPERIENCE (NDE) as a silver cord; it resembles an umbilical cord and is attached at the solar plexus, heart, or top of head.

SIMPLICITY. Increased clarity, diminished distortion or illusion, realizing a state wherein uncomplicated understanding results because more integration of Self has occurred.

Sin. A way of learning by following the NON-SELF and the prompting of the senses. From the Greek *amartia,* which translates "to miss the mark." The word used in religious teachings for a breach of prescribed moral codes, dogmas, or specific doctrines. Minor violations are determined by denomination or sect, while major errors are set by Commandment. Sin (Self-Inflicted Nonsense) is identified by various world religions and cultures, with many differences and many similarities. *See* Self-Inflicted Nonsense; Seven deadly sins.

Sinai. A triangular peninsula in Egypt, extending from the Mediterranean to the Red Sea, to Gulf of Suez and the Gulf of Aqabar. In the south is Jehel Musa (in Arabic, Mount of Moses) or Mt. Sinai. On its slope is the famed Greek Orthodox monastery of St. Catherine, founded ca. 250 A.D. The Codex Sinaiticus, one of the oldest manuscripts of the New Testament, was found here in the 19th century.

Sirius. Believed by many mystics and metaphysicians over the ages—especially kabalists and Esoteric Christians—to be the spiritual central sun of our universe and the director of our evolutionary forces. From the ancient Egyptians, we have traces of their reverence for Sirius, but it is believed they inherited the idea from much older and more profound traditions. Sirius (in Canis Major) is depicted as a five-pointed star, representing fire, air, water, and earth, plus time (eternal) as the fifth or over-seeing point. Contemporary esotericism teaches that Earth receives her RAY influences from Sirius through the fixed star of the Great Bear.

> "There has been much debate as to whether their teachers [of ancient Egypt] actually came from the region of Sirius itself—in other worlds they were extraterrestrials . . . or whether their origins were nearer home, in Atlantis . . . . My own premise, which combines both empirical research and inborn 'memory', is that this solar system was seeded from the binary stars Sirius A and B, the archetypes of which preprogrammed their knowledge into the genetic structures of the . . . highly advanced prehistoric people who were capable of understanding and technology."[21] *Also see* Sothis.

Sita. The consort of Lord Ram and the ideal of Hindu womanhood.

Siva. *See* Shiva.

Skrying. The technique of focusing on a bowl of water, a mirror, a flame, or any reflective surface for the purpose of psychic impression or reaching an altered state for meditation. Recently Dr. Raymond Moody has built a contemporary PSYCHOMANTEUM for research into techniques to explore making contact with the deceased.

Smudging. A preparation of sweet grass or herbs burned for the purpose of cleaning the astral level of a person or area, usually in preparation for a spiritual service or to attend a spiritual ceremony. Often used to help clear the consciousness of negative influences of heart and mind.

Sohin. An elevated Hierarchy operating on an intergalactic level as commander of Alpha

Spacecraft. Its task, linked to that of the Space Gardeners, includes the implantation of the new genetic code—GNA (genetic nucleic acid)—in rescueable (advanced) beings, the preparation of their bodies for the deliverance and the transformation of the levels of consciousness of the Earth. *Also see pp. 349–55,* Etheric Dimensions; GNA.

SOLAR ANGEL. A member of the HIERARCHY (not of the angelic kingdom) having knowledge of the PLAN and dedicated to the protective care of Earth's evolving human souls, the true "GUARDIAN ANGEL." At an early time of crisis, these patient and wise ones volunteered to assist humanity—a threatened and sluggish new kingdom. The Solar Angel on its own path of SOLAR INITIATION earns merit for its work with humanity. Its principal duties are to act as a transformer for the powerful streams of energy from the Soul to the personality and to vibrate the Plan for humanity at the edge of conscious mind. A Solar Angel for an individual soul is the SILENT WATCHER until the individual matures (the fourth INITIATION in ESOTERIC CHRISTIANITY). *Also see* Manasaputras.

SOLAR DEITY. A heavenly being embodied in a solar system and advancing through the expanded consciousness of each planet within the system. This divine one contains all of our planets, or centers of awareness, the sun being its heart.

SOLAR FIRE. Electricity animating forms or groups of atoms, resulting in: coherent groups, the radiation from all groups, the magnetic interaction of these groups, the synthesis of form.[22]

SOLAR INITIATION. Differentiates between the lunar-astral development that guided humanity during INVOLUTION and the development of the conscious mind on the evolutionary path of ascent. Also, advanced INITIATIONS of the SOUL that follow the human initiations when the mature soul continues its experience in service through yet another evolving set of experiences to better reflect the MONAD. The monad completes the cycle as it satisfies COSMIC INITIATION requirements.

SOLAR LOGOS. A cosmic entity who affects all lesser life in evolution within our solar system through application of will, love, and intelligence. The sun is the physical vehicle of the Great Life, the Solar Logos through which divine will is radiated toward each planet. This RING-PASS-NOT comprises the entire circumference of the solar system and everything included within the sun's sphere of influence. The Solar Logos is the aggregate of all manifestation within that sphere—from the lowest and densest physical atom to the most radiant and cosmic, ethereal DHYANI CHOHAN. Contained within our solar system are seven PLANETARY LOGOI, whose physical bodies are the PLANETS of our solar system, the centers through which the Solar Logos emanates its force and purpose.

SOLAR MEDITATION. A spiritual approach emphasizing the sun as home of the solar

deity and source of life. A meditation technique practiced

outdoors at sunrise to receive the personal energy of the newly risen sun to inspire and energize both inner and outer life, as taught by Master Mikhael AÏVANOV.

SOLAR MYSTERIES. The inner teachings to which the conscious mind must awaken on the path of evolution. Also, the three primary unknowns of the solar system: 1) the mystery of electricity, 2) the mystery of polarity, and 3) the mystery of fire itself—the secrets of the third, second, and first aspects of divine life, respectively.

SOLAR PLEXUS CHAKRA. The third CHAKRA, as we ascend, is usually identified with power, control, the degree of confidence and sense of self one embodies; the home of will and lower mind for the individual. The psychic sense it provides is CLAIRSENTIENCE and is the most easily ignited. "Gut feelings" and "butterflies" resonate there.

SOLAR PLEXUS PATH. A path with specific defined rules and regulations of "thou shalt" and "thou shalt not." A clearly stated record of expectations, such as the Ten Commandments, the FOUR NOBLE TRUTHS, or 12-step programs.

SOLAR YOGA. See Yoga.

SOLEMNITY. An Agni term. Respectful thought, honor, and nobility of intent; appropriate regard for concepts to be revered and exalted. The ability to see why each concept is holy and to respond in kind. *See* Reverence.

SOLOMON, KING. A name perhaps derived from *salom,* meaning "peace" and "prosperity"—so appropriate, for Solomon's long reign (ca. 961–922 B.C.) was one of peace, prosperity, foreign trade, and building. The son and successor of David, Solomon is considered the father of Israelite wisdom and wisdom literature.

SOLSTICE. When the sun is the most distant from the equator—southernmost or northernmost—the longest and the shortest days of the year occur in the respective hemispheres. Summer solstice is celebrated in the northern hemisphere as the sun moves from Gemini to Cancer, at the height of the growing and flowering season. At winter solstice, when the light is hidden, we go within and renew our commitment as the sun moves from Sagittarius to Capricorn.

SOMATIC BRIDGE. A regression technique that moves the client in an altered state of consciousness from present to past by way of a physical sensation, i.e., "Remembering this discomfort, allow your mind to wander back to another time when you experienced this same physical sensation. Take a breath; now feel, and follow that feeling." As defined and taught in PSYCHOGRAPHY.

SONS OF GOD. A way of speaking of sparks of God that descend to embody and learn through experience within matter.

SOPHIA. In the original Greek writings of Scripture, *sophia* means "wisdom." Also understood as a female expression or being, an aspect of the Creator. Many GNOSTIC systems depict her as WISDOM that becomes distorted in the false world of creation. Sophia is rediscovered as we clear distortions such as MAYA, GLAMOURS, and ILLUSIONS, and learn to listen inwardly, to know higher will. Sophia is she who dwells within and directs through intuited guidance—more simply, the wisdom abiding within deeper levels of Self that emerges as our personal inner knower. "In the Wisdom of Solomon, Sophia is herself 'mother' (7:12), sits by God's throne (9:4) and can do all things. (7:27)."[23]

Proverbs, Wisdom of Solomon (APOCRYPHA), and Song of Solomon especially refer to this feminine aspect of Spirit, sometimes as Lady Wisdom. See Prov. 8 to understand the many facets of Sophia present in creation. CHRISTO-SOPHIA acknowledges the wisdom aspect of CHRIST CONSCIOUSNESS, or LOVE-WISDOM, as the androgyny of the divine masculine and feminine natures. Sophia may be best known in Eastern Orthodox Christianity as the "THEOTOKOS" (Greek). Sophia—once again appearing with some prominence upon the world scene in Western approaches to Christianity—is considered most often as the WORLD SOUL. *See pp. 268–77,* Introducing the Sophia Teachings.

No. 45. The Realm of the Fire Queen. From original pastel painting © 1989 Barrington Coleby.

SOPHIANIC. Relating to the study or understanding of Sophia. Streams of revelations and a growing impulse of the divine feminine began reemerging about the end of the 19th century and will gain strength as we enter the Age of Aquarius. *See* Aquarius, Age of; *pp. 180–3,* Mothers and Goddesses of the World; Mysteries, feminine; Polarity, expressing as gender collectively.

SOPHIA OF JESUS CHRIST. An overwriting of the *Eugnostos the Blessed* found as part of the NAG HAMMADI Library. A Gnostic text believed to be from the 1st century and a teaching given by Master Jesus after his Resurrection—"not in his previous form, but in the invisible spirit." This mystic document describes the HIERARCHY of the world of creation and the fall of humanity into the denser world. The Savior is sent for the purpose of redemption. In *Sophia of Jesus Christ,* the Savior is Jesus; in *Eugnostos the Blessed,* the name is not given.

SOPHIA, THE FALL OF. The decline into the world of physicality that Wisdom experienced as she descended plane by plane into denser reality, taking on veils and wrappings until she fell unconscious. Metaphorically called the WORLD SOUL, as each human begins unaware and must evolve into conscious awareness. Her reemergence has been brought about by the awakening of humanity to hidden wisdom.

SOPHIOLOGY. The science and theology of Sophia, who is the feminine aspect of the Divine. This unique philosophy enriches the understanding of the whole of Creation.

SORCERY. Can be positive or negative. In some groups, particularly of Mexico and South America, the word pertains to "shaman." Often implies the selfish use of transformational knowledge—BLACK MAGIC—

Introducing the Sophia Teachings

In this first century of a new millennium, we enter the era of the divine feminine wherein Sophia will reveal herself to more and more of humanity. Many believe we are to follow a literal, or dictated, path; yet, the mystic knows of another. The lay mystical approach for Christians of sensitivity is to follow Sophia, the way of Wisdom. This natural process—inner directed—emerges gradually. Intuitively revealed, it is the equivalent of SUFISM in Islam or KABALAH in Judaism—that sacred journey individuals "just know" as they discover their soul path. In this wisdom a new culture will blossom and flourish under the inspiration of Divine Sophia. In time a Christianity of a new era will emerge, a Sophianic Christianity that will flourish, bringing an awakening of humanity and a turning point in spiritual evolution. Thus Sophia signifies the beginning of transformation and spiritualization of the whole Earth.

The following is excerpted and paraphrased from *The Sophia Teachings: The Emergence of the Divine Feminine in Our Time*[24] by Robert A. Powell, a contemporary researcher, writer, and authority on Sophia. We are indebted additionally to Robert for *The Most Holy Trinosophia and the New Revelations of the Divine Feminine.*

In the 2,000 years since the birth of Christ, revelations and actual manifestations of Divine Sophia have occurred sporadically. We will review significant historical contributions to the Sophia tradition.

St. Augustine (354–430) plays an important role because, among the Church fathers, he was the one most occupied with Sophia. His influence has touched many subsequent theologians and prominent figures in Christian history.

In the Middle Ages, we find an extraordinary revelation of Sophia. From early childhood, St. HILDEGARD of Bingen (1098–1179) was aware of being surrounded by divine light and able to see beyond the natural world into heavenly realms. Among her most powerful and inspiring visions were those of Divine Sophia. For Hildegard, Sophia was on one hand the mother and soul of the world and on the other the bride of Christ and mother of the Church.

The question is often raised whether Sophia is an attribute of God as Divine Wisdom or an actual person. Some think the words of Sophia in the Old Testament, Proverbs and The Song of Solomon, and from the Apocrypha's Wisdom of Solomon show her to be a personification of God's wisdom who addresses humanity. If we study the actual words and indications of Sophia in these wisdom books, however, it becomes clear that Sophia is a being with a spiritual nature, having human qualities,

(cont.)

attributes, and functions such as reason and free will. Furthermore, she is described as being created female and as dancing before God. She is different from God and acts independently with respect to God. To Creation she is depicted as guiding, renewing, and ruling everywhere with reason, power, and goodness. To humanity, she admonishes, leads, and assists us as mother, teacher, and beloved.

Church fathers to the present have usually understood Sophia as a person, even if interpretations about her vary. Some theologians identify her with the Logos and others with the Holy Spirit. Mystics such as Hildegard and Jakob BOEHME (1575–1624) make it quite clear they had direct, living experiences of Sophia as an actual being—not simply as a personification of divine wisdom.

Sophia was often depicted as an actual being in the art of the Middle Ages. She is shown as queen of the seven liberal arts, sitting on a royal throne and surrounded by grammar, rhetoric, dialectic, music, arithmetic, geometry, and astronomy. A stream of water pours from each side of her body, and below her are the philosophers Plato and Aristotle, receiving the living waters of Sophia's wisdom.

Jakob Boehme's visions and experiences of Sophia are powerful and extraordinary testimony to a divine Sophia existing in spiritual realms and with whom we can have communication and relationship. For Boehme, Sophia is the exhalation, the out-breath of God's power, God's mirror, the image of God's goodness. She dwells in pious souls and is the friend, betrothed, bride, mistress, and teacher to those who seek her in the appropriate manner.

Due to his inspiring visions that testify to the Divine Sophia, Boehme became known as the father of Sophiology in the West. A key element in his teachings of Sophia concerns her profound relationship with the Virgin Mary. Boehme was perhaps the first to intuit an incorporation, even an incarnation of the Divine Sophia in Mary.

Boehme's testimony has inspired numerous individuals since his time, including John Pordage (1607–1681) and Jane Leade (1623–1704) in England. In Germany Gottfried Arnold (1666–1714), the poet Novalis of the 12th century, and the great idealist philosopher Friedrich Wilhelm Joseph von Schelling (1775–1854) were all touched by his works. Vladimir Solovyev (1853–1900), the great Russian philosopher, was also influenced by Boehme. The relationship between Sophia and the Virgin Mary became of central importance to Russian Sophiologists.

One of the most gifted clairvoyants of all time, Anne Catherine Emmerich (1774–1824), bears witness to Divine Sophia and her relationship with the Virgin Mary. She began to receive visions

(cont.)

day by day, describing the life of Christ, which led to the discovery of the historical, validated house of the Virgin Mary near Ephesus in Turkey. Emmerich's visions include a testimony to Sophia as the wisdom of God and as a being who incarnated qualities of Sophia into the Virgin Mary.

A few years after the death of Emmerich, philosopher Vladimir Solovyev emerged as a great prophet of the Sophia tradition in Russia. He believed a divided Church was a scandal for Christianity and through Sophia a reunification between East and West might come about. He inspired many Russians, among them poets and theologians. The tradition now known as Sophiology came to birth in Russia through Russian Orthodox priests who carried it further. Solovyev saw Sophia as the soul of the world, having three aspects, which allow her to unify, connect, and direct everything. She possesses a higher divine part, a lower earthly part, and a middle part, which creates and directs space, time, and causality.

Vladimir Solovyev is the last great 19th century herald in the Sophia tradition extending from St. Hildegard through Jakob Boehme and to the modern age. Despite being held back from mainstream Christian development, Divine Sophia continued to reveal herself to chosen individuals. Today, in the first century of a new millennium, we can see a turning point, a beginning of an age in which Sophia is gradually revealing herself to more and more human beings.

The Sophia teachings had a profound influence in the East, and the mystery of the PALLADIUM, a Sophianic symbol, led us back to the East. Early in the 20th century, followers of Rudolf Steiner went to Istanbul and began excavations to locate the Palladium—without success.

One of the greatest monuments of Christianity is the great basilica of HAGIA SOPHIA, constructed by Byzantine emperor Justinian (483–565) in Constantinople. For a long time Hagia Sophia—the very name means "Holy Sophia"—possessed the largest dome in the world. Justinian was of the school that viewed Sophia as identical with the Logos, the Christ. So the Hagia Sophia, built not far from the site of the Palladium, is really a basilica dedicated to Christ as the wisdom of the world.

When Christianity spread to Russia in 988, its orientation was not to the Roman Catholic world but to the Greek Orthodox tradition centered at Constantinople. The great temple of Holy Sophia inspired the Russians, but they interpreted Sophia not as the Logos or Christ but as Divine Sophia, the feminine side of God. So from the very beginning of Christianity in Russia and the Ukraine, we find a true Sophianic quality within Christianity.

Sophia has been at the root of Russian Orthodox Christianity; but within the

(cont.)

Church there was little understanding of the nature of Divine Sophia until the time of philosopher and mystic Solovyev in the 19th century. The presence of the Divine Sophia in the Russian Orthodox tradition points to the future Sophianic culture that is prophesied to emerge in Russia.

Vladimir Solovyev (1853–1900) was the first within Russian Orthodoxy to reveal, on a conscious level, the mystery of Divine Sophia as the WORLD SOUL, the mother, guide, and inspiration of future humanity. Following Solovyev, two key figures in the development of Russian Sophiology were two Russian Orthodox priests, Pavel Florensky (1882–1937) and Sergei Bulgakov (1871–1944).

Born in Georgia, Florensky was an extraordinarily gifted child, a brilliant mathematician who became a priest. In the 1930s, he was sent to a concentration camp on the White Islands in the far north of Russia; he was executed there in 1937. In today's Russia he is regarded as a hero. In his major work on Sophia, *The Pillar and the Foundation of Truth*, he describes Sophia as the soul of the world.

Florensky also pointed to the central significance of the Virgin Mary as a manifestation and incarnation of the Divine Sophia. His views concerning Mary as the incarnated Sophia are identical to those of Jakob Boehme.

Florensky was a personal friend of the Russian priest Sergei Bulgakov, perhaps the most prodigious of the Sophianic theologians. At the time of the Bolshevik Revolution, Bulgakov was exiled to France, where he later became head of the Russian Orthodox Seminary in Paris. His work was the most comprehensive body of knowledge on Sophiology. Like Florensky, his purpose was to present Sophia in a way that would be acceptable to fellow priests and theologians. Bulgakov did not derive any of his teachings from Gnostic sources but concentrated solely upon the Church tradition. Nevertheless, in his exposition of the nature of Divine Sophia, he ran into conflict with Moscow authorities and was condemned for his Sophia teachings.

Bulgakov continued to write and carry out his functions as a priest, but from this time forward his writings bore the stigma of heresy. Hope remains within the Russian Orthodox Church that there will be a great council dedicated to Sophia. A concept first held by Solovyev, the dream to unite East and West, still persists.

Valentin Tomberg (1900–1973) was of central significance for the Russian Sophia tradition, and his teachings will occupy humanity for millennia, just as the teaching of the holy trinity within the Christian tradition has. Going a stage further, Tomberg's teachings completely transform Florensky. Based on the wisdom books of the Old Testament, Sophia is the first created being. (Prov. 8.22–23) As the first created being, she came forth

(cont.)

from the womb of the Holy Trinity, and therefore has a relationship to each member of the Holy Trinity. Tomberg talks of Sophia not simply as having three aspects but as being three persons.

He speaks of a Sophianic Trinity parallel to the Holy Trinity: arising out of the primordial Godhead begotten from the Divine Father and the Divine Mother are the Divine Son and the Divine Daughter, Christ and Sophia, the Logos and Sophia. Just as we may understand the incarnation of the Logos, Christ, which took place in Jesus, so, according to Jakob Boehme and the Russian Sophiologists, there also took place an incarnation of Divine Sophia into Mary. In Tomberg's Sophia teaching of the Divine Feminine Trinity—Mother, Daughter, and Holy Soul—we reach the pinnacle of the Sophia tradition of Russia.

Prominent Teachers of the Sophianic Tradition

St. Augustine (354–430) distinguished between two Sophias. The *uncreated* Sophia, he considered to be the Logos, the Christ; the *created* Sophia, divine wisdom, has existed since the beginning of Creation. The uncreated Sophia is the illuminating light of existence, he believed, and the created Sophia is the illuminated light. His distinction has influenced many Christian theologians.

Hildegard of Bingen (1098–1179) was aware of being surrounded by divine light from early childhood. Among her most powerful and inspiring visions were those of Divine Sophia. On one hand Sophia was the mother and soul of the world; on the other Sophia was the bride of Christ and mother of the Church.

Herrad von Landsberg, 12th century author of *The Garden of Delights,* depicts Sophia as queen of the seven liberal arts. Sitting upon a royal throne, she is surrounded by grammar, rhetoric, dialectic, music, arithmetic, geometry, and astronomy. A stream of water pours from each side of her body. Below her are the philosophers Plato and Aristotle receiving the living waters of Sophia's wisdom.

Jakob Boehme (1575–1624) had a direct, living experience of Sophia as a divine being existing in spiritual realms, with whom we can have communication and a relationship. The son of a poor German farmer, in his first mystical experience Jakob felt himself bathed in supernal light and a blessed sense of peace. Around 1600, with his second mystical experience, while watching the splendid glow of sunlight on a pewter jug, he became aware of forces active in the foundation of things. He continued to have visions and realizations but remained silent until a third experience around 1610 seemed to unify everything.

(cont.)

Attacked from the pulpit of his Lutheran pastor (Gorlitz, Germany) he was branded a heretic and forbidden to write of his experiences. Urged on by his friends and inner voice, he began to record his visions again. One of his most significant visions was of an appearance of the Divine Sophia. His knowledge of her qualities increased after this and he ascribed to her seven qualities: keen, soft, firm, serious, clear, pure, and persuasive. To Boehme, Sophia was the exhalation or out-breath of God's power, God's mirror, dwelling in pious souls as friend, betrothed, bride, mistress, and teacher to those who seek her in the appropriate manner. His teachings, a seed impulse with great influence upon German cultural tradition, crossed over to England and extended to Russia.

John Pordage (1607–1681) possibly earned a doctor of medicine at Oxford, England, in 1640, but his calling was to be a religious. He entered the order of the Anglican Church and became a rector. His wife began having unusual visionary experiences, and he soon followed. He experienced remarkable phenomena, including angelic apparitions witnessed by others who joined him and his wife in a prayer group.

Difficult circumstances resulted and persecution meant that for some years he and his group lived surrounded by wrath, suffering something akin to "the dark night of the soul." They avoided public view and therefore censure. He wrote elaborate, lucid, and concisely expressed metaphysical treatises, the exemplary of which is entitled *Sophia.* His works had a private circulation both in England and on the Continent; his primary works were published only in German under the name Johannes Pordaschens.

Jane Leade (1623–1704), born to a wealthy English family, received a fine education. At age 15, she was dancing and celebrating with her family when she heard a voice. Her mystical experiences began. She married William Leade, a merchant with whom she shared spiritual concerns and had four daughters, two of whom died. At his death she found herself destitute and she threw herself on the mercy of God. She became a member of John Pordage's circle and slowly assumed leadership, eventually coming to live with him; the circle became a community.

After Pordage's death in 1681, she continued the work and had some of his more important treatises published, as well as her own. Leade's group began to call itself the "Philadelphian Society." She often experienced direct visions of Sophia and her better writings are based upon these.

The Poet Novalis (1772–1801), known as the wisest, most profound, and most childlike of the early Romantics, lived his life inspired by his experience of Sophia.

(cont.)

Gottfried Arnold (1666–1714), a great and gifted German scholar and student of Boehme, wrote almost totally on quotations from early Christian writers and from Pordage, whose work inspired him. He wrote some of the first influential modern theological history taking seriously early Christian Gnosticism, particularly Valentinian Gnosticism.

He declared the true history of the Church was that of the spiritually reborn through Gnostic experience, a concept that includes and transcends being "born again" in contemporary Protestantism. More scholar than Gnostic, Arnold's treatise is rooted in works like the *Book of Wisdom.* His influence stretched from Germany to Russia as his writing, *The Mystery of Divine Sophia,* is described in scripture (part 1) and poetry (part 2). He struggled for a clear picture of Sophia and found in his speculative Sophiology he was not able to come to terms fully with the Sophia of Scripture; yet his work carries powerful mystical profundity.

Friedrich Wilhelm Joseph von Schelling (1775–1854), the great idealist philosopher, was inspired by Jakob Boehme.

Anne Catherine Emmerich (1774–1824), a nun of the Augustine order, received the stigmata and began to receive visions describing the life of Christ. She is best known for her historic discovery of the Virgin Mary's house near Ephesus in Turkey, now a famous place of pilgrimage. She also gave testimony of Sophia as the wisdom of God, a being who incarnated qualities of Sophia into the Virgin Mary.

Vladimir Solovyev (1853–1900), a philosopher greatly influenced by Boehme, emerged as the great prophet of the Russian Sophia tradition. He had three profound experiences of Sophia: the first, as a youth at age 9, inspired him to seek the path of spiritual study; the second, in London at the British Museum, Sophia's face appeared to him, and the words "go to Egypt" gave him direction; and the third in Cairo, his greatest vision of Divine Sophia.

This last experience became the central motivation for his life's work as a philosopher to the Russian people and to work for the reunification of the Eastern and Western churches. He believed it was scandalous for Christianity to be divided and that reunification could occur through Sophia. Solovyev inspired many poets and theologians, bringing together the tradition known among Russian Orthodox priests as Sophiology.

He saw Sophia as the soul of the world, having three aspects, which allow her to unify, connect, and direct everything. She possesses a divine part, a lower earthy part, and a middle part, which creates and directs space, time, and causality. Solovyev is the great 19th century herald of the Sophia tradition extending from

(cont.)

Hildegard through Boehme down to the modern age.

Sergei Bulgakov (1871–1944) is perhaps the most prodigious of Sophianic theologians. At the time of the Bolshevik Revolution, he was exiled from Russia and went to France where he became head of the Russian Orthodox Seminary in Paris. He sought to present Sophia in an acceptable way to his fellow priests and theologians. He concentrated solely upon the Church tradition; however, he ran into conflict with Moscow authorities and was condemned.

Bulgakov was viewed as a heretic for the idea of *ousia* (Greek)—a substance common to each of the three persons of the Trinity. The idea aroused suspicion that he would put Sophia forward as a fourth hypostatic equal to the Father, Son, and Holy Spirit. Bulgakov denied the idea, but it is for this he was condemned. He continued to serve as a priest and to write, but his teachings continued to bear the stigma of heresy.

Pierre Teilhard de Chardin (1881–1955), a Frenchman who was ordained a Jesuit priest in 1911, was a scientist who affirmed the concept of evolution and sought to integrate it into Christian theology. His "Hymn to the Eternal Feminine" relates his concept of a primordial entelechy (dictionary) to Sophia of the Old Testament and through her to Mary of the New Testament who clearly exists in a polar relationship to Christ. In his essay "The Soul of the World" he acknowledges the cosmological and religious point of contact to God and Christ that exists through Sophia, as the Soul of the World. His great understanding of science, religion, and mysticism led him to know Sophia in all her aspects.

Nicholas Berdyaev (1874–1948) was one of the great Sophianic writers of modern time. His writing is vivid and lucid, emerging out of a fiery creativity that sometimes outstripped his capacity to write. Born of Russian nobility, he grew up in luxury, moved to St. Petersburg, and published a journal entitled *The New Way*. Exiled by the communists in 1922, he moved to Berlin and then to Paris where he lived out his life in exile.

Deeply influenced by Boehme, Berdyaev is most faithful to the Sophianic tradition. He loved to discuss its central issues: Eros, sexuality and gender, and certain questions such as the androgyny and conditions the indwelling of God in humanity raises.

Pavel Florensky (1882–1937), born in Tiflis in Georgia, was a gifted child—a brilliant mathematician, who became a priest and one of the key figures in the development of Russian Sophiology. In 1930 he was sent to a concentration camp on the White Islands in the far north of Russia where he was executed in 1937. His major work on Sophia is called "The Pillar and Foundation of Truth," in

(cont.)

which he describes Sophia as the soul of the world. He draws his teachings from the tradition of the entire Church back to its foundation and from the books of wisdom from the Old Testament. He tried to find a pure teaching of Sophia that would be acceptable within the Russian Orthodox Church. He also pointed to the Virgin Mary as a manifestation and incarnation of Divine Sophia. Although Florensky came to his perspective independently, his views concerning Mary as the incarnated Sophia are identical with the teachings of Jakob Boehme. He was also a personal friend of Russian priest Sergei Bulgakov.

Valentin Tomberg (1900–1973) goes further than Florensky. Based on the Old Testament's wisdom books, Sophia was the first created being issuing forth from the womb of the Holy Trinity and therefore has a relationship to each member of the Holy Trinity. Tomberg speaks of Sophia not simply as having three aspects but as being three persons—a Sophianic Trinity parallel to the Holy Trinity. He teaches that arising out of primordial Godhead begotten from the Divine Father and the Divine Mother are the Divine Son and the Divine Daughter, or Christ and Sophia.

Tomberg teaches that the heart of the Divine Mother is to be found in the center of the Earth and that the plant kingdom resonates with the very heartbeat of the Mother. The Divine Daughter is the wisdom of the cosmos, extending from the realm of the fixed stars down to the planets and the moon. This awe-inspiring image of Sophia as the World Soul can be found in the Book of Revelation, where she is depicted as a woman clothed with the sun, with the moon under her feet, and upon her head a crown of twelve stars. In this Sophia teaching of the Divine Feminine Trinity—Mother, Daughter, and Holy Soul—we reach the pinnacle of the Sophia Tradition of Russia.

Contemporary writers and teachers of the Sophianic tradition

Arthur Versluis is a modern author of *TheoSophia: Hidden Dimensions of Christianity* and editor and compiler of *Wisdom's Book, the Sophia Anthology*, a remarkable collection of rare texts. He offers an exposure of this lay mystical approach for Christians of an inner bent, the equivalent of Sufism in Islam and Kabalah in Judaism. Many of the texts in the anthology have never been published broadly before. Versluis holds a doctorate in American Literature and is an assistant professor at Michigan State University and editor-in-chief of *Esoterica*, an electronic journal.

Thomas Schipflinger, a German priest, compiled over two decades a timely, indispensable source of reference—a veritable Sophia encyclopedia—to meet the growing interest in

Sophia outside the Russian Church. The golden thread running through the material is the relationship of Sophia to the Virgin Mary. *Sophia-Maria, A Holistic Vision of Creation* originally published in German in 1988 is now available (since1998) in English.

SUSANNE SCHAUP, author of *Sophia,* published in both German and English, was born in Vienna. She studied languages, psychology, and philosophy at Vienna University, continued her studies in the U.S. on a Fulbright scholarship, returned to Germany to complete her Ph.D. at Salzburg University. Her successful series of broadcasts on "The Transformation of the Feminine" and the feminine nature of God led to her writing on Sophia. She places emphasis on the work of Otfried Eberz, another contemporary Sophiologist who makes a radical appeal to modern women to reclaim the consciousness of the Goddess.

ROBERT POWELL joins the growing number of Germans researching Sophia and sharing their inspiration. Powell is author of *Divine Sophia: Holy Wisdom* and *The Sophia Teachings, the Emergence of the Divine Feminine in Our Time,* and *The Most Holy Trinosophia and the New Revelations of the Divine Feminine,* plus a number of volumes on the life of Christ.

CAROL E. PARRISH-HARRA, author and spiritual teacher, established Sancta Sophia Seminary in 1978 following the prompting of her inner contact. A frequent lecturer on "Sophia, the Intuitive Guide" and "ChristoSophia," Carol believes the emerging Sophia is leading the second reformation of the Church, enriching Christianity with an innovative mystical influence (a Sophianic revival), as well as bringing a new spirituality to all of humanity.

The Lord created me [wisdom] as the first of his creations, before all of his works.
Prov. 8.22 (Peshitta)

for personal gain, money, or fame. The abuse of spiritual powers for the benefit of ego or to another's disadvantage or detriment.

SOTHIS. "The old name for Sirius, a large, bright blue-white star approximately eight and a half light years away from the Earth in the constellation of Canis Major, called the 'Dog Star' by the ancient Egyptians who calculated the annual spring floods of the Nile River according to its heliacal rising."25

SOUL. A projection of the MONAD that creates personality and experiences through it while becoming conscious. The vehicle of experience that contains the entire history of the journey through incarnations—often represented in writings as EGO (capital E). As awareness increases, the mature human soul becomes less reflection and more the monad itself, a fragment of the OVERSOUL, a spark of the Flame imprisoned within form. Some use "Soul" to designate an enhanced, deepened control over lower aspects, having achieved first INITIATION, birth of the CHRIST-WITHIN. Others reserve the right to capitalize Soul for the fourth initiation when it is said that we live as a Soul or ADEPT. The soul is considered feminine in nature, that part of the human that births the inner Christ.

In Kabalah, named as three: NEPHESCH, RUACH, and NESCHAMAH. The souls, all of which are aspects of the One, strive toward unity once again. Progress is achieved as the sephiroth Yesod, Tiphareth, and Daath on the middle PILLAR are integrated.

The candle of God is the soul of man.
—Prov. 20.27

SOUL ALIGNMENT. The goal of all MEDITATION. Specific techniques have evolved as the receiver set is built and expanded to be responsive to increasingly subtle influences. Alignment leads to response to impressions, RAY influence, higher will, and greater love. Thus we align to our individual and GROUP SOUL purposes.

SOUL ASTROLOGY. An understanding held in ESOTERIC ASTROLOGY of a method to determine the purpose the soul seeks to realize in a particular incarnation.

SOUL ATTUNEMENT. The harmonizing vibration of two or more souls for the purpose of assisting one another. A name for a reading regarding the purpose of the soul and/or facilitating the goal of establishing personality in right-alignment to soul.

SOUL EXCHANGE. An appropriate description of the event known as WALK-IN (coined by Ruth MONTGOMERY), whereby one soul departs from a human body, allowing it to be used by an incoming soul. Other names have been given to the theory: "monadic transmutation" (Trigueirinho, *see pp. 349–55),* "divine obsession" (The TIBETAN), "exchange of inner selves" (STEINER), "messenger" (this author, Parrish-Harra).

SOUL GROWTH. A more conscious use of soul power and more complete expression of soul qualities at personality level. The development and integration of the physical, emotional, and mental bodies—personality—into a mechanism through which the human soul anchored in the SPIRITUAL TRIAD can express itself in the three lower worlds and use them as a field of service.

SOUL INFUSION. The state in which a coworking relationship between the soul and the personality has been achieved. When the real personality, the totality of the three LOWER BODIES, has been developed and integrated with the soul. The process of soul infusion—in which the light of the unit created by Soul and SOLAR ANGEL illumines the personality—stimulates a greater radiation of the divine within matter. This stage, also known as the MYSTIC MARRIAGE, is associated with the third INITIATION of the esoteric Christian tradition, TRANSFIGURATION. Also called CHRISTO-SOPHIA.

SOULMATES. Two or more personalities/souls of such a close vibrational frequency they assist each other in realizing desired growth pursued by either or both during incarnation.

Also see Cosmic relationships; Karmic relationships; Worthy opponent.

SOUL PURPOSE. The goal of an incarnation; the experience the soul desired that prompted it to create and experience through a personality.

SOULSTAR. A symbol of a bright star over the head represents the presence of the soul (and SOLAR ANGEL) from which the personality has descended, and continues to be overlighted—an archetype to constantly remind personality of its source of power and true nature. Imaged over a person's head when invoking soul influence, this soul energy is significant to the process of emanation and TRANSFORMATION.

SOUND CURRENT. The generative first word that went forth—the sacred sound, the OM—continues to ever reverberate while creation exists. This silent, mystic tone underlying manifested life and emanating as "the Word" or "divine sound" can be heard with the inner ear as it continues to create and maintain the universe. As we attune to this stream of vibration, we are brought into higher alignment and harmony with it.

SOURCE, THE. A generic term for God, usually recognized easily and without specific religious association.

SPACE. The seemingly empty, receptive void. More commonly, the openness in which the planets revolve. There is no true emptiness, however, for all Creation is manifestation, but a less dense cup is necessary for a space to invite or to be receptive to purpose. Less dense space allowed manifestation to enter its womb for the purpose of spirit. Thus space, the void, is the divine feminine, the receiver, and the participator with spirit in the act of creation.

SPACIAL BEINGS. A parallel kingdom evolving in dimensions of the Earth humanity does not frequently explore. Extended by definition to other evolving intelligences transferred to Earth from other planets in the greater space of the universe. This family has its center on the mental plane, and its beings are able to project into denser dimensions. Also known as extraterrestrials, ETs, space brothers, meta-terrestrials. *See* Manasadevas; Star people; Tiamat.

SPARK OF GOD. The MONAD; a particle of the creative FOHAT that travels into dense realities in INVOLUTION, returning to the Source through the process of EVOLUTION. Also known as the "divine spark."

SPARKS OF SPACIAL CONSCIOUSNESS. This Agni term is used with "super-radiant fires of space" to describe FOHAT, imaged as a form of primal energy-matter. It emphasizes the energy pouring forth to permeate all of creation: the innate consciousness we often call the "SPARK OF GOD."

SPARROW HAWK. The KESTREL, a small falcon honored as the symbol of Egyptian god OSIRIS. It represents holy consciousness because it can hover in mid-air and fly straight up. Sparrow Hawk Village has adapted the kestrel as its logo because the village is built on Sparrow Hawk Mountain (named by the native people) and along the Illinois River where a hatchery once existed.

Sparrow Hawk Village. An intentional community with a spiritual educational focus, established 1981 by this author, located a few miles outside of Tahlequah, Oklahoma. For additional information: 22 Summit Ridge Drive, Tahlequah, 918 456-3421, or e-mail lccc@sanctasophia.org

Specific works (of meditation). Meditation can be employed for a wide variety of needs, purposes, and experiential works: healing, directing energy to others, opening the heart center, sustaining another, telepathy. The purpose determines the technique used.

Speculative. Describes a spiritual method employing the mind in a variety of techniques: illumination, meditation, contemplation, pondering, or thinking about diverse aspects of a given subject.[26] *See* Spirituality, approaches to Christian.

Sphinx. This gigantic sculpture is said to represent the quest of humanity, for each is to embody the courage of a lion, heightened awareness that can take flight as the eagle, the persistence of the bull, and the enlightened mind of humanity. Some now believe the head was originally that of a woman with much hair and was reshaped at a later period of time, which may explain why the head is small in proportion to the body; Greek myth supports this idea. While Egyptologists of this era claim its origin to be about 4500 B.C., today's scientists—challenged by damage from rains and floods—believe it is of a much earlier period.

Spirilla. One of seven delicate threads of energy projected by each PERMANENT SEED ATOM, each thread being anchored on one of the seven sub-planes of the permanent atom's home plane of manifestation within the human being, as used in Alice A. BAILEY'S *Treatise on Cosmic Fire.* They are referred to as "Seven Deva Lords" or "Lords of the Sub-planes."[27]

Spirit. From the Latin word *spiritus* for "breath." The divine spark within each soul, the breath, or spirit, of God, i.e., Holy Spirit. Also widely used as meaning all nonmaterial beings.

Spirit attachment. A point of consciousness that becomes attracted to another and takes up a parasitic relationship, using or affecting the energy of another. The host may or may not be aware of this attachment. EXORCISM or SPIRIT RELEASEMENT is needed to free both host and parasite. *Also see* Psychography.

Spirit guides. One or a number of friends in spirit who collect around a human to provide encouragement and assistance.

Spirit releasement therapy. Techniques developed to disengage attachments and free the host; a modern term for exorcism.

Spiritual. Having to do with the evolving soul. Distinguished from "religious" dogma and doctrine by following the prompts and personal teachings of the spirit within self.

Spiritual alchemy. *See* Alchemy, spiritual.

Spiritual disciplines. Practices embraced to enhance an awareness of the spirit within. Most religious, as well as spiritual, traditions encourage disciplines—specific exercises and rules of conduct, e.g., diet (vegetarian-ism), prayer, meditation, silence, poverty (owning no property), celibacy, service to others. These may be either or both additions and/or subtractions to daily life.

SPIRITUAL EMERGENCY. A phenomenon that so distresses one's usual consciousness that malfunctioning or major disturbances occur. Happenings known to trigger such events are: contact with DISCARNATES, UFOs, or ETs; NDEs; spontaneous psychic openings; and awakening the KUNDALINI. A major difficulty is that such happenings change one's reality too rapidly, as well as at times create confusion with pathology.

SPIRITUAL EVOLUTION. The process of ever-increased awareness and transformation of each vehicle into increased sensitivity as it integrates with higher vibrations in preparation for its reunion with the Source, the One, or All That Is.

SPIRIT KINGDOM. Non-physical life that exists in planes other than the material plane.

SPIRITUALISM. A religious approach—Christian or otherwise—with a focus on contact with DISCARNATES and the nonphysical reality. Spiritualism began its current popularity in the U.S. around 1850 when the Fox sisters made contact with a discarnate through a series of knocks used to indicate "yes" or "no." It rapidly spread to Great Britain where it developed further religious potency and scientific investigation. After stabilization in Great Britain, spiritualism returned to the U.S. in the late 19th century and became a denomination of the Christian tradition with an emphasis on life after death and spiritual communication with discarnates.

SPIRITUALITY, APPROACHES TO CHRISTIAN. *Affective:* illumination of the heart, emotions, and feelings attributed to an idea. *Apophatic:* negative, denying, emptying. *Kataphatic:* imaginal, forming mental images of what is not actually present. *Speculative:* illumination of the mind, meditating, pondering, thinking about various aspects of a given subject.[28]

SPIRITUAL LAW. Derived from the HERMETIC PRINCIPLES—seven great laws that guide all life in its EVOLUTION of consciousness and express through numerous lesser laws, ever just, ever imprinting justice upon humanity. Collective influences that maintain and support life through processes of chaos, creation, orderliness, and destruction. Within the framework of these laws, numerous variations have been defined by religions and cultures. The Hermetic Principles are 1) Mentalism, 2) Correspondence, 3) Vibration, 4) Polarity, 5) Rhythm, 6) Cause and Effect, 7) Gender.

SPIRITUAL POLITICS. A new grasp of the work of RAY 1 is emerging as the true nature of politics is understood. The concept is that everything begins in mysticism and ends in politics. As we comprehend with spiritual insight, we realize that spiritual politics explores the effects from the inside to the outer, not from the outer to the inner. Politics is the art of helping people live together; spiritual politics seeks to explain the interconnectedness of all events. See *Spiritual Politics*, a book by Corrine McLaughlin and Gordon Davidson.

SPIRITUAL SCIENCE. A term coined by Rudolf STEINER for wisdom teachings of an esoteric nature, which he perceived as an extension of the science of a purely matter nature, making available and understanding other dimensions of matter. A methodology to evolve higher consciousness as it relates to the human being, to the universe, and to all creation, as taught by the AGELESS WISDOM, OCCULT studies, and THEOSOPHY.

SPIRITUAL TEACHER. An individual sufficiently evolved spiritually to share with others what s/he has *realized* in order to give comfort and assurance, marking the route of spiritual conquest for others.

SPIRITUAL TRIAD. The reflection of the divine Trinity within the human being: spiritual will, intuition, HIGHER MIND—or ATMA, BUDDHI, MANAS. Also, the "spiritual human" levels that are built with atmic, buddhic, and manasic, or light, substance. The expression of the MONAD—the germinal seed containing divine potential that unfolds during the course of evolution—that creates the soul, which in turn creates the personality.

SPIRITUAL WARRIOR. A person consciously on the spiritual path. Some say the term comes from the struggle between the good and the bad residing within. The MAYA say when the forces of fire and water within mix, it is called "war." The one in whom this transformation is occurring is the "spiritual warrior."

SPIRITUAL WILL. The will of soul or spirit within self with which we seek to blend personality will, that the higher may be expressed.

SPONTANEITY. Freedom to release barriers and limitations that restrict the full flow of the animated spirit and its creative consciousness.

SQUARE. In astrology, a square involves two planets 90 degrees or three signs apart (allowable orb 7 degrees). These can be difficult stumbling blocks or can bring forth potential and become building blocks, wherein lies potential.

SRI. Hindu title of respect used to address a holy man of the East; sometimes spelled "Shri."

SRI RAMA. A well-known AVATAR in the Hindu tradition. One of the principal avatars of Vishnu; next to Krishna, the most popular deity of Vishnuism.

STARCHESTVO. The practice in Eastern churches of laymen appealing for spiritual counsel to certain monks known for their wisdom and piety, the STARTSI.

STARETS. Practitioners of the Eastern churches who rarely have any outward status or rank and instead are cloaked in their humility. There is no equivalent in Western churches.

STARFOLK. A term used by Carl Sagan in director-producer Stanley Kubrick's movie "Discovery," symbolizing the emergence of a new state of evolution: the development of the coming race—the offspring of humanity, the star child, as a citizen of the cosmos—no longer ego-centered or even Earth-centered, but universally centered and cosmically conscious.

SPIRITUALITY

An evolutionary impulse, when one's focus moves from personality issues to an awareness of oneself as a divine being expressing one's essence. As activity is focused on the innermost dimension of an individual, the essence—called Self, soul, or spirit by most esoteric traditions—shares its transcendental nature of reality. Specifically designed practices explore this core and facilitate greater expression of the sacred within—the consciousness or soul maturity.

JOHN WHITE ADDRESSES SPIRITUALITY

The New Age is characterized by spirituality. In essence, spirituality is simply living with intention to realize God in every circumstance of your being—thoughts, emotions, words, deeds, relations, aspirations—in short, the totality of your life, right through its very end (as saints and sages do by "dying the good death"). As I have said before: That attitude, that stance in life is the only thing which can truly create a better world. There will never be a better world until there are better people in it. The way to build better people is to begin with yourself by realizing God. To realize God means to know God on every level of reality and in every mode or aspect of God's being. Thus, spirituality can be defined, level by level of reality, this way:

In *physical* terms, spirituality is recognizing the miraculous nature of matter and the creative source behind the mystery of matter.

In *biological* terms, spirituality is realizing that a divine intelligence underlies all life-change and that such change is evolving all creation to ever greater degrees of wholeness in order to perfectly express itself.

In *psychological* terms, spirituality is discovering within yourself the ultimate source of meaning and happiness, which is love.

In *sociological* terms, spirituality is giving selfless service to others, regardless of race, creed, color, gender, caste, or nationality.

In *ecological* terms, spirituality is showing respect for all the kingdoms in the community of life—mineral, vegetable, animal, human, spirit, and angelic.

In *cosmological* terms, spirituality is being at one with the universe, in tune with the infinite, flowing with the TAO.

In *theological* terms, spirituality is seeing God in all things, all events, and all circumstances, indwelling as infinite light and unconditional love, and seeing all things, events, and circumstances in God as the matrix or infinite ocean in which the universe occurs.[29]

The Meeting of Science and Spirit

Star of David. *See* Star, six-pointed.

Star people. Those believed to have incarnated in the human family, having transferred to planet Earth from elsewhere in the universe. Native Americans—Cherokees specifically, but others as well—refer in their legends to visitors from the stars. Esoteric teachings call such people SPACIAL BEINGS. Zecharia Sitchin, scholar and scientist, provides rational information and theory to sustain the idea of humanity being the result of genetic engineering between humanoids and the ANNANUKI or the NEFILIM of Gen. 6.4.[30] *See pp. 337–47,* Humanity's Genesis.

Startsi. Elders of the monastic republic of Athos, true professors of inner knowledge; spiritual researchers known for their piety and wisdom.

Stations of the Cross. Fourteen steps taken by Jesus, the Christ, in the journey to the cross represent the mysteries of the PATH OF INITIATION. The first seven focus on the WATER MYSTERIES, the last seven on the FIRE MYSTERIES. Walking the symbolic stations is a Lenten practice, when we become mindful of initiations and truly express love for the Wayshower and the service he rendered to the Christ and humanity. Rarely understood for its esoteric meaning and a practice that may easily degenerate into a mere recognition of the suffering of Jesus. The stations are depicted by Corinne Heline as: 1) Christ Jesus is condemned to death; 2) He carries his cross; 3) He falls the first time; 4) He meets his mother; 5) Simon of Cyrene helps him carry the cross; 6) Veronica wipes his face; 7) He falls the second time; 8) the daughters of Jerusalem weep for him; 9) He falls the third time; 10) He is stripped of his garments; 11) He is nailed to the cross; 12) He dies on the cross; 13) He is taken down from the cross; 14) He is laid in the sepulcher.[31]

Steiner, Rudolf. b. Austria, 1861, d. 1925. Mystic, clairvoyant, and founder of the Anthroposophical Society, which drew on ROSICRUCIAN, THEOSOPHICAL, and Christian traditions that expressed belief in a spiritual world available to those possessing the highest faculties of intellect, though accessible through training to all. He believed that the mind had to be made to rise above its material preoccupations to experience spiritual reality. Steiner's lectures led to widespread interest in biodynamic farming and the use of natural fertilizers. WALDORF SCHOOLS with instruction based on color, form, rhythm, and nature studies are still actively attended today. EURYTHMY, the art of movement to speech and sound, also conceived by Steiner, has led to music therapies and healing-with-sound techniques in current use. *Cosmic Memory Prehistory: of Earth and Man,* 1968; *Man as Symphony of the Creative World,* 1970; *Art in the Light of Mystery Wisdom,* 1970; *The Inner Nature of Music and the Experience of Tone,* 1983.

Stellium. In astrology, three or more planets all CONJUNCT one another. Creating their own emphasis and action, these planets enhance the power of the sign and the house.

Stigmata. From the Greek word meaning "brand." Spontaneous wounds, bleeding, or marks—corresponding to those Jesus, the Christ, suffered on the cross—that appear on

Star

Star, eight-pointed. Considered the star of the Mother, usually identified in orthodoxy as Sophia.

Star, five-pointed. The pentagram—traditionally one point up, two down, and two across, and enclosed in a circle—is a familiar symbol of mystery teachings, first dating back to around 3500 B.C.E. in ancient Mesopotamia; symbolizes the human being made ready for spiritual development. Its occult meanings translate in various ways but generally relate to the five areas of life to be refined: physical, emotional, mental, spiritual, and social, and the recognition of one's nature as being fivefold in elements: earth, air, fire, water, and ether.

Pythagoreans considered its geometric qualities to be symbolic, both mathematically and metaphysically—of absolute perfection. To the Hebrews the five points are tied to the Pentateuch, the first five books of the Bible, and represent the concept of truth as a whole.

Star, nine-pointed. A symbol of the diamond body of the Adept, the highest state of human consciousness.

Star, six-pointed. The six-pointed star, the Star of David, or hexagram, is comprised of two triangles. In esoteric wisdom this "Star of the Disciple" indicates an initiated one who has succeeded in aligning the physical, emotional, and mental aspects of personality to the down-pouring trinity of the soul—the monadic, atmic, and intuitional planes. Closely identified with the Jewish people since the 17th century, it is the well-known motif of Israel's flag.

the physical bodies of mystics. "Impression with the stigmata may even be a more common MIRACLE than levitation. According to Dr. A. Imbert-Gourbeyre, a French physician and authority on the subject, 312 appearances* can be traced from the beginning of Christianity up to the end of the 19th century." *See pp. 246–51,* Saints: Francis of Assisi; Padre Pio.

"(*This figure is open to question. [He] based his calculation on cases of both visible stigmata and invisible stigmata {i.e., cases in which the sufferer felt the pain of the Passion wounds but never developed visual lesions or bleeding}. . . .)"[32]

STONE CHURCH. A term used by Jakob BOEHME to mean an exoteric or intellectual Christian perspective—the church of the outer world rather than the inner church of the PARACLETE.

STONEHENGE. A unique circle of stones located in Salisbury Plain, Wiltshire, England, believed to have been used as a giant clock for maintaining an awareness of the movement of heavenly bodies. The full purpose is not yet understood. Estimated to have been erected about 2800 B.C.

STRAIGHT KNOWLEDGE. Revelation; intuitive knowledge received directly from higher realities.

STRAIT GATE. A biblical reference to the PATH OF INITIATION. The narrow entry between two poles of duality that one is to achieve to advance on the spiritual path. Related to the idea that any good thing to excess becomes a negative; for the majority, a MIDDLE-ROAD PATH is preferable.

STRIVING. An Agni theme. Maintaining a state of creative tension and using passion to propel the self toward high consciousness. As we strive, the astral body becomes purified and provides strength with which to live a refined life. Correlates to the energy of the number 1. *See* Numerology.

SUBCONSCIOUS, THE. The storehouse of knowledge held individually or collectively to be utilized by various levels of mind, consciously or not.

SUBJECTIVE. Describes an awareness held within, not readily apparent but real and often significant to the individual concerned. Opposite of "objective," which characterizes material more readily detected and grasped by rational thought or by another.

SUB-PLANE. A division of individual vibratory frequencies creating step-like layers within an individual PLANE.

SUB-RACE. Each ROOT RACE, or "wave of consciousness," it is said, has seven great sub-races. The fifth sub-race of any given root race gives birth to the next root race, and the sixth and seventh sub-races perfect the expression of their particular root race. The current era is considered the fifth sub-race of the fifth root race. Remnants of the third root race are few (Aborigines); remnants of the fourth (native people of the Americas) are more populous. An oft-heard expression today, the "new kind of children coming in," refers to those of the sixth sub-race of the Aryan consciousness (which can be any ethnicity) who are better able to integrate both right and left hemispheres of the brain, i.e., endowed with both rational and intuitive awareness. *See* Hemispheres, right and left, of the brain; Root race, Aryan; Three-brain concept.

SUB-RAY. The influence of a RAY expressing in a shorter cycle within the greater cycle of the Ray.

SUBTERRANEANS. Beings who work within the body of the Earth with the elementals in sustaining the planet—generally of a lesser-evolved nature than humanity.

SUBTLE MIND. The intuitive mind of the higher world, existing for both the individual and the collective.

SUBTLE WORLD. One of three divisions of manifestation in Agni Yoga: the physical, the subtle, and the fiery worlds—each closer to the Source and more intense. In this system the subtle world would be the realm of the developing soul: higher astral, mental, and intuitive.

SUCCUBUS. *See* Incubus.

SUDRA VARNA. The vocational class of servants and laborers in the Hindu culture.

SUFI. A Muslim ascetic, or mystic; originally associated with Islamic tradition (8th century Persian), now often meant as a mystic free of formal tradition.

SUKKOTH. For this Jewish Feast of Tabernacles open-roofed huts are built on porches and in backyards to remember the makeshift lodgings of the biblical Israelites as they wandered the desert.

SUMER. An ancient civilization that flowered suddenly nearly 6,000 years ago, developing a number of city-states (Erech, Kisti, Lagash, Ur) with a great deal of power based on flourishing agriculture with irrigation, pottery, metal works, fine arts. This society ended as Babylonia became a nation, forming the foundation for three ancient languages: Mesopotamian, Egyptian/Hamitic, and Indo-European. Sumerian tablets attribute the TOWER OF BABEL to a decision of the gods, initiated by Enlil. *See pp. 337–47,* Humanity's Genesis.

SUMERIAN SCRIPTURE. The Sumerian culture began CUNEIFORM writing, recording the story of creation and leaving a great many clay tablets to which the first eight chapters of Genesis refer. These clay tablets contribute greatly to the scientific study of early human civilization, also forming a foundation for the theories of Zechariah Sitchin. *See pp. 337–47,* Humanity's Genesis.

SUN BEHIND THE SUN. The source of life (power) hidden behind the visible sun, which is its densified light and form. This hidden sun, the storehouse for all the energy of our universe, is the heart of the solar system, the ever-hidden, attracting, and emitting life center—the primal source of being wherein divine radiance is focused. According to esoteric teachings, behind the physical sun is the Great Heart, the source of the outpouring love of the Creator. Hidden behind that sun is the invisible central spiritual sun which is the source of all life in the universe. Acknowledged by astronomical science as the presence in space of a central body in the Milky Way, a point unseen and mysterious. The physical sun is regarded as the expression of the central spiritual sun which is hidden by the brilliance of the visible manifestation. In esoteric literature the "True Sun" or "Heart" who sustains the universe, from whom all proceed and to whom all return. The universe is believed to have evolved from this central point, which is the ever-concealed germ of life. Therefore, it is the source not only of our sun but of all the suns and of all universes—the mighty Solar Being that pulsates its creative will pursuant to the rhythm of the divine Plan. *See* Yoga, Solar.

SUN OF RIGHTEOUSNESS. An ancient title given to the sun, the heart of the solar system and the reflection of the COSMIC CHRIST which loves, energizes, and sustains our universe.

SUN SIGN. The constellation in which the sunis located at the time of an event or birth. Considered to be the principal point of a personal chart, the sun sign represents our inner developing self, the personality, or EGO. The MOON SIGN and the ASCENDANT are the other two most significant points of the personal trinity. Sun signs, 12 in number, divide the year into periods exhibiting similar qualities and attributes. An EPHEMERIS is used to establish exactness of the position of planets at any given time. Astrology teaches that each person is evolving into his or her sun sign and so must consciously attempt to build the virtue of that sign. *See* Agni virtues; Astrological sun sign profiles.

SUPERCONSCIOUS. The part of the God-self at which we connect to the whole.

SUPERMIND. Truth consciousness, as used by Sri AUROBINDO and the MOTHER; as it appears in the Vedas, one who possesses knowledge without seeking it. In the UPANISHADS, a step above the mental being, the soul that arose and attained perfect bliss of spiritual existence. When humanity achieves this evolutionary step, full spiritual living could be realized in body and/or a divine life could be realized on Earth. The aspiration of HEAVEN ON EARTH

SUPERSTITION. The belief that anything outside ourselves can have supernatural power over us or provide intuitive guidance. Psychic tools are used to reflect inner awareness and hold no power in themselves. Wise spiritual students recognize these tools are merely a means to help us see more clearly. Such techniques are especially helpful when we are caught up in pain, emotionally involved, or confused by personal issues. Those who attribute psychic power to the tool, rather than recognizing the power exists in one's own nature, are being superstitious. Superstition is contrary to spiritual wisdom.

SUPRA-PHYSICAL. Dimensions of the etheric that overlap and interpenetrate the physical, wherein portals exist through which passage can be gained to other dimensions, planets, parallel worlds, or extraterrestrial satellites. *Also see pp. 349–55,* Etheric Dimensions.

SURVIVAL OF THE FITTEST, LAW OF. That which can best cope adapts in order to continue; all else is swept away.

SUSHUMNA. One of the channels in the subtle body through which the KUNDALINI power ascends when awakened along the spinal column. This central canal in the finer body is located and traversed by means of spiritual practice according to the careful instructions of a teacher. The current on the left is the IDA, and that on the right, the PINGALA.

SUTRATMA. This one of three threads forming the ANTAHKARANA is anchored in the heart. When it is withdrawn, the physical body dies. Also known as the life thread. *See* Consciousness thread; Cord, silver.

SVADHARMA. The truth of one's own path, the inner path of spiritual truth, addressed in the Hindu's Bhagavad Gita, 18.47: "Better to follow one's own svadharma (inner law), however humble, than to follow another's, though great. By engaging in the work prescribed by one's own soul, one does not miss the mark."

SWAMI. A title given to one spiritually prepared to serve; much like a Hindu priest. Traditionally swamis are trained in an apprentice style, working closely with their guru and very aware of their lineage. *See* Yogananda, Paramahansa.

SWARM. A collective—evolving together and operating upon a GROUP MIND—often associated with reaching a more advanced state.

SWASTIKA. A symbol used in both East and West for the cyclic flow of time and energy. The swastika represents the four truths (facts); the four seasons; the four directions; and the four life-stages: birth, childhood, adulthood, and death. The "feet" turn in different directions in different systems, but all are indicative of life energy in movement. The original sign used by ancient Hindus is clockwise (shown here). The swastika was considered a positive mystic symbol until Hitler used it for the Nazi Party and for black magic purposes, but tilting it to the left.[33]

SYLPH. *See* Nature spirits.

SYMBOLOGY. The study of pictures, images, designs, and glyphs as a means of awakening vast amounts of archetypal knowledge in a simple and usually universal manner. These pictures from the subconscious form the language of dreams, visions, intentions, and psychic impressions. An international, cross-cultural nomenclature of MYTHS, DREAMS, VISIONS, and RITUAL, timeless and limitless compared to words—a principal tool for the SUB- and SUPERCONSCIOUS as we evolve from unconscious to conscious awareness. *Also see* Senzar.

SYMEON THE NEW THEOLOGIAN. *See pp. 246–51,* Saints.

SYNASTRY. In astrology, the comparing of two charts.

SYNCHRONICITY. A Jungian term: the coincidences of life that reveal a greater, unitive pattern existing outside normal awareness or perception. What appears as separate actions developing and moving toward a single point of connection, often considered divine timing, sometimes recognized, sometimes not.

SYNERGY. A number of factors harmonizing in order to create or result in a significant event or thing that has depth of meaning for a principle, individual, or purpose.

SYNPAN.™ A book by George Charles Pappas. The word is the fusion of two Greek words for "synergy" and "for all." The basic meaning, "One for all and all for one," affirms synthesis.

SYNTHESIS. The dovetailing of diverse actions and manifestations of life to create an evolution of awareness. These energies blend into a new integration of subtle, related actions.

An Agni term to describe a moment of coming together, a time of achievement brought about by a unique blending of energies. It is the work of Rays 1 and 7 to synthesize forces present and to create anew.

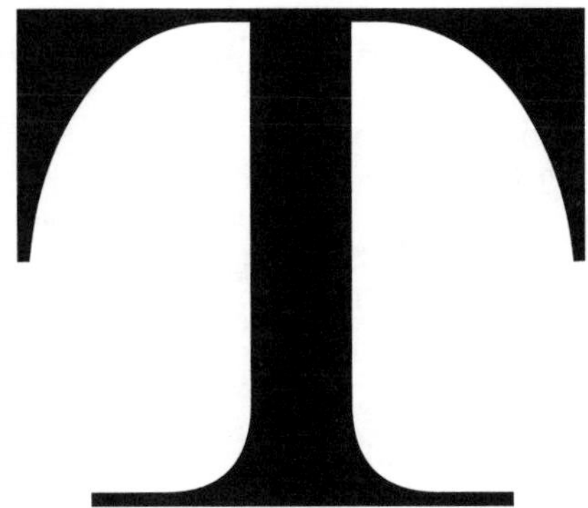

T'AI CH'I CH'UAN. A system of graceful, gentle, dance-like postures, facilitating the movement of life force *(ch'i)* throughout the body. Health- and strength-giving, the practice is often referred to as a "moving meditation."

TALMUD. This collection of writings constituting Jewish civil and religious law consists of two parts: the Mishna (oral law) and the Gemara (commentary). An edited anthology of the deliberations of academics where Judaism is explicated, it records views that indicate a consensus among the rabbis on a specific subject of discussion. Much of the Talmud involves intricacies of scripture-derived law on every aspect of life, as well as nonlegal material about human character, heroes, scientific observations, advice, and the nature of transcendent experiences. Often the information is expressed in a veiled manner. Its organization was largely geared to the original necessity for memorization.

TAMAR. Feminine principle represented by women of the Old Testament. Tamar (Gen. 38.1–30) means "palm tree," a symbol of soul. She corresponds to a lover, companion, friendly psychic structure, with the task of creating and relating to right relationship with inner instinct, the PSYCHE. Confronted by God the Father, she must learn to deal with her masculine side in a patriarchal world.

TAMAS. The lowest of the three GUNAS, the influence of electric qualities affecting all of life. The influence of tamas is sluggishness or inertia. *Also see* Rajas; Sattva.

TANKA. An Eastern icon or sacred picture used for the purpose of meditation, contemplation, or inspiration; comparable to a MANDALA.

TANTRAS. The scriptures and practices of VAJRAYANA Buddhism.

TANTRIC YOGA. *See* Yoga; Disciplines, sexual.

TAOISM. A Chinese mystical world religion following the teachings of LAO TZU. The Tao (pronounced with a d rather than t sound), or the "Way," emphasizes passivity and living gently: "By non-action everything can be done." "Be humble and you will remain entire; be bent and you will remain straight." And, "He who knows does not speak; he who speaks does not know."

TAO TE CHING. Lao Tzu's *Book of the Way* is the Taoist classic manual on the art of living, in 81 brief chapters.

TAPAS. An intense practice of any YOGA for a lengthy period of time.

TAPES. Memories of impressions and experiences of the earlier years in this life or of previous lives, held at a less-than-conscious level of mind. Often referred to as "programming." "Old tapes"—relating to the mind's re-enactment of past experience—impede spiritual advancement.

TARA. This Sanskrit term, popular to Buddhism, translates "fountain" and refers to a female MASTER, a representation of the DIVINE FEMININE, divine SHAKTI. Known to the Tibetans as Dolma, the Savioures, the Great Goddess of Mercy; revered by Mongolians and Tibetans as a female emanation of the great Master AVALOKITA. Tara is the cosmic Mother of All Creation, the fountain from whom all potential flows. In Tibetan Buddhism Tara correlates to SOPHIA in Greek, SHEKINAH in Hebrew, and other contemporary concepts of the divine feminine.

TAROT. A method of divination related to KABALAH, using 78 pictured cards, believed by many to be based on the esoteric philosophy of ancient Egypt, astrology, and numerology. It is said the Hebrews preserved the wisdom of Kabalah by conveying its mysteries in this art form.

TEACHER OF ANGELS AND OF HUMANITY. A title given the Lord Christ in Esoteric Christianity; correlates to TIPHARETH, the Holy Consciousness, in Kabalah.

TEACHER OF RIGHTEOUSNESS. A title given in the updated teachings of the Essene tradition for the holy one who would provide guidance from God. Some suspect the ESSENES saw Master Jesus as destined to serve in this capacity.

TEACHINGS. *See* Ancient wisdom teachings.

TEALEAF READING. A form of divination based on shapes and designs created by the dregs of tea leaves, stems, and twigs left after the liquid is drunk or drained.

TEILHARD DE CHARDIN, PIERRE. b. Sarcenat, France, 1881, d. 1955. Jesuit priest, theologian, and paleontologist (he participated in the discovery of Peking man while on expedition in China), noted for his interpretation of Christianity in the perspective of cosmic evolution, which became central to his scientific and religious thought. He acknowledged SOPHIA as "Soul of the World" and her relationship to Mary and Jesus. He also envisioned a new advance of humanity toward the Omega Point—Christogenesis, the goal of the evolutionary process. At this point, all things reach a supra-personal unity in God, in which AGAPE, or self-transcending, love prevails. *Phenomenon of Man,* 1959; *The Divine Milieu,* 1960. *See pp. 268–77,* Introducing the Sophia Teachings.

TELEGNOSIS. Direct clairvoyant observation of objects or events beyond the range of somatic senses.[1]

TELEKINESIS. The movement of articles without physical touch; called a "MIRACLE" and one of the GIFTS OF THE SPIRIT. A major interest in PARAPSYCHOLOGY.

TELEPATHIC COMMUNICATORS. Those with the ability to convey thoughts from mind to mind. Also, a category of WORLD SERVERS working through integrated head, heart, and throat to step down the higher PLAN for humanity.

TELEPATHY. Mind-to-mind communication, intentional or not, considered natural for humanity at an advanced stage of building the SUBTLE MIND.

TELEPORTATION. The movement of articles (aports) from plane to plane without physical interaction; considered a "MIRACLE" and a GIFT OF THE SPIRIT. Of major interest in PARAPSYCHOLOGY.

TELESMATIC IMAGES. These IMAGES have been deliberately built through the ages by generations of psychic or mystic practitioners concentrating and visualizing until a semi-autonomous state is achieved. Such images have become impersonal universal symbols, serving as reflections of the greater light—wisdom and knowing. *Also see* Mantic images; Phosphoric images.

TEMAZCAL HEALING. A traditional Zapoteca Mexican Indian herbal steam bath used by the Nahuatl, Mixteca, Zapoteca, and Mayan people to treat illness. Nearly destroyed by the Spanish because the healing techniques were associated with indigenous goddesses, the practice survived underground. Temazcals can be built in three shapes: Aztecan-style dome roof, Mayan-style rectangular building, or Sioux-style triangle. A low ceiling holds the heat as the steam hovers over seated bathers. A healer, usually a woman, controls the level of heat. The treatment is especially helpful for women with disorders of the menstrual cycle, those wanting to increase fertility, or those who suffer from cysts. The baths—combining herbs, heat, humidity, rest, and massage as a remedy for body, mind, and spirit—are usually located in a garden or in the forest, capitalizing on nature to help balance the temperament of the client.

TEMPLE. A dwelling place for the holy. An area within ourselves—such as a dedicated heart—or in the outer world that has been purified and dedicated to spiritual purposes.

TEMPLE NOT MADE BY HUMAN HANDS. A reference to the transmuting power of the SOLAR ANGEL and its influence as it creates a domain wherein abides the divine SHEKINAH, the glory of the eternal who prevails over the seat of justice in the HOLY OF HOLIES.

TEMPLE OF IBEZ. An ancient outpost for the Shamballa fraternity located in the center of South America, according to THE TIBETAN.[2] Its energy is currently nourishing the feminine PLANETARY CENTERS once more. *Also see pp. 349–55,* Etheric Dimensions.

TENSION. An Agni term. The movement of consciousness toward evolution that results first in psychological stretch and, in time, spiritual transformation. This evolutionary tug creates a degree of pull throughout creation—between the lowest level of consciousness and the highest, such as spirit and matter, soul and personality, persona and shadow, and so on.

TERESA, MOTHER. b. Albania, 1910, d. 1997. Known as the Saint of Calcutta (India). When I visited M. Teresa, a Hindu proverb hanging near her office door read: "If you have two loaves of bread, give one to the poor; sell the other, and buy hyacinths to feed your soul." Mother Teresa modeled the love of the Christ and the strong will of Sophia in the boldness of her response to her call.

TERESA OF AVILA. *See pp. 246–51,* Saints.

TESHUB. Among the HITTITE gods, a deity name translated "wind blower," or storm god, also nicknamed Taru ("bull"). Like Jupiter after him, Teshub was depicted as god of thunder and lightning, mounted on a bull. *Also see pp. 337–47,* Humanity's Genesis.

TERRESTRIALS. Earthlings that belong to terra firma. Also, there are two types of SPACIAL BEINGS: EXTRATERRESTRIALS and META-TERRESTRIALS.

TESLA, NIKOLA. b. Croatia, 1856, d. 1943. Physicist and electrical engineer who worked at Menlo Park. After quarreling with Thomas Edison, he left to devote himself to his own inventions: improved dynamos, transformers, electric bulbs, and the Tesla high-frequency coil. Today many feel they are being inspired by Tesla from spirit to investigate alternative sources of energy to help humanity with current ecological challenges.

TESTS. Our opportunity for progression, to learn to look with detachment at current life situations in order to see them in a new light; learning to make our struggles a positive, constructive action.

TETRAGRAMMATON. The holy name of God written as four letters: YHWH, Yod Hey Vau Hey (pronounced yod hay vah hay).

TETRAHEDRON. One of the five three-dimensional Platonic solids in which its lines, angles, and four surfaces are equal. Used in the context of SACRED GEOMETRY and the ageless wisdom teachings to help demonstrate the process of spiritual evolution.

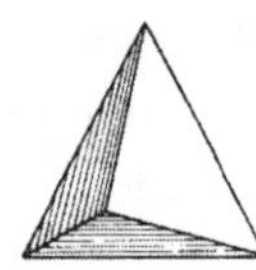

THANATOLOGY. The formal study of death, a major area where science and spirituality converge. *See* Death and dying, stages of.

THAT. A title for the Absolute used by some Eastern traditions; used by Western traditions in "I Am That I Am."

THAT ABOUT WHICH NAUGHT CAN BE SAID. This ancient wisdom phrase affirms the NO-THING as the source of life, the higher reality as

Infinite. The Infinite cannot be comprehended by the finite.

THAUMATURGY. Lower magic. The utilization of psychic energy and abilities to serve personality rather than soul purpose. *Also see* Theorgy.

THEANTHROPOS. *The-* or *theo-* means "God"; *anthrop-* and *anthropo-* are Greek for "human being"; acknowledges the divine manifestation of God, from which Rudolf STEINER drew the term ANTHROPOSOPHY.

THEISM. Belief in the existence of one creative source in the universe: God, or called by whatever name.

THEOLOGY. The study of God or the divine.

THEORGY. Higher magic, depending upon the grace of God. *Also see* Thaumaturgy.

THEORIA. Greek for "CONTEMPLATION." Intellectual assent and viewing. The cessation of mental activity at which point one sees God in everything.

THEOSIS. The dissolution of the individual self into the perfect union with the GODHEAD.

THEOSOPHIA. Defined by Blavatsky as "divine wisdom"—*theo,* "God," *sophia,* "wisdom."

THEOSOPHICAL SOCIETY. An association established in 1875 by Helena BLAVATSKY, Charles LEADBEATER, Annie BESANT, and Charles OLCOTT. It still thrives worldwide today, with a large audience. Its American headquarters are in Wheaton, Illinois.

THEOSOPHY. The philosophy of the revealed teachings given to Madame Helena P. BLAVATSKY by the Trans Himalayan MAHATMAS covering the nature, structure, origin, destiny, and operation of the universe, and meaning "divine wisdom." Mme. Blavatsky was inspired greatly by ancient Tibetan and Hindu beliefs.

THEOTOKOS. A Greek word meaning "God" and "childbirth"—therefore, "the one who bore God," or "God bearer." Used in both Orthodox and Roman Christian traditions as a title for the "Mother of God," awarded at the Third Ecumenical Council in Ephesus in 431. It was confirmed that Mary is the mother of Christ's human and divine natures because the two cannot be divided. The Council also recognized that Mary lived in Ephesus, Turkey, with St. John. *See* Seven Churches of Asia Minor.

THERAPEUTAE. A sect of the mysteries of Alexandria, Egypt, similar to the Essenes, emphasizing learning, austerity, a high moral code, and contemplation. Means "those who heal the diseases of the soul."

THERE ARE NO ACCIDENTS. Acknowledging "Higher will, not mine," and revealing an underlying perception that the Higher (or our own SUB- or SUPERCONSCIOUS) has a reason for all actions. Nothing happens without a cause. There are no accidents—only ways and means of calling us to higher awareness through insights, experiences, and actions.

THEURGY. Latin, *theurgia,* literally means "miracle worker" and is the root of "theology." The art or technique of compelling or persuading a supernatural or metaphysical power to do or refrain from doing something; the work of a divine agency in human affairs; also, the communication with such divine beings. The practice of sacramental and magical rites to INVOKE or EVOKE such presences, generally by direct intervention.

THINKETH IN THE HEART, FEELETH IN THE MIND. An adage reminding us that we must integrate the attributes of heart and mind, our emotional and mental bodies. Esoterisists have long taught that a subtle sensitivity to the soul exists in the head center. Similarly, today HEARTMATH™ is teaching there is a "mind" in the heart.

THIRD EYE. The instrument of true spiritual vision and insight to be developed in etheric matter. The etheric correspondence of the pineal gland which sees, creates, communicates, heals, destroys obstacles, unveils mysteries, and controls and directs energies. This faculty allows us to see the blueprint of creative imagination on the mental level and to visualize creatively on that plane. This etheric center of energy and force, an instrument of will or spirit, is the eye of inner vision through which we can direct and control the energy of matter, see all things in the eternal now, and be aware of causes more than effects. This hidden organ is the medium through which direct and certain knowledge is obtained; it does not convey clairvoyance, but knowing. Also known as the single or spiritual eye, Eye of Shiva, EYE OF HORUS, and the ruby eye of the serpent. *See* Alder, Vera Stanley.

THOMAS AQUINAS. *See pp. 246–51,* Saints.

THOUGHTFORM. The etheric picture, pattern, or form created on the mental plane by the active mind—somewhat like an etching—which dissolves easily unless energized by the emotional nature. Learning to visualize is one of the skills to be mastered in the LESSER MYSTERIES. We progress from understanding the power of thoughtforms to creating positive thoughtforms, always recognizing our relationship to all we create—positive or negative. Real deliberation, or pondering, is the life-principle of any thoughtform. Once the thoughtform is created, if it is not anchored, it is released and another may perceive and manifest it. When all vital components are withdrawn, the thoughtform exists for a while as a "corpse" in the mental frequencies until it disintegrates. Everything that has been given form was originally a thoughtform in some mind—human or divine.

THOUGHTOGRAPHY. The power of the mind (kinekinesis, "to move") to project thoughtforms that can be photographed. This has been achieved under laboratory conditions with scientists present: Edgar Mitchell, Andrei Purharich, Uri Geller, and others.

THREADS OF CONSCIOUSNESS. *See* Antahkarana.

THREE BECOMES SEVEN. As it leaves the realm of the MONAD (the one), the Creator becomes the TRINITY (the three) and animates at the ATMIC level by expressing seven types of will, or RAYS. The three now becomes seven in

Three-brain concept

The animal part of our being operates from the REPTILIAN BRAIN (1), i.e., the sympathetic autonomic nervous system that keeps us breathing, digesting, and performing other involuntary functions. Its greatest concern is survival. The MAMMALIAN (2), or mid-brain, knows the need for socialization; this is the seat of self-esteem. The NEOCORTEX (3) is the center of EGO structure as a result of human INDIVIDUALIZATION and is divided into left and right hemispheres, each with its own characteristics.

Left hemisphere	***Right hemisphere***
• masculine in nature	o *feminine in nature*
• rational	o *artistic*
• cognitive	o *intuitive*
• analytical	o *playful*
• positive	o *imaginative*
• sequential	o *physical*
• linear	o *gentle*
• active	o *spontaneous*
• goal-oriented	o *diffuse*
• concrete	o *visual*
• explicit	o *holistic*
	o *emotional*
	o *nonverbal*
	o *integrative*

expression. *See* One becomes three; Seven becomes twelve.

THREE JEWELS, THE. According to Buddhism, 1) Buddha, embodiment of enlightenment; 2) dharma, the teachings of the Buddha; and 3) sangha, the community of those committed to the practice of these teachings.

THREE KINGS OF OLD. Represents, first, the three races of the Mideast, which are to signify the people of the world. Second, the MAGI symbolize the three lower vehicles of personality—matter, emotion, and mind—bowing to the divine. The third mystery is held in the prophetic gifts of GOLD, FRANKINCENSE, AND MYRRH they brought. Gold is the symbol of power and nobility. Frankincense represents emotion and beauty, cleansing and purification—used especially in religious rituals. Myrrh, the symbol of suffering and death of the body, is used in embalming.

THREE PEARLS IN THE LOTUS. Adapted by Sancta Sophia Seminary as its logo to represent three significant sets of WISDOM TEACHINGS to modern spiritual students: ESOTERIC CHRISTIANITY; KABALAH, the Western Judaic mysteries of the past; and AGNI YOGA, a more current set of dictation from the Masters.

THREE, THE LAW OF. One of the most important kabalistic principles concerning the nature of the universe. Reality is founded upon three forces represented by the right, left, and central PILLARS of the kabalistic TREE.

- Right-column energy corresponds to the sharing aspect of the Light of the Creator.
- Left-column energy relates to the desire of the vessel (person) to receive.
- Central-column energy pertains to the act of resisting the Light by the vessel, which produced the "big bang" of our universe.

In the filament of a lightbulb the right column is the positive pole, the left is the negative, and the central is the resistor. It is the resisting function of the filament that keeps the light aglow.

In human terms the right column refers to the soul and the desire to share; the left column corresponds to the egoistic desire to receive for self alone; the central column relates to the free will to resist the desire to receive for self alone and to transform it into a desire to receive for the sake of sharing.

THRONES. The hierarchical rulership of the Lords of Karma, the LIPIKAS, expressing through the constellation of Taurus. These angels represent the force of God through which divine law and judgments are generated. The Thrones represent the function of rulership and are associated with Ray 1—universal will as expressed in evolution, or God the Father. They contemplate the glory and equity of supreme judgments, teach humanity to rule with justice, and act as the bridge between destiny and karma.

TIAMAT. In Sumerian texts the planet located between Mars and Venus that encountered a renegade planet from another solar system and was largely destroyed. The remnant healed and evolved into planet Earth.

TIBETAN BOOK OF THE DEAD. This centuries-old guide to spiritual wisdom teaches the journey through the BARDO taken by each soul after death.

TIBETAN, THE. *See* Djwhal Khul.

TIKKUN. Literally, "fixing." Lifting sparks of holiness to new levels. "The Restoration." Tikkun ha-nefesh: mending the soul; tikkun ha-olan: mending the world. The process of correction made by the soul through its lifetimes of existence in the physical world—somewhat like KARMA—emphasizing the cosmic energy available to help us turn or remove misfortune.

TIPHARETH. The sixth sephirah on the kabalistic TREE, Beauty, is the principal sephirah of the Tree, for here the sun/son is represented and the tree's upper and lower faces overlap. Home of divine consciousness. Symbolized by the Holy Grail in Western traditions; by Ma'at in Egyptian mysteries, Goddess of Truth (represented by golden scales), who weighs the soul at the death of an incarnation; and in Christian art by archangel Michael holding scales to weigh souls at JUDGMENT.

TITHE. Money and/or service contributed; a spiritual discipline practiced by many religions in diverse ways. While methods and amounts—usually 10 percent—vary, the goal is to remind the practitioner that the Source of life provides all. The giver returns a dedicated portion in the spirit of joy and thanksgiving. We are to learn to share and return, just as the Source does. Tithing supports the Law of

ABUNDANCE: as we give more freely, so too will we receive more freely.

TOB. The Aramaic word Jesus used, meaning "to return or to flow back into God," or "to repent." Mistranslated today, most often as "to feel sorry for one's sins," a debasement of the original meaning.

TONGUES, SPEAKING IN. The Pentecostal experience of speaking and hearing in a variety of languages or nonlanguages. One of the GIFTS OF THE SPIRIT. (1 Cor. 12) A practice of some Christian denominations to demonstrate spiritual status. In exoteric Christianity an experience that occurs when a great deal of emotion/devotion moves through the astral nature, manifesting in an altered state of consciousness and a stimulated throat chakra. The words spoken may or may not be understood by the speaker or listener(s), but biblical teaching is that one will always be present who can understand "the soul crying out to its God."

TONING. A technique using sound to move energy through the personality to release blocks and balance the centers. Ascertained by Laurel Elizabeth Keyes, author of *Toning—the Creative Power of the Voice,* who developed and taught a psychological approach—toning—to many.

Root chakra—sound O, as in Om
2nd chakra—sound U, as in oo
Solar plexus chakra—sound A, as in ah
Heart chakra—sound E, as in ay
Throat chakra—sound I, as in ee
Brow chakra—sound MMM or NNN
Crown chakra—sound NNG, or silence

TORAH, THE. This book of instruction—the Pentateuch, or five books of Moses—is the oldest text of the Jewish faith, given as a means of purifying humanity. Based on tribal myth, saga, history, and divine revelations, the scriptures form a multi-leveled body of literature designed to be understood esoterically as well as practically. The Torah became the outer aspect of a spiritual tradition that was imparted in full only to those who sought its deeper meaning. (Sefer Torah, or Scroll of the Law, md. Jewish Museum, London.)[3] It is commandment and wisdom, instruction and law—God's revealed will.

TO SET ONE'S HOUSE IN ORDER. A biblical command (Isa. 38.1), "Thus says the Lord, Set your house in order: for you shall die, and not live," which refers to the body as the temple of the living God, our "house" on the Earth plane. We are to align our physical, emotional, mental, and spiritual bodies with clarity and purification to persevere in the evolutionary perfecting of the LIGHT BODY.

TOTEM. An animal symbol or protective influence recognized for its animal nature that becomes personalized.

TOUGH LOVE. A bold application of true caring, discipline, and protection, with boundaries clearly defined so as not to be misunderstood.

TOWER OF BABEL. A structure built to reach God but destroyed (Gen. 11.9), as well as humanity's common language (inner connection)—to be reconstructed as spiritual matu-

rity increases. Used in Tarot as a symbol of ego strengths (path 27, "Peh," runs horizontally between Netzach and Hod) that are struck by lightening and destroyed (by light, awakening) so one can rebuild the life from higher consciousness earthward. Jakob BOEHME used the term as a state of ignorance dependent upon outside sources, hearsay, or books for understanding spiritual matters.

TRAINED OBSERVERS. Specific WORLD SERVERS who work through integrated head, heart, and solar plexus to step down the higher PLAN for humanity.

TRANCE. An altered state of consciousness. States may vary from a light and slight brain wave frequency change to a significant alteration wherein the entranced person cannot recall the event, words, or what happened during the experience. Entering a trance can be accomplished while alone or with the assistance of another and for a variety of reasons.

TRANSCENDENTAL. Surpassing the senses; mystical. *See* Transcendental Meditation.

TRANSCENDENTAL FIELD. An arena of mystical awareness beyond rational knowing in which we can interact and encompass new realities

TRANSCENDENTAL MEDITATION™(TM). The registered name for a SIDDHA yoga approach to meditation brought to the United States by Indian physicist Maharishi Mahesh Yogi in 1957. A simplified approach with a MANTRA is given to initiates, along with techniques and instructions for their use. This approach, emphasizing human potential and scientific evaluation, has resisted the religious connotations of Hinduism to a great degree. It does, however, utilize Eastern culture and mystique.

TRANSFIGURATION. The process of creating a new vehicle of expression through the use of fire (purification) and light (of the soul), particularly by the practice of focused meditation. The new VEHICLE, once evoked, is to serve the purposes of soul and spirit more perfectly. Transfiguration occurs as the ELECTRIC FIRE of the SPIRITUAL TRIAD pours into the mind of personality, thereby releasing the light of the atoms within the three lower bodies of personality to produce enlightenment. The recreated new vehicle may be called the "mystical WEDDING GARMENT," the "ROBE OF GLORY," or the "coat of many colors," for it is created of higher frequencies so that it may reflect more perfectly the energies of the soul and, in time, the spirit. It is this vehicle that can be lifted into other planes and come and go without decay.

TRANSFORMATION. A personality change aligning to a pattern appropriate to spiritual life which so sensitizes the recipient that incoming spiritual forces have significantly increased impact. Contemporary churches try to influence this receptivity to change. Transformation requires the use of will and practices to clear and cleanse the astral and mental vehicles. As the astral purifies and the focused mind expands, their refined frequencies capture and reflect higher awareness. In transformation, devotion clears the astral vehicle, and love fills the life with aspiration; as illusions clear, the mind more faithfully reflects high consciousness. These changes emerge as a series of reforms in daily life, initiated by the aspirant.

An Agni virtue for Scorpio. The processes of magic, alchemy, and change of personality are aspects of transformation. Beginning with self-discipline, we invoke will and choose a path of light, using the forces of heart (aspiration) and mind (inspiration) to transform both consciousness and lifestyle.

TRANSITING. In astrology, the personified movement of planetary bodies in the heavens. This influence impacts natal planets and patterns to trigger responses both beneficial and challenging.

TRANSITION (AS DEATH). Acknowledging the demise of the body, the passing of consciousness from the physical realm into the nonphysical. As death approaches, we are encouraged to do the necessary work to release negatives and bring into balance events, attitudes, and emotions—our "unfinished business"—in preparation for the inner life to follow, as well as the next incarnation.

TRANSMIGRATION. Belief that human souls can incarnate into the bodies of animals. Taught by PLATO in his early works, he appears to have abandoned the belief later. Similarly, the UPANISHADS suggest the possibility of animal incarnation after a human life. Most Western wisdom teachings do not accept a backward movement of evolving egos into lesser kingdoms.

TRANSMUTATION. The continuing process of change in the very substance of the VEHICLE of personality that begins with the second initiation. Clearing and cleansing bring about an actual transmutation from denser to lighter. The etheric body, now much more reflective of heart and mind, continues to become a more delicate receiver set for high frequencies. Both matter and consciousness vibrate increasingly to the soul. As the etheric body is so sensitized, it has greater impact on the body, the aura increases in glow and vibrancy, and higher energy flows to the physical body. In time, the astral body, as a separate vehicle, disintegrates, and the energy released moves to create the MYSTICAL MARRIAGE of heart and mind. Without a separate astral body, the initiate is now a more objective, realistic, and just viewer of emotional issues.

TRANSMUTATION, MONADIC. A term used by Trigueirinho to indicate an advanced consciousness, a messenger, or WALK-IN, who is spared going through building the physical vehicle when that is superfluous to the life purpose. This one remains incarnated as long as needed to carry out the task for which it is responsible. Some EXTRATERRESTRIAL beings employ this means of entry into human form. *Also see pp. 349–55,* Etheric Dimensions.

TRANSPERSONAL. Reaching beyond, or transcending, the individual nature.

TRANSPERSONAL SELF. The inner presence, the SELF, the CHRIST-WITHIN, the ATMAN.

TRANSPERSONAL WILL. As free will is transcended and the soul-infused personality is able to move in accordance with higher will without feeling a sense of loss, transpersonal will is activated. The universal human surrenders free will in accordance with the evolutionary PLAN.

The Tree—A Universal Symbol

Tree, kabalistic. Kabalah utilizes two symbolic trees: the Tree of Knowledge of Good and Evil and the Tree of Life. The first, most commonly used, provides a map of energies descending through the four WORLDS and creating a world of duality.

Tree of Knowledge of Good and Evil. The kabalistic glyph upon which ten SEPHIROTH are placed, each of a different energy, or quality. As it descended, the life force created the four WORLDS, each of which contains a tree. This tree acknowledges involution and the PATH OF INITIATION for a humanity dealing with polarity. It is one of two trees mentioned in Gen. 2.9, reminding us that we gain experience in this world by using the two PILLARS of force and form to learn "good" and "evil." This well-known kabalistic glyph is the tree most commonly seen.

Tree of Knowledge of Good and Evil

Ain

Ain Soph

Ain Soph Aur

Tree of Life. In Kabalah the second tree mentioned in Gen. 2.9 refers to the pathways traveled as one on the path ascends the tree, integrating the side PILLARS and returning to the higher realities after mastering the lower. Also known as the corrected tree, the return tree, and other descriptive words to name its purpose, to record our progress in reintegrating duality toward a single upward path. The Tree of Life is a specific model that serves to hold the goal before us. In Prov. 3.18 SOPHIA is described as "a tree of life to those who lay hold of her."

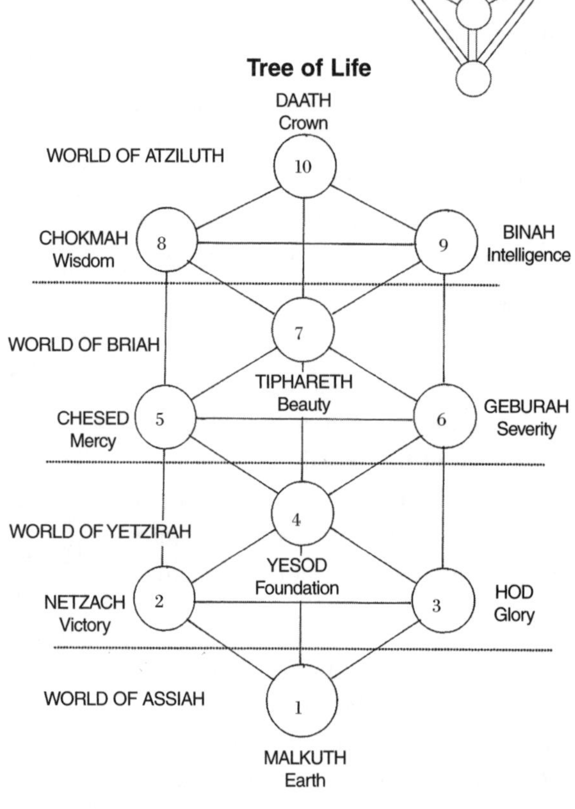

The Essene Tree of Life

Tree of Life, Essene. This tree presents the idea of 14 positive forces, seven of them heavenly, or cosmic, and seven earthly, or terrestrial. The tree is pictured as having seven roots reaching into the soil and seven branches extending toward the heavens, symbolizing humanity's relationship to both heaven and Earth. Each branch represents a different force or power. The human position is in the center of the Tree, learning to use harmoniously the available forces.

Trees of Life. A mythological symbol prevalent in many ancient and current indigenous world belief systems. Mystical approaches often use the concept of the tree upon which to hang symbols or glyphs representing a variety of energies, i.e., the tree in the Garden of Eden. The Druids, the Maya, and others had their sacred tree—sometimes considered the center of the known world, at other times depicted with its roots in heaven and its branches unfolding in the physical plane. Also called the "world tree."

Trefoil. St. Patrick used nature's example of the shamrock in the trefoil, with its three equal lobes depicting the doctrine of the Trinity.

Triad. The kabalistic Tree depicts a triad of three triangles—as do many systems—which are known as, from lowest: 1) Nephesch, the mundane triad of the emotional, mental, and psychic bodies; 2) Ruach, the ethical triad of evolution, the Higher Self, inspiration, and guidance; and 3) Neschamah, the supernal triad of cosmic knowledge and the true spiritual self. The highest is, of course, composed of the subtlest energies. Similarly, in a sequence located on the human body, the three lower chakras create the physical triad; the three middle chakras create a psychological triad; and the three upper centers create a spiritual triad.

Triangle. The perfect archetypical and earliest known symbol of the holy Trinity. The three sides, being of the same length, represent the equality of the three aspects of Divinity.

Tribulation. A period of severe affliction or acute trial for an individual or a group. Many believe we are currently undergoing such a time, as predicted by the Bible.

Trine. In astrology, the formation of two planets 120 degrees, or about four signs, apart (allowable orb 7 degrees). Considered favorable.

Triquetra. A design of three equal arcs, representing the holy Trinity. Its continuous form symbolizes eternity, and the intertwining represents the indivisibility of

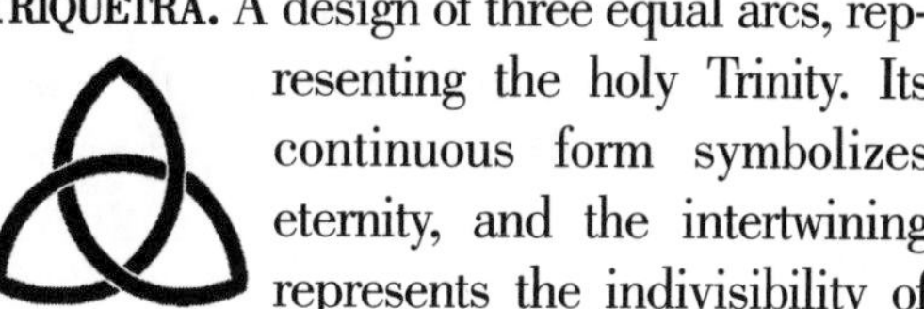

Trinity

The three persons known traditionally as the Father, Son, and Holy Spirit in the Christian Logos. Esotericists believe the "masculine-feminine polarity lives in dynamic harmony in all three persons . . . . Working in harmony with great rhythms of earthly evolution, the GODHEAD reveals in different planetary

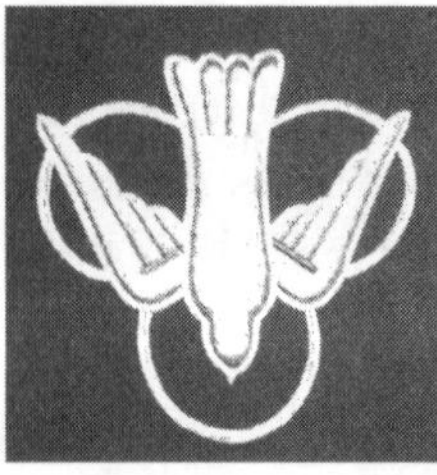

incarnations and epochs more the masculine or feminine forces contained in the Trinity. Human beings worshipping [*sic*] God on Earth are shaped by these forces according to what is needful in any given epoch on the way to evolving into the ideal, the universal, human being."[5]

The LOGOS is illustrated as three-in-one to portray the generating power, the maintaining force, and the destroyer aspects. The Christian tradition, as well as other world religions, recognizes the concept of deity as Trinity in the Father (-Mother), Son, and Holy Spirit. Brahma, Vishnu, and Shiva comprise the Hindu Trinity. In ancient Druidism the one God is called Duw, with three aspects known as the one without darkness who pervades the universe, represented by the Trinity of Beli, the Creator of the past; Taran, controller of the present; and Yesu, the expected savior of the future. Kether, Chokmah, and Binah comprise the Trinity of Kabalah. In astrology personality reflects the trinity by its SUN, MOON, and ASCENDANT. In numerology the three aspects, known by various terms according to the system, are determined by the numerical values of the totals of vowels, then consonants, then the combined total.

TRINITY, FIRST PERSON OF CHRISTIAN. The Creator, the Source, usually identified as the Father, represents the androgynous Creator—both masculine and feminine—by whose power creation was set into motion.

TRINITY, SECOND PERSON OF CHRISTIAN. The Christ, reflection of the divine Father and Mother in the subtle world, is called "the Son." The physical sun is believed by esotericists to be the radiant body for the Great Lord Christ, planetary guide for our stream of life. The CHRIST-WITHIN, or MYSTICAL CHRIST, is the reflection of the holy in individual lives.

TRINITY, THIRD PERSON OF. The Paraclete, or Holy Spirit, advocate who guards and guides the lesser worlds and its inhabitants back to the Source. Symbolized by the dove, the Holy Spirit is the feminine nurturing influence of Sophia. In Kabalah the home of the Holy Spirit is BINAH, the Mother.

the holy Trinity. Used frequently today to represent the interlocking relationship of body, mind, and spirit.

TRUTH. We think of truth as inflexible; however, it is UNIVERSAL LAW that is uncompromising. Truth changes, unfolds, and evolves as we do. What we may have avowed as our position or even a "fact" a decade or two or three ago probably has altered or amplified with experience and maturity. The process of realizing truth advances in three steps. First, we gain information; utilizing it, we become knowledgeable; and, when we are able to comprehend how the pieces fit, we achieve wisdom, which we use to see through distortions and thus discover truth.

TSE-BUM. Tibetan equivalent of the GRAIL, the sacred urn that contains the elixir of life, whose lid is decorated with a fan of PEACOCK feathers. An actual act of empowerment occurs when the guru-initiator places it upon the candidate's head, upon the thousand-petaled crown. This act is highly significant because the "skullcap" is said to contain the nectar of the Gods. The CRYSTAL SKULLS of MesoAmerica also symbolize this teaching, enlightened consciousness.

TUMAH. Negative packets of energy.

TURIYA. Sanskrit for the ultimate state of consciousness, God realization, or enlightenment.

TURN THE OTHER CHEEK. (Matt. 5.39) An admonishment not to react to misuse or abuse with vindictiveness but to respond without offense rather than add negative energy that will prolong the battle. We could say, do not set adverse KARMA into action; attempt to end the pattern by setting good into motion.

TWELVE-STEP PROGRAM(S). A contemporary path of awakening, referred to as the probationary path in spiritual teachings. Developing will and choosing direction and focus are major parts of the probationary effort. The first twelve-step program, created by Bill Wilson and Dr. Bob Silkworth, became a highly successful support group known as Alcoholics Anonymous, after which many comparable groups have been patterned.

TWELVE TRIBES OF ISRAEL. Relates esoterically to zodiacal influences (as twelve perfected stages of the One Being). Stages are realized in an unpredictable process, not sequentially, so growth is always pictured as a circular journey, rather than linear.

TWITCHELL, PAUL. b. Paducah, Kentucky, 1908, d. 1971. Founder of ECKANKAR in 1965. As with many spiritual leaders, his biography is often confusing and inconsistent. Few facts of his personal life are available. An adventurer, he traveled extensively in search of occult teachings. He married at least twice and served in the U.S. Navy during World War II, after which he became involved with magazines, public relations, and ultimately became the author of numerous books, including *The Drums of ECK; The Tiger's Fang; In My Soul I Am Free; ECKANKAR—The Key to Secret Worlds.*

TYPTOLOGY. The ability to communicate with spirit, utilizing a formula or predetermined code of rappings.

TZADDIK. An entire universe of awareness of adamic purity, out of which individual tzaddikim, or saints, come.

TZADDIKIM. Righteous persons, saints. A "lamed-vav tzaddikim" is one of the 36 hidden saints who quietly do their work in this world in a way that holds the universe together.

TZORECH G'VOAH. That which is projected by the wise of the higher world to those of humanity who are karmically qualified to receive, i.e., the call to "come up higher." Also known as the science of the sages.

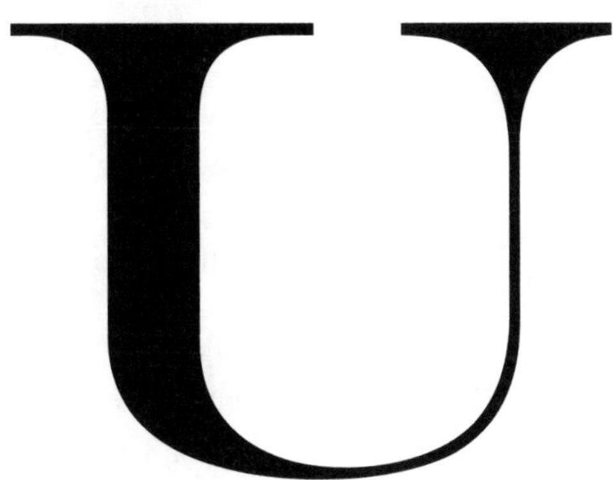

UFO. This early acronym for an "unidentified flying object" is related to the concept of unknown species of life suspected of existing in other dimensions, planes, or planetary systems, with the capability of traveling into our solar system and to our planet. *Also see* Reverse spectrum photography technique.

UFO/ALIEN PHASE. Unidentified flying objects awaken humanity to the unknown still under investigation. The term has evolved to denote an alien culture from outside our planet, awakening inquiries about the ramifications of that presence and contact. Many archaeologists/scientists believe this has occurred before and that we are entering a possible contact phase once again.

UFOLOGY. The study of little-understood phenomena categorized as "Unidentified Flying Objects" (UFOs). Such sightings may be terrestrial, extraterrestrial, or cosmic, and include experiences that convention often considers hoaxes, hallucinations, and/or crafts built by some human means.

UNCONSCIOUS DARKNESS. A state of evolution in which we are guided by involution, or instinctual nature; KALI YUGA is the period of purification at this level of planetary life.

UNCONSCIOUS, THE. A level of self of which most are unaware but which contains instinctual awareness (knowledge that has slipped beneath the level of consciousness), repressed material, and unawakened potential. Each person has an individual unconscious but also taps into the unconscious of the human race. Also refers to those not yet awakened, considered asleep to higher worlds.

UNDEVELOPED SOULS. Young souls who have had little experience on the Earth plane; usually required to reincarnate several times in one SUB-RACE.

UNDINES. The water sprites of the nature kingdom. *See* Nature spirits.

UNFORGIVINGNESS. This barrier to spiritual growth, the nonreleasing of either self or another, causes us to stay bound in ourselves. Without granting freedom, we cannot make progress to become all we might be.

UNICORN. A fabled creature of mystical meaning, symbolizing one who has accessed higher reality and refined the basic nature by bringing the subtler awareness down to the physical. The single horn represents the developed and focused spiritual center of the forehead, or third eye.

UNICORN EYE. Made of two crescent moons point to point with a dot in the center is the glyph of the BLACK MOON, the archetype for the multiple principle necessary for transformation. The WHITE SUN and Black Moon represent "AS ABOVE, SO BELOW," male and female, etc., as parts of the necessary interplay of extremes in which spiritual energy is never destroyed but transformed. The symbol of the sun (circle w/dot) is quite similar; the Black Moon incorporates it as well.

UNITY. The ability to increasingly see beyond separateness, finding the principles that link perspectives in order to heal and affirm the oneness of life.

UNIVERSAL BEING. One whose consciousness has merged into the timeless, endless pool of awareness of the Infinite, God, or Source.

UNIVERSALITY. The thread of sameness that flows through all aspects and experiences of life.

The Agni virtue for Gemini. A state of non-separativeness. Both a blessing and a challenge, for ultimately universality—the wholeness—is the guiding consciousness of all life. The awareness that no separation or abrupt break exists between opposing forms of life because each flows into the other, overlapping and embracing. People of high consciousness stand for one spirit, one life, and one existence to express these interlocking bonds of life.

UNIVERSAL LAW. A way of designating the sustaining axioms of spiritual reality as we can understand them within the human experience. These laws are determined within the framework of the HERMETIC PRINCIPLES. *Also see* Spiritual law.

UNIVERSAL MIND (OR CONSCIOUSNESS). The mind of God; the consciousness of the Supreme Being which permeates the macrocosm. A state of God-consciousness in which the great will or purpose of the Logos is known. Union with God; a state in which the Soul consciously knows itself to be one with the ALL. The vast consciousness with which we are identified, the totality of consciousness. The divine thinker, or principle of intelligence, which makes itself known as the will-to-be, desire, or love-of-being, and that active, intelligent purpose which animates the solar system.

UNIVERSE. A spiritual system governed by the laws of higher reality that reflects divine law at work, from the smallest particles to the rhythm of the planets themselves.

UNSELF, THE. Another name for "ego," the nonself.

UPANISHADS. Spiritual writings of the East; a part of the Vedas from which emerged the Vedanta, a system of philosophy and spiritual teachings. The esoteric wisdom of Hinduism is held largely in the Upanishads, which means "at the feet of," suggesting a dialogue between the wise and those who sit receptively at their feet.

URANTIA BOOK, THE. Extensive channeled material about the development and evolution of the universe and humanity, received by a variety of personalities and published in 1955 by the Urantia Foundation, Chicago.

URIEL. *See* Archangels.

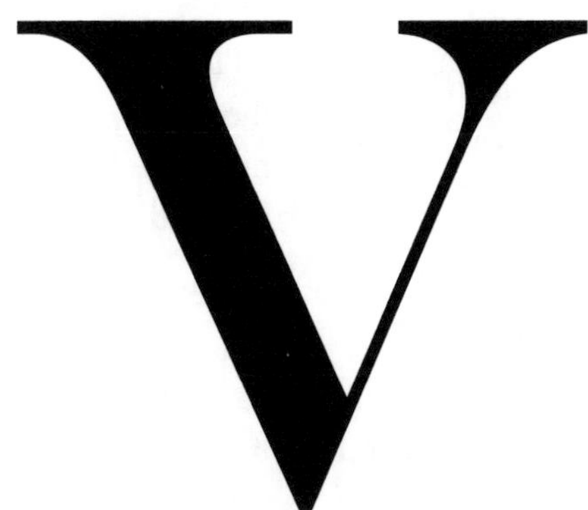

VAISYA VARNA. The vocational class of farmers and merchants in India.

VAJRAYANA. Third school of Buddhism; practices for the realization of emptiness, the nature of mind and oneness with all things. This indirect Eastern path is also known as tantra; its practitioners are SIDDHA yogis who actualize the tantras—not sex magic, but ALCHEMY that utilizes sexual symbolism to sublimate and transform the instinctual. The importance of the LAMA is emphasized. *See other two schools:* Mahayana, Hinayana.

VARNA. External appearance, covering, type, species, kind, color, or caste.

VARNA DHARMA. The law of color; the Vedic law of the four inherited occupational classes—the highest rank, Brahman, the kings and military, the merchants, the laborers.

VARUNA. The Vedic guardian of the natural and moral order, Savior, and forgiver of sins, regarded as the god of water and symbolizing the Water of Space.

VEDANTA. A Hindu philosophy derived from the teachings of the UPANISHADS—the latter part of the Vedas—summaries that form the doctrinal basis of the Hindu religion, that all reality is a single principle, BRAHMA. The believer's goal is to transcend the limitations of self-identity and realize unity with Brahma. One of the oldest spiritual paths on the planet. Arthur SCHOPENHAUER praised them as "deep, original, sublime thoughts." "Access to the Vedas," he said, "is the greatest privilege this century may claim over all previous centuries."

VEDAS. The most ancient sacred literature of the Hindus, consisting of four collections:

1) Rig Veda, hymns to the gods, 2) Sama Veda, priests' chants, 3) Yajur Veda, sacrificial formulae in prose, and 4) Atharva Veda, magical chants. Considered revealed literature, they contain philosophical insights and are regarded as the final authority.

VEGAN. One who is a strict vegetarian, which includes no animal food or dairy products.

VEHICLE. In esoteric terminology, "body." The vehicle of mind expresses thought; the astral (emotional) vehicle expresses feeling; the physical vehicle expresses action.

VEHICLES OF PERSONALITY. Personality expresses through three bodies, or vehicles, during incarnation. From the lowest to the highest: 1) physical body (includes the etheric body) deals with sensory reactions and actions; 2) astral body deals with emotions, feelings, desires; 3) mental body deals with ideas and concrete thoughts. As it evolves, the goal of personality is to become sensitive to the intuitive nature, dealing with ideals and abstract thought.

VEHICLES OF THE SOUL. The SOUL, empowered by the MONAD, receives its impulse from the atmic level where it steps down RAYS 1, 2, and 3 into a formation of an additional four rays, 4, 5, 6, and 7. This flow descends into the intuitive plane (also known as the Buddhic level or Christ consciousness) to blend with the essence of the abstract levels of mind. Here in the subtler frequencies of the mental body, the EGOIC LOTUS forms. This delicate area of mental frequencies and soul essence is called the CAUSAL BODY. From here, the soul develops the personality that has been projected into the dense world of physical experience.

VEIL. A protective covering used to conceal the perception mechanism of the expanding mind. Veils dissolve as consciousness heightens and perception clears.

VEILS, FOUR. The veils that separate three inner-plane segments known as the HALLS OF LEARNING are defined by MASTER DJWHAL KHUL. These curtains over the windows of vision prevent the realization of that which is beyond our capability; they block the light of consciousness. They protect the human kingdom from the burning energies it may not yet be able to contact. As we experience INITIATION, we are attuned to handle the fiery currents and can safely rend the veil and advance.

THE 1ST, the Veil of Impulsion, obscures the Hall of Concentration. This is the veil the average person meets. It is made up of the four OBSTACLES ON THE PATH. The energy of the veil is Law. To go beyond it, we must realize the purpose of SPIRITUAL LAW and respect it.

THE 2ND, the Veil of Distortion, prevents entrance to the Hall of Choice. This veil distorts our picture of reality beyond the physical dimension. The Christ rent this veil by his power of love, symbolizing that those who love (without glamours) can advance to the fourth initiation. When this occurs, the DWELLER is released and the soul meets itself on the BUDDHIC PLANE. The energy of this veil is love, and we must know love as a great and powerful force to advance.

THE 3RD. As the Veil of Separation (between the Hall of Choice and the Hall of Blinded Men) is rent, a brilliant charge of light is released, revealing the union of all. The energy of this veil is union, or synthesis, and it enables progress.

THE 4TH, the Veil of Aspiration, will be rent by humanity itself when it stands as "massed intent," as the EXTERNALIZATION OF THE HIERARCHY occurs. The energy of the veil is life, and it will pour forth in a renewed way when the Hierarchy takes physical residence upon the planet once again.

The veils of the temple are representative of the separation formed by outer participation and the inner mystery hidden even from ourselves.

VENERATED. Describing those valued not for their own divinity, but because they turn others toward that which is truly holy (different than worship).

VENETIAN, THE. *See pp. 170–1,* Masters.

VENKATESANANDA, SWAMI. d. 1982. A highly respected SWAMI from Johannesburg, South Africa, who has written a popular commentary to the Bhagavad Gita, *The Song of God;* a book of guidance entitled *Multiple Reflections;* and *Christ, Krishna, and You,* published by the Chiltern Yoga Foundation, San Francisco. *The Yoga Sutras of Patanjali* is a commentary compiled from the swami's many talks. He credited his legacy to his teacher Swami Sivananda of Rishikesh, frequently reminding others, "I am a disciple and not a guru." He was very well-educated, possessing a grasp of several languages and a vast knowledge of the Vedas; his Sanskrit was as refined as his English. His wisdom is greatly venerated by those inclined toward interfaith understanding.

VESICA PISCIS. An integral component of SACRED GEOMETRY. This figure is constructed by drawing two equal circles so the center of each lies on the circumference of the other. Used to create a balanced relationship between masculine and feminine energies and a connection between the physical plane of thought and the planes of universal awareness, intuition, and higher will.

The chapel at SPARROW HAWK VILLAGE was designed in this configuration in order to best utilize the interaction of the intersecting leys upon which it rests and to assist in balancing the masculine and feminine aspects of the consciousness of the devout.

VESSEL. Symbolically, the receptive consciousness formed through spiritual exercises necessary for advancement. Also referred to as the GRAIL, cup, or chalice.

VIBES. Intuitive sensing of emotional climate, probably telepathic; short for vibrations.

VIBRATION (HERMETIC PRINCIPLE OF). All is in movement—some slower, to be known as matter; some faster, so as to be invisible. Simply stated, "motion." From an occult perspective, any vibration becomes significant to the process of spiritual evolution, including REINCARNATION and KARMA. *See* Hermetic Principles.[1]

VICE. A negative distortion of pure, undefiled energy moving through a chakra in an unclear expression. Its opposite is "virtue," the clear expression.

VIGIL, PRAYER. Prolonged period of uninterrupted invocation, meditation, or adoration of the holy, usually for a specific intent and length of time or for a celebration. It may be designated as short as an hour or as long as the length of a war, for example. The structure is defined by the purpose.

VIRGIN MARY. A title given to the mother of Jesus and the foundation of the idea of the virgin birth. In the esoteric tradition, however, "virgin" does not mean celibate but a state of purity in which one's life is lived: pure, chaste, honorable. *See pp. 180–3,* Mothers and Goddesses of the World; Mary, mother of Jesus.

VIRTUES. Working under the ARCHANGELS and with the concrete mental and abstract astral substances, this advanced order of ANGELS bestows MIRACLES, evokes integrity, and releases the flow of grace upon humanity.

A soul quality clearly expressed is drawn into the personality and flows without distortion through one's consciousness into the physical world. This ability to bring a soul quality into the personality is called "building a virtue or facet of the soul." *See* Astrology.

VISHNU. The Vedic god of justice, the preserver and protector, and the second member of the Hindu Trinity, the Son of the creator; compares to the Christian Son. It is said the LOGOS manifests as a Trinity to perform the work required for each ROOT RACE. Lord KRISHNA is considered an incarnation of Vishnu. The Hindu Trinity comprises Brahma, Vishnu, and Shiva.

VISHNU, INCARNATIONS OF. The concept of God descending into the world of humanity. Vishnu, second god of the Hindu Trinity, is considered an AVATAR. The nine incarnations as given by Manly Palmer Hall in *Man—The Grand Symbol of the Mysteries* (1931), suggest the myth of the avatar "signifies the Divine Spirit either in the universe or of man" moving from form to form and is "the true explanation of transitions constantly taking place in Nature." (p.107)

The first incarnation was Matsya the Fish; the second was Kurma the Tortoise; next Varaha the Boar; the fourth, Narasimha the Lion-Man; fifth, Vamana the Dwarf. Parashu Rama is the sixth; Ramachandra, hero of the Indian epic, the Iramayana, was seventh; while Krishna (sometimes known as Balarama the Plowman) was the eighth. Buddha is considered by Hindus to be ninth, but Buddhists do not use the term avatar nor identify Buddha as one. The tenth, Kalki, has yet to appear, it is believed, but will do so when a righteous age begins.

Viewed as a history of evolution, we get an entirely different meaning to the above list. Symbolically, the fish is the earliest form of life; amphibians gain ascendance in the tortoise. Next is the boar, the mammal; then the half-man–half-lion represents a developing humanity. The dwarf, better understood as the short man, is the not-yet-completed man; next comes the man with the axe—the Neanderthal beings with their primitive tools. The hero of the *Ramayana* was a hunter with bow and arrow. As humanity evolves to the hunter-gatherer stage, the plowman appears. Krishna, with his flute, is artistic and represents spiritual consciousness; certainly Buddha models human potential. Kalki will symbolize the full appearance of potential flowering throughout the human race as a higher humanity—HOMO NOETICUS.

VISION. An experience of higher reality, usually while in an altered state that inspires or conveys direction, response, or action.

VISIONARY. One who perceives through spiritual senses a glimpse or cognizance of the future or another reality.

VISIONING. Seeing in the mind's eye activates, accompanies, and encourages the use of the spiritual senses. This CLAIRVOYANCE, or clear seeing, can be a strong inner awareness of an impression. HUGH OF ST. VICTOR taught that we have three ways of seeing: we use our physical eyes to see outer objects or scenes; we see with our minds to grasp concepts, ideals, and principles; and we have a spiritual eye with which to see God's PLAN at work.

VISION QUEST. Withdrawal from daily life patterns for the purpose of seeking a spiritual experience or perception—often a journey into a wilderness. The Native American tradition used these periods to contact the spirit world for INITIATION, guidance, or to honor spirit as the supporter of those in the physical.

VISUALIZATION. Creating in the mind's eye a picture, symbol, or design—sometimes spontaneously through the power of the mind screen to receive impressions and sometimes by act of will when the mind is focused and affirming. Visualization is an extension of the creative power and a major tool when awakened to the power of mind and our relationship to UNIVERSAL MIND.

As a spiritual discipline, a technique applied by spiritual disciples to train the inner nature in a particular way. Usually one closes the eyes and engages the image-making ability to see oneself performing or behaving in a particular manner. To see oneself in one's mind in a specific act or manner empowers one to bring that behavior into outer manifestation. Spiritual teachings suggest that to act "AS IF" assists one to become.

VIVEKANANDA, SWAMI. b. India, 1863, d. 1902. Indian yogi and chief disciple of the Christlike Ramkrishna Paramahansa (1836–1886), known for bringing VEDANTA to the West with his famous addresses at the Parliament of Religions held in Chicago in 1893. Vivekananda established one of India's leading charities, the Ramkrishna Mission, and carried on the work of Ramkrishna who stressed "not mercy, but service," which helped touch the Western heart.

VOID OF COURSE. Astrologically, a period of time when the moon does not progress in its forward movement but rests or stalls.

VOODOO. A form of ritual used to act upon a person or situation on the material plane through use of astral energy; known for its negative impact or influence, it is often regarded as detrimental. *Also see* Sorcery.

VOW OF POVERTY. The spiritual meaning, "Gives all and expects nothing." A promise taken by those who choose to own no material property, reminding us we have no worth but our true value as a SOUL.

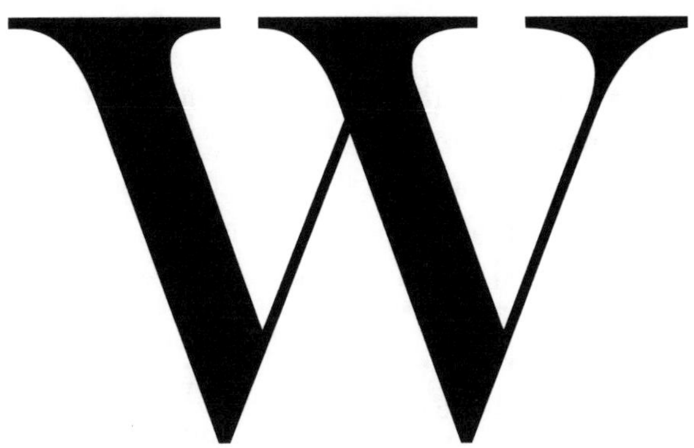

WALDORF SCHOOLS. These institutions, based upon Rudolf STEINER'S ANTHROPOSOPHY, emphasize preparing children for sensitivity, creativity, independence, moral and spiritual consciousness. The first schools opened in Stuttgart, Germany, in 1919 and in North America in 1928.

WALK-IN. A term coined by Ruth MONTGOMERY (d. 2001) which she introduced in *Strangers Among Us* and used in *Threshold to Tomorrow* to designate the exchange of souls when the builder of the body withdraws and a different soul—assisted by the LORDS OF KARMA—is allowed to enter and use the personality for a humanitarian purpose. In the *Gospel of St. Luke* Rudolf STEINER said that when reaching a certain age, a human being could fall into a dead faint and the Inner Self leave the body and a new Inner Self take over.[1] In 1920 MASTER D.K., The Tibetan, referred to this phenomenon as a "DIVINE OBSESSION" and assured that it would become increasingly common in the years ahead.[2] Such changes are carried out under the benign aura of liberated beings who serve as mainstays of the energy factors. Trigueirinho calls this change MONADIC TRANSMUTATION. Such SOUL EXCHANGE events occur more frequently in times of collective crisis. *Also see* Messenger, *for delivering a message is indeed the purpose of such an exchange.*

WARRIOR, SPIRITUAL. Esoterically, one who enters into the conscious struggle between levels of self—light and darkness, good and evil—within one's own nature. The warrior is developing the strengths, qualities, and persistence needed to do battle with the DWELLER ON THE THRESHOLD. Every battle is preparation for the next. The MAYAN people say that when the forces of fire (will) and water (sensitivity) within mix, it is called "war." Thus the one in whom this occurs is the spiritual warrior.

Watcher (or Silent Watcher). Spiritual guide(s) of the worlds. That part of eternal or divine life that never identifies with form, ever conscious of its holy nature. This eternal magnet ceaselessly draws the separated self, the fallen spark, homeward along the path of return to the Source. Also, the Great Being, head of Hierarchy, the most evolved of a system or group. This Great One, whose radiance pervades the entire system over which this Watch extends, provides the home for innumerable beings. Lofty though a Great Being's surveillance may be, in every case an even Greater Being encompasses creation to an even greater magnitude.

Waterbearer. A modern term for Aquarian consciousness, implying the time and awareness for pouring living waters upon humanity. In both John 4.10 and 7.38, Jesus, the Christ, says he brings the living water to humanity that it may awaken to the will of the Creator. Esoterically, *living water* means "awakening human will to higher will."

Water mysteries. The gentle, emotional teachings of love, appreciation, respect, consideration, and esteem to aid in the development of positive emotions in the astral body. Centered around Advent, the birth of the Christ (Christmas), and Epiphany. As these are raised to higher astral frequencies, they will in time blend with the mental nature in transmutation to become love-wisdom.

Waxing and waning. The phases of the moon as it moves from new to full, then fades. Waxing is before full moon, as its power builds. Waning is the lingering influence after full moon, as the moon diminishes to darkness.

Wayshower. A prophet or enlightened one who, by virtue of evolutionary progress, can lead humanity in spiritual development. Master Jesus serves as the wayshower for the Christian tradition. Each wayshower serves as a guide who goes before others to take them toward self-realization and expression of the divine within.

Weatherhead, Dr. Leslie D. A great theologian and leading British pulpit voice in the first half of the 20th century. He preached in the famed City Temple in London to cabinet ministers, slum dwellers, middle-class Londoners, and visitors from around the world. The temple was destroyed by incendiary bombs during World War II. He wrote over a score of books. A specialist in psychology, he applied that knowledge and contemporary techniques to both preaching in his pastorates and counseling. "It is evident in his writings that he has seen Christ, however obscured, in every human soul," reads a book cover. *The Christian Agnostic*, 1965; *The Meaning of the Cross*, 1945; *Psychology of Religion and Healing*, 1952; *A Plain Man Looks at the Cross*, 1945; *The Will of God*, 1944.

Web, etheric. The mechanism that connects the energy fields of the less dense physical to the astral, the astral to mental, and so on. These connecting threads are often said to hold together or to hold apart the vehicles until TRANSFORMATION begins. Subtle energies flowing through the web from body to body register on the personality. Integration advances through TRANSMUTATION toward the building of the transfigured body, fully integrated into one celestial body guided by the soul.

WEDDING GARMENT. In the Christian mystery tradition, this is the radiant light formed through purification of the astral and mental natures as we approach SOUL INFUSION. This transmuted subtle body must be developed before we can stand in the presence of the Christ or become a Christed One. The garment of the soul is the sublimated essence of the physical body, together with the spiritualized forces of the etheric sheath: an ETHERIC BODY capable of functioning on the physical and etheric planes without a dense body.

WELLNESS. The optimum condition or point of wholeness—harmony and balance—one can realize at any given time through an integration of physical, emotional, mental, and spiritual awareness.

WELLNESS GUIDE. One prepared for a private practice or specific role of providing direction to others regarding the integration of body, mind, and spirit as they strive for wholeness.

WELLNESS UNIVERSE. This concept, becoming more prevalent, applies to holistic well-being and integration of physical, emotional, mental, and spiritual components (body, mind, and spirit) in the life of humanity in relationship to planetary and universal expression. An awareness of harmony to be achieved as collectives of life abide in accord with UNIVERSAL LAW.

WESAK. A festival said to occur in the Himalayas at the FULL MOON of Taurus in which all members of the planetary hierarchy are present for a special blessing bestowed by the BUDDHA as he renews his bond with the work of planet Earth. The blessing is accepted for the planet by the Christ as head of HIERARCHY and distributed to humanity through the MASTERS.

WESTERN YOGA. *See* Yoga.

WHAT GOES AROUND COMES AROUND. A reference to the law of KARMA, inevitably just.

WHEEL OF KARMA. An Eastern term for cycles of experiences we attract in order to achieve the wisdom and insight needed until there is no further reason for incarnation; thus we are off "the wheel."

WHEEL OF REBIRTH. Cycle of REINCARNATION; returning to earthly existence repeatedly until all experiences of the physical plane are registered at the soul level, all intended lessons are learned and absorbed, and all issues of karma are resolved.

WHEN THE STUDENT IS READY, THE TEACHER APPEARS. Here we confront the realization that indeed the higher PLAN is withheld until we have advanced enough to realize the richness of the opportunity at hand. We may have to go through an agonizing process of breaking through our own barriers (usually not acknowledged) before we are ready, in position, and at a level of consciousness to appreciate the answer or teacher that resonates in such a way we are drawn to awakening spiritually. *See* Yoga, Krishna.

Whirling dervishes. Members of a sect of Islamic mystics who use movement and dance to alter the consciousness. They are known to whirl in a circle for long periods of time to enter an altered state and then follow with meditation and contemplation.

White Lodge. *See* Brotherhood, White.

White magic. Specific acts of goodness for the purpose of higher consciousness, through affirmation, prayer, visualization, meditations, and "how-to" techniques. Acts must be unselfish, of positive benefit, and with good intent. *Magick* is an earlier word for alchemy; now "transformation" is used.

White magician. One who does the work for which s/he has incarnated, working in the light of one's own soul and soul purpose to assist the Plan to manifest for self and others.

White Moon. In alchemy, an astrological reference to the repository of souls after death, known as heaven in most religions.

White Sun. In alchemy, the white light of the One Mind. *See* Unicorn eye.

Wholeness. An integration of the personality vehicles: physical, emotional, and mental natures are now ready for the spiritual self to lead the way toward higher consciousness—holiness.

Wicca. The Anglo-Saxon root of "witch," the European shaman tradition. Many contemporary witches of all varieties use this term as a less misunderstood word for "witchcraft."

Wiccan. A practitioner of the old religion of Wicca or witchcraft. Technically, applied only to British traditionalist witches, but widely used as a synonym for "witch."

Will. The Ray 1 quality of focused spiritual power that initiates action. The energy of ignited will creates action, often resulting in leadership. Ray 1's color is generally accepted as red. It is labeled as masculine.

Will of God. Known as a Plan for creation, understood in the council chamber of Shamballa as the purpose and goal toward which evolution is carrying creation. To cooperate with this flow is to align one's will toward higher will.

Will-to-be. An Agni term. One of the qualities of Ray 1 energy directed to each disciple as a specific command to affirm the potential to be lived out in an optimum way day by day—to be all we can be.

Will-to-good. An Agni term. One of the qualities of Ray 1 energy directed specifically to the "Common Good," an oft-used term for higher will or God's will, aligned to the purpose and the Plan to be manifested by humanity.

Winnowing technique. A style of questioning inviting further detail to obtain a clearer perspective; a clarification technique to search for what is real, for a more distinct recall. Think of "fishing for specifics." As defined and taught in Psychography.

WISDOM. An advanced level of comprehension. Steps taught in spiritual understanding are: information—data and concepts; knowledge—use of; and wisdom—the ability to synthesize, to see relationships of event to event, of "this to that." The dedicated observation and practice of knowledge result in wisdom. The mystic's wisdom comes from experience that causes personal expansion, thus engendering greater insight. When the expansion unites the separate and the One, all perspectives change. *See* Truth.

WISDOMKEEPER. The Mayan SHAMAN, or DAYKEEPER. Other lineages of the Americas use this term for their wise ones as well.

WISDOM PRINCIPLE, BUDDHA'S. The use of mind—in meditation, visualization, affirmation, and contemplation—to offset the power of instinct and emotion.

WISDOM TEACHINGS. A body of practical knowledge about the hidden nature of humanity and the world held sacred through all time. The purpose of studying these teachings is to attain such knowledge in the intellect as may be contemplated and to awaken the spiritual memory of the soul held within the COLLECTIVE UNCONSCIOUS of humanity.

WISE GUARDIANS. Those from inner worlds who watch human progress, guiding and protecting as they can without interfering with humanity's free will.

WISE MEN, THREE. *See* Magi.

WISE ONES. A common title signifying those trained in the wisdom of the esoteric; certain Masters, saints, and sages in the Western tradition, and gurus in the East. High initiates who step down the scheme of evolution to the less evolved.

WITCH. One who worships the goddess in an Earth religion, working with forces of nature and following the disciplines of Wicca. Both male and female practitioners may be called "witches"; more correctly, males are called "warlocks." WICCAN is the older term; the more recent, "witch," began as a sign of disrespect.

WITCHCRAFT. The most common practice of NEO-PAGANISM. A magical Earth religion with many traditions derived from various cultural sources around which covens and individual practitioners converge. Modern witchcraft traditions include Gardnerian, Alexandrian, Dianic, Celtic, Circle, Faerie, Shamanic.

WITCHES OF SALEM. A large number of individuals, mostly women, were put to death for practicing ancient folk wisdom such as spiritual healing, herbology, gifts of intuition, or natural psychic abilities for the benefit of their families or others. In the U.S. in the 1690s, a particular focus became Salem, MA, which resulted in the murder of 20 and the arrest of 141 people. Witch hunts became so fanatical, there was no defense and almost any accusation resulted in persecution. Related to the period of the Inquisition (which began in 1233 in Europe).

WITNESS CONSCIOUSNESS. An impersonal level of awareness created through objectivity and spiritual insight; a developed chosen perspective from which we observe life at work.

WIZARD. Magician, sorcerer, or a highly skilled person in a particular area.

WORD, THE CREATIVE: *OM*. The sacred word from ancient Sanskrit is said to be *OM*, deemed to be the generative first word or tone that vibrated through the receptive void to shape and maintain creation. This keynote went forth from the Source to set creation, as we know it, into motion. Considered the sum of all vibrations of the universe, *Om* is the sound of both INVOCATION and EVOCATION in meditation, the witness of a divine presence, the sacred word that was with God. Just as the *Om* issued forth from God to create all that is, the *Om* restores and magnifies God's presence within creation. Thus it is an especially effective POWER WORD as a MANTRA.

WORKERS IN THE FIELD OF RELIGION. A particular category of WORLD SERVERS who work through head, heart, and solar plexus to step down the higher PLAN for humanity.

WORKING *AS IF*. A self-explanatory technique for aiding perception from an other-than-personal perspective. Working "AS IF" provides an opportunity to see if a given circumstance may be made feasible, a learning process to reveal what is advantageous and what is not.

WORLD MOTHER. The divine feminine in working partnership with the divine masculine in manifestation. Many personifications are recognized by different traditions as her representations. *Also see pp. 180–3,* Mothers and Goddesses of the World.

WORLD PERIOD. Represents the period of time required for the passage of seven ROOT RACES, including each of its seven SUB-RACES.

WORLD SERVERS. Those in all arenas of life and service who knowingly or unknowingly play their part in the divine PLAN, seeking to further the work of the HIERARCHY and dedicated to the well-being of humanity. While working in the outer world, they maintain a deep, inner life from which they can draw all that is needed for dynamic spiritual work. Modern disciples who perceive their part in a planetary transformation. Once called the NEW GROUP OF WORLD SERVERS, this company provides a training ground and a field of experience for those who choose to grow in spiritual stature and to ready themselves for active, directed service to the Christ.

World servers can be categorized as: telepathic communicators, trained observers, magnetic healers, educators of the new age, political organizers, workers in the field of religion, scientific servers, psychologists, financiers and economists, and creative workers *(see individual definitions),* according to the teachings of MASTER DJWHAL KHUL. It is said that these functions seek to satisfy humanity's needs and promote the development of the individual chakra systems of the world server.

WORLDS, FOUR. In Kabalah, each "world"—of which there are four—is represented by a complete TREE. From highest to densest, they are: Atziluth, the archetypal home; Briah, the world of soul; Yetzirah, the psychological realm; and Assiah, the etheric/physical plane. *See individual world names.*

WORLD SOUL. The Earth as an entity—Mother Earth, mother matter, Gaia—is seen as the personality: physical, emotional, and mental levels of density animated by the spiritual essence or soul of the planet. A level of knowing innate within creation is the consciousness called the soul of the world or SOPHIA.

WORLD TEACHER. Christ is the world teacher—not Jesus, as the exoteric Christian tradition teaches, but the Great Lord Christ, teacher of angels and of humanity. In the Orient he is known as the BODHISATTVA, as Lord MAITREYA, and as Imam Madhi, the one looked for by the devout Muslim. This one is committed to the guidance of humanity and the development of each human, the realization that the SPARK OF GOD resides within. The world teacher is charged to develop that inner presence so each will know s/he is the offspring of the Most High.

WORRY STONE. Small pebble used in the HUNA system for invoking spiritual power, especially employed in rites of healing or saying affirmations.

WORTHY OPPONENT. Each of us, in our principal relationship, needs one who is deserving of us if we are to grow to our potential. By meeting our counterpart in love and respect, we bless each other—a desired state for precious marriages or relationships. A title for a spouse or a significant other; also perceived as SOULMATES. *See* Cosmic relationships; Karmic relationships.

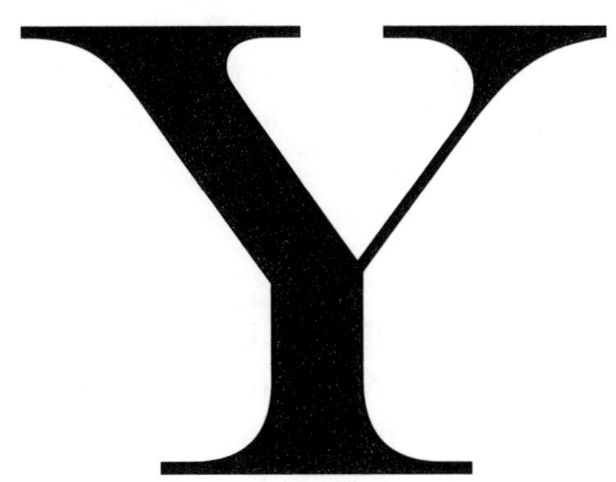

Yahweh. God of the Hebrews who later became Jehovah. *See* Tetragrammaton; Yod Heh Vau Heh (YHWH).

Yarrow stalks. A type of straw or sticks used in I Ching for purposes of divination.

Ye are Gods. We are reminded in both Old and New Testaments that we are Gods; the FEMININE PRINCIPLE, the SOUL, is to bring about the birth of the Christ-Within. Jesus quoted the Psalm to reinforce humanity's awareness of its divine nature. In Psalm 82.6, RSV, we read, "I say, You are Gods, and all of you are children of the Most High," and in John 10.34 of the Peshitta Bible, "Is it not so written in your law, 'I said, you are gods'?"

Yearning to perceive. An Agni expression. A great desire to know, to connect with the innate consciousness, and to proceed on the path of evolution. Often called DIVINE DISCONTENT.

Yemen-Yah. *See pp. 180–3,* Mothers and Goddesses of the World.

Yeshiva. A school in which to study holy wisdom in the Jewish tradition.

Yeshua. The name for Jesus in Aramaic translates, "He shall save"; the Greek word is *Jesus.*

Yesod. This ninth sephirah on the kabalistic Tree equates with "foundation" and is understood as that which is held in the unconscious depths of mind.

Yetzirah. A Chaldean term denoting the formative world. In kabalistic tradition the third of four lower WORLDS. The astral or psychological reality behind the world of Assiah, the world of physical reality.

YOGA

From the Sanskrit *yug*, meaning "union." The realization of union of spirit and matter (soul and personality) leading to the realization of AT-ONE-MENT. Also, various schools or methods which aim at union through spiritual exercises, practices, and meditation. Popularly refers to Hatha Yoga, which emphasizes physical training but is only one of many yoga systems.

A yoga emerges on a certain RAY influence. Over the centuries, some approaches survive and flourish even when the major influence of the time period changes with the needs of humanity. Therefore, with the exception of Agni Yoga (the most contemporary), *the yogas listed below are according to Ray.* Agni Yoga is a synthesis of all Rays but especially compatible to Rays 1 and 7, bridging will and orderliness as we move into a Ray 7 era.

AGNI YOGA. A contemporary school of thought emphasizing the everyday practice of ethical living, devotion, and purification of the physical, emotional, and mental bodies to aid the process of synthesis. This modern path utilizes the practice of meditation to connect with the inner self and the work of clearing GLAMOURS and ILLUSIONS. Practitioners work at their own pace, using a series of themes rather than rigid disciplines. The formation and application of a living ethic and the development of virtues within the personality characterize this still-emerging yoga and spiritual lifestyle associated with the birth of a new age in human history. Combines Rays 1 and 7, both of which create synthesis. *Also see p. 5.*

RAJA YOGA. A system of yoga typified by development of psychic and spiritual powers and union with the higher self through will and spiritual intellect. A practical and experimental approach involving the exercise, regulation, and concentration of thought. Known as the "royal yoga" for its high ethical standards and its goals to master the mental subplanes and to link one's higher nature with the higher world, achieving realization of or oneness with the Soul. A Ray 1 approach, utilizing a code of honor and integrity, invoking will as a principal tool.

KRIYA YOGA. A style of yoga related to Ray 1, similar to raja and karma yogas; will is invoked with specific disciplines to be added and subtracted from daily life. Spiritual practices/living taught by Herakhan Babaji, Yogananda, and others, based on the 18 SIDDHAS.

KARMA YOGA. This system of yoga emphasizes the practice of service, work, and the fulfillment of duty without attachment to selfish interest or expectations for the results of our labor. As a path of discipline or action, the aspirant uses will and wisdom in order to comprehend the law of cause and effect and the creation of effects. Selflessness and union with God are achieved through consecrated action and alignment with the High Self. A karma yogi chooses carefully the seeds to plant or set into motion. Also related to Ray 1.

KRISHNA YOGA. Based on the Bhagavad Gita, a Ray 2 approach of LOVE-WISDOM of the Krishna school of consciousness. Two great truths are used as guidelines: to love without ceasing and to remember many have become great through doing their duty without personal desire. Teaches the belief in being in a place for a reason, and that WHEN THE STUDENT IS READY, THE TEACHER APPEARS. Fulfillment of duty is seen as a prerequisite for discipleship.

JNANA YOGA. Jnana means "wisdom," and this Ray 3 system of yoga emphasizes intellectual philosophy, theological in nature. This approach seeks union with God through the path of discerning the real from the unreal and establishing the relationship of the parts to the whole. The power of intellect is used to gather knowledge, which, with love, is to be used for the benefit of all.

HATHA YOGA. This yoga system consists chiefly of physical postures (ASANAS) and exercises to keep the body fit and to influence the relationship between spirit and matter. In Sanskrit *ha* means "sun" and *tha* means "moon"—hence, the uniting of sun and moon, the physical and the etheric bodies, or balancing the male and female currents in the body. A Ray 4 healing technique.

WESTERN YOGA. A set of prescribed exercises descending to current times through the Zoroastrian Mideast, designed for the more sensitive etheric bodies of today's disciples. Said to have been presented to the fifth ROOT RACE so disciples could, without harm, anchor the intense energy with which they would connect. Ray 4 in nature and similar to calisthenics, the exercises are vigorous in nature, peppy, and with controlled, counted breaths. Brought to and taught in the U.S. by author and teacher Peter Roche de Coppens.

LAYA YOGA. This system of yoga involves the development of the chakras of the etheric body. Also called "kundalini yoga," or the "yoga of energy," laya yoga is an advanced technique that requires close guidance by an experienced teacher. The purpose of this path is to unfold and harmonize the etheric centers and to awaken the kundalini force in order to contact higher levels of consciousness. The cultivation of phenomena or altered states of consciousness in the Hindu tradition. A Ray 5 spiritual science approach designed to produce nonphysical, nonscientific results.

KUNDALINI YOGA. A Western variance to the laya school of yoga. Again, Ray 5 in nature and designed specifically to facilitate an advantageous arousal of the kundalini.

SIDDHA YOGA. Related to laya yoga, the teaching of awakening psychic abilities to develop extended sense awareness, called "siddhas." TRANSCENDENTAL MEDITATION™ is the registered name for this Ray 5 approach established by Maharishi Mahesh Yogi in the United States in the 1960s.

BHAKTI YOGA. This Ray 6 yoga system aims at union with God through the practice of love and devotion. A natural pathway for those whose spiritual orientation is primarily devotional, this yoga utilizes the desire to love and worship the divine and to surrender to God's will and compassion. A particular Master, saint, or teacher is often used as a point of focus for adoration of the One God manifest in all forms. One's lover can become that focus—as to be one with the god within another.

TANTRIC YOGA. Literal meaning is "loom." A spiritual school of yoga in the Hindu tradition that uses the sexual energy within humanity as its transformational emphasis. While the approach generally begins with two partners, once understood, the discipline can be performed alone. An ecstasy experience created by bringing energy to the head centers is the goal, rather than releasing sexual fluids. Practiced as a path to enlightenment, this powerful Ray 6 yoga needs to be practiced under the guidance of an experienced and knowledgeable teacher as a protective measure.

MANTRA YOGA. This particular practice uses affirmations, chants, words, and prayers to increase the connection to God and to experience the Holy Presence. This yoga system utilizes sound, or vibration, to affect matter, body, emotions, and mind. Based on the science of sound, specific mantras are used to create forms, manipulate matter, and control the energies of nature and of the self. In its most sacred form it becomes a powerful tool for the expansion of consciousness to further the evolution of humanity. This school of yoga, a Ray 7 approach, seeks union with the divine through the use of mantras to increase the power of worship and adoration by releasing the God-self within each person, making each more sensitive to higher energies.

INTEGRAL YOGA. A contemporary method delivered to the world through the teachings of Sri AUROBINDO—the existence and application of spirituality to daily life. A comfortable path for people both East and West. It combines the best elements of traditional yogas in a manner suited to the modern temperament containing many practical instructions and has a compelling vision of the spiritual evolutionary process leading the entire human race to the SUPERMIND, as it is called in the teachings of John White. Seemingly a Ray 2, sub-ray 3 approach.

SOLAR YOGA. A yoga technique named, developed, and taught by Master Omraam Mikhael AÏVANHOV that all yogas are contained in the sun, that we draw our energy from the sun and, through meditation, we unite ourselves with the spirit of the Christ which dwells within the sun. Those who practice the discipline of witnessing the sunrise find a source of awe and inspiration for thought, meditation, and prayer; they find in the sun the strength to live their daily lives in harmony and the courage and will to transform. Once having achieved divine knowledge through meditation, we are never the same. Knowing even a few aspects of the truth, we are enabled to help others.

YIN/YANG. An Eastern designation for feminine and masculine energy—yin being female and yang being male. The symbol depicts the goal of balance of these energies in every person and every situation.

YOCHAI, RABBI SHIMON BAR. A mighty mystic who is said to have received the hidden wisdom directly from Moses and Elijah, the prophet. His writings are found in the *ZOHAR*, the major text of kabalistic wisdom.

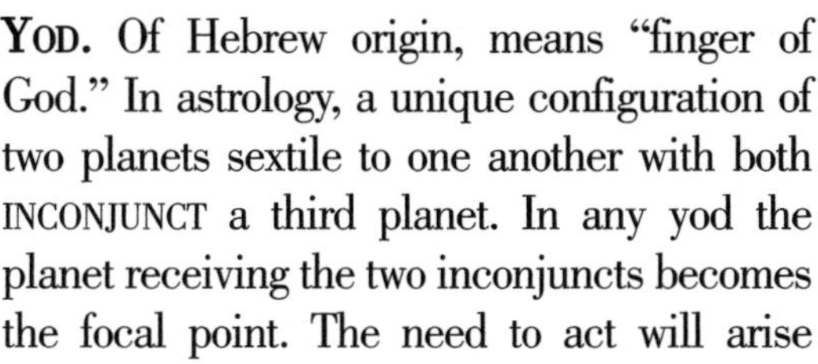

YOD. Of Hebrew origin, means "finger of God." In astrology, a unique configuration of two planets sextile to one another with both INCONJUNCT a third planet. In any yod the planet receiving the two inconjuncts becomes the focal point. The need to act will arise through this focal planet whereas the opportunity to act lies in the two planets sextile to each other. A yod often produces undisciplined thinking, even as it forces the native into some sort of action.

YOD HEH VAU HEH (YHWH). In the Kabalah, the TETRAGRAMMATON, the name of the One Almighty God, becoming commonly known as "Yahweh."

YOGANANDA, SWAMI PARAMAHANSA. b. India, 1893, d. 1952. Great spiritual teacher of the KRIYA YOGA lineage who immigrated to the United States as a young man and founded the Self-Realization Fellowship. He taught that the key to liberation is in the arousal of the KUNDALINI energy by meditation. His ancient meditation techniques were confirmed by contemporary scientific discoveries about energy and the functioning of the brain. *Autobiography of a Yogi,* 1946.

Yoga Sutras of Patanjali. Said to be both the textbook for the inner schools and the most ancient of all the yogas; also known as the ancient teachings of RAJA YOGA.

Yom Kippur. The most solemn day of the Jewish year, the Day of Atonement, a High Holy Day.

Younger kingdoms. The mineral, plant, and animal kingdoms are considered to be younger than humanity in consciousness—"younger" implying less self-conscious, not length of existence.

YoYo technique. Taking a client back and then forward from a certain area in the life to relieve tension. Used when a regression is becoming too painful or deep. As defined and taught in Psychography.

Zarathustra. *See* Zoroaster.

Zen. A discipline of meditation practiced under the direction of a Zen master, considered an ACTIVE MEDITATION, rather than PASSIVE.

Zen bench. A low wooden bench designed to support the body in a kneeling position and

encourage an erect spine; considered beneficial to bring about a relaxed state for meditation.

Zen Buddhism. This Japanese Buddhist sect teaches self-discipline, meditation, and the attainment of enlightenment through direct intuitive insight.

Zendo. An ASHRAM wherein Zen practitioners live a life of spiritual discipline.

Zenzar. *See* Senzar.

Zeroids. Exobiological life in "free space," which "could easily have trod many different evolutionary paths, so that they may now range in dimensionality from the microscopic to the macroscopic, with morphologies varying from the utterly simple to the extraordinarily complex," according to Dr. Franklin Ruehl, nuclear physicist, in a 1979 *Canadian UFO Report* article.[1]

Zodiac. A band in the celestial sphere that represents the path of the principal planets, moon, and sun of our solar system, extending about eight degrees to either side of the ECLIPTIC. According to the tropical zodiac, this band is divided into 12 parts, or "signs," each of which is 30 degrees wide and designated by the constellation for which it originally was named. The zodiac provides a systematic arrangement of the 12 astrological influences that affect all of evolving humanity. Thus personality types are determined by birth sign. In esoteric philosophy planetary position provides insights to the rhythms, strengths, and weaknesses of the inner and outer nature. *See* Astrology; Planets.

ZODIACAL ARCHANGEL. The spiritual archetype of the Great Beings who step down the influences of each CELESTIAL HIERARCHY to the world of lower vibrations or lesser intelligences.

ZODIACAL TRINITY. The three major astrological influences acting upon an individual, according to the sign, or constellation, in which the sun, moon, and ascendant are positioned in the natal chart. Establishes goals to be achieved for the growth of the personality in this lifetime.

ZODIAC ANIMAL NAMES. From Greek *Zodiakos kyklos,* assigned by SUMERIANS to the 12 zodiacal constellations. The pictorial representation and names have remained much the same since introduction in Sumer.

ZODIAC, SIDEREAL. "Sidereal means 'referring to stars'. The sidereal zodiac is a coordinate system in the circle of 'living starry intelligence' as present in the Sun soul's (or solar logos's) field of vision. It constitutes the cosmic intelligence as grasped by or in the Sun soul's contemplation."[2]

ZODIAC, TROPICAL. "The tropical zodiac provides a coordinate system in which the Earth 'orientation' is crucial. One meaning of the term *trope* . . . refers to the 'turning' points of the Earth orientation we call the solstices (and the balance points of the turning called equinoxes). . . . mathematically organized into the 360-fold symmetry of the tropical degrees. Throughout history there have been various attempts to symbolize in image the 360 degrees of the tropical zodiac. By contemplating the degree symbols, we may get a glimpse of the ideas and their meanings in our lives."[3]

ZOHAR, THE. A great work of Spanish-Jewish Kabalah in the late 13th century, the body of all sacred scrolls and scriptures which have been used to keep alive a parallel tradition of direct teaching concerning Jehovah's worlds. The teachings allow the believer to be transfigured in a dimension of space-time beyond conventional space-time in awe of the Father's many mansions reserved for soul advancement within the infinite way. The symbolism is dense and the Aramaic prose in which it is presented is often abstruse. It has been described as "the science of the thinking star intelligence."[4]

ZOMBIE. A human being reduced to a robot state of being.

ZOROASTER. Greek name for Zarathustra, Persian prophet, ca. 600 B.C., who sought to abolish pagan religious practices and initiate a new morality. Zoroastrianism, the oldest living religion in the world, seeks to uphold two principles: to maintain life and to combat evil. AHURA-MAZDA and his angels and archangels struggle against evil, Ahriman, his demons and archfiends. It teaches a heavenly journey of the SOUL, a belief in a heavenly book of record, bodily resurrection, and a paradise. Its sacred scriptures are contained in the *Avesta,* a collection of hymns which, in relating stories of the creation, are strikingly similar to the Old Testament. The teachings of the

Avesta were said to be revealed to Zoroaster as he meditated.

ZOROASTRIANISM. A great temple religion which preserved ANCIENT WISDOM TEACHINGS six centuries before the birth of Jesus. The three Magi are believed to have been mystics and astrologers of the Zoroastrian tradition. Zoroastrianism continues today among those known as the Parsees (or Parsis).

Integrating the
Ancient and the Future

An Introduction to the Works of

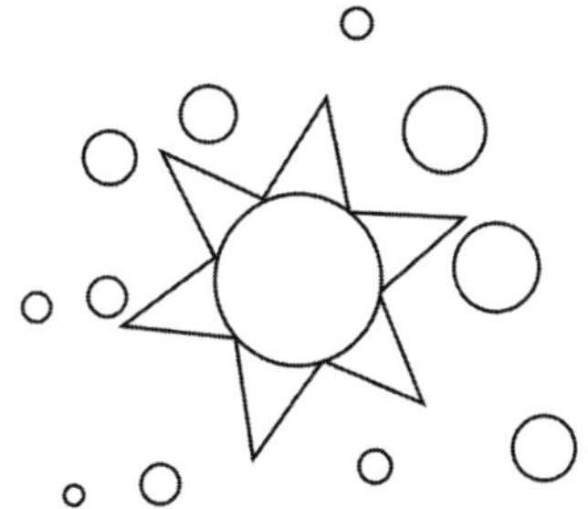

Zecharia Sitchin

and

José Trigueirinho

Humanity's Genesis: A Space Chronicle

With a visionary's ardor and a scientist's attention to the detail within age-old Sumerian texts, Zecharia Sitchin presents a stunning account of primordial human interaction, the ANUNNAKI, with celestial travelers in eight books. *The Earth Chronicles* series (in paperback, from Avon Books, New York, 1976–1998) includes: *The 12th Planet, The Stairway to Heaven, The Wars of Gods and Men, The Lost Realms, When Time Began,* and *The Cosmic Code.* In addition, *Genesis Revisited,* 1990, and *Divine Encounters,* 1995, offer commentary, insights to expand upon the premise.

Social critic and philosopher Dr. Neil Freer, a Sitchin associate, has developed and defined related concepts. They are identified below with an asterisk (*). To assist Sitchin students in locating a context for particular ideas, pagination references follow each entry (using book title abbreviations above).

The following definitions give only a glimpse of Sitchin's intriguing analysis and interpretation of ancient texts. Having attended a Sitchin workshop to become certified as a teacher of his materials, it seemed imperative to discuss his work in a book intended to open and expand concepts that may be new to many readers.

With the public's ever-increasing interest in spacial contact, we find his material speaking to many questions. Ancient literature addresses spacial-human contact in amazing detail. These selected definitions introduce Sitchin's retelling of the story of humanity's creation by the insemination of an APEWOMAN by beings from the planet Nibiru (later, renamed Marduk by revisionist Babylonian scribes).

ABZU. Place of the gold mines (a project overseen by ENKI) in which the ANUNNAKI toiled under difficult and backbreaking circumstances for "40 counted periods" (40 orbits of their planet NIBIRU), or 144,000 Earth years.

ADITYAS. The offspring of Aditi (meaning "Boundless"), consort of Kasyapa. She begot many. The Adityas have been known and revered since Vedic times. Numbering seven at first, they were Vishnu, Varuna, Mitra, Rudra, Pushan, Tvashtri, and Indra. Agni, another son of Kasyapa, was also birthed by Aditi (some texts say by Kasyapa's mother). The number of Adityas rose to 12 on Earth, mirroring ANUNNAKI practice. Among them was Bhaga, believed to be the Supreme Slavic god, Bogh. The last god/child born to Aditi was Surya, father uncertain.

AKKAD, AKKADIANS. In MESOPOTAMIA, INANNA/Ishtar promoted the kingship of Sharru Ken, "Righteous Ruler," Sargon the First (ca. 2400, they built a city, Agade, and established the kingdom of Akkad). Their language, written in a cuneiform (wedge-shaped) script, became the mother tongue of all the Semitic languages.

ALALU. Ruler on NIBIRU overthrown by ANU, possibly on Earth for a time. Anu's grandson, Teshub, the Storm God, and Alalu's grandson KUMARBI, continued the feud.

ANAKIM. A Hebrew term for the people of NIBIRU—the ANUNNAKI (of Sumerian texts). GR/19

ANU. Nibiru's ruler (rank: 60). Father of Enlil and Enki, who became polarized concerning the fate of humanity. A Hittite epic, *Kingship in Heaven*, recounts pre-mortal events involving the "12 olden gods," establishing that in antiquity, gods were of both heaven and Earth. Space beings were called the "sons of god who came down." Anu visited Earth on occasion.

ANUNNAKI. Cosmic astronauts from NIBIRU; literally "Those of Heaven Who Are on Earth." Also called "Guardians." They colonized the planet and created an "adam" who revered them. Texts refer to an Anunnaki population of "50" passing near Saturn. A text from the Third Dynasty of Ur speaks of *anunna ninnubi* (the 50 Anunnaki of the city ERIDU), suggesting that the group of NEFILIM there numbered 50. These were "directed," so says a Babylonian text, by MARDUK, Enki's son. Conceivably the Nefilim arrived on Earth in groups of 50. As visits became regular, some left and others arrived; the number involved with Earth grew to 600 or more. Those who remained in the skies (some 300) were called IGIGI.

APEWOMAN. Term used for female Homo erectus upon whom the NEFILIM image was bound or implanted to bring forth HOMO SAPIEN.

ASURAS. Elder gods whose mothers bore them to Kasyapa before the ADITYAS were born. Those bearing a non-Aryan name of Near

Eastern origin eventually were assigned the role of evil gods ("demons") in the Hindu tradition.

ATRA-HASIS EPIC. An unambiguous account told inter alia in this Mesopotamian text (which includes stories of the Flood and the gods' drawing of lots to determine regions of authority) concerns disgruntled, rebellious ANUNNAKI mining in the Abzu (ca. 300,000 B.C.). Ninharsag, as chief medical officer, takes up her brother Enki's challenge to fashion a primitive worker using Apewoman to produce an ANUNNAKI-hominid hybrid.

***BICAMERAL.** As in genetics, the mind, or the collective unconscious, embracing two perspectives; also, "of two minds" names our earth/sky racial genetic heritage: Homo-erectus plus Nefilim.

ELOHIM. Hebrew for "deities" (plural) who said, "Let us make Man in our image," and, who instructed Moses (as the singular "Yahweh") during the Sinai sojourn.

ENKI/EA. Leader of the first astronauts who came to Earth from NIBIRU, Ea (meaning "Whose Home Is Water") was honored in ancient times with two constellations, Aquarius and Pisces. He established Eridu, the first Earth station and assumed the title Enki, "Lord of Earth," but was replaced in command by Enlil. Firstborn of Anu, Enki (rank: 40) created humankind with Ninhursag. Unlike his half-brother Enlil, he had compassion for Earth's people when a foreseen catastrophe (flood) was forthcoming (ca. 11,000 B.C./Age of Leo). He instructed a Noah-like man (called Ziusudra in the Sumerian original) in the building of a submersible ship to preserve humankind and the genetic codes of Earth's animal life. Enki, a master engineer, built ships and sailed to far-off lands. A great jealousy existed between Enki, the father of Marduk/Ra, and Enlil, the father of Ninurta, as their sons contended for succession privileges. Enki bequeathed Africa to his six sons: Nergal, Great Watcher (spouse, Ereshkigal); Gibil, The One of Fire; Ninigal, Prince of Great Waters; Dumuzi, Son Who Is Life, nicknamed the Herder. Another son, likely Ningishzidda/Thoth (Lord of the Tree of Life), is in dispute among scholars. Enki's legal heir was firstborn Marduk: Son of the Pure Mound (honored by the Ram/Aries).

ENLIL. Second most powerful deity (rank: 50), son and heir of Anu, ruler of the ANUNNAKI. Anu sent Enlil to Earth to oversee Enki's mining project when he suspected Enki could not succeed. He appointed Enlil to rule, for he was born of the preferred bloodline, through Anu's half-sister wife, Antum. Enki, however, was Anu's firstborn (by Id, a concubine).

ENLIL

ERIDU. First Earth station (meaning "House in the Faraway Built"), a settlement established by 50 ANUNNAKI and directed by Enki, says a text from the third dynasty of Ur.

***FOUR-DIMENSIONAL CONSCIOUSNESS.** "Habitual direct perception of the Einsteinian fourth dimension, space-time, in addition to the three (Cartesian) dimensions of length, width and depth we normally perceive . . . In *Voyages Towards the Great Attractor* Alan

Dressler has speculated that, if our brains had evolved to be able to distinguish down to a billionth of a second, we could probably perceive the fourth dimension." It is suggested we are evolving rapidly to that point.

***GENETIC ENLIGHTENMENT.** "The realization that we are a genetically engineered species and the ramifications of that fact for religion, philosophy, science, world unity and the new age concept."

***GOD GAMES.** "Activities worthy of the new human who is genetically enlightened, knows he or she wears 'designer' genes, is free to create his or her own realities one-on-one with the universe determining his or her own unique evolutionary trajectory."

***GODSPELL.** A term (also the name of a Broadway play) "indicating a subservient, looking-to-the-sky-for-Daddy-to-return-to-tell-us-what-to-do attitude, the result of our being created originally as slave animals by and for the NEFILIM, which has given rise to its sublimation into religion."

HAMMURABI. King of Babylon, 1792–1750 B.C., known for his code of law. Expanded his kingdom on the command of ANU, with ENLIL leading the army. MARDUK granted Hammurabi a powerful weapon, called "Great Power of Marduk."

HOMO SAPIENS. "Thinking man," a neutral term, used in the context of Earth's evolving hominid (from homo habilus, to erectus, to sapiens). Sitchin shows that humanity appeared on Earth suddenly (about 300,000 years ago) as a thinking being, without any "evidence of gradual change." "The Adam" was developed in stages by the ANUNNAKI after Anu's first Earth visit. Decisions made then (regarding mtDNA especially) set the course for human history for millennia. Some pre-Deluvian models of "modern man" are referred to as "cavemen" because they created lasting art in caves from about 30,000 to 13,000 B.C.

IGIGI. Literally, "Those Who Observe and See." The 300 true astronauts of the ANUNNAKI, they stayed on the spaceship without landing on Earth. Although they lobbied for time off, they generally did not contact humanity. Texts say they were "too high up for [hu]mankind," (perhaps in vibration) or "too lofty" (in their philosophy) to be concerned with humanity. Parallel term in Greek, Titans.

INANNA/ISHTAR. Firstborn of NANNAR/Sin (and his spouse Ningal) "when only the gods inhabited Earth." Her twin brother Utu, by reason of gender, was named legal dynastic heir and outranked her. One love interest was Dumuzi (the biblical Tammuz). Above the Earth during the Great Flood, the goddess openly wept, "The olden days, alas, are turned into clay."

KASYAPA. "He of the throne." Made himself chief of the devas (the shiny ones) seizing the title Dyaus-Pitar (Sky Father) from which came the Greek title Zeus (Dyans).

KUMARBI. Grandson of Alahu, an adversary of Anu on NIBIRU. He fought battles with Teshub, the Hittite's supreme deity (and a grandson of Anu), carrying on a family feud begun long before. The defeat of Kumarbi did not end the struggle, for he managed to impregnate a goddess who birthed his avenger, the Stone God (stone, meaning "mineral"), Ullikummi.

LILLU. A term for "birdlike" demons (meaning both "to howl" and "of the night"). The Lillu's female leader, Lillitu (Lilith), is depicted as a naked, winged goddess with bird-like feet—spirits seen as forerunners of evil sorcerers and harmful witches.

LULU AMELU. "Primitive Worker." Enki suggested APEWOMAN be used to create slave laborers. NINHURSAG/Sud mixed the purified essence of a young male ANUNNAKI with an egg of Apewoman. The fertilized egg was implanted in a female ANUNNAKI for gestation. When the "mixed creature" was born, the Mother Goddess lifted him and shouted, "I have created! My hands have made it!" Thus HOMO SAPIENS came into being. Sumerian texts suggest the "missing link in human evolution" was a feat of genetic manipulation in a laboratory.

MARDUK (THE GOD). The ambitious firstborn son of Enki who proclaimed himself supreme deity of Babylon. Marduk engaged in numerous wars, leading kings and rulers into mighty battles both before and after the Earth's first nuclear catastrophe in 2024 B.C. There is evidence the god called RA by the Egyptians and Marduk by the MESOPOTAMIANS is one and the same.

MARDUK (THE PLANET). In the teaching myth regarding Creation, two primeval celestial bodies gave birth to a series of gods. As the number of celestial beings increased, they made too much noise, disturbing the Primeval Father. When the Primeval Mother sought revenge, the son was invited to join the assembly of the gods (planets) and fight against the mother. The young son was Marduk, the planet, who vanquished the mother, Tiamat, splitting her in two: one part is in heaven (the asteroid belt) and the other part is now Earth.

MARDUK

MESOPOTAMIA, FIRST CITIES OF.

ERIDU. House in Faraway Built (first city; a gold-extracting facility)

BAD-TIBIRA. Bright Place Where the Ores Are Made Final (for smelting and refining)

LARAAK. Seeing the Bright Glow (a beacon city of unknown location)

SIPPAR. Bird City (the landing place)

SHURUPPAK. Place of Utmost Well-Being (the medical center)

NIPPUR/NIBRUKI. Earth's Crossing (a later mission control center)

LARSA. "Seeing the Red Light" (a southwest beacon city for landing shuttle craft)

LAGASH. "Seeing the Halo at Six" (a northeast beacon city)

***MONO ATOMIC GOLD.** The single atom form of gold (which requires two atoms in its ordinary, metallic form). Like other rare earth elements on the periodic chart, such as rhodium and iridium, it is a fluffy white powder. Rediscoverer David Hudson claims this substance (known to the ANUNNAKI and the ancients) was lost to us and sought by alchemists because it was believed to bestow physical immortality.

***MYTHOGENIC ZONE.** A center of culture where myths originate. The term was used by Joseph Campbell in *The Masks of God* series to describe Sumer as a primary myth-producing area.

NANNAR. Enlil's firstborn son on Earth (rank: 30); also called by his Akkadian/Semitic name, Sin (and assigned the Moon as his planet). Father of INANNA (Venus) and Utu/Shamash (the Sun). His half-brother NINURTA, born on NIBIRU, was elevated to receive Enlil's rank of 50, while his other brother Ishkur/Adad (Mercury) was ranked 10. Nannar, entitled "Lord of the Oath," was granted sovereignty over Ur, Sumer's best-known city-state.

NANNAR/Sin

NEFILIM. A Hebrew word (found in Gen. 6.4), sometimes translated as "giants." It literally means "those [eternal sons of the ELOHIM] who came down," descending to Earth from the heavens. (The Genesis context suggests those in particular who intermarried with the daughters of humankind.) These beings are also reported in Sumerian, Babylonian, Assyrian, Hittite, and Canaanite histories and languages. Sumerian texts speak clearly of them as astronauts who arrived on Earth, giving the names of their leaders, relationships, loves. Ancient texts struggle to explain the nature of their seeming immortality and their creation of humanity as part of a master plan. Writing extensively on these cosmic travelers, the ANUNNAKI, Sitchin suggests the Old Testament actually refers to them as "people of the rocket ships." The people of the SHEM, of the rocket ships, were those "cast down upon Earth." They were capable of space flight 450,000 years ago. The Semitic root NFL, meaning "to be cast down," was erroneously translated previously as "giants upon the earth." Recent translators simply leave the word *Nefilim* intact.

NETER. The name given by the Egyptians to the celestial beings of NIBIRU, meaning "One Who Watches." *See also* Igigi.

NIBIRU. Planet X ("Planet of Crossing"), the original home of the ANUNNAKI; major subject of Sitchin's *The Twelfth Planet.* This forgotten planet of our solar system is twelfth when counted with the sun and Earth's moon, as the ancients often did. NIBIRU's symbolic emblems are the celestial disk, the winged globe, and the cross. Ancient civilizations recorded a trans-cultural god's visit to Earth and the eventual seeding and nurture of civilization here. The extreme elliptical orbit of this planet brings it into the region of the known planets every 3600 years. One clue as to when NIBIRU might be seen again in Earth's skies appears in *The Cosmic Code*. Names given to the beings ("gods") of NIBIRU, in Sumerian: ANUNNAKI, Igigi; in Egyptian: Neter; in Hebrew: Anakim, NEFILIM, Elohim.

NINHURSAG. A title bestowed on Ninmah by her son NINURTA, meaning "Lady of the Head Mountain" when the Sinai spaceport was entrusted to her care. She is the sister of Enlil and Enki, equal with them as a daughter of Anu. As the NEFILIM mother goddess and geneticist (sometimes called Sud/nurse or "Lady Life"), she created, the ATRA-HASIS EPIC says, HOMO SAPIENS. We may think of her as having fashioned Lucy, the apparent genetic ancestress of all humanity, from out of the continent of Africa (*see* Abzu). Sumerian texts speak of the "Black-Headed People" she brought into being.

NINKI. The title "Lady of Earth," given to Enki's spouse, Damkina (rank: 35).

NINLIL. A goddess, who through feminine wiles and trickery became the bride of ENLIL on Earth. Entitled as "Lady of the Airspace" or "Lady of the Command" after marriage (rank: 45). Mother of Enlil's favorite son, Nannar/Sin. Called Sud/nurse, in some texts.

NINURTA. Literally, "Lord Who Completes the Foundation." The heroic warrior son of ENLIL by his half-sister NINHURSAG was his legal heir (on Earth, though born on NIBIRU). Called "the Foremost Son," he was revered as one who taught farming to humanity after the Deluge. Hero of *The Myth of Zu.* He contended with ENKI's firstborn son MARDUk for supremacy among the new generation of incoming gods on Earth.

NINURTA

***OOPARTS.** Purportedly out-of-place-in-time artifacts—toys, tools, technical devices, depictions, and documents which have come to light through archaeological excavation or discovery, e.g., clay pot batteries; flyable model airplane; 1,000-ton precision-cut blocks of stone; ancient relief frieze from Abydos temple depicting rockets, airplanes, even a helicopter.

RANK. The gods' hierarchical position (indicated by an odd or even number) in the official Assembly of Twelve was a divine secret revealed only to certain priestly initiates. The highest number of the sexagesimal system then in use, 60, was assigned to Anu. The remaining six male deities took 50, 40, 30, 20, 10 and the females, 55, 45, 35, and so on.

SAR. One orbital period of the planet NIBIRU, about 3,600 Earth years.

SARGON OF AGADE. *See* Akkad; Sharru Kin.

SEMITE. Peoples of greater MESOPOTAMIA descended from Noah's son Shem. Pillaging bands of western Semites were labeled "Hapiru" (bandits) in the 18th and 17th centuries B.C.

SHALMANESER III. Ninth century B.C. Assyrian victor over Babylon, Sumer, and Akkad; led into battle by the great lord Ashur, carrying weapons provided by lord Nergal.

SHARRU KIN. "Righteous Ruler," Sargon the First, who established the kingdom of Akkad. He reigned 54 years in 2400 B.C. as overseer of Inanna/Ishtar; appointed as a priest of Anu and great righteous shepherd of Enlil.

Believed by some scholars to be the biblical Nimrod.

SHEM. Fiery rocket or sky vehicle. Also the name of the firstborn son of Noah deemed to be of Abraham's lineage. *See* Semite.

SIN. *See* Nannar.

SUD/NINMAH. *See* Ninhursag. One of the original group of ANUNNAKI pioneers on Earth. As Anu's daughter, she bore the title Nin.mah, "Great Lady." In time, given domain over the Sinai Peninsula spaceport. Came to Earth young and beautiful (rank: 15), lived to be old and nicknamed "the Cow" (rank: 5). Not to be confused with Enlil's wife, Sud. Enki forced himself on her and she mothered one of his daughters to whom he also then made love. Resentful of her half-brother Enki's explorations with various young women, NINHURSAG eventually put a temporary curse on him. As "Lady Life"/Nin.ti, chief medical officer, she created a primitive worker to "bear the yoke," using APEWOMAN.

SUMER. Olden MESOPOTAMIA; literally, "Land of the Guardians" or, from *The Book of Enoch,* "Land of the Watchers." (Its biblical name is Shin'ar.) Historic civilization flowered suddenly here nearly 6,000 years ago. Its language became the foundation of all the ancient languages: Mesopotamian, Egyptian/Hamitic, and Indo-European. 12P/370 Sumer was home to the earliest extraterrestrial settlements on Earth (*See* Mesopotamia, first cities). Some 432,000 years before the Deluge, the Din.Gir (righteous ones from the rocket ships) came down to Earth from their planet, Nibiru. Records of this dim pre-historic past (events from before the Flood) are gradually being unearthed, and historic Sumer emerges under the god-appointed kings of Ur as the center of an empire encompassing the entire ancient Near East. Toward the end of the third millennium B.C., that great civilization—humanity's first known—succumbed to a catastrophic nuclear event of unprecedented proportions, believed to have been the result of a decision by the Great Gods sitting in council. Modern Western civilization (as well as its religions and histories) goes well back beyond Greece and Judea of the first millennium to Sumer.

SUMERIAN SCRIPTURE. Numerous clay tablets and pictorial cylinder seals from the Sumerian culture record its stories and histories. Scholars readily see parallels in them to texts contained in the Bible (especially the opening chapters of Genesis).

TABLETS OF DESTINIES. Vital celestial charts and orbital data panels used for complex space operations of the ANUNNAKI were installed in the most restricted area, "mission control center" in Nippur (under the control of Enlil). This chamber was accessed by one named Zu who seized the valuable Tablets. Zu means "He Who Knows," or an expert in a given field.

TIAMAT. According to Sumerian/Babylonian sources, a planet originally located beyond Mars. It encountered a renegade moon from a planet (NIBIRU) that had escaped from another solar system and was largely destroyed. The largest remnant healed and evolved into planet Earth.

TWELFTH PLANET. Using a Sumerian astronomy system, one counts the sun in the center, our moon, the nine planets we know today (including those only recently "discovered"), and one more, a large wandering planet, the twelfth, whose elliptical orbit requires 3,600 Earth years to complete. This orbit takes the planet to a "station" in the distant heavens, before bringing it back to Earth's vicinity where it crosses between Mars and Jupiter. From this comes its name NIBIRU, meaning "crossing," and one of its symbols, the cross.

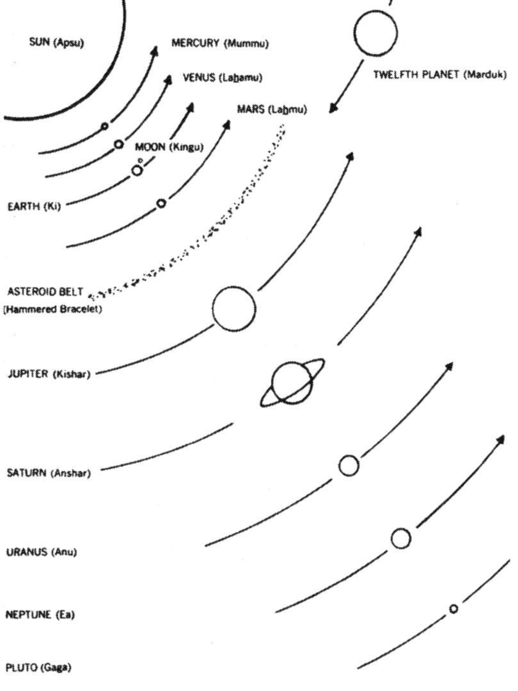

Z. Sitchin, *The 12th Planet,* fig. 110.

WEAPON OF BRILLIANCE. A device that emitted an intense, blinding brightness, worn by gods as part of their headgear. Hammurabi is said to have received one from MARDUK to aid in expanding his kingdom. Esarhaddon and Ashurbanipal made similar claims. The Old Testament frequently refers to a blinding weapon like the one used by "the angels" in the story of Sodom's visitation by two emissaries of the Lord. One was stolen by Zu. Zeus was said to hurl lightning, and a "fire weapon" was fashioned for the Hindu god, Agni.

ZU. Literally, "He Who Knows [the Heavens]," a god who gained access to the control room of ANUNNAKI operations in Nippur, seizing its TABLETS OF DESTINY. Orphaned, Zu had been adopted by the IGIGI who instructed him in the secrets of space travel and asked him to appeal to Enlil to establish a place where the Igigi could get some rest and relaxation. But Enlil was suspicious. Enki meddled, magnifying the problem. Zu escaped to the mountains, well-armed, but was chased down and defeated by Ninurta, Enlil's Foremost Son who unceremoniously beheaded him (establishing his own right to rule). *The Myth of Zu* became part of an elaborate Babylonian reenactment ritual in which a bull was slain, representing the evil Zu.

PARALLELS BETWEEN HOPI AND SUMERIAN CULTURES

by Robert Morningsky

The Hopi believe the Creator of Man is a woman. The Sumerians believed the Creator of Man was a woman.

The Hopi believe the Father Creator is KA. The Sumerians believed the Father Essence was KA.

The Hopi believe Taiowa, the Sun God, is the Creator of the Earth. The Sumerians believed TA.EA was the Creator.

The Hopi believe two brothers had guardianship of the Earth. The Sumerians believed two brothers had dominion over the Earth.

The Hopi believe Alo to be spiritual guides. The Sumerians believed AL.U to be beings of Heaven.

The Hopi believe Kachinas (Kat'sinas) are the spirits of nature and the messengers and teachers sent by the Great Spirit. The Sumerians believed KAT.SI.NA were righteous ones sent of God.

The Hopi believe Eototo is the Father of Katsinas. The Sumerians believed EA.TA was the Father of all beings.

The Hopi believe Chakwaina is the Chief of Warriors. The Sumerians believed TAK.AN.U was the Heavenly Destroyer.

The Hopi believe Nan-ga-Sohu is the Chasing Star Katsina. The Sumerians believed NIN.GIR.SU to be the Master of Starships.

The Hopi believe Akush to be the Dawn Katsina. The Sumerians believed AK.U to be Beings of light.

The Hopi believe Danik to be Guardians in the Clouds. The Sumerians believed DAK.AN to be Sky Warriors.

The Hopi believe Sotunanga is a Sky Katsina. The Sumerians believed TAK.AN.IKU were Sky Warriors.

The Hopi name for the Pleaides is ChooChookam. The Sumerians believed SHU.SHU.KHEM were the supreme Stars.

The Hopi believe Tapuat is the name of Earth. The Sumerians believed Tiamat was the name of Earth.

The Hopi call a snake Chu'a. The Sumerians called a snake SHU.

The Hopi word for "dead" is Mokee. The Sumerians used KI.MAH to mean "dead."

The Hopi use Omiq to mean above, up. The Sumerians used AM.IK to mean looking to Heaven.

The Hopi believe Tuawta is One Who Sees Magic. The Sumerians believed TUAT.U was One from the Other World.

The Hopi believe Pahana was the Lost Brother who would one day return to assist the Hopi and humankind. The Sumerians would recognize PA.HA.NA as an Ancestor from heaven who would return.[1]

Etheric Dimensions: The Expanding Reality

In 1988 José Trigueirinho Netto of Brazil experienced a SOUL EXCHANGE—in his teachings, a "MONADIC TRANSMUTATION." During the first phase of his work, he had especially addressed self-knowledge, prayer, and instructions for spiritual transformation. Already an author and teacher, he now made contact with information from the inner world about the currents of planetary life shifting from the masculine force at Shamballa to the reawakening feminine force anchored in the Andes and empowering a number of new PLANETARY CENTERS.

Transmitting information regarding civilizations—intraterrestrial and extraterrestrial centers that presently support and guard the Earth—he addressed spiritual Hierarchies and the coming of a new life on Earth. He reinforced concepts regarding initiations of the soul, a continuation of ancient teachings expanded to bring in new information appropriate to these times, as he fulfills the need foreseen by Alice A. Bailey and other teachers in previous periods.

Trigueirinho amplifies the subtle aspects of healing, as well as an expansion on ANCIENT WISDOM TEACHINGS, astrology, numerology, color, and SACRED GEOMETRY. Among the factors that contribute to an imminent, more luminous cycle, he states, will be the introduction of a new genetic code (see GNA below) being developed on the supraphysical levels of consciousness in a part of humanity.

Trigueirinho founded Figueira, a spiritual center in Brazil, where he and approximately 120 others live, study, heal, create natural medicines, and publish books. His many varied activities always focus on the seeding of a new state of consciousness and distribution of their agricultural produce, healing essences, clothing, tools, and health education to the poorer population of the region.

Today he is one of the most published live authors in Portuguese and Spanish with 69 books (a million and a half copies in print): *The Esoteric Lexicon* (520 pages in its fourth edition); *Our Life in Dreams,* 12th printing; *Death Without Fear or Guilt; Ways to Inner Healing;* and *Signs of Contact,* to name a few. Some of these are currently being translated into English.

The following definitions present a mere sampling of his superb teachings.

CHAKRAS, FUTURE

As revealed to Trigueirinho by a Pleiad, "In the new cosmogony one will not be bound to free will; therefore, one need no longer be concerned with the chakras. Instead, one must remain stable on three levels: the head (symbol of the thinking man), the heart (symbol of this new astral condition) and the cosmic plexus (situated below the last rib on the right side of the body, a symbol of contact with cosmic energies)." A person's consciousness, he added, should transcend free will to embrace a deeper will, inwardly and outwardly.

In addition, major changes will occur to the seven chakras, reforming themselves into three major centers: cosmic plexus (will), cosmic heart (astral/feeling), and cosmic mind (thinking). The lower three chakras combine into a greater center which responds to higher will, the cosmic heart responds to the dynamic love nature, and cosmic mind responds to Divine Mind. These changes are now beginning to develop in the new humanity. José Trigueirinho uses terms left-sided consciousness for the traditional chakra system and right-sided consciousness for the restructuring of traditional centers into three centers of the body, which are anchored at these locations on the human body:

This shows the front side of the body, the new cosmic being ascending as it returns to the Source.

Right-sided Consciousness Centers

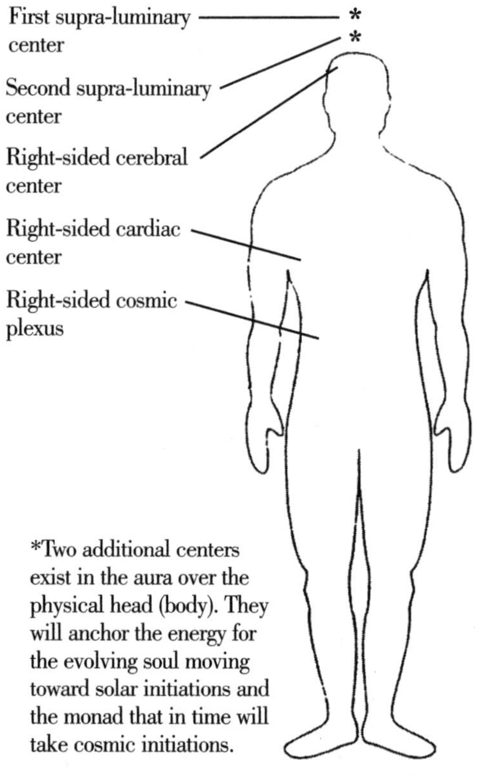

COSMIC PLEXUS. The new physical energy center replacing the solar plexus—a sign that one has joined the New Humanity in achieving (the emerging) right-sided consciousness. This level incorporates the three lower chakras, which then manifest as one. Cosmic will becomes the new consciousness.

FATHER. In Christian writings, often used as a blind for the MONAD, the dynamic expression of the fiery GODHEAD whose sparks (human beings) seek exploration of the denser planes.

GARDENERS, THE More highly evolved spacial beings assisting humanity and all planetary life in their evolutions. *See* Pleiad.

GARDEN OF EDEN. Esoterically speaking, in the mystery teachings the Garden is the ASTRAL PLANE, where all of humanity's needs were met and when interaction with the Divine was natural. Expulsion from the Garden represents the descent from unconscious to a conscious state. Now we must travel through humanity's PATH OF INITIATION to regain entrance to the subtler planes.

GNA (GENETIC NUCLEIC ACID). The new genetic code replacing DNA (in about 10 percent of humanity at the turn of the millennium) is currently appearing many places simultaneously. Trigueirinho began to use this specific designation some years ago due to information provided by beings who are visiting Earth. They assist humanity on three levels: the physical level, preparing individuals for the change in genes and the implanting of new micro-organs in each organ of their present body; the spiritual level, purifying all supraphysical planes as needed; and the cosmic level, expanding the consciousness of beings to be able to contact universal knowledge.

HIERARCHY OF LINEAGES. Seven types of workers (disciples)—or lines of work advancing human consciousness—often unrecognized as they serve in the world: contemplatives, healers, mirrors (reflectors), governors, warriors, prophets/sages, and priests. The inner MONAD leads each to her or his vocation. The lineage of the MONAD defines the task or kind of service one is to do. This corresponds somewhat to the seven RAYS; as an example, we would say leaders, teachers-healers, philosophers, etc.

INTRATERRESTRIALS. Beings who live in the center of the Earth, subject to other laws. In terms of conscious development, some are more primitive than humanity on the surface, following an even more rigorous path of purification than humanity. There are EXTRATERRESTRIALS who have not yet reached a stage of evolution that attunes them to UNIVERSAL LAWS, thus controlled by the cosmic center which governs all things. Numerous levels of life exist in various stages of development.

MONADIC TRANSMUTATION. The process of soul exchange, as called by José Trigueirinho, popularly known as the "walk-in" experience. This experience will be increasingly common in the future.

PLANETARY CENTERS

Just as various subtle centers of energy are in the human body, an analogous condition occurs on the planet. Planetary centers—points of focus of the universal energy of the planet—channel to Earth the energies and impulses emanating from the Planetary Logos, from the Solar Logos, or from even wider cosmic sources. They work together, forming a subtle network which manifests the internal government of the planet, that is, the Spiritual Hierarchy of the Earth. The Ascended Masters are part of this hierarchy. Planetary centers are expressed through intraterrestrial and intra-oceanic centers, which exist in supra-physical dimensions, as well as through spiritual centers and other nuclei active on the surface of the Earth. The main planetary centers, at this time of awakening of the feminine polarity of the planet, are: Anu Tea, Aurora, Iberah, Lis-Fatima, Mirna Jad, Erks, and Miz Tli Tlan. These names also designate the intraterrestrial centers and civilizations linked to the planetary centers. These seven centers compose specific junctures of energy, influencing the various levels of existence of the Earth by transmitting the Ray qualities specific to each cycle.

Miz Tli Tlan, Aurora, and Erks are the three main centers and form an energy triangle called the Major Center, which is being activated in a special way in order carry out the current transition of planet Earth. Intraterrestrial and intra-oceanic civilizations have always been mysterious to humans of the surface of the Earth. They are worlds that exist in dimensions parallel to the physical but which can manifest on it.

MIZ TLI TLAN. Current regent center of the planet, its nucleus is located in the intraterrestrial dimensions of the Peruvian Andes. It expresses the feminine polarity of logoic energy, the polarity which will predominate during the new Earth cycle. It has been in action as of the present planetary transition, replacing Shamballa, which manifested the masculine polarity and is now withdrawn. Miz Tli Tlan, the most potent center in manifestation on the planet, receives the divine purpose for the Earth. The divine emanations radiating from Miz Tli Tlan become laws and principles when disseminated to the other centers, which then assume the task of guiding manifestation according to archetypal patterns. The consciousness of Miz Tli Tlan is omnipresent light, permeated by pure divine life. In these emanations humanity can recognize and base its life on the spiritual. Miz Tli Tlan responds to cosmic laws and makes it possible for divine love to flow throughout the Earth.

AURORA. Its specific function is to bring the essence of cosmic healing into the planet. Aurora aids humans in their integration into the world in which they are living and into intraterrestrial dimensions, leading them to surpass human limitations. When Aurora's subtle radiation reaches humanity, it stimulates equilibrium and health, which is possible when there is faith. One of its tasks is to remove conflictive forces from the Earth's aura. Certain branches of the hierarchy of devas act under the direction of this center, one of the decodifiers of the archetypal patterns of the planet. Nowadays it is polarized in the intraterrestrial dimension of Salto, in Uruguay. It radiates impulses of transmutation and transformation to all the kingdoms of nature on the planet. It even manifested on the physical plane, with the participation of humans from the surface. The Hierarchy of Aurora currently works under the governance of Amhaj, a consciousness which made itself known as Master Morya, channeling the First Ray to humanity. Extraterrestrial civilizations converge to, and unite with, Aurora's own intraterrestrial civilization.

ERKS. On the inner planes Erks receives those who *see*k spiritual fulfillment. As a planetary center and intraterrestrial civilization, its present function is broad. Erks is the seat of knowledge of initiation and of the awakening of the new spirituality. The influence of its energy reaches every corner of the planet, contributing to the inner formation of individuals, preparing them to recognize and consciously contact their immaterial essence. Through its invisible work, it channels the energy of instruction to all parts and introduces human conscious-

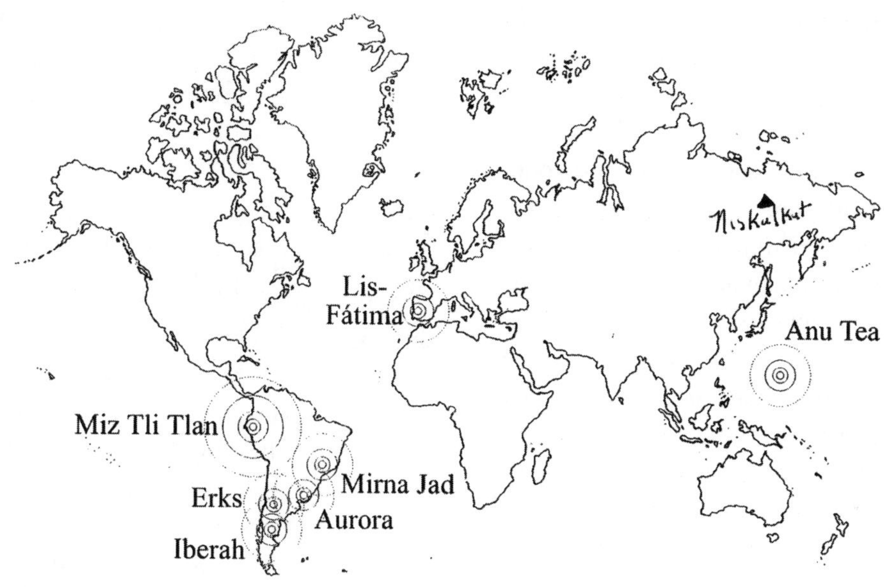

ness to the new philosophy, the new spirituality, and the new education. Erks is in charge of directing the evolutionary path that humanity is to tread today. A source of impulse for the path of initiation, in this sense it is one of the guardians of the mysteries of the cosmos. The Hierarchy polarizes here when it is to define the steps for each stage of the planet. Thus Erks receives its inner congregations and councils, as well as the awarenesses of distant worlds that come to aid the Earth.

IBERAH. A planetary center that with Erks and Anu Tea forms an energy triangle called the Guardian of the Sacred Mysteries. Erks is the core of this work. Iberah has been active since the very beginning of the Earth, working toward the redemption of matter. It is the most mysterious and occult of the planetary centers revealed to date. The primordial junction of spirit and matter expressed by Iberah has not yet been understood by humans of the surface of the Earth; therefore, they have not been able to contact this center directly. Iberah is one of the occult nuclei which sustained the spiritual development of the planet. An antecedent of Shamballa, Iberah became a regent center of the Earth in times so remote, they have become legendary. Iberah holds the custody of the true science of alchemy, which will be available to humans when their consciences will have become sufficiently refined so as to apply it without distortions.

ANU TEA. In ancient times Anu Tea aided in the establishment of the bases for humanity's mental development. It influenced civilizations that flourished around the Mediterranean Sea, for its energy was projected into that region by a subtle nucleus present there. From Anu Tea came revelations disseminated as noble truths of culture, philosophy, and religion. Today some extensions of Anu Tea are located in the etheric region situated between Japan and Oceania. Its work is especially linked to the kingdom of devas and to the formation of the individualized soul, for it prepares the transition of lives from the animal to the human kingdom. In regard to the human kingdom, Anu Tea acts in the field of instruction and revelation, as well as in the formation and development of individual consciousness through stimulating the formation and refinement of the body of the soul.

MIRNA JAD. Revealed as an advanced civilization on the supraphysical levels of certain regions of South America, Mirna Jad receives and synthesizes energies from the three Major Centers: Miz Tli Tlan, Erks, and Aurora. A direct extension of Miz Tli Tlan, it works mainly on the MONADIC level; however, it also projects its energies on material levels. Its task is to stimulate the evolution of humanity, and it is currently mediating the emissions of other intraterrestrial centers to humanity of the Earth surface. The energy vortex that influenced several evolved civilizations in the past and that gave rise to the Essenes can be found today in Mirna Jad. Inner healing is another of its tasks. Members of humanity are taken to Mirna Jad in their subtle bodies in order to be harmonized, have their energies transmuted, or be prepared to be transported to subtle dimensions. Because of its intrinsic attunement with the nucleus of the Sun, the civilization of Mirna Jad radiates love to the Earth in a special manner. The way to Mirna Jad is through the spirit. It prepares the human being for a higher line of evolution, while healing and expanding consciousness.

LIS. With a significant role in the purification and preparation of the Earth for the coming cycle, the energy of Lis mainly encompasses a circle that includes Western Europe and, in a unique way, the Iberian Peninsula. The intraterrestrial center of Fatima (which manifested its energies in the area of Fatima, Portugal) is an extension of Lis. France is also among the areas magnetically linked to Lis, and the work manifested in Lourdes is fruit of this radiation. From the intraterrestrial center of Lis comes the stimulation which includes apparitions in Medjugorje, in ex-Yugoslavia. Lis is the way of ascent for humankind—from the first awakening to inner fulfillment to the final consecration as a divine being. Human evolution on the terrestrial circle is focused on and stimulated by Lis. Its energy reaches human beings who are permeated by a natural humility and attracts them by its simplicity. Celestial and angelic hosts hold this center as a point of support and draw from it the standards to create the subtle patterns to be implanted in humanity. This construction of the New Being counts on the joint action of Aurora, Lis, and Mirna Jad, which, besides holding contact with the inner schools, provides instructions on as-yet-unknown extra-planetary communication.

PLEIAD. A highly evolved EXTRATERRESTRIAL being who has come from the subtler regions of the cosmos. A generic name given to every consciousness that comes from immaterial worlds, that is to say, from dimensions beyond the cosmic physical plane. The plural is Pleiades, but the term does not refer only to those from a specific location in space.

TRANSPERSONAL WILL. As free will is transcended and the SOUL-INFUSED personality is able to move in accordance with higher will without feeling a sense of loss, the transpersonal will is activated. The universal human surrenders free will in accordance with the evolutionary PLAN.

Endnotes

A

1. Sarah Leigh Brown, *Cosmic Fire Revealed—A Student Guide to Alice A. Bailey's* A Treatise on Cosmic Fire (Tahlequah, OK: Sparrow Hawk Press, 2001).
2. John White, *The Meeting of Science and Spirit—Guidelines for a New Age* (New York: Paragon House, 1990), 262–3.
3. Louis Richard Batzler, "A Brief Survey of Christian Spirituality," *Spiritual Frontiers,* vol. 31, nos. 1/2.
4. Brown, *Cosmic Fire Revealed.*
5. Ibid.
6. Ibid.
7. Trigueirinho, *Lexico Esoterico (Esoteric Lexicon)* (Sao Paulo, Brazil: Pensamento, 1994), currently being translated.
8. Ibid.
9. H. P. Blavatsky, *The Voice of Silence* (London: Theosophical Publishing Co., 1889).
10. H. P. Blavatsky, *Theosophical Glossary* (Los Angeles: The Theosophy Company, 1st ed. 1892, 1973).
11. G. de Purucker, *Occult Glossary: A Compendium of Oriental and Theosophical Terms* (Pasadena: Theosophical University Press, 1933, 1969).
12. Webster's New World™ Encyclopedia (New York: Prentice Hall General Reference, 1993).
13. Triguerinho, *Lexico Esoterico.*
14. Torkom Saraydarian, *Christ—The Avatar of Sacrificial Love* (Sedona, AZ: Aquarian Educational Group, 1974).
15. Dennis William Hauck, *The Emerald Tablet—Alchemy for Personal Transformation* (New York: Penguin Putnam Inc., 1999).
16. Saraydarian, *Christ—The Avatar of Sacrificial Love.*
17. Batzler, "A Brief Survey of Christian Spirituality."
18. Raymond Moody, M.D., *Reunions—Visionary Encounters with Departed Loved Ones* (New York: Random House, Inc., 1993).
19. Robert Powell, *Hermetic Astrology,* vol. 1 (Kinsau, Germany: Hermetika, 1987). Page 63 gives exact dates of the zodiacal ages and also of the corresponding cultural epochs.
20. Samuel D. Cioran, *Vladimir Soloviev and The Knighthood of The Divine Sophia.* (Waterloo, Ontario: Wilfrid Laurier University Press, 1977).
21. Rudolf Steiner, *The Course of My Life* (Hudson, NY: Anthroposophic Press, 1951), 276.
22. Andrew Harvey, *The Return of the Mother* (Berkeley, CA: Frog, 1995).
23. Thomas Schipflinger, *Sophia-Maria* (York Beach, ME: Samuel Weiser, 1997).
24. Sandra L. Zimdars-Swartz, *Encountering Mary* (Princeton, NJ: Princeton University Press, 1991).
25. Robert A. Powell, *The Most Holy Trinosophia and the New Revelations of the Divine Feminine* (Great Barrington, MA: Anthroposophic Press, 2000), 84–86.
26. Z'ev ben Shimon Halevi, *kabbalah, Tradition of hidden knowledge* (New York: Thames and Hudson, 1979).
27. Anthony Damiani, *Astronoesis: Philosophy's Empirical Context, Astrology's Transcendental Ground* (Burdett, NY: Wisdom's Goldenrod, Ltd., by Larson Publications, 2000).
28. Triguerinho, *Lexico Esoterico.*

29. Laurence Tunstall Heron, *ESP in the Bible—the Psychic Roots of Religion* (Garden City, NY: Doubleday & Company, Inc., 1974).

B

1. Bill S. Ballinger, *The 49 Days of Death* (Los Angeles: Sherbourne Press, Inc., 1969).
2. *Fiery World 1933,* n.a. (New York: Agni Yoga Society, Inc., 1982), 615.
3. Manly P. Hall, *The Blessed Angels—The Reality of Things Unseen* (Los Angeles: The Philosophical Research Society, Inc., 1996).
4. Godwin, Cash and Smith, *Paul Brunton: Essential Readings,* as reproduced on the internet on 4/25/01 under http://www.paulbrunton.org/pb.html.

C

1. Lord Alfred Tennyson, *Idylls of the King* (London, 1859 [publisher unknown, book currently in Scripps College Library, Claremont, CA]).
2. Lawrence Bendit and Phoebe Paine, *Our Psychic Sense* (Wheaton, IL: The Theosophical Publishing House, 1983).
3. Alice A. Bailey, *Esoteric Healing* (New York: Lucis Publishing Company, 1984).
4. From the Mantram of Unification, as given to Alice A. Bailey by The Tibetan.
5. Richard W. Noone, *5/5/2000: Ice, the Ultimate Disaster* (New York, Three Rivers Press, 1982).
6. White, *The Meeting of Science and Spirit.*

D

1. Christian de la Huerta, *Coming Out Spiritually* (New York: Jeremy P. Tarcher/Putnam, 1999).
2. Anthony Damiani, *Astronoesis.*
3. H. P. Blavatsky, interpreter, *The Book of Dzyan* (Ferndale, MI: W. Q. Judge, 1980), 7–15.

E

1. Paul Twitchell, *The Shariyat-Ki-Sugmad Book One* (Las Vegas, NV: The Illuminated Press, 1972), 131.
2. Ibid., 6.
3. John DuBocq, dean and professor of world religions, George Williams College, and member of the Council's [International Council of Community Churches] Faith and Order Commission, quoted in the ICCC newsletter, The Christian Community, Winter 1998.
4. Dennis W. Hauck, *The Emerald Tablet* (New York: Penguin Putnam Inc., 1999).
5. From a periodical published by En-humanity—The One Humanity, Hari Homaro, ed., Kalamata, Greece, vol. 9, no. 23, Jan. 2000.
6. John White, "Enlightenment and the Judeo-Christian Tradition," *Body, Mind & Spirit,* Nov.–Dec. 1987, 36–39.
7. Triguerinho, *Lexico Esoterico.*
8. Brown, *Cosmic Fire Revealed.*
9. White, *Meeting of Science and Spirit,* 129, 133.

F

1. Raymond Moody, M.D., *Reunions—Visionary Encounters with Departed Loved Ones* (New York: Random House, Inc., 1993).
2. Brown, *Cosmic Fire Revealed.*
3. Helena Roerich, *Agni Yoga* (New York: Agni Yoga Society, 1954).
4. P.M.H. Atwater, *Future Memory* (Charlottesville, VA: Hampton Roads Publishing Company, Inc., 1999), 32–3, 37.

G

1. Webster's New World™ Encyclopedia
2. Trigueirinho, *Lexico Esoterico.*

3. Don Webb, "How to Do Good: A Satanic Perspective," *Gnosis Magazine,* Winter 1998, 35.
4. Noone, *5/5/2000, Ice: The Ultimate Disaster,* 130.
5. Kathleen Riordan Speeth, *The Gurdjieff Work* (New York: Gulf and Western Corporation, 1976), 25.

H

1. World Book Encyclopedia (Chicago: Field Enterprises Educational Corporation, 1977).
2. Doc Childre and Howard Martin, *The HeartMath Solution* (San Francisco: HarperCollins Publishers, 1999), 10.
3. Source unknown.
4. Joseph Campbell, *The Hero with a Thousand Faces* (Princeton, NJ: Princeton University Press, 2d ed., 1968).
5. Maggie Oman Shannon, "Overwhelmed by the World?" *Utne Reader,* Nov–Dec. 2000, 90.
6. Brother Philip, *Secret of the Andes* (London: Neville Spearman Limited, 1961).
7. Paraphrased from http://www.geoffreyhodson.one.net, 6-14-01.
8. Ken Wilber, *Eye to Eye* (Garden City, NY: Anchor Books, 1983), 3.
9. Noone, *5/5/2000: Ice, The Ultimate Disaster.*

I

1. Triguerinho, *Lexico Esoterico.*
2. Ibid.
3. Ibid.
4. Ibid.

J

1. David Goddard, *The Tower of Alchemy* (York Beach, ME: Samuel Weiser, Inc., 1999).
2. Damiani, *Astronoesis.*
3. J. J. Van der Leeuw, *The Fire of Creation* (Adyar, India: The Theosophical Publishing House, 1947).
4. The Catholic Encyclopedia, vol. 8, Online Edition© 1999 by Kevin Knight, 1-23-01.

K

1. Brown, *Cosmic Fire Revealed.*
2. Batzler, "A Brief Survey of Christian Spirituality."
3. Lewis Spense, *An Encyclopaedia of Occultism* (New York: New Hyde Park, 1960), 408.
4. Brown, *Cosmic Fire Revealed.*

L

1. Lamsa, George M., trans., Holy Bible from the Ancient Eastern Text (the Aramaic of the Peshitta), (San Francisco, CA: Harper & Row, n.d.; orig. © A. J. Holman Company, 1933), ii.
2. Marcus Bach, *Major Religions of the World* (Marina del Ray, CA: DeVorss & Co., 1959), 82.
3. Triguerinho, *Lexico Esoterico.*
4. Manly P. Hall, *How to Understand Your Bible* (Los Angeles: The Philosophical Research Society, Inc., 1996).
5. Reprinted from *Glossary of The Tibetan's Terms* by Meditation Mount, P.O. Box 566, Ojai, CA 93023, rev. 1989.
6. White, *Enlightenment 101.*

M

1. Brown, *Cosmic Fire Revealed.*
2. David Anrias, *Through the Eyes of the Masters* (New York: Samuel Wieser, 1971).
3. Aryeh Kaplan, *The Sepher Yetzirah* (York Beach, ME: Samuel Weiser, 1993).
4. Halevi, *kabbalah, Tradition of hidden knowledge.*
5. Three Initiates, *The Kybalion—A Study of the Hermetic Philosophy of Ancient*

Egypt and Greece (Chicago: The Yogi Publication Society, 1940).

6. Heron, *ESP in the Bible.*
7. Larry Dossey, M.D., *Recovering the Soul: A Scientific and Spiritual Search* (New York: Bantam Books, 1989).
8. Larry Dossey, M.D., *Be Careful What You Pray For . . . You Just Might Get It: What We Can Do About the Unintentional Effects of Our Thoughts, Prayers, and Wishes.* (HarperSanFrancisco, 1997).
9. Carl Jung, *Man and His Symbols* (New York: Doubleday, 1988), 33.
10. Craig Hamilton, "Toward Homo Noeticus," an interview with John White, *What is Enlightenment?* 19 (2001): 89.
11. Popular British historian, poet, and professor dedicated to Peace Initiatives of the '90s. A world traveler who frequently teaches the virtues, muses material.
12. n.a., "Letters of Rav Yehuda Brandwein," kabbalah, Fall/Winter 1999, 28–29. 20th century kabalist Rav. Yehuda Brandwein, disciple of Rav. Yehuda Ashlag. A gentle and kind soul who paved the way for kabalistic teachings to be released to the masses. Born in Safed (Tzefut) in 1904, d. 1969. Teacher of kabalist Rav. Berg; in a letter to Rav. Berg his eventual successor and the one who has directed the teachings to the four corners of the world for the first time in history.

N

1. Atwater, *Future Memory.*
2. *Influence on St. Augustine*
3. Merriam Webster's Collegiate Dictionary, 10th ed., 1994.
4. Powell, *The Most Holy Trinosophia.*

O

1. C. W. Leadbeater, *The Masters and the Path* (Adyar, India: The Theosophical Publishing House, 1925; 4th ed. 1984).
2. Ibid.
3. Rosemary Ellen Guiley, *Harper's Encyclopedia of Mystical & Paranormal Experience* (Edison, NJ: Castle Books, 1991).
4. Torkom Saraydarian, *The Science of Meditation* (Sedona, AZ: Aquarian Educational Group, 1971).
5. G. A. Gaskell, *Dictionary of All Scriptures and Myths* (New York: The Julian Press, Inc., 1973), 527.
6. Damiani, *Astronoesis.*

P

1. John G. Hargrave, *The Life and Soul of Paracelsus* (Chicago, IL: William Benton, 1951).
2. MaryBeth Rapisardo, on a card by Aurora Visionary Art, Woodacre, CA, 2000.
3. Reprinted from The Holy Bible from Ancient Eastern Manuscripts, by George M. Lamsa.
4. Brown, *Cosmic Fire Revealed.*
5. Moody, *Reunions.*
6. Damiani, *Astronoesis.*
7. *Breakthrough to Higher Psychism* (Sedona, AZ: T.S.G. Publishing Foundation, Inc., 1990).

R

1. Swami Nikhilananda, *The Gospel of Ramakrishna* (New York: Ramakrishna-Vivekananda Center, 1958).
2. Three Initiates, *The Kybalion.*

S

1. Carol E. Parrish-Harra, *How to Use Sacred Space for Problem-Solving and Inner Guidance* (Tahlequah, OK: Sparrow Hawk Press, 1994).

2. Robert Ellsberg, *All Saints—Daily Reflections on Saints, Prophets, and Witnesses for Our Time* (New York: The Crossroad Publishing Company, 1999).
3. Sabina Flanagan, *Hildegard of Bingen* (London: Routledge, 1989), 13.
4. Ellsberg, *All Saints.*
5. John Funchion, compiler, 1-23-01.
6. Ellsberg, *All Saints.*
7. Emily Mitchell. 1999. Bleeding-hands man gets star treatment. *Time,* May 10, 1999, 20.
8. The Catholic Encyclopedia, vol. 9.
9. Internet, Britannica.com, Symeon The New Theologian, Saint, Jan. 8, 2001.
10. Michael Wood, *Legacy, the Search for Ancient Cultures* (New York: Sterling Publishing Co., Inc., 1992) as quoted in pre-print edition by Robert Cox, *The Pillar of Celestial Fire and the Lost Science of the Ancient Seers,* to be published by Sunstar Publications, Fairfield, IA.
11. Veronica Ions, *The World's Mythology in Color* (Secaucus, NJ: Chartwell Books, Inc., 1987).
12. Ralph Metzner, *Maps of Consciousness* (New York: The Macmillan Company, 1971).
13. Internet accessed 8/8/01.
14. Carl Jung, *Memories, Dreams, Reflections* (New York: Random House, 1965), 69.
15. White, *The Meeting of Science and Spirit,* 136.
16. John Curtis Gowan, *Development of the Psychedelic Individual* (Buffalo, NY: State University College, 1974).
17. Vera Stanley Alder, *Initiation of the World* (London, England: Rider and Company Limited, 1939).
18. Joseph Campbell, *The Power of Myths* (New York: Doubleday, 1988).
19. Robert Cox, *The Pillar of Celestial Fire and the Lost Science of the Ancient Seers,* pre-print edition (Fairfield, IA: Sunstar Publications, to have been published 1997).
20. M. Govindan, M.A., *Babaji and the 18 Siddha Kriya Yoga Tradition* (Montreal, Quebec, Canada: Kriya Yoga Publications, 1991).
21. Murry Hope, *The Sirius Connection—Unlocking the Secrets of Ancient Egypt* (Rockport, MA: Element Books, Inc., 1996).
22. Brown, *Cosmic Fire Revealed.*
23. James H. Hindes, *Renewing Christianity* (Hudson, NY: Anthroposophic Press, 1996), 106.
24. Robert Powell, *The Sophia Teachings: The Emergence of the Divine Feminine in Our Time* (New York: Lantern Books, 2001.)
25. Hope, *The Sirius Connection.*
26. Batzler, "A Brief Survey of Christian Spirituality."
27. Brown, *Cosmic Fire Revealed.*
28. Batzler, "A Brief Survey of Christian Spirituality."
29. White, *Meeting of Science and Spirit,* 239—40.
30. Zecharia Sitchin, *The Earth Chronicles,* 6 vols. (New York: Avon Books, Inc., 1976-98).
31. Corinne Heline, *Mystery of the Christos,* vol. 7 of New Age Bible Interpretations (Santa Monica, CA: New Age Bible & Philosophy Center, 1961), 97–8.
32. D. Scott Rogo, *Miracles, A Parascientific Inquiry into Wondrous Phenomena* (Chicago: Contemporary Books, 1983), 51.
33. Author unknown, Metta newsletter, vol. 8 No. 3 Oct-Dec. 2000.

T

1. Heron, *ESP in the Bible.*
2. Alice A. Bailey, *Treatise on White Magic* (New York: Lucis Publishing, 1934, 1951).
3. Halevi, *kabbalah, Tradition of hidden knowledge,* 66.
4. Edmond Bordeaux Szekely, *From Enoch to the Dead Sea Scrolls* (Nelson, B.C., Canada: International Biogenic Society, 1999), 51.

V

1. Three Initiates, *The Kybalion.*

W

1. Rudolf Steiner, *Gospel of St. Luke* (Hudson, NY: Anthroposophic Press, 3d ed., 1964), 114.
2. Alice A. Bailey, *Letters on Occult Meditation* (New York, Lucis Publishing Co., 1950).

Z

1. White, *Meeting of Science and Spirit,* 266–7.
2. Damiani, *Astronoesis.*
3. Ibid.
4. J. J. Hurtak, The Keys of Enoch (Los Gatos, CA: The Academy for Future Science, 1977), 612.

Humanity's Genesis

1. Morgana's Observatory, ca. 1997–2000. "The Web source for this article is no longer active. Voyage to the Observatory to visit my Home—and for the Main Index."

Bibliography

Alder, Vera Stanley. *Initiation of the World.* London, England: Rider & Company Limited, 1939.

Anrias, David. *Through the Eyes of the Masters—Meditations and Portraits.* New York: Samuel Weiser, 1971.

Atwater, P.M.H. *Future Memory.* Charlottesville, VA: Hampton Roads Publishing Company, Inc., 1999.

Bach, Marcus. *Major Religions of the World.* Marina del Ray, CA: DeVorss & Co., 1959.

Bailey, Alice A. *Discipleship in the New Age II.* New York: Lucis Publishing Company, 1955.

———. *Esoteric Healing II.* New York: Lucis Publishing Company, 1953.

———. *A Treatise on White Magic.* New York: Lucis Publishing Company, 1934, 1951.

Batzler, Louis Richard. "A Brief Survey of Christian Spirituality," *Spiritual Frontiers,* Vol. 31, No. 1/2.

Bendit, Laurence, and Phoebe Paine. *Our Psychic Sense.* Wheaton, IL: Theosophical Publishing House, 1958; 1st Quest edition, 1967.

Blavatsky, Helena P. *The Theosophical Glossary.* Los Angeles: The Theosophy Company, 1892, reprinted 1973.

———. Interpreter. *The Book of Dzyan.* Ferndale, MI: W. Q. Judge, 1980.

———. *The Voice of the Silence.* London: Theosophical Publishing Co., 1889.

Britannica.com, *Symeon The New Theologian, Saint,* Jan. 8, 2001.

Brown, Sarah Leigh. *Cosmic Fire Revealed—A Student Guide to Alice A. Bailey's* A Treatise on Cosmic Fire. Tahlequah, OK: Sparrow Hawk Press, 2001.

Campbell, Joseph. *The Hero with a Thousand Faces.* Princeton, NJ: Princeton University Press, 2d ed., 1968.

———. *The Power of Myth.* New York: Doubleday, 1988.

Course in Miracles, A. Tiburon, CA: Foundation for Inner Peace, 1975.

Damiani, Anthony J. *Astronoesis: Philosophy's Empirical Context, Astrology's Transcendental Ground.* Burdett, NY: Wisdom's Goldenrod, Ltd., Larson Publications, 2000.

de la Huerta, Christian. *Coming Out Spiritually.* New York: Jeremy P. Tarcher/Putnam, 1999.

de Purucker, G. *Occult Glossary: A Compendium of Oriental and Theosophical Terms.* Pasadena: Theosophical University Press, 1933, 1969.

Dossey, Larry, M.D. *Be Careful What You Pray For . . . You Just Might Get It: What We Can Do About the Unintentional Effects of Our Thoughts, Prayers, and Wishes.* HarperSanFrancisco, 1997.

———. *Recovering the Soul: A Scientific and Spiritual Search.* New York: Bantam Books, 1989.

DuBocq, John. *International Council of Community Churches* newsletter, "The Christian Community," winter 1998.

Ellsberg, Robert. *All Saints: Daily Reflections on Saints, Prophets, and Witnesses For Our Time.* New York: The Crossroad Publishing Company, 1999.

Flanagan, Sabina. *Hildegard of Bingen.* London: Routledge, 1989.

Freer, Neil. Internet. http://www.neilfreer.com/index5.htm. 9-27-00.

Gaskell, G. A. *Dictionary of All Scriptures and Myths.* New York: The Julian Press, Inc., 1973.

Goddard, David. *The Tower of Alchemy.* York Beach, ME: Samuel Weiser, Inc., 1999.

Govindan, M., M.A. *Babaji and the 18 Siddha Kriya Yoga Tradition.* Montreal, Quebec, Canada: Kriya Yoga Publications, 1991.

Gowan, John Curtis. *Development of the Psychedelic Individual.* Buffalo, NY: State University College, 1974.

Guiley, Rosemary Ellen. *Harper's Encyclopedia of Mystical & Paranormal Experience.* Edison, NJ: Castle Books, 1991.

Halevi, Z'ev ben Shimon. *kabbalah: Tradition of hidden knowledge.* New York: Thames and Hudson, 1979.

Hall, Manly P. *The Blessed Angels—The Reality of Things Unseen.* Los Angeles: The Philosophical Research Society, Inc., 1996.

———. *How to Understand Your Bible.* Los Angeles: Philosophical Research Society, Inc., 1943.

Hargrave, John G. *The Life and Soul of Paracelsus.* Chicago, IL: William Benton, 1951.

Hauck, Dennis William. *The Emerald Tablet—Alchemy for Personal Transformation.* New York: Penguin Putnam Inc., 1999.

Heron, Laurence Tunstall. *ESP in the Bible—The Psychic Roots of Religion.* Garden City, NY: Doubleday & Company, Inc., 1974.

Hindes, James H. *Renewing Christianity.* Hudson, NY: Anthroposophic Press, 1996.

Homaro, Hari, ed. Enhumanity—The One Humanity, a periodical, Kalamata, Greece, vol. 9, no. 23, Jan. 2000.

Hope, Murry. *The Sirius Connection—Unlocking the Secrets of Ancient Egypt.* Rockport, MA: Element Books, Inc., 1996.

Hurtak, J. J. *The Keys of Enoch.* Los Gatos, CA: The Academy for Future Science, 1977.

Ions, Veronica. *The World's Mythology in Color.* Secaucus, N.J.: Chartwell Books, Inc., 1987.

Jung, Carl. *Man and His Symbols.* New York: Doubleday, 1988.

Kaplan, Aryeh. *The Sepher Yetzirah.* York Beach, ME: Samuel Weiser, 1993.

Knight, Kevin. *Catholic Encyclopedia, The,* vol. 8. Online Edition© 1999. www.newadvent.org, 1-23-01.

Lamsa, George M., trans. The Holy Bible from the Ancient Eastern Text, translated from the Aramaic of the *Peshitta.* Philadelphia: A. J. Holman Co., 1933.

Leadbeater, C. W. *The Masters and the Path.* Adyar, India: The Theosophical Publishing House, 1925; 4th ed., 1984.

McLaughlin, Corinne and Gordon Davidson. *Spiritual Politics.* New York: Ballantine Books, 1994.

Meditation Mount. *Glossary of The Tibetan's Terms.* Ojai, CA, rev. 1989.

Metta newsletter, vol. 8 no. 3 Oct.–Dec. 2000. Author unnamed.

Metzner, Ralph. *Maps of Consciousness.* New York: The Macmillan Company, 1971.

———. *Opening to Inner Light.* Los Angeles: Jeremy P. Tarcher, Inc., 1986.

———. *The Unfolding Self—Varieties of Transformative Experience.* Novato, CA: Origin Press, 1998.

Mitchell, Emily. Bleeding-hands man gets star treatment. *Time,* May 10, 1999.

Moody, Raymond, M.D. *Reunions—Visionary Encounters with Departed Loved Ones.* New York: Random House, Inc., 1993.

Nikhilananda, Swami. *The Gospel of Ramakrishna.* New York: Ramakrishna-Vivekananda Center, 1958.

Noone, Richard W. *5/5/2000: Ice, the Ultimate Disaster.* New York: Three Rivers Press, 1982.

Pappas, George Charles. *Synpan.* Tahlequah, OK: Sparrow Hawk Press, 1999.

Parrish-Harra, Carol E. *Adventure in Meditation—Spirituality for the 21st Century,* vols. 1, 2, 3. Tahlequah, OK: Sparrow Hawk Press, 1995, 1996, 1997, respectively.

———. *The Aquarian Rosary—Reviving the Art of Mantra Yoga.* Tahlequah, OK: Sparrow Hawk Press, 1988.

———. *Book of Rituals—Personal and Planetary Transformation.* Tahlequah, OK: Sparrow Hawk Press, 2d ed., 1999.

———. *How to Use Sacred Space for Problem-Solving and Inner Guidance*. Tahlequah, OK: Sparrow Hawk Press, 1994.

———. *Messengers of Hope—The Walk-in Phenomenon.* Tahlequah, OK: Sparrow Hawk Press, 2d. ed., 2001.

———. *The New Age Handbook on Death and Dying.* Tahlequah, OK: Sparrow Hawk Press, 1989.

———. *The New Dictionary of Spiritual Thought.* Tahlequah, OK: Sparrow Hawk Press, 1994.

———. *Reflections [of].* Compiled by Maggie Webb-Adams. Tahlequah, OK: Sparrow Hawk Press, 1997.

Philip, Brother. *Secret of the Andes.* London: Neville Spearman Limited, 1961.

Powell, A. E. *The Etheric Double—The Health Aura of Man.* Wheaton, IL: The Theosophical Publishing House, 1983.

Powell, Robert A. *The Most Holy Trinosophia and the New Revelations of the Divine Feminine.* Great Barrington, MA: Anthroposophic Press, 2000.

———. *The Sophia Teachings: The Emergence of the Divine Feminine in Our Time.* New York: Lantern Books, 2001.

Rapisardo, MaryBeth. *Immortal Dance.* Woodacre, CA: Aurora Visionary Art, 2000.

Roerich, Helena. *Agni Yoga.* New York: Agni Yoga Society, 1954.

———. *Fiery World 1933,* vol. 1. New York: Agni Yoga Society, Inc., 1943.

______. *Letters of Helena Roerich 1929–1938,* vol. 1. New York: Agni Yoga Society, Inc., 1954.

———. *Mother of Agni Yoga, 1956.* New York: Agni Yoga Society, Inc., 1956.

———. *Woman: 1958.* New York: Agni Yoga Society, Inc., 1958.

Rogo, D. Scott. *Miracles, A Parascientific Inquiry into Wondrous Phenomena.* Chicago: Contemporary Books, 1983.

Saraydarian, Torkom. *The Science of Meditation.* Sedona , AZ: Aquarian Educational Group, 1971.

———. *Breakthrough to Higher Psychism.* Cave Creek, AZ: T.S.G. Publishing Foundation, Inc., 1990.

———. *Christ—The Avatar of Sacrificial Love.* Sedona, AZ: Aquarian Educational Group, 1974.

Shyam, Radhe. *I Am Harmony.* Crestone, CO: The Spanish Creek Press, 1989.

Sitchin, Zecharia. *Divine Encounters.* New York: Avon Books, Inc., 1995.

———. *The Earth Chronicles,* 6 vols., New York: Avon Books, Inc., 1976–98.

———. *Genesis Revisited.* New York: Avon Books, Inc., 1990.

Speeth, Kathleen Riordan. *The Gurdjieff Work.* New York: Gulf and Western Corporation, 1976.

Spense, Lewis. *An Encyclopaedia of Occultism.* New York: New Hyde Park, 1960.

Steiner, Rudolf. *Gospel of St. Luke.* Hudson, NY: Anthroposophic Press, 3d English ed., 1964.

Tennyson, Alfred. *Idylls of the King.* London, publisher unknown, 1859; book currently in Scripps College Library, Claremont, CA.

Three Initiates. *The Kybalion—A Study of the Hermetic Philosophy of Ancient Egypt and Greece.* Chicago: The Yogi Publication Society, 1940.

Trigueirinho, José. *Lexico Esoterico* (Esoteric Lexicon) Sao Paulo, Brazil: Pensamento, 1994.

Twitchell, Paul. *The Shariyat-Ki-Sugmad Book One.* Las Vegas: The Illuminated Press, 1972.

Van der Leeuw, J. J. *The Fire of Creation.* Adyar, India: The Theosophical Publishing House, 1947.

Venkatesananda, Swami. *The Song of God.* Cape Province, South Africa: The Chiltern Yoga Trust, 1972.

Webster's New World™ Encyclopedia. New York: Prentice Hall General Reference, 1993.

White, John. *The Meeting of Science and Spirit—Guidelines for a New Age.* New York: Paragon House, 1990.

———. *Enlightenment 101.* Forthcoming.

Wilber, Ken. *Eye to Eye.* Garden City, NY: Anchor Books, 1983.

World Book Encyclopedia. Chicago: Field Enterprises Educational Corporation, 1977.

Yogananda, Paramahansa. *Autobiography of a Yogi* (Babaji). Los Angeles: Self-Realization Fellowship, 1946.

Sancta Sophia Seminary

A Contemporary Mystery School

How It Came to Be

In 1982, Carol E. Parrish-Harra was revealed to the greater public by author Ruth Montgomery in the best-selling *Threshold to Tomorrow*. The book elaborated upon Carol's remarkable pychic and spiritual abilities, and it described her role as a messenger for a new era.

Carol already had moved the school she established in 1978 from Florida to the beautiful Ozark Mountains of eastern Oklahoma.

Today, in addition to her personal teaching of Sancta Sophia students, Carol is academic dean and coordinates seminary classes, several post-graduate programs, faculty, and advisors. She continues to minister and publish widely acclaimed books and audiocassette programs. She is a highly sought international speaker and world traveler, leading many pilgrimages to sacred places.

Spiritually Charged Location Enhances Growth

The magnificent, wooded, 400-acre mountaintop setting where Carol was inspired to build the seminary is also the location of Sparrow Hawk Village. This intentional spiritual community has an educational focus, providing a supportive atmosphere for the practice of ethical living. The village, established in 1981 in the foothills near Tahlequah, Oklahoma, by Carol, her husband, Charles C. Harra, and her friend, Rev. Grace B. Bradley, is a harmonious environment of fifty homes, office buildings and church. It has lovely gardens, good drinking water, and a sophisticated infrastructure. Villagers are self-supporting people who live, learn, meditate, and worship together. Although over half of the 168 potential lots have been sold, homes and home sites are still available.

The church sanctuary is centered on a vortex of special energies created by a star-shaped convergence of Earth ley lines. This unique enclosure of spiritual energies enhances the synergy of living, learning, and personal growth for every Sancta Sophia student. The village is a sacred space, helping those who visit to heal and to make their lives whole and holy. The spiritual energies create an environment for preparation in spiritual vocations.

Programs Create Personal Transformation through Educational Preparation

A combination of off-campus retreats, home-study, and on-campus classes forms the basis of participation in both graduate and undergraduate studies. This integrative experience begins with a format of meaningful home study and techniques tailored to personal

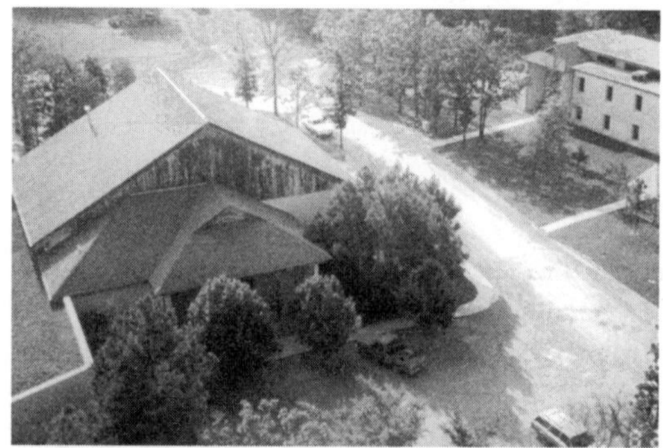

goals. The focal point of every student's program is a unique transformational process guided by master teacher Dean Parrish. Individually assigned advisors become month-by-month spiritual mentors, communicating by telephone sessions or personal meetings, or electronic or postal mail. The entire process catalyzes during residential class weeks when students come to study and enjoy the unique atmosphere of the courses and campus at Sparrow Hawk Village.

The distinctive process of home study, meditation, spiritual guidance, and periodic classes at the village produces students capable of planetary service on one of several paths. The basic seminary program, Foundations of Spirituality, prepares individuals for lay ministry certification called Practitioner. From here one proceeds to consider graduate-level study by entering one of several combined master's degree programs, including certification as a Wellness Guide, Spiritual Director, Teacher of Esoteric Philosophy or ordination through Light of Christ Community Church.

Teachers of Esoteric Philosophy become educators for the new paradigms of spirituality now emerging around the planet, and ordination prepares ministers in Esoteric Christianity to bring the true Ageless Wisdom into metaphysical and mainstream settings. Ordinations are endorsed by the International Council of Community Churches. For students with the requisite background, commitment, and high creativity, individually designed programs can lead to one of three doctoral degrees. All programs are moderate in cost.

If you are interested in more information
we invite you to call **800 386-7161**
e-mail the school at
registrar@sanctasophia.org
or write to Sancta Sophia Seminary
11 Summit Ridge Drive
Tahlequah, Oklahoma 74464

Keep informed of Sancta Sophia events or
contact the affiliated center, church, or class
nearest you online at
www.sanctasophia.org